PROGRAMMED RUDIMENTS OF MUSIC

ROBERT W. OTTMAN

FRANK d. MAINOUS

School of Music
North Texas State University

PRENTICE-HALL, INC., ENGLEWOOD CLIFFS, NEW JERSEY 07632

Library of Congress Cataloging in Publication Data

Ottman, Robert W.
Programmed rudiments of music.

Includes index.
1. Music–Theory, Elementary–Programmed instruction.
I. Mainous, Frank, joint author. II. Title.
MT7.0816 781'.07'7 78-17256
ISBN 0-13-729962-1

Printed in the United States of America

10 9 8 7 6 5 4 3 2 1

Prentice-Hall International, Inc., *London*
Prentice-Hall of Australia Pty. Limited, *Sydney*
Prentice-Hall of Canada, Ltd., *Toronto*
Prentice-Hall of India Private Limited, *New Delhi*
Prentice-Hall of Japan, Inc., *Tokyo*
Prentice-Hall of Southeast Asia Pte. Ltd., *Singapore*
Whitehall Books Limited, *Wellington, New Zealand*

CONTENTS

PREFACE

Almost everybody can hum, whistle, or sing a good tune after hearing it a few times. In this sense, almost every person has at least a minimum of musical talent. A smaller number of fortunate people can actually go to an instrument, such as the piano or clarinet or violin, and "play by ear" with various degrees of success, even with no formal music instruction.

These activities are the simplest accomplishments in musical performance. Most of you who are reading this have found musical performance so enjoyable that you have enlisted the aid of someone more experienced than yourself in the expectation of heightening your enjoyment even more.

If you are one of these, you have seen that your teacher helps you learn a new piece of music in one or more ways. In the simplest way, your teacher sings, or plays on an instrument, the piece you are to learn, and you simply imitate the demonstration. If you play an instrument, your teacher probably has provided you with a list of fingerings or a chart so that when you look at a note on the staff, you will know what key to depress, or the approximate location of the finger on a string, or the position of the trombone slide, and so forth.

Finally, your instructor will begin to teach you some of the *theory* of music even if only such simple theory as note values, how to count time, the names of lines and spaces, etc.; the instructor may also suggest that you take a course in *music theory*. This is in order that you can become literate in the art of music, thereby increasing your skill in reading and performing music and ultimately enhancing your enjoyment of music to the fullest extent.

Music theory is a study of the materials composers use when they write music. We might say that music theory covers the technical aspects of music. But don't let the word "technical" alarm you. A recipe for chocolate cake is one of the technical aspects of baking, and quite necessary if a delicious product is to be expected. We can carry the analogy further: many people cook adequately without written recipes, just as many people play music by ear with pleasant results. But the cook who studies food materials and their combinations (the "theory" of the culinary arts) will ultimately become a better cook and provide many more and varied culinary treats. Likewise, the musician, with whatever degree of native untutored performance ability, will find greater accomplishments through study of materials and devices used to create a musical composition.

This book is for beginners in music theory; the material covered in this volume is often known under such titles as "Elements of Music," "Rudiments of Music," or "Basic Principles of Music," and precedes more advanced theoretical studies such as Harmony, Counterpoint, and Orchestration. In this book, we will study the most elementary aspects of music notation: pitch, scales, intervals, keys and key signatures, note values, meter, time signatures, rhythm, and basic harmonic structures.

R. W. O.
F. D. M.

HOW TO USE THIS BOOK

This is a "programmed" textbook using a concept of learning different from that of the conventional textbook. *Programming* allows you to learn at your own rate of understanding and comprehension. A programmed textbook can be used with or without the guidance of a teacher, and can be used in class or by an individual at home.

Observe the horizontal and vertical lines dividing the pages of this book. The horizontal lines divide a page into sections called *frames.* The vertical line, separating a page into two columns, divides each of the frames into two parts. The part on the right (righthand column) contains a simple bit of information, a question on that information, and a space for an answer.* The part on the left (lefthand column) shows the answer to the question.

Proceed through the book in this manner:

1. Cover left column. Read right column.
2. Answer question at bottom of the frame.
3. Uncover correct answer and compare your answer with it.

**Some frames may contain review or questions on a previous frame.*

In this way you will know either that you are correct and can proceed confidently, or that you need to go back several frames and review up to the point of error.

Here is a frame demonstrating the learning of a bit of information from a non-musical subject area.

Step 1. Cover left column. Read frame at right.

Keep covered	01. Solar energy is so called because the energy is derived directly from the sun. When the sun is the direct source of energy, this energy is known as __________ energy.

Step 2. Supply answer in space provided at bottom of the frame.

Keep covered	01. Solar energy is so called because the energy is derived directly from the sun. When the sun is the direct source of energy, this energy is known as ___solar___ energy.

Step 3. Check your answer by uncovering left side of frame.

solar	01. Solar energy is so called because the energy is derived directly from the sun. When the sun is the direct source of energy, this energy is known as ___solar___ energy.

You may already know some of the material covered in *Programmed Rudiments of Music.* To determine if this is so, a Pre-Test is found preceding each chapter. Completing a test with a satisfactory score will allow you to skip that chapter, thereby shortening the time needed to complete the book.

R. W. O.
F. D. M.

PRE–TEST
THE STAFF AND CLEF SIGNS

1. Name this device: ________________

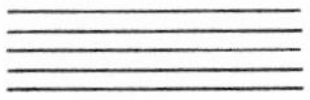

2. This sign alone, 𝄞, is called ________ ________

3. This sign alone, 𝄢, is called ________ ________

4. With this combination, 𝄞 (on staff), the sign, 𝄞, is called a ________ ________

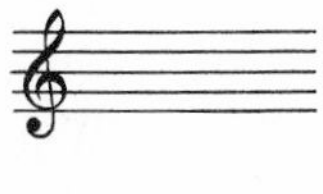

5. With this combination, 𝄢 (on staff), the sign, 𝄢, is called a ________ ________

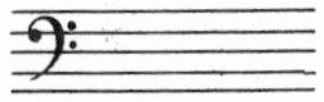

6. The short lines above and below the five parallel lines are called ________ ________

7. Identify by letter name the lines and spaces indicated by the numbers:

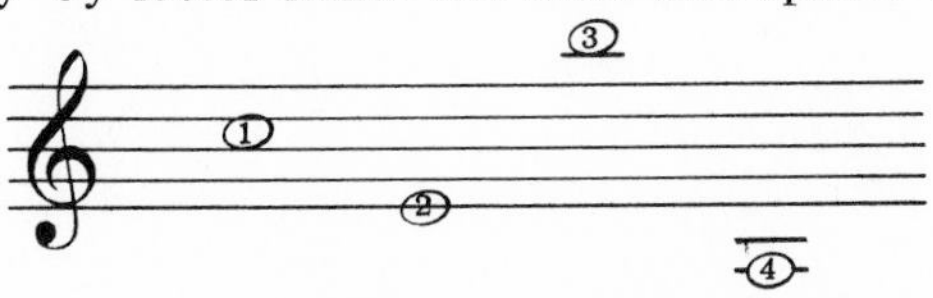

(1) ______ (2) ______ (3) ______ (4) ______

8. Name the lines and spaces indicated by the numbers:

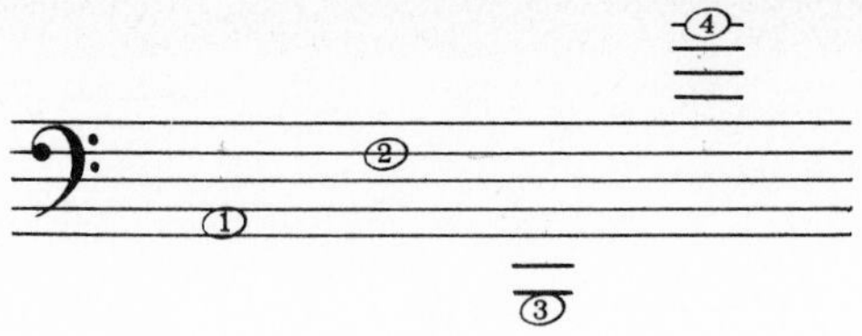

(1) ______ (2) ______ (3) ______ (4) ______

9. Both notes shown have the same name: ______

ANSWERS

A score is given at the end of each answer. If your answer is correct, place that score in the column at the right. Add this column for your score.

	Score
1. Staff (8)	______
2. G clef (10)	______
3. F clef (10)	______
4. Treble clef (10)	______
5. Bass clef (10)	______
6. Ledger lines (10)	______
7. ① C, ② E, ③ B, ④ A (4 each)	______
8. ① A, ② F, ③ B, ④ B (4 each)	______
9. Middle C (10)	______
Total score:	______
Perfect score:	100

If your score is 80 or above, turn now to Chapter 2, page 18. If your score is less than 80, continue with Chapter 1.

THE STAFF AND CLEF SIGNS

Obviously the most important aspect of music is its sound, *and all study of music should have as its primary goal the production of correct and beautiful sound. One important approach to this goal is the study of the symbols used to notate sound on paper. Notation of sound, even in its most elementary aspect, involves several factors, as you have already discovered in reading the Preface. We will begin our study with one of these factors,* pitch.

DEFINITION OF PITCH

	1. When we hear a musical sound, we usually evaluate it in terms of how "high" or how "low" it seems to be. When we hear two sounds, one seems "higher" or "lower" than the other. This property of sound, its seeming highness or lowness, is called *pitch,* or in acoustical terms, *frequency.* (See Appendix 1, Frames 1059–1067 for an acoustical explanation of this phenomenon).
highness or lowness	The term *pitch* refers to the seeming ________ or ________ of a sound.
pitch	2. To describe the highness or lowness of a sound, we use the term ________.

THE STAFF

	3. To indicate on paper the difference in pitch in musical sound, we use a device called the *staff.* The music *staff* (plural, *staves*) consists of five parallel horizontal lines and the four resultant spaces.
staff	A device for indicating pitch, employing five parallel lines and four resultant spaces, is called a ________.
pitch	4. The staff is used to indicate differences in ________ in the musical sound.
	5. The lines and spaces of the staff represent successively higher pitches when progressing from the lowest line to the highest line.
higher	Upper lines and spaces of the staff indicate ________ pitches.

pitch	6. The lines of the staff are numbered from the bottom to the top, 1 through 5. Spaces are similarly numbered from the bottom, 1 through 4. 5th line / 4th line / 3rd line / 2nd line / 1st line — 4th space / 3rd space / 2nd space / 1st space The lower the number of the line or space, the lower will be the __________.
1	7. The bottom line of the staff is numbered __________.
1	8. The bottom space of the staff is numbered __________.
higher	9. The higher the number of the line or space, the __________ will be the pitch.
5	10. The top line of the staff is numbered __________.
4	11. The top space of the staff is numbered __________.
lower	12. The third line of the staff is (higher/lower) __________ than the third space.

THE MUSICAL ALPHABET

pitches	13. The pitches represented by lines and spaces are identified by letters of the musical alphabet: *A B C D E F G.* The letters of the musical alphabet are used to identify ________ on the staff.
A B C D E F G	14. The musical alphabet consists of the letters ____ ____ ____ ____ ____ ____ ____.

CLEFS

clef	15. The letters of the musical alphabet are used to name the lines and spaces of the staff, but what letter name is assigned to a specific line or space is determined by a symbol called a *clef,* appearing at the beginning of a staff. Each of the several clef signs designates a certain line to carry a certain letter name. A symbol used to indicate a specific letter name for a specific line is called a ________.

THE TREBLE CLEF

G clef	16. The G clef, 𝄞, is so called because its lower loop encircles a line of the staff to be designated as G. The symbol, 𝄞, is known as a ____ ________.
G	17. When the lower loop of the G clef encircles the second line, designating that line as G, the clef is known as a *treble clef.* The treble clef indicates that the second line of the staff is ____.

18. To facilitate drawing the G clef, think of it as in two separate parts, (1) and (2), and then combined, (3). Observe in (2) and (3) how the loop encircles the second line.

(1) (2) (3)

(G)

Place four examples of the treble clef on this staff:

---

19. By fixing G on the staff by means of the G clef, names of the other lines and spaces are determined, since the lines and spaces are found in ascending alphabetical order.

(G) E F G A B C D E F

The treble clef indicates that the ______________ line of the staff is G.

second

---

20. Name the ascending successive lines and spaces of the staff with the treble clef, beginning with the lowest line.

____ ____ ____ ____ ____ ____ ____ ____ ____

E F G A B C D E F

---

21. The lowest line with the treble clef is ____.

E

---

22. To name the lines with the treble clef, begin with the letter name of the lowest line and skip every other letter.

The names of the lines are ____ ____ ____ ____ ____.

E G B D F

---

23. The lowest space with the treble clef is ____.

F

24. To name the spaces with the treble clef, begin with the letter name of the lowest space and skip every other letter.

The names of the spaces are ____ ____ ____ ____.

F A C E

---

25. Beginning with the highest line with the treble clef, name the descending lines and spaces of the staff.

____ ____ ____ ____ ____ ____ ____ ____ ____

F E D C B A G F E

---

26. Beginning with the highest line, name the descending lines.

____ ____ ____ ____ ____

F D B G E

---

27. Beginning with the highest space, name the descending spaces.

____ ____ ____ ____

E C A F

---

28. A pitch on the staff is usually indicated by a note which is then named according to its location on the staff. A note is a symbol based on an oval shape (o •) to which may be added stems (e.g., ♩) and flags (e.g., ♪) in varying combinations which express not only pitch but also duration of sound, as will be studied later.

To express pitch on a staff, a ________ is used.

note

---

29. On the staff, place notes to represent these pitch names.

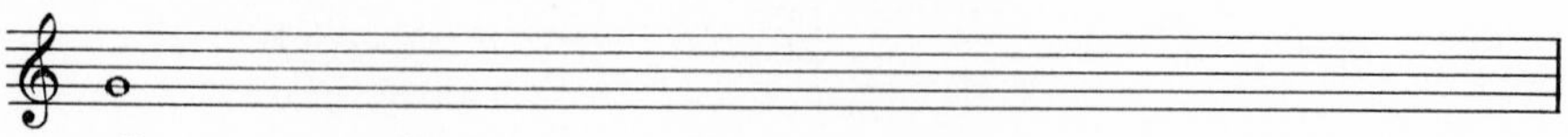

G B D C A

G B D C A

E F (low) E F (high) F (low) E (high) E (low)	30. E and F each appear twice on the staff. Place these on lower line/space or higher line/space as indicated: E F (low) E F (high) F (low) E (high) E (low)

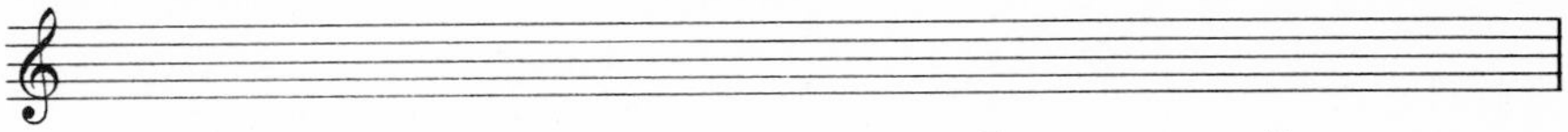

THE BASS CLEF

F	31. Pitches lower than those which can be accommodated by the treble clef are often placed on a staff with an F clef, 𝄢 . It is so called because the two dots are placed on either side of a line designated as the pitch F. When the fourth line of the staff is so designated, the clef is known as a *bass clef.* The bass clef indicates that the fourth line of the staff is ____.
	32. Here is a staff on which is placed a bass clef, an F clef with its two dots on either side of the fourth line. (F) Place four examples of the bass clef on this staff:
fourth	33. By fixing F on the staff by means of the F clef, names of the other lines and spaces are determined, in the same way as with the treble clef. (F) G A B C D E F G A The bass clef indicates that the ________ line of the staff is F.
G A B C D E F G A	34. Name the successive lines and spaces of the staff with the bass clef, beginning with the lowest line. ___ ___ ___ ___ ___ ___ ___ ___ ___

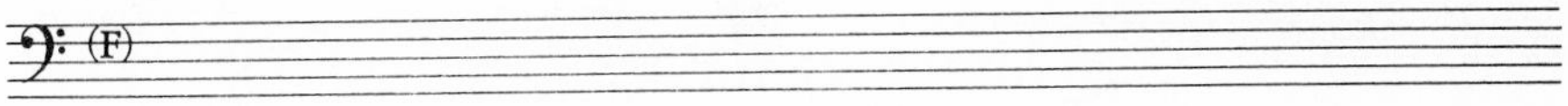

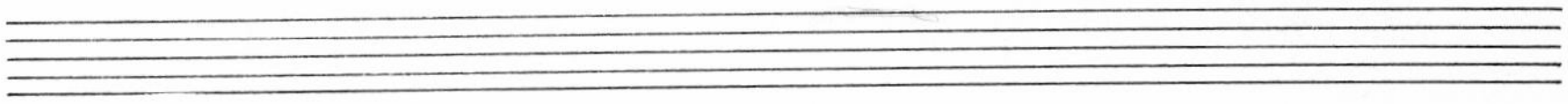

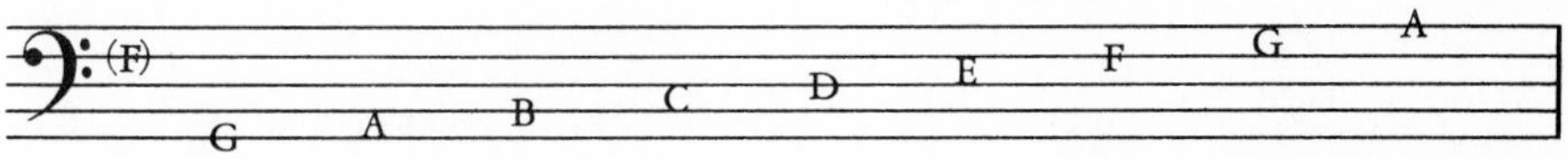

GBDFA

35. Name only the successive lines of the staff with the bass clef, beginning with the lowest line.

____ ____ ____ ____ ____

ACEG

36. Name only the successive spaces of the staff with the bass clef, beginning with the lowest space.

____ ____ ____ ____

AGFEDCBAG

37. Name the descending successive lines and spaces of the staff with the bass clef, beginning with the highest line.

____ ____ ____ ____ ____ ____ ____ ____ ____

D C F B E

38. On the staff, place notes to represent these pitch names.

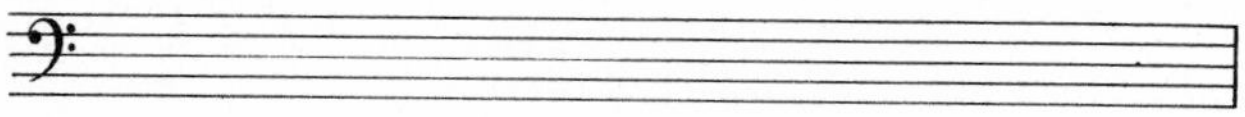

D C F B E

GA (low) GA (high) A (low) G (high) G (low)

39. With the bass clef, G and A appear twice on the staff. Place these on lower line/lower space or higher line/higher space as indicated:

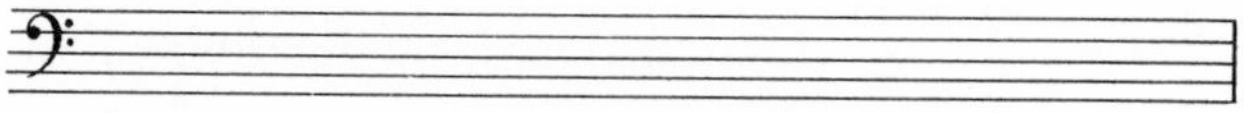

GA (low) GA (high) A (low) G (high) G (low)

E E B B

40. On the lines and spaces of the staff, place notes indicated by these letter names. Where a letter name occurs twice on a staff, show both notes. Observe that both treble and bass clefs are used.

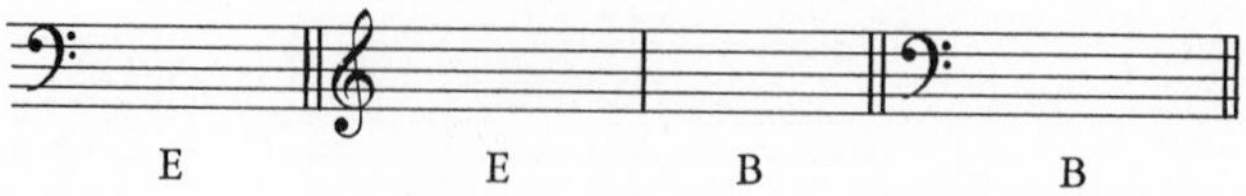

E E B B

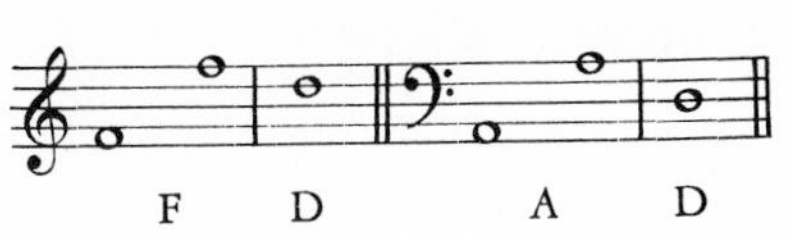

41. Continue as above.

LEDGER LINES

42. When necessary to indicate pitches either higher or lower than the limits of the five-line staff, short lines called *ledger* (*leger*) *lines* may be added above or below the staff. These lines and resultant spaces are drawn equidistant from the lines and spaces of the staff.

Ledger lines and spaces are used to indicate pitches __________ or __________ than the limits of the five-line staff.

higher or lower

43. The alphabetical succession of pitch names continues both above and below the staff. Fill in the pitch names in the blank spaces below.

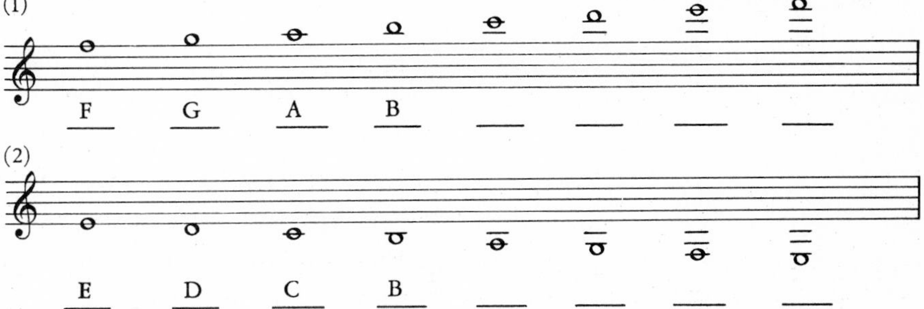

(1) C D E F
(2) A G F E

44. Fill in the pitch names in the blank spaces below.

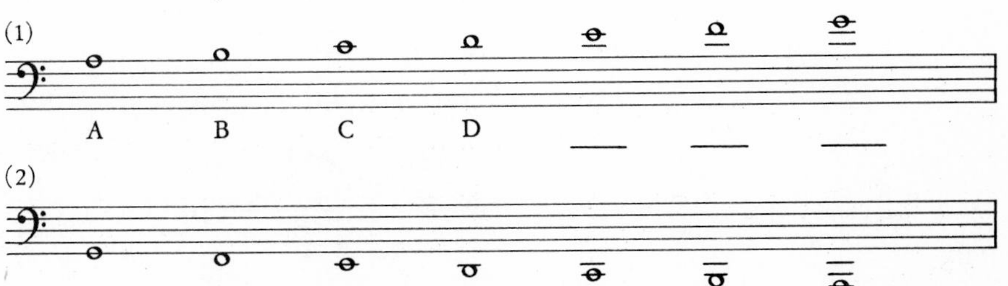

(1) E F G
(2) C B A

45. Observe that the space above the staff and the space below the staff do not require ledger lines, regardless of the clef used.

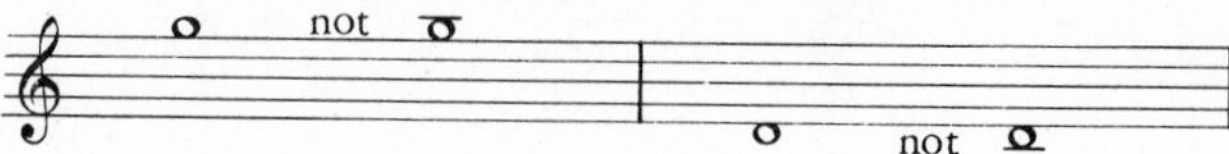

(1) In the treble clef, the notes above and below the staff not requiring ledger lines are ____ and ____.

(2) In the bass clef, the notes above and below the staff not requiring ledger lines are ____ and ____.

(1) G, D
(2) B, F

MUSIC EXAMPLES

46. Here, in Frames 46, 48, and 50, are some actual musical examples of the preceding concepts. Answer the question in the frame following each example. The signs ♯ and ♭, found at the beginning of the staff and also immediately preceding a few of the notes, will be explained later and should be disregarded at this time.

*Beethoven, Quartet for Strings, Op. 18, No. 5**

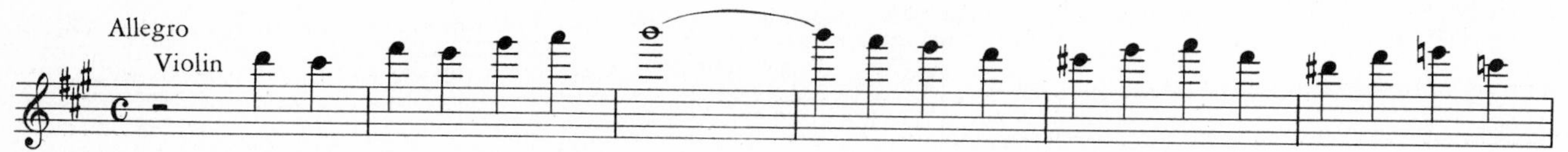

**Op.: Opus (Latin,* work*). The abbreviation, together with a number, identifies a composition, and is usually supplied by the composer.*

47. From Frame 46, name the lines and spaces on which the first seven notes are found.

____ ____ ____ ____ ____ ____ ____

D C F E G A B

48. *Bach,* Brandenburg Concerto No. 3

49. From Frame 48 name the lines and spaces on which the first four notes are found.

C D C B

____ ____ ____ ____

50. *Chopin, Nocturne, Op. 27, No. 2*

Piano

51. From Frame 50, name the lines and spaces on which the first six notes are found.

D F A F D F

____ ____ ____ ____ ____ ____

THE GREAT STAFF

52. When two staves are used together and are joined by a *brace* (a vertical line and a bracket), the combination is known as a *great staff*, or *grand staff*, or *piano staff*. In its most common form, the great staff displays a treble clef on the upper staff and a bass clef on the lower staff.

brace

The great staff is created by joining two staves with a__________.

53. The two staves of the great staff have an easily recognizable pitch in common. A note placed on the first ledger line below the treble staff is the same pitch as a note placed on the first ledger line above the bass staff. Both pitches are named C, and both are the same C. Because of its location, this pitch is known as *middle C* on either staff.

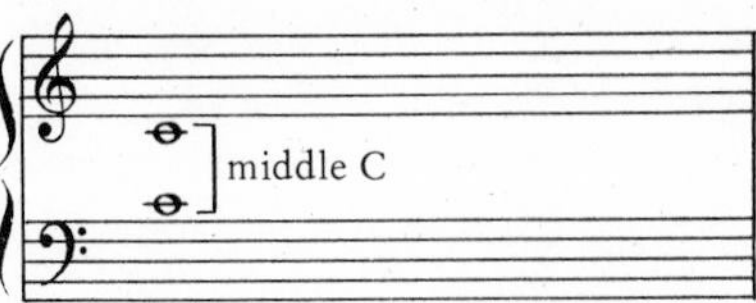

Middle C can be found on the first ledger line (above/below) ______ the treble staff and on the first ledger line ______ the bass staff.

below, above

54. On the treble staff of the great staff, notes below middle C can be written using ledger lines and spaces as in Frame 43. Similarly, on the bass staff, notes above middle C can be written using ledger lines and spaces as in Frame 44. In this example, the pitches in the treble clef are identical in sound to those in the bass clef.

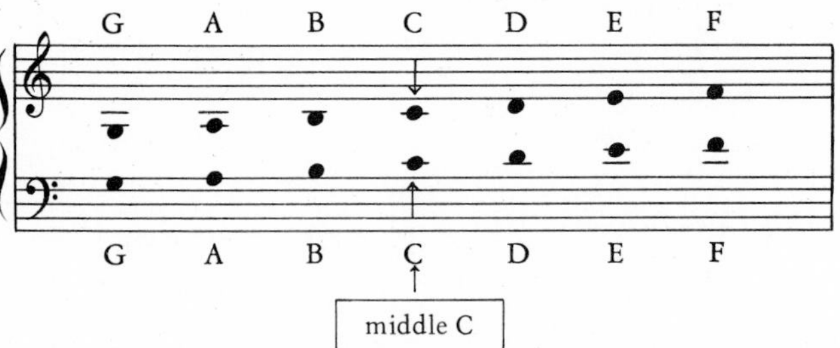

A note two ledger lines below the treble staff represents the same pitch as the ______ line of the bass staff.

fifth (or, highest)

55. Write notes on the blank bass staff that will sound the same as those given on the treble staff. Name each pitch.

C B A D F E G B C

56. Write notes on the blank treble staff that will sound the same as those given on the bass staff. Name each pitch.

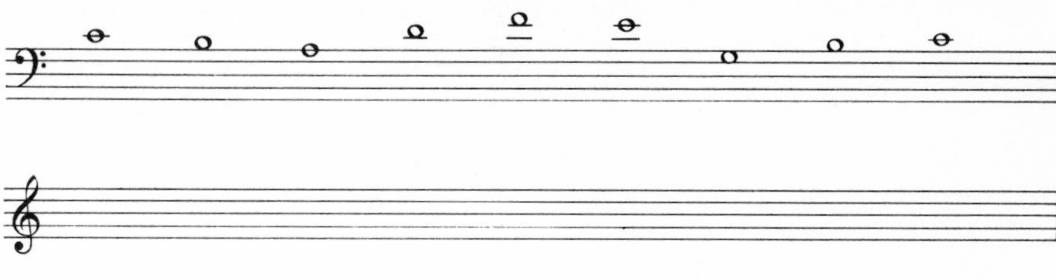

57. In drawing a great staff, it is necessary that the two staves be well separated so that it is possible to include necessary ledger lines. In the treble clef below, follow the given note F with descending notes E, D, C, B, A, G. Then add a staff with the bass clef below these to create a great staff (include the vertical line and the brace).

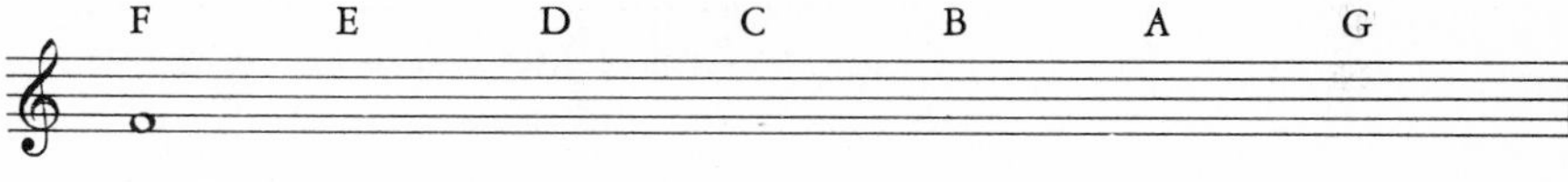

MUSIC EXAMPLES

58. The great staff may be found in several forms. In Frames 58–61 are some examples from music literature showing these. Questions on these examples are found in Frames 62–65.

Beethoven, Sonata for Piano, Op. 2, No. 1

59. *Mozart, Sonata for Piano, K. 279**

Allegro

**K.: abbreviation for Ludwig von Köchel, who in 1862 made a chronological listing of Mozart's works. Mozart did not give his works opus numbers.*

60. *Chopin, Prelude, Op. 28, No. 20*

61. *Mozart, Sonata for Piano, K. 576*

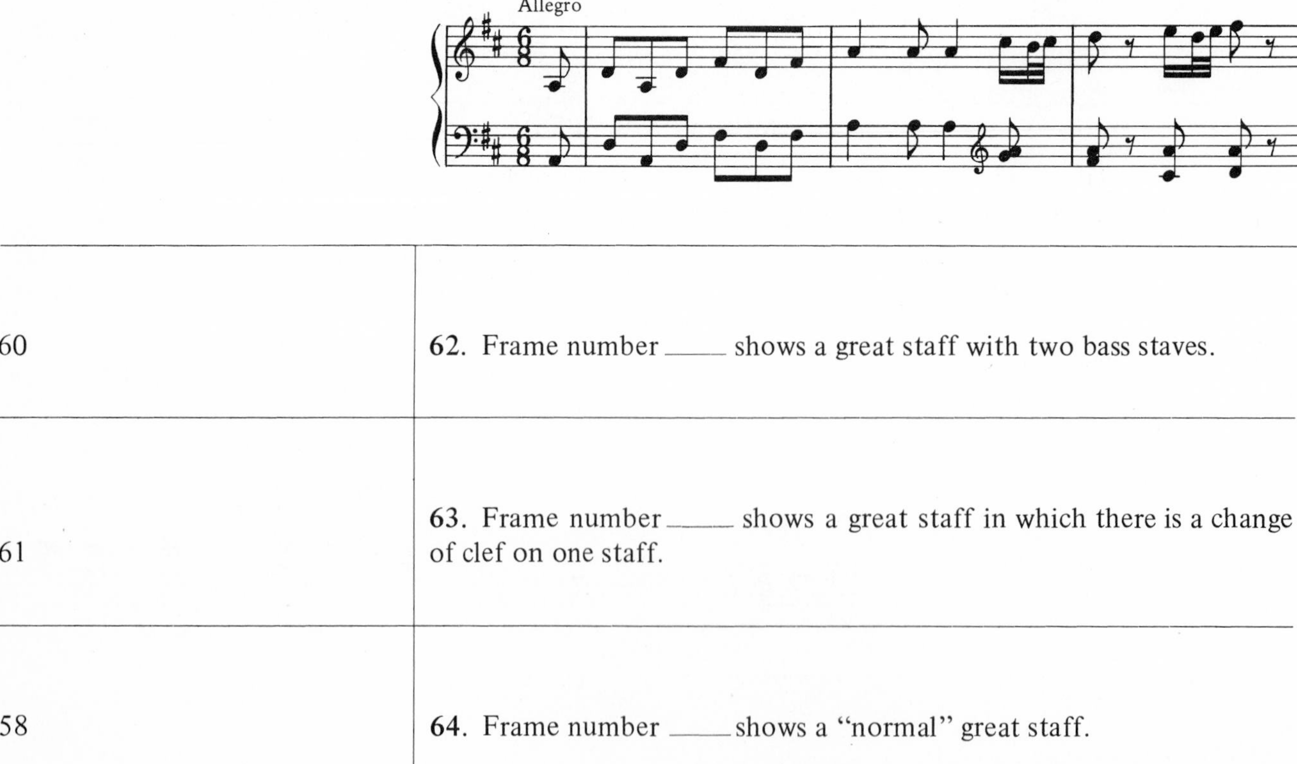

60	62. Frame number ____ shows a great staff with two bass staves.
61	63. Frame number ____ shows a great staff in which there is a change of clef on one staff.
58	64. Frame number ____ shows a "normal" great staff.

59	**65.** Frame number ____ shows a great staff with two treble staves.

CHAPTER SUMMARY

1. The term *pitch* refers to the seeming highness or lowness of a sound.

2. A staff, five parallel lines and the resultant four spaces, is a device used to indicate differences in pitch.

3. The lines of the staff, starting with the bottom line, are numbered consecutively from 1 to 5; the spaces, starting with the bottom space, are numbered consecutively from 1 to 4.

4. Pitches are represented by letters of the musical alphabet, A B C D E F G.

5. Letter names of the lines and spaces of the staff are assigned by a clef sign at the beginning of the staff.

6. The *G clef,* 𝄞, placed on a staff so that its lower loop encircles the second line, indicates that line to be G. In this position it is known as a *treble clef.*

7. The *F clef,* 𝄢, placed on a staff so that the two dots are on either side of the fourth line, indicates that line to be F. In this position it is known as a *bass clef.*

8. The *great staff* consists of two staves joined by a *brace.* Commonly the upper staff carries a treble clef, and the lower staff a bass clef.

9. *Ledger lines,* short lines and spaces above and below the staff, indicate pitches higher or lower than the limits of the five-line staff.

10. Middle C is found on the first ledger line below the treble staff and on the first ledger line above the bass staff.

PRE–TEST
THE KEYBOARD

1. Name the first nine white keys of the piano keyboard beginning with the bottom key. ____ ____ ____ ____ ____ ____ ____ ____ ____
1 2 3 4 5 6 7 8 9

2. The white key immediately to the left of any group of three black keys is named ____________.

3. Middle C on the keyboard corresponds to middle C on the great staff (T/F)____.

4. A whole step is the smallest interval on the keyboard. (T/F)____.

5. From any white key to its adjacent white key is a whole step. (T/F)____.

6. Match the answers:

a. ♭ ________ natural

b. ♮ ________ sharp

c. ♯ ________ flat

7. Name this symbol: 𝄫 ______________________________.

8. Draw the symbol for the accidental which raises a pitch a whole step ____________.

9. Draw an arrow connecting each note to its key.

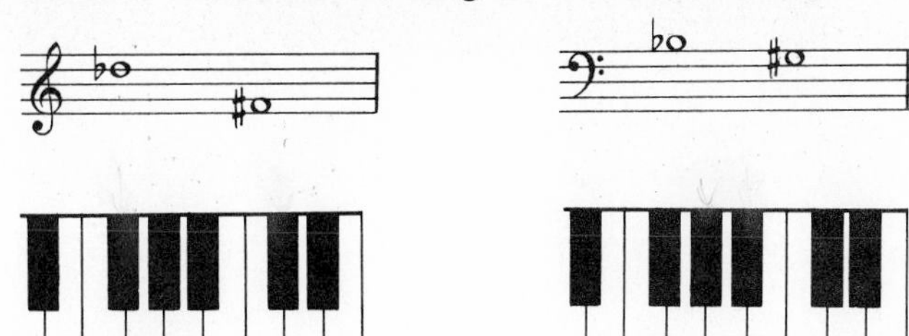

10. Circle the two pitches which are enharmonic. G#–G♭ B♭–A# D–D#

ANSWERS

A score is given at the end of each answer. If your answer is correct, place that score in the column at the right. Add this column for your score.

Score

1. A B C D E F G A B (10) The complete answer must be correct. ___
   1 2 3 4 5 6 7 8 9

2. F (10) ___

3. True (T) (10) ___

4. False (F) (10) ___

5. False (F) (10) ___

6. b (2) ___
   c (2) ___
   a (2) ___

7. Double flat (4) ___

8. 𝄪 (10) ___

9. 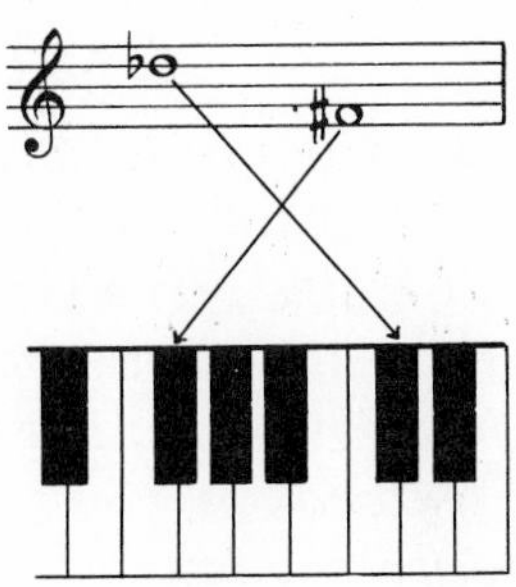 (5 each) ___

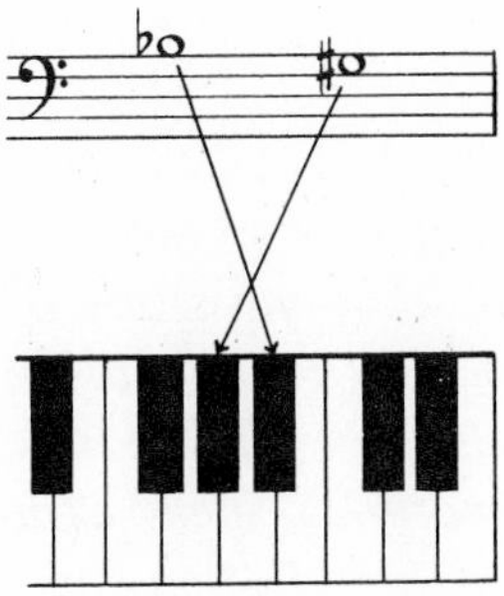

10. B♭–A# (10) ___

Total score: ______

Perfect score: 100

If your score is 80 or above, turn now to Chapter 3, page 34. If your score is less than 80, continue with Chapter 2.

CHAPTER TWO

THE KEYBOARD

Knowledge of the construction and layout of the piano keyboard is most valuable as an aid to understanding theoretical concepts. Since it is important that the study of sound itself be the primary reason for theoretical study, it follows that for this purpose the piano offers a readily available source of all the pitches used in most of the music performed today. Theoretical ideas expressed in a textbook as words become immediately meaningful when connected to musical sounds.

Even if you are not a pianist you can easily develop enough familiarity with the keyboard to make your study of music theory easier and more useful.

Ex. 2.1. *The Standard Piano Keyboard.*

bottom-lower pitches — higher pitchs-top

a b c d e f g a b c d e f g a b c d e f g a b c d e f g a b c d e f g a b c d e f g a b c d e f g a b c

left — right

up (ascending) →

← down (descending)

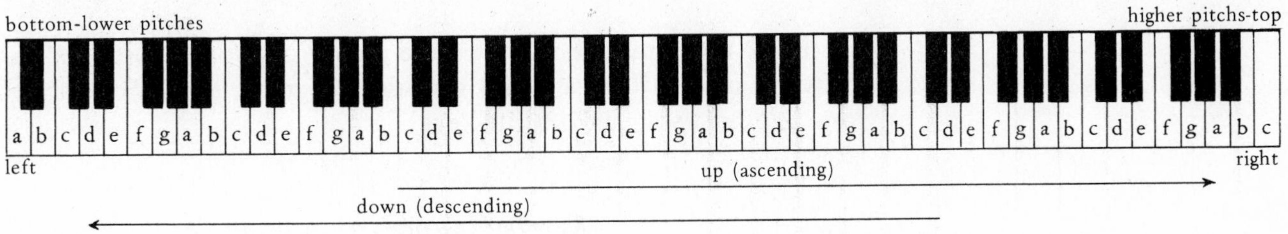

Refer to this illustration as often as necessary when working with the frames of this chapter.

THE KEYBOARD

88	**66.** The standard piano keyboard has 88 keys consisting of 52 white keys and 36 black keys. The standard piano keyboard has a total of ____ keys.
lower	**67.** Keys at the left of the keyboard sound the lower pitches while keys at the right sound higher pitches. Keys at the left of the keyboard sound (higher/lower) __________ than those at the right.
left	**68.** Pitches at the extreme left are said to be at the *bottom* of the keyboard; pitches at the extreme right are said to be at the *top* of the keyboard. When you are seated at a keyboard, the bottom of the keyboard is to your __________.

69. Black keys are found in alternate groups of two and three and can easily be seen on the keyboard because one group is always separated from another by a pair of white keys.

Keyboard Groups of Two and Three Black Keys.

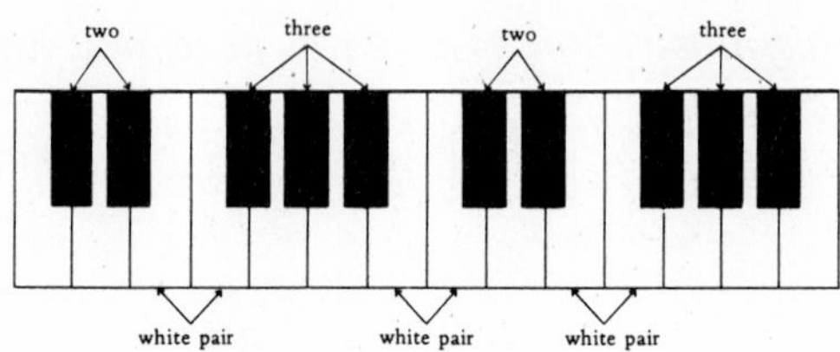

One group of black keys is always separated from another by a

pair | ______ of white keys.

NAMES OF WHITE KEYS

70. Each white and black key of the keyboard is identified by name. White keys are named with the seven letters of the musical alphabet, A B C D E F G. The key at the far left side, at the bottom of the keyboard, is a white key and it is named A. See Example 2.1.

A | The key at the bottom of the keyboard is named ____.

71. The next white key to the right of A is named with the next letter of the alphabet, B. This application of the alphabet in naming white keys continues in order up the keyboard.

C | The next white key to the right of B is named ____.

72. After G, which is the seventh and last letter of the musical alphabet, A occurs again.

A | The next white key to the right of G is named ____.

73. The process of the application of the alphabet is repeated through all succeeding white keys ending with the highest pitch, C, at the top of the keyboard. Observe that any C (except the topmost) is located at the immediate left of any group of two black keys.

Location of C at Left of Two Black Keys.

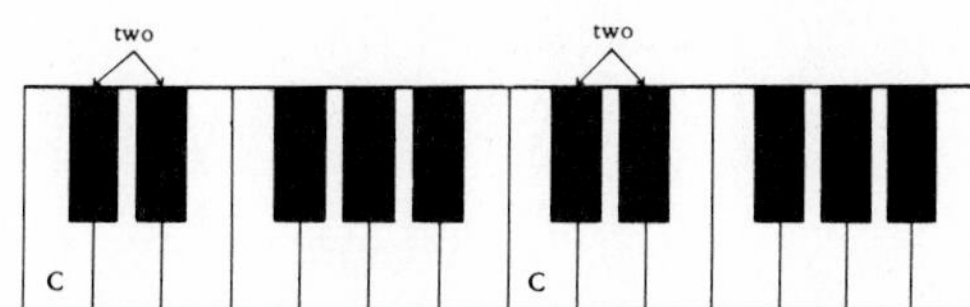

The white key at the immediate left of any group of two black keys is named ____.

C

74. When studying the keyboard in more detail, we will often use the key named C as a point of orientation, or as a starting point when playing at the keyboard. Write in names of white keys. C is given.

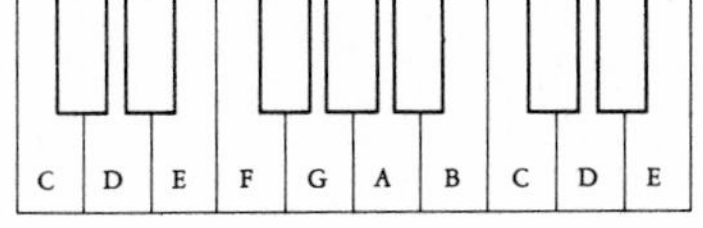

75. Write in names of white keys. Locate C first.

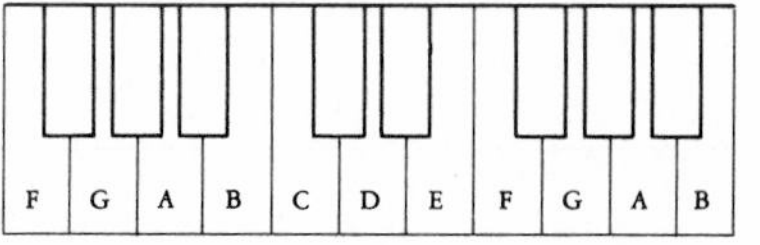

76. The C nearest the center of the keyboard is called *middle C.* Middle C on the piano corresponds to middle C on the great staff, as shown below.

Middle C on the Keyboard and Great Staff.

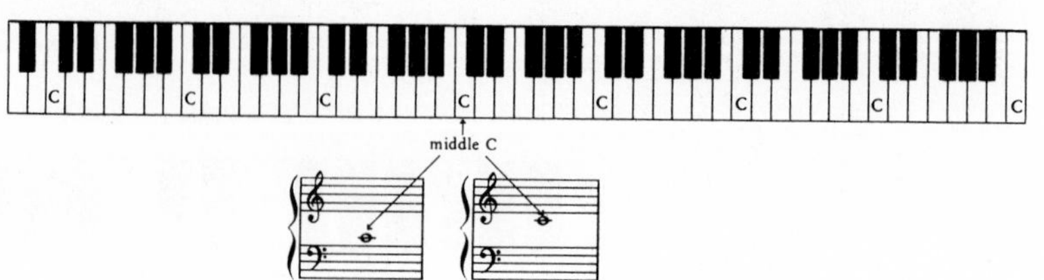

The C nearest the center of the keyboard is called ____________ C.

middle

77. Pitches of white keys to the right of (above) middle C are represented as notes in ascending order on lines and spaces of the staff. Fill in blanks with names of white keys corresponding to notes on the staff.

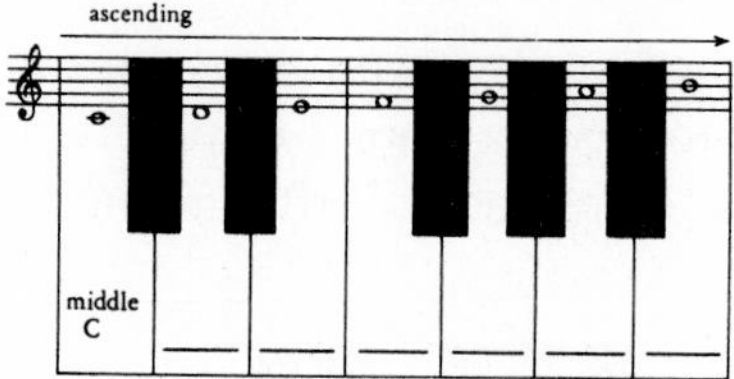

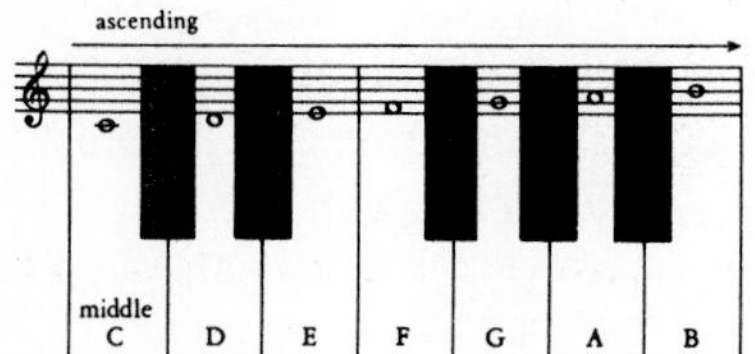

78. Fill in blanks with names of white keys corresponding to notes.

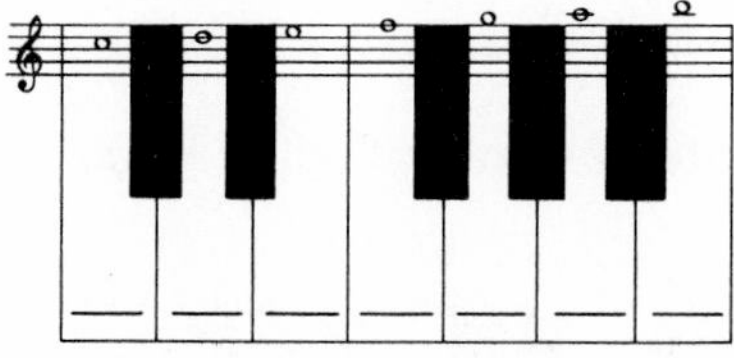

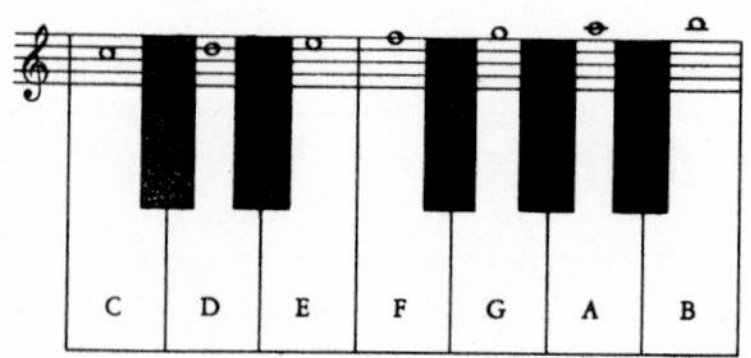

79. Fill in blanks with names of white keys corresponding to notes on the staff. Locate C first.

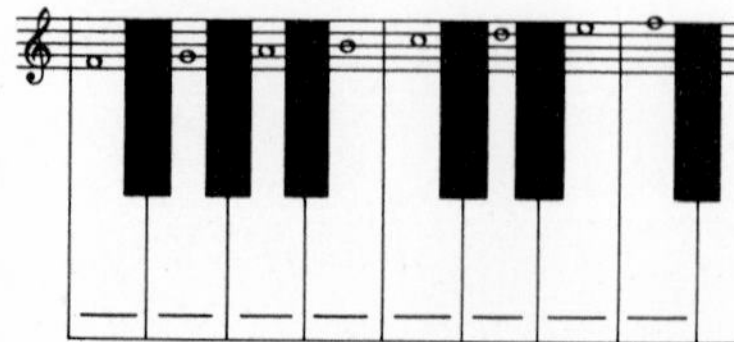

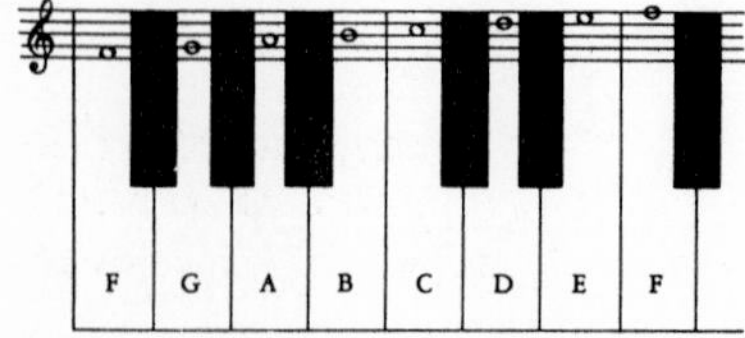

80. Pitches of white keys to the left of (below) middle C are represented as notes in descending order on lines and spaces of the staff. Fill in blanks with names of white keys corresponding to notes on the staff.

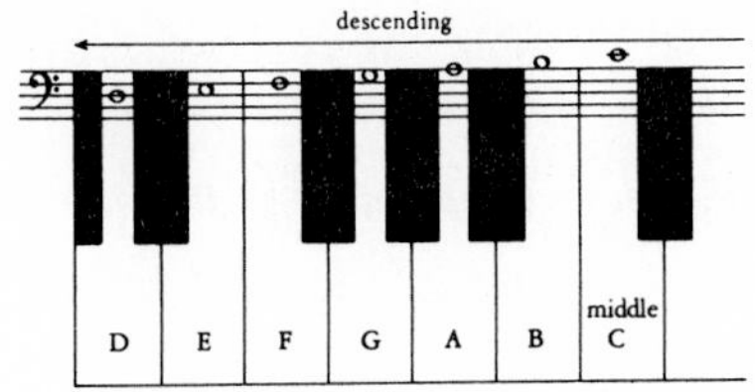

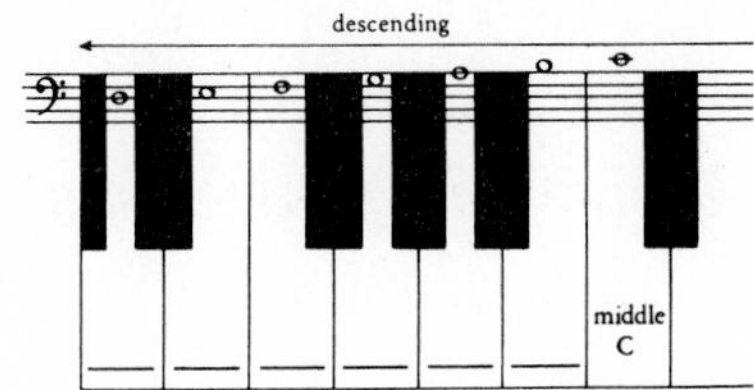

81. Fill in blanks with names of white keys corresponding to notes.

E F G A B C

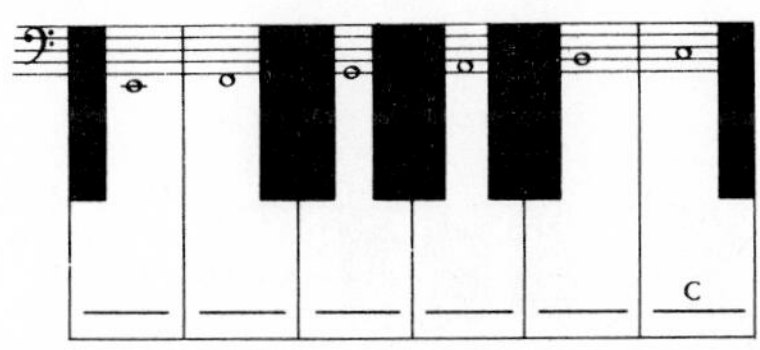

82. Fill in blanks with names of white keys corresponding to notes on the staff. Locate C first.

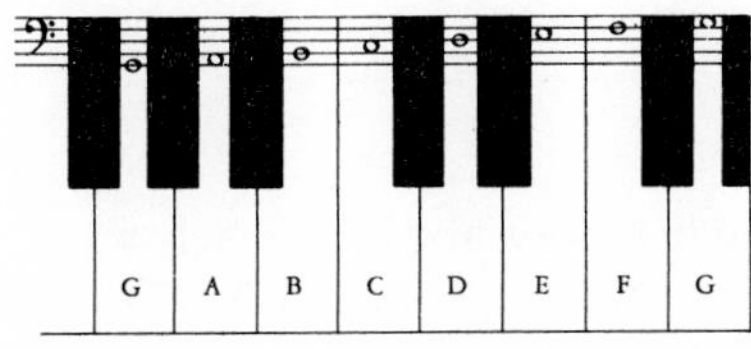

INTERVALS: HALF STEPS AND WHOLE STEPS

83. In music an *interval* is the distance between two different pitches, or between two different notes on the staff, or between two different keys on the piano.*

interval

The distance between two different pitches is called an ____________.

**Musical intervals are actually acoustical, but the graphic and spatial aspects of notation and the keyboard are commonly used by musicians in relating to intervallic concepts. Intervals are treated as ratios of frequencies in Appendix 1, Acoustics. This information is not needed at this time.*

half step	84. You can see on the keyboard many intervals* between different keys, but our present study will be limited to two: first, the smallest interval, a *half step,* and then the next larger interval, the *whole step.* The smallest interval on the keyboard is a______ ______. **A complete study of intervals will be covered later in Chapters 13 and 14.*
half step	85. On the keyboard, a half step is the interval from *any key to its adjacent key,* whether that key be white or black. ***Half Steps on the Keyboard.*** ½ ½ ½ ½ C D E F G A B C etc. From C, a white key, to the next higher pitch, a black key, is the interval of a ______ ______.
half step	86. From any black key to the adjacent white key above (or below) is the interval of a ______ ______.
F, C	87. Notice that there is no black key between E and F or between B and C; therefore, these adjacent white keys are half steps apart. ½ ½ ½ ½ C D E F G A B C etc. A half step above E is ____; above B is ____.

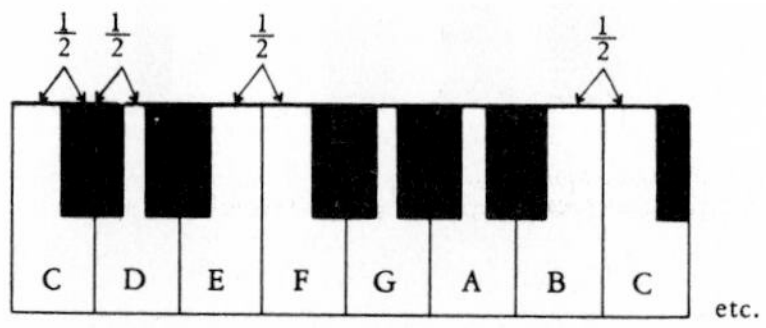

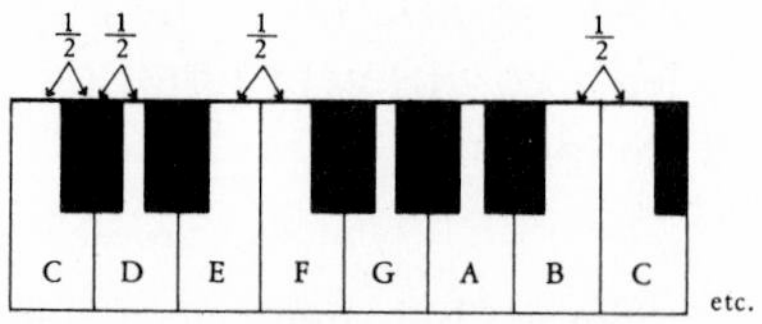

	88. Two half steps in succession equal *one step,* usually called a *whole step.*
whole step	Two half steps equal a ________ ________.
	89. Between C and D is a black key, producing two half steps.
	½ ½ C D
whole step	Therefore, the interval from C to D is a ________ ________.
	90. Because of the irregularity of the keyboard with its black keys in groups of two and three, whole steps on the keyboard are found in three different combinations of white and black keys. Whole steps exist (1) from white key to next white key, (2) between a white and black key, or (3) between a black and another black key. There will always be a single key, black or white, between the two keys that produce a whole step. The following illustration shows one example of each of the combinations.
	Whole Steps on the Keyboard.
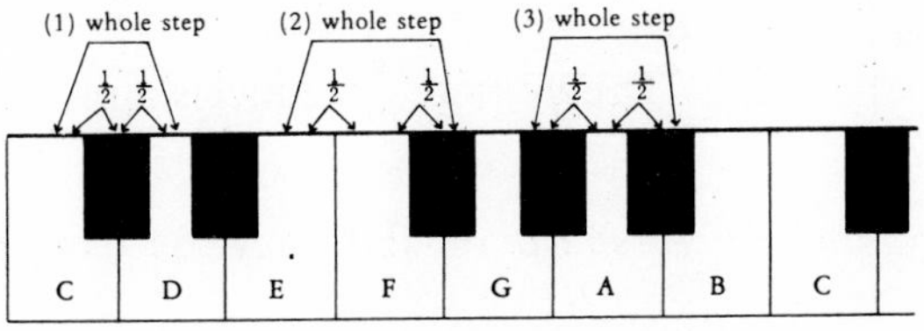	(1) whole step (2) whole step (3) whole step ½ ½ ½ ½ ½ ½ C D E F G A B C
	In the preceding illustration, a whole step between a white key and
2	a black key is shown at (1/2/3)________.
	91. In the illustration in Frame 90, a whole step between a black key
3	and another black key is shown at (1/2/3)________.

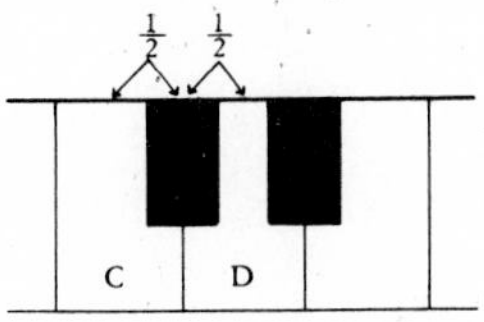

1	92. In the illustration in Frame 90, a whole step between a white key and another white key is shown at (1/2/3)__________.

ACCIDENTALS

♯ sharp	93. An accidental is a symbol (sign) which alters the pitch of a note. There are five accidentals. The *sharp,* ♯ , raises the pitch of a note one half step. The pitch of a note is raised one half step by the symbol______, called a __________.
♭ flat	94. The *flat,* ♭ , lowers the pitch of a note one half step. The pitch of a note is lowered one half step by the symbol______, called a __________.
♮ natural	95. The *natural,* ♮ , cancels a preceding accidental. A sharp or flat may be cancelled by the symbol_____, called a __________.
𝄪 double sharp	96. The *double sharp,* 𝄪 , raises the pitch of a note two half steps or one whole step. The pitch of a note is raised a whole step by the symbol______, called a __________ __________.

𝄫 double flat	97. The *double flat,* 𝄫, lowers the pitch of a note two half steps or one whole step. The pitch of a note is lowered a whole step by the symbol ______, called a ______ ______.
(c)	98. In music writing, the accidental is placed immediately to the left of (before) the note to be altered and precisely on the same line or space occupied by the note.* Circle whichever is correct: a b c. a. b. c. **Accidentals are studied further in later chapters.*
C flat	99. When an accidental is to be written in notation, it is, without exception, placed *before* the note. But, in speaking the name of an altered note the accidental comes *after* the letter name. Therefore, is spoken "C-sharp." is spoken "______ ______."
C natural	**100.** is spoken "______ ______."
C double sharp	**101.** is spoken "______ ______ ______."

C double flat

102.

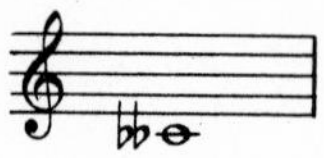

is spoken "_____ __________ __________."

NAMES OF BLACK KEYS

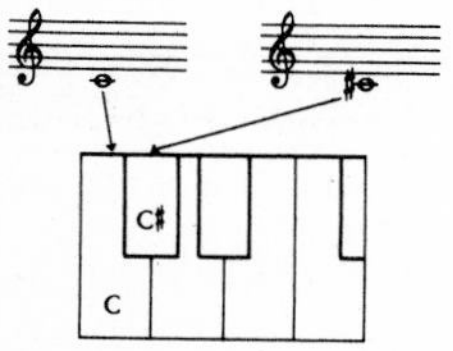

103. On the piano keyboard, black keys are named in relation to the white keys. The black key one half step above C is named C-sharp.

Draw an arrow connecting C♯ on the staff to its key.

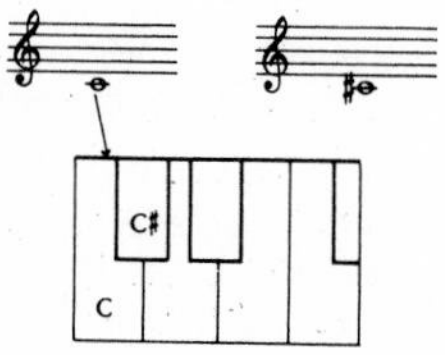

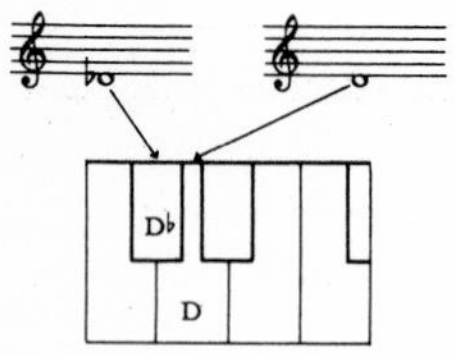

104. The black key one half step below D is named D-flat. Draw an arrow connecting D♭ on the staff to its key.

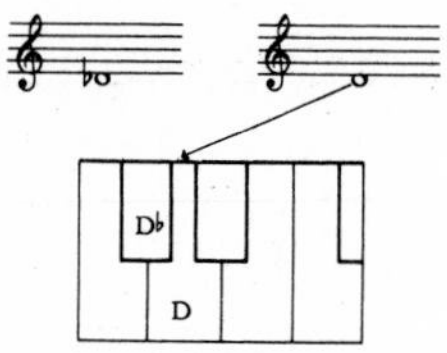

C-sharp (♯)

105. Observe that the same black key is named both C-sharp and D-flat.

The black key D-flat may also be named _____ __________.

D-sharp (♯)

106. The other black keys are named in a similar manner.

The black key one half step above D is named _____ __________.

E-flat (♭)

107. The black key one half step below E is named ____ ________.

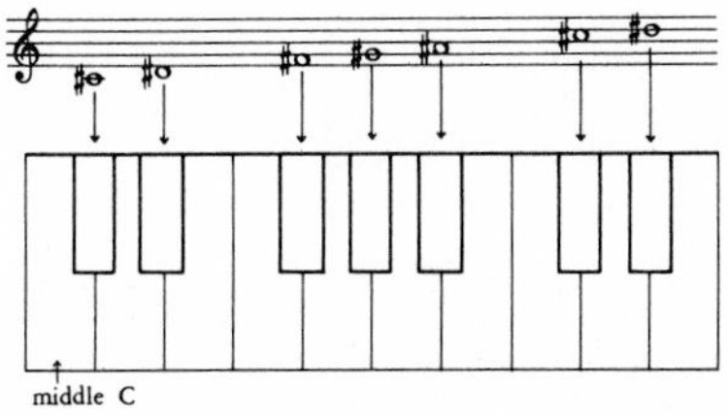

middle C

108. Draw arrows connecting sharped notes on the staff (treble) to their black keys.

middle C

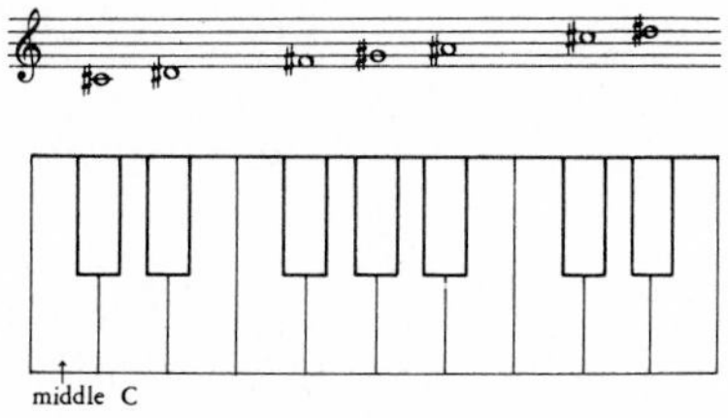

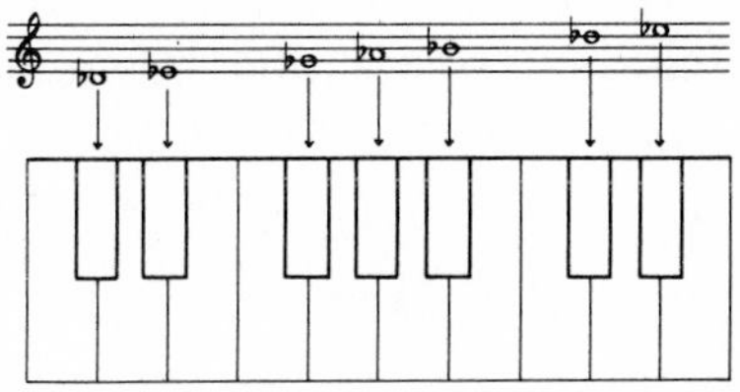

109. Draw arrows connecting flatted notes on the staff (treble) to their black keys.

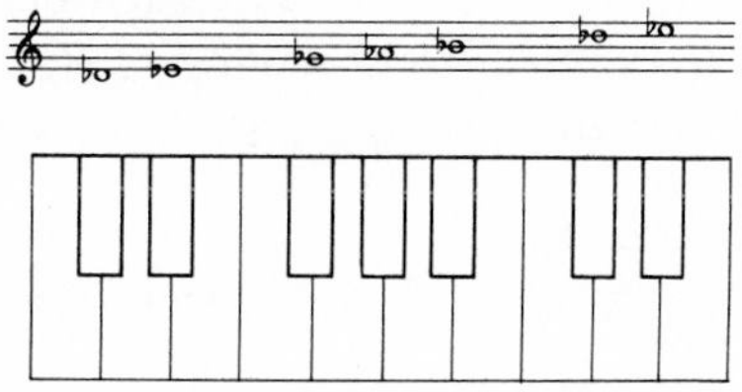

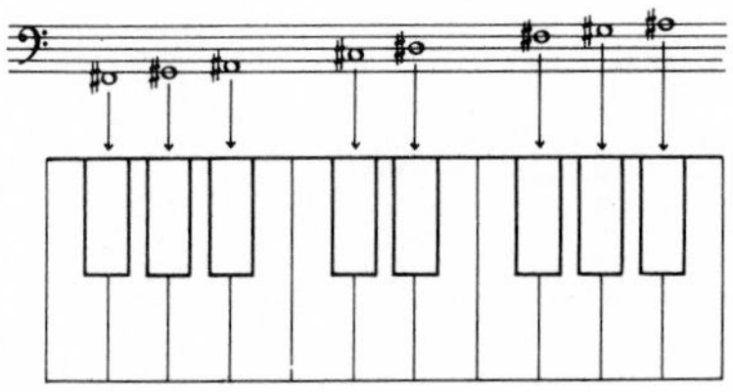

110. Draw arrows connecting sharped notes on the staff (bass) to their black keys.

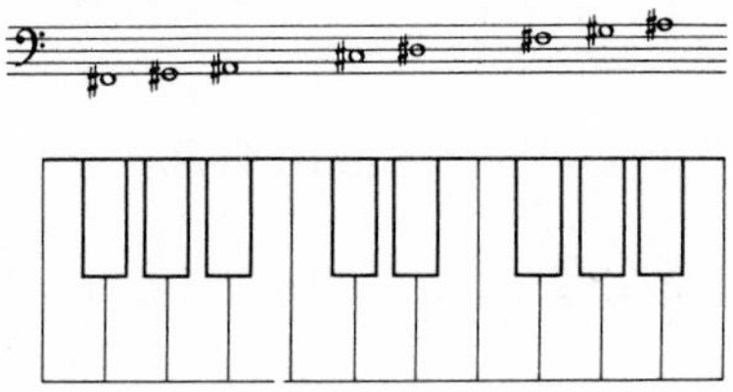

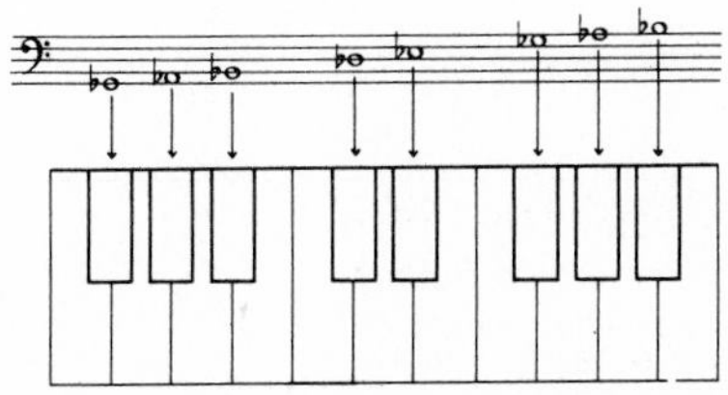

111. Draw arrows connecting flatted notes on the staff (bass) to their black keys.

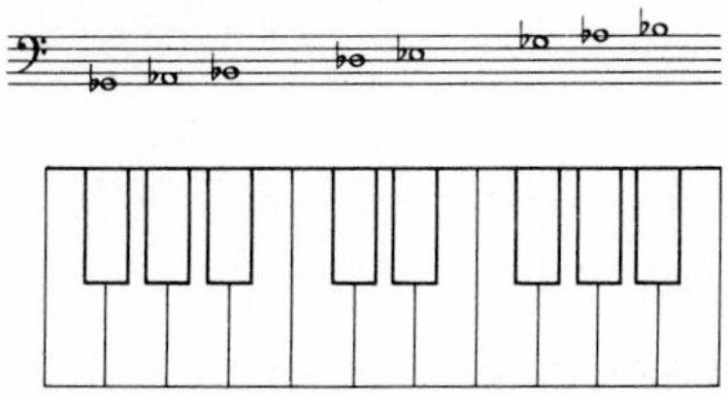

ENHARMONIC PITCHES

112. Examine these illustrations with particular attention to all black keys.

The Keyboard and Treble Notes on the Staff.

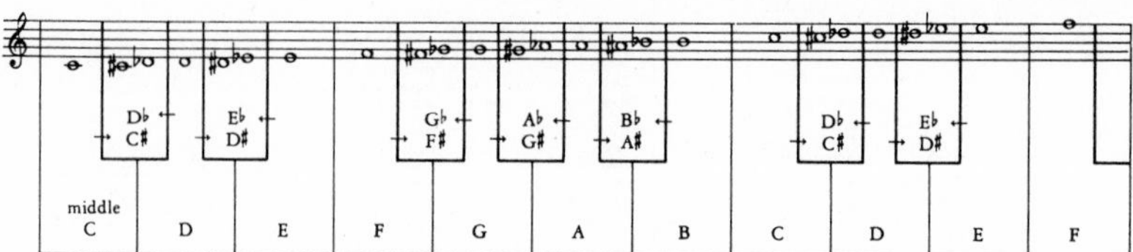

The Keyboard and Bass Notes on the Staff.

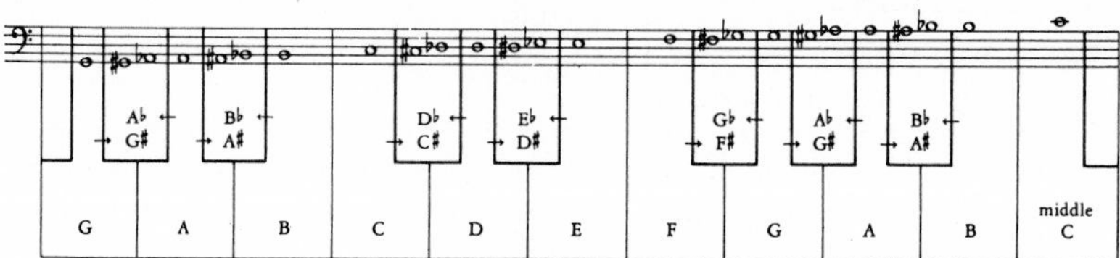

You have noticed that each black key has two different names, one and the same pitch having different spellings. To describe this and similar situations we use the term *enharmonic.**

C-sharp and D-flat, occupying the same black key, are said to be____________________.

enharmonic

**White keys may also have enharmonic spellings, either by use of ♯ or ♭, or 𝄪 or 𝄫. These will be studied later.*

---

113. The enharmonic of E-flat is____ ________.

D-sharp

---

114. The enharmonic of F-sharp is ____ ________.

G-flat

---

115. The enharmonic of G-sharp is ____ ________.

A-flat

---

116. The enharmonic of B-flat is____ ________.

A-sharp

CHAPTER SUMMARY

1. The standard piano keyboard has 88 keys/pitches.

2. Each white and black key is identified by name. White keys are named in order with letters of the musical alphabet.

3. C, located at the left of a group of two black notes, is commonly used as a point for keyboard orientation.

4. *Middle C* is that C nearest the center of the keyboard and corresponds to middle C on the great staff.

5. In music an *interval* is the distance between two different pitches. The smallest interval on the keyboard is the distance from any key to its adjacent key (either white or black), called a *half step.* Two half steps in succession comprise the interval of a *whole step.*

6. An *accidental* alters the pitch of a note. There are five accidentals: ♯, ♭, ♮, 𝄪 and 𝄫.

7. Black keys are named in relation to white keys; for example, the black key one half step above C is C♯; the black key a half step below d is D♭.

8. When one key (pitch) has two different names, such as C♯ and D♭, the names are said to be *enharmonic.*

PRE–TEST
NOTATION OF PITCH

1. Place on the staff a note an octave *higher* than each of those at a) and b). At c) and d) place the note an octave *lower*. (Do not use 8va sign.)

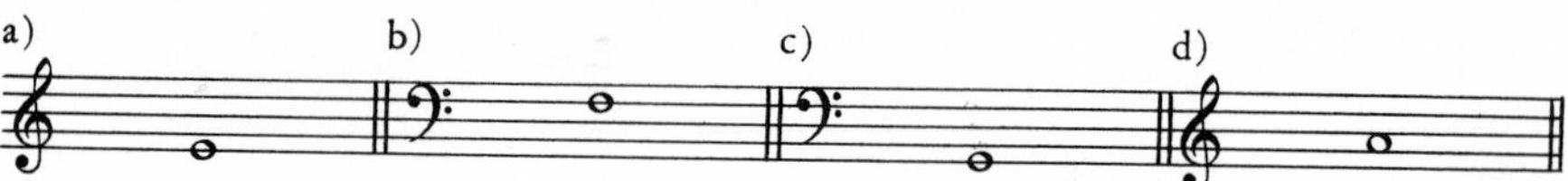

2. Using *octave register* designations, name each of these notes:

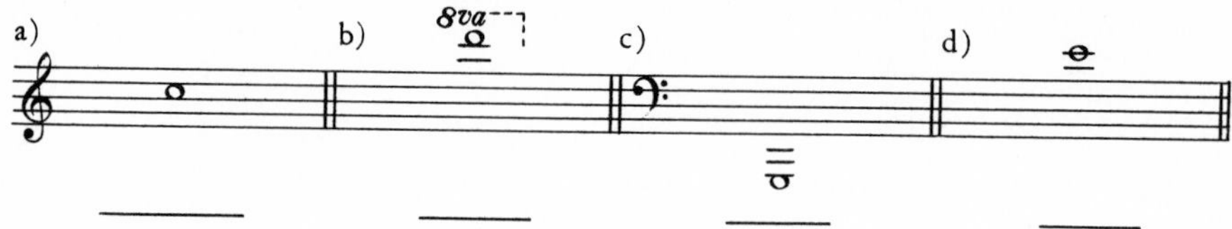

3. The pitch CC is also called ____________C.

4. Locate with an arrow a key an octave above that shown on this keyboard:

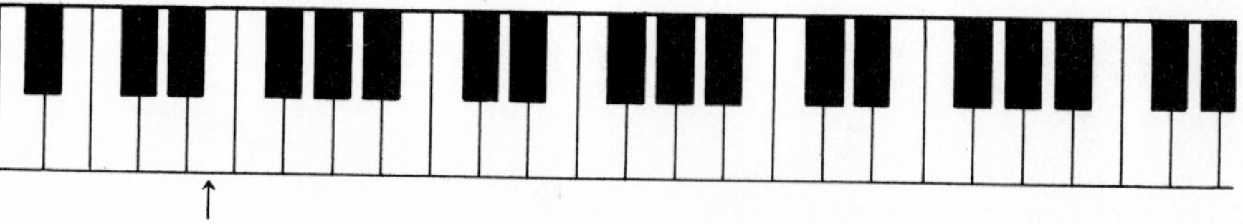

ANSWERS

Score 10 points for each of the four parts of questions 1 and 2. Score 10 points each for questions 3 and 4. Place your scores in the column at the right. The total of this column is your score.

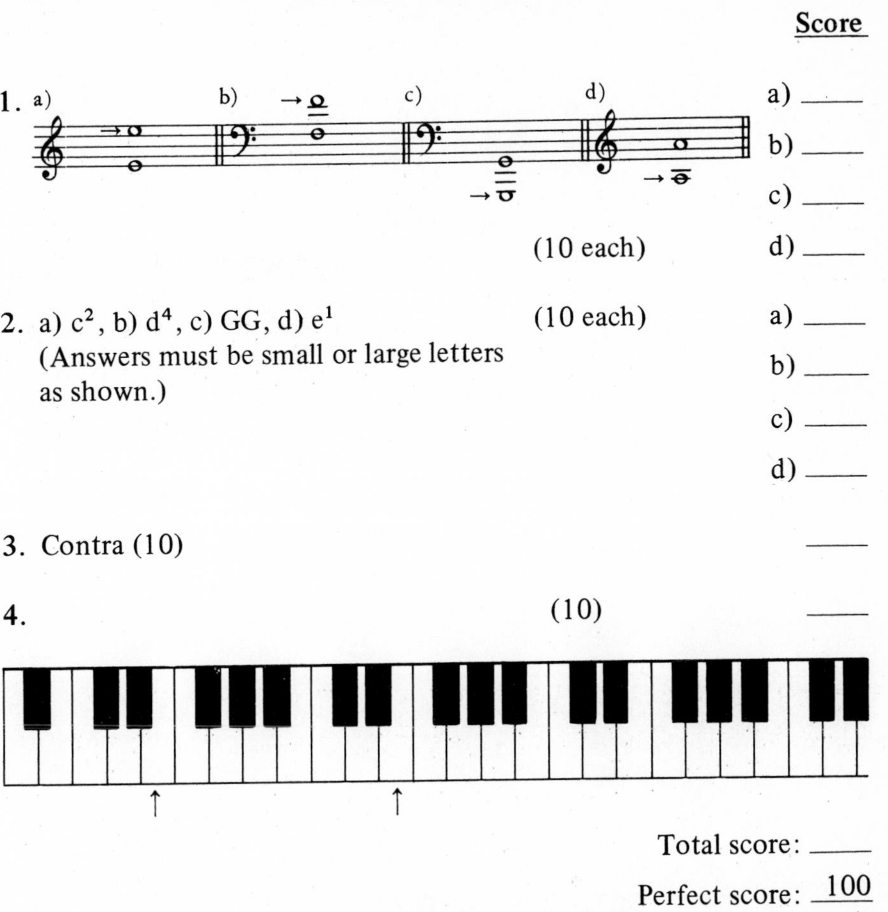

Score

1. a) b) c) d) (10 each) a) ____ b) ____ c) ____ d) ____

2. a) c^2, b) d^4, c) GG, d) e^1 (10 each) a) ____ b) ____ c) ____ d) ____
(Answers must be small or large letters as shown.)

3. Contra (10) ____

4. (10) ____

Total score: ____

Perfect score: 100

If your score is 80 or above, turn now to Chapter 4, page 47. If your score is less than 80, continue with Chapter 3.

NOTATION OF PITCH

In studying the keyboard in Chapter 2, you have noticed that each letter name is used more than once in naming the keys of the piano. In fact, there are eight A's, eight B's, and eight C's, plus seven each of the remaining letters of the musical alphabet. Therefore, there is a need for a system whereby any one pitch can be designated distinctly from any other pitch of the same letter name. A system of octave registers *fulfills this need. While working on this chapter, frequent reference should be made to Example 3.1 on page 37.*

OCTAVE

117. The word *octave** refers to an interval and is derived from the Latin *octo,* meaning eight. The interval of the octave consists of two pitches encompassing eight staff degrees.

The interval whose two pitches encompass eight staff degrees is called an ____________.

octave

**The acoustical explanation of the octave may be found in Appendix 1, Frames 1068–1072.*

Ex. 3.1. ***Octave Registers.***

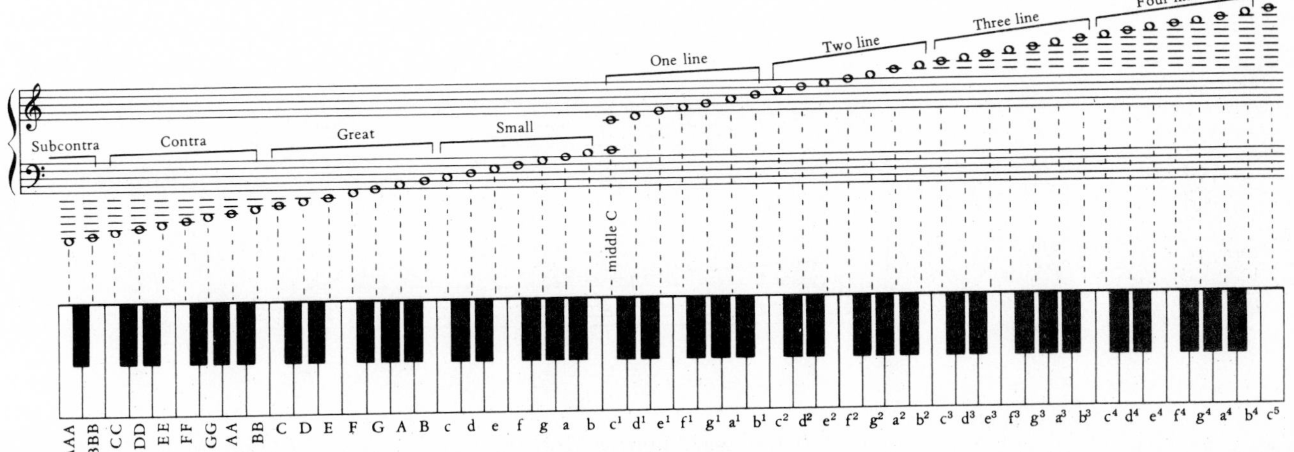

Courtesy of Raymond Elliott, Fundamentals of Music, *2nd edition (Englewood Cliffs, N.J., Prentice-Hall, Inc., 1965).*

118. An octave can be clearly seen on the piano keyboard. Refer to the picture of the piano keyboard, Example 3.1, page 37. Find middle C, consider it as 1 and count up (to the right) the white keys to 8, at which point you will arrive at another C. 1 and 8, using the same letter name, are an octave apart. (If you have access to a piano, try this at the real keyboard and then play the two notes. Notice each sounds the same except that one is higher than the other.)

An octave above C is also called ________.

C

119. In similar fashion, it can be shown that the interval from any pitch to the next pitch of the same letter name, either up or down, is an octave. For example, A up to A is an octave.

F

F up to ____ is an octave.

---

octave

120. D down to D is an ____________.

---

121. An octave on the staff can be located by counting up or down eight staff degrees from a given note.

1 2 3 4 5 6 7 8
C C

1 8
C C

8 7 6 5 4 3 2 1
A A

8 1
A A

On the staff below, find the note an octave *above* the given note by numbering the staff degrees from 1 through 8. You will be correct if the note represented by 8 is the same letter name as 1.

1

Answer: 1 2 3 4 5 6 7 8
(G) (G)

---

122. Find the note an octave *below* the given note by numbering the staff degrees 8 descending through 1.

8

Answer: 8 7 6 5 4 3 2 1
(E) (E)

OCTAVE REGISTERS (ABOVE MIDDLE C)

123. Refer to Example 3.1, page 37. Observe in the letter names below the keyboard that each C has a different designation. All the pitch names from one C up to the next higher C constitute an *octave register.* There are seven complete octave registers plus two incomplete ones.

All pitch names above a given C up to the next higher C are in the

same ______________ ______________.

octave register

---

124. Middle C is designated as c^1, spoken "one-line c" or "c-one."

c^1 refers to the pitch ______________ ______.

middle C

---

125. Each C above middle C is designated by a successively higher number until the highest note on the keyboard, c^5, is reached.* Observe that all the letter names from c^1 to c^5 use lower-case (small) letters. These names are spoken "one-line c" or "c-one" for c^1, "two-line c" or "c-two" for c^2, etc.

c^3 is an ______________ higher than c^2.

**There exist several similar systems but with different numbering: e.g., middle C is c with c^1 an octave higher, or middle C is c^4 when counting C's from the bottom of the keyboard, etc.*

octave

---

126. The highest key on the piano is ________.

c^5

---

127. Identify each C by its octave register.

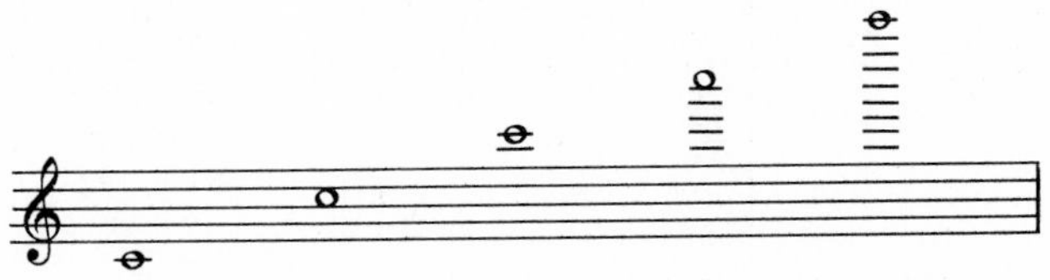

c^1 ____ ____ ____ ____

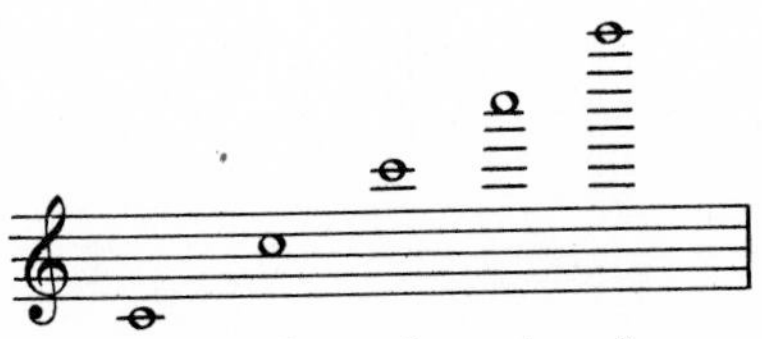

c^1 c^2 c^3 c^4 c^5

128. Letter names above c^1 but lower than c^2 are designated as one-line: c^1 d^1 e^1 f^1 g^1 a^1 b^1 // c^2. Similarly, all letter names above c^2 but lower than c^3 are designated as two-line, etc.

Fill in these blanks:

(1) The d next above c^3 is ________.

(2) The a♭ next above c^2 is _______.

(3) The f♯ above c^4 is ________.

(1) d^3

(2) $a♭^2$

(3) $f♯^4$

---

129. Identify each note by its letter name and its octave-register designation.

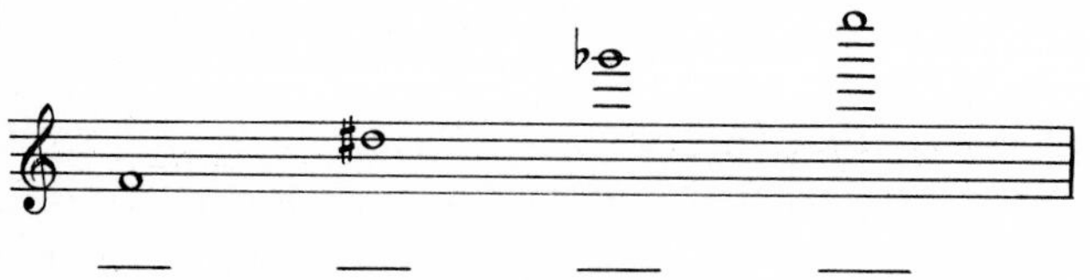

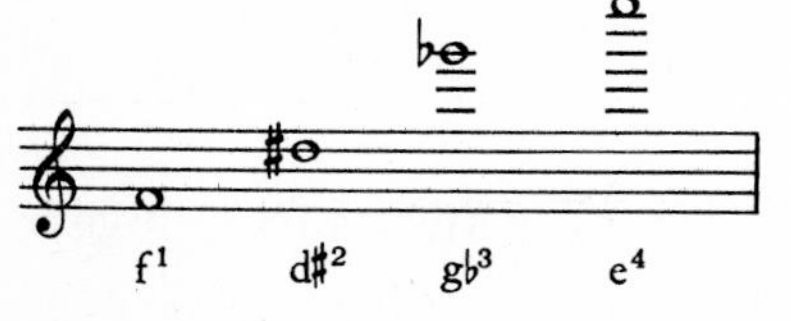

THE 8VA SIGN

130. Observe from Frames 127 and 129, and from Example 3.1 on page 37, that many notes above the treble staff require a large number of ledger lines. To reduce the number of these lines, making the music easier to read, a sign is available. 8va-----┐ or 8-----┐ over a note or notes indicates that the pitches are intended to sound an octave higher than written. (8va is an abbreviation for the Italian *all' ottava,* at the octave.) The dotted line extends over the note or notes affected and ends at a short vertical line extending down from the end of the dotted line.

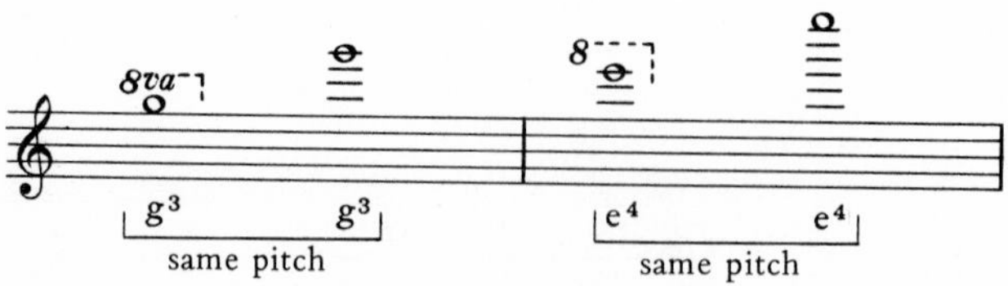

When the 8va sign is used above a note, the note sounds as though written an octave (higher/lower) _____________.

higher

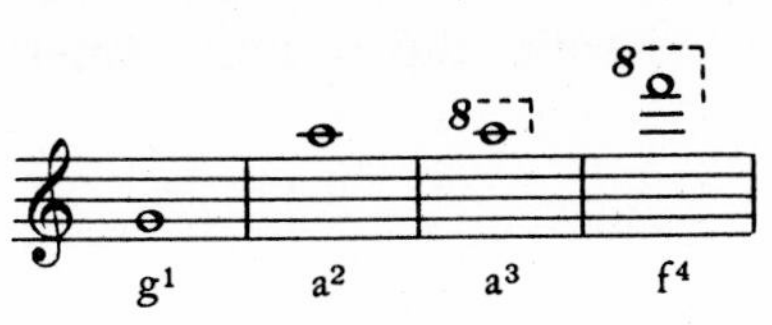

131. Identify each note by its letter name and octave-register designation.

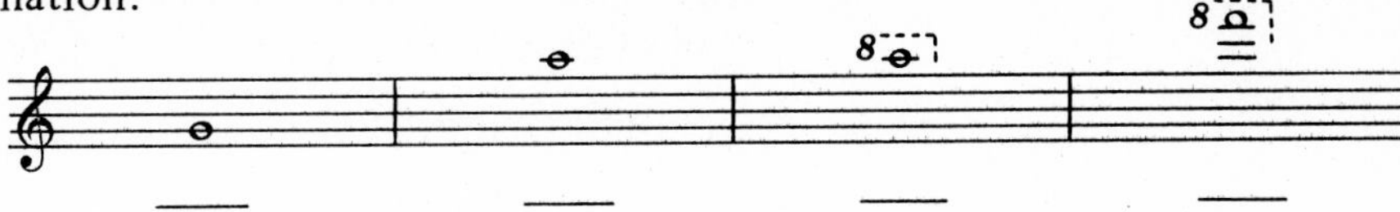

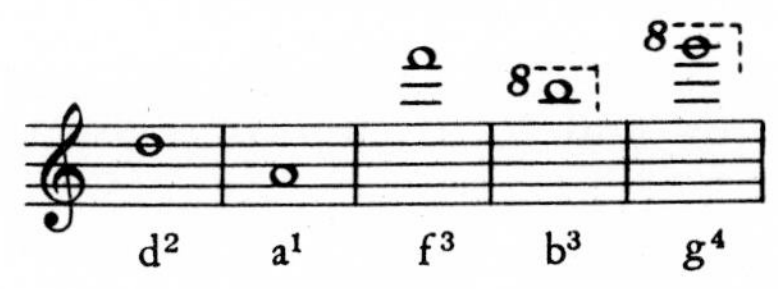

132. Place notes on the staff. Use 8va or 8 for notes g^3 or higher.

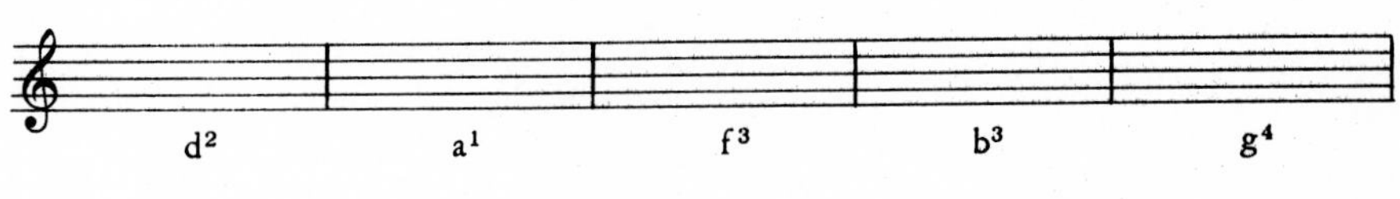

OCTAVE REGISTERS (BELOW MIDDLE C)

133. The C's below middle C receive different designations. In the list below, c^1 is again middle C and each following C is one octave lower than the previous C. (Refer again to Example 3.1, page 37). Observe that small c is a lower-case letter while the others are upper-case (large) letters.

- c^1 one-line c or c-one
- c small c
- C great C
- CC contra C
- AAA subcontra A (lowest key on piano)

C (great C) is an octave (higher/lower) ________ than c (small c).

lower

134. The lowest key on the piano is ________.

AAA (or, subcontra A)

135. Identify each C and the final note A by octave-register designation.

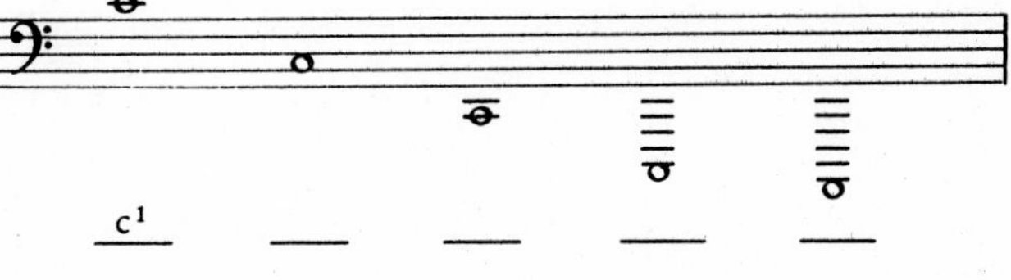

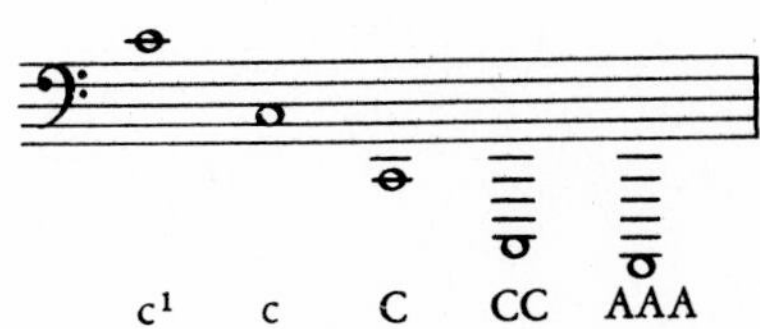

(1) GG

(2) b

(3) D

136. Below middle C, the designation of any C is also used to identify pitches in the octave above that C. For example, the E above CC is EE. Fill in these blanks:

(1) The G above CC is ________.

(2) the B above d is ________.

(3) The D above C is ________.

---

f G AA DD BBB

137. Identify each note by its letter name and by its octave-register designation.

___ ___ ___ ___ ___

---

lower

138. The 8va sign can also be used below the bass staff. (It is also occasionally used above the bass staff and infrequently below the treble staff.) Observe that the final vertical dash extends *up* from the end of the dotted line.

CC CC — same pitch

AAA AAA — same pitch

When the 8va sign is used below a note, the note sounds as though written an octave (higher/lower) ____________.

BB e♭ CC♯ A

139. Identify each note by its letter name and octave-register designation.

___ ___ ___ ___

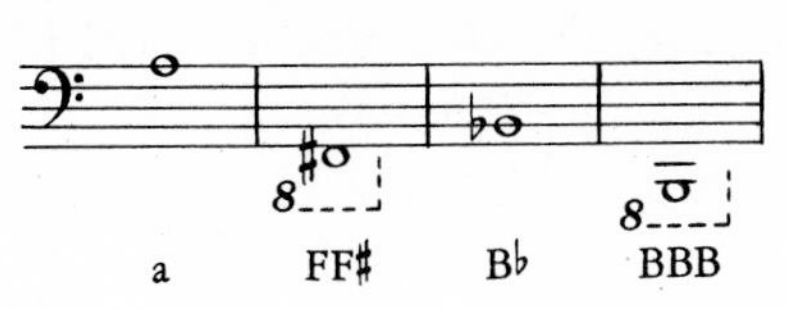

140. Place notes on the staff. Use 8va for notes GG and lower.

MUSIC EXAMPLES

141. Here in Frames 141–146 are examples showing music in various octave registers. Questions on these examples are found in Frames 147–152.

*Mozart, Symphony No. 36 in C Major (*Linz*), K. 425*

142.

Stravinsky, The Firebird

143.

Tchaikovsky, The Nutcracker, *Op. 71, "Dance of the Sugar Plum Fairy"*

144.

Beethoven, Symphony No. 5 in C Minor, Op. 67

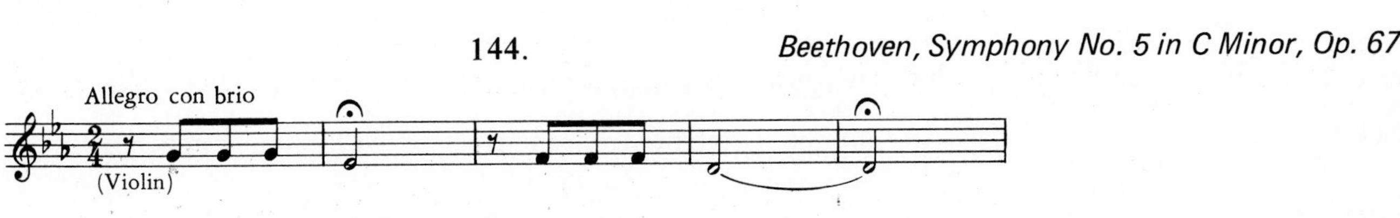

145. *Dvořák, Cello Concerto, Op. 104*

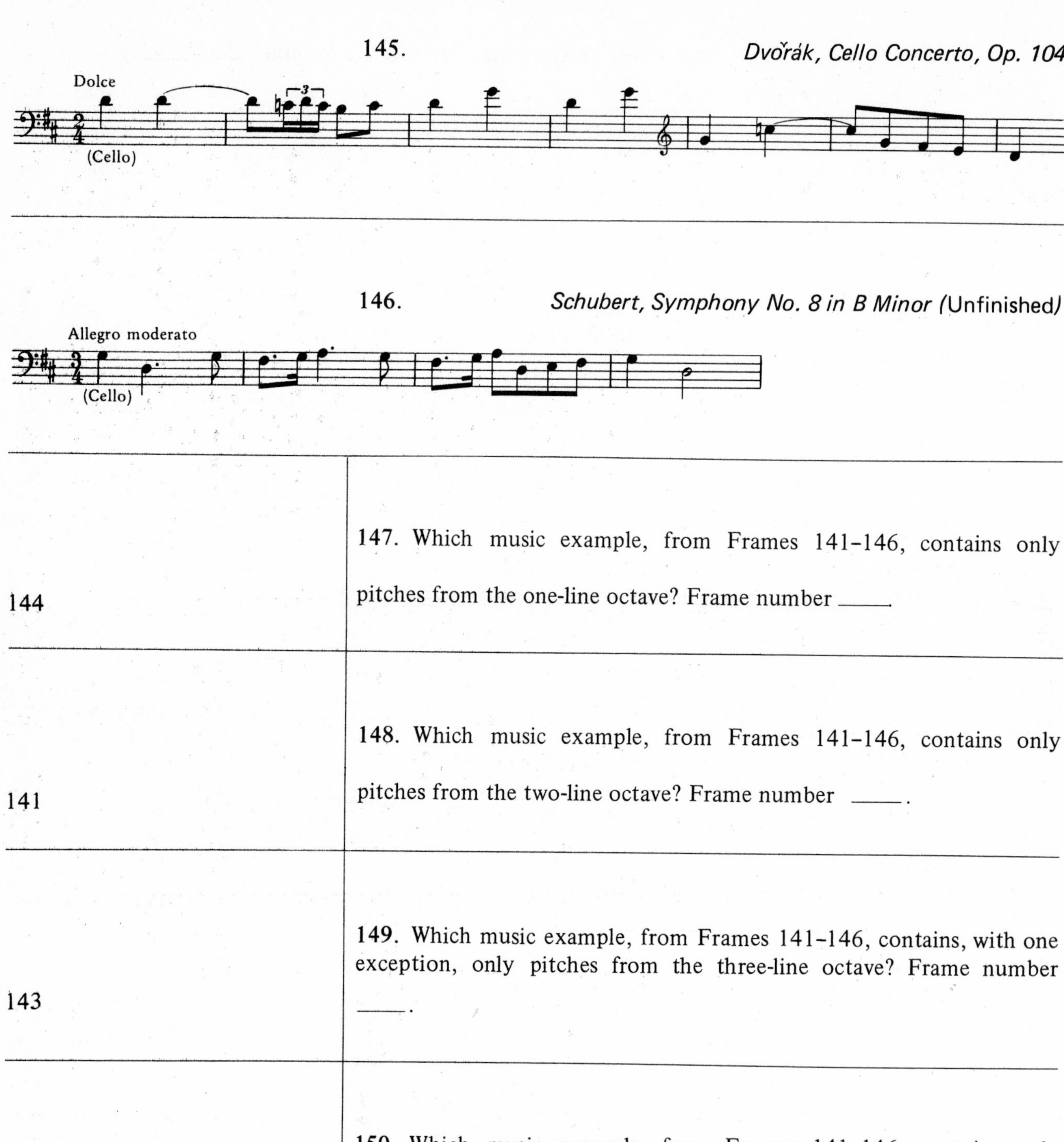

146. *Schubert, Symphony No. 8 in B Minor (Unfinished)*

144	147. Which music example, from Frames 141–146, contains only pitches from the one-line octave? Frame number ____.
141	148. Which music example, from Frames 141–146, contains only pitches from the two-line octave? Frame number ____.
143	149. Which music example, from Frames 141–146, contains, with one exception, only pitches from the three-line octave? Frame number ____.
146	150. Which music example, from Frames 141–146, contains only pitches in the small octave? Frame number ____.
142	151. Which music example, from Frames 141–146, contains, with one exception, only pitches from the great octave? Frame number ____.

(1) 145
(2) g^1
(3) g^1

152. (1) Changing a clef sign to avoid excessive ledger lines is shown in frame number ____.

(2) The last note before the change of clef is ____.

(3) The first note after the change of clef is ____.

153. The remaining three music examples are shown using the great staff. A question regarding each example is found in the frame following each example.

Saint-Saens, Piano Concerto No. 4 in C Minor, Op. 44

c^4 e^4 g^4 c^4 e^4 g^4 c^5

154. Name each of the highest notes under the 8va sign, using octave-register designations.

____ ____ ____ ____ ____ ____ ____

155. *Debussy,* Images I, *"Hommage à Rameau"*

AA | EE CC AAA DD | GG

156. Name the lowest notes on the lower staff, using octave-register designations. Omit accidentals.

——| —— —— —— ——| ——

157. *Schubert, Sonata in A Major for Piano (1828)*

e^3 e $g\sharp^2$ e^1 b^2 $g\sharp^1$ |

e^3 e b^3 $g\sharp^2$ $d\sharp^4$ b^2 |

e^4 e

158. Name each note on the upper staff, using octave-register designations. Note the clef changes.

—— —— —— —— —— ——|

—— —— —— —— —— ——|

—— ——

CHAPTER SUMMARY

1. An *octave* is an interval encompassing eight staff degrees. Both notes of the octave carry the same letter name.

2. The term *octave registers* refers to a system which designates any given pitch by a name distinctly different from any other pitch using the same letter name.

3. Each C has a distinctive designation. Starting with the lowest C on the keyboard, they are CC (contra C), C (great C), c (small c), c^1 (one-line c, or c-one), c^2, c^3, c^4, and c^5. c^1 is middle C.

4. All letter names within the octave above a given C receive the designation of that C. Above c^2 are d^2, e^2, etc.; above CC are DD, EE, etc. The two lowest white keys on the keyboard are AAA and BBB (subcontra).

5. The *octava* sign (*8va*- - - -┐ or *8*- - - -┐) over a note in the treble clef indicates that the note sounds an octave higher than written. If it is placed below a note in the bass clef, the note sounds an octave lower than written. The device is used to eliminate the need for many ledger lines.

PRE–TEST
NOTATION OF TIME

1. Name each of these notes:
   a) ♩ __________
   b) 𝅝 __________
   c) 𝅘𝅥𝅯 __________

2. Name each of these rests:
   a) 𝄼 __________
   b) 𝄾 __________
   c) 𝅀 __________

3. Are these notes written correctly? Answer Yes or No.
   a) ________
   b) ________
   c) ________
   d) ________
   e) ________
   f) ________

a) b) c) d) e) f)

4. A quarter note equals how many sixteenth notes? ________

5. A half rest equals how many thirty-second rests? ________

6. Are these notes and rests written correctly? Answer Yes or No.

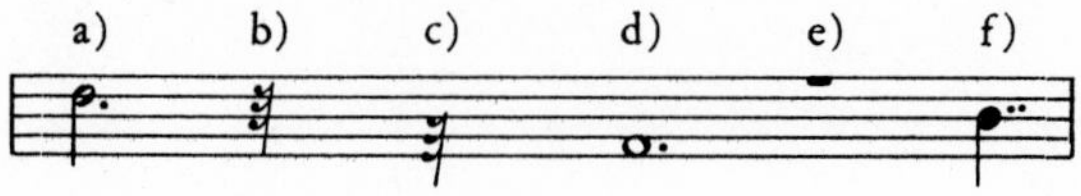

a) ________
b) ________
c) ________
d) ________
e) ________
f) ________

ANSWERS

Place a score of 5 for each correct answer in the right-hand column. Add this column for your score.

	Score
1. a) quarter	___
b) whole	___
c) sixteenth	___
2. a) whole	___
b) eighth	___
c) thirty-second	___
3. a) Yes	___
b) No	___
c) No	___
d) No	___
e) Yes	___
f) No	___
4. four	___
5. sixteen	___
6. a) No	___
b) Yes	___
c) No	___
d) Yes	___
e) No	___
f) Yes	___
Total score:	___
Perfect score:	100

If your score is 85 or better, turn now to Chapter 5, page 69. If your score is less than 85, continue with Chapter 4.

NOTATION OF TIME

Another primary characteristic of sound, other than its pitch, is its duration. When hearing a pitch or other sound, we are usually aware that it has a time value; we notice that sounds last a very short time, a very long time, or somewhere in between. In music, there must be a way to measure these time values, and there must be a system of symbols to represent these measured time values. Such a system does exist, so it is possible to express on paper the length of time a pitch, or a silence, is to be held. We will begin our study of time by learning the symbols used to express duration of sound.

duration	159. Duration refers to the length of time, long or short, that a pitch is sounded, or that a silence between.sounds lasts. The length of time a pitch is sounded is called its ________.
notes	160. Duration of a sound can be represented on the staff by the use of notes (review Frame 28). So far, in representing pitch on the staff, we have used only one type of note, 𝅝 . Several other types exist, however, for the purpose of indicating duration. Different durations of a pitch can be represented by different types of________.
relative	161. These various types of notes do not indicate absolute lengths of time, but rather how long one type of note lasts in relation to another type of note. More exact measurement is dependent upon *tempo* and *time signature,* to be studied in subsequent chapters. Various types of notes indicate (absolute/relative)________ durations of time.
twice	162. The note used in previous chapters (𝅝) is called a whole note. Other note names indicate a fractional relationship to the whole note, such as a half note (𝅗𝅥) whose duration is half that of a whole note, or a quarter note (♩) whose duration is one-quarter that of a whole note. If a whole note has twice the duration of a half note, then a half note has________ the duration of a quarter note.
half	163. Two quarter notes have the same duration as one ________ note.

four	**164.** How many quarter notes are equal in duration to one whole note? ________

CONSTRUCTION OF SINGLE NOTES

whole	**165.** With an understanding that a relationship exists between various note values, and before describing the function of these note values in greater detail, we will describe the construction of the various note values. A note is made up of one, two, or three elements: (1) the *note head,* (2) the *stem,* and (3) the *flag* (or *hook*). The note head is a tilted ellipse, either white (open) or black: white (open) black The white note head above is the same as the ________ note seen in Frame 162.
stem	**166.** The *stem* is a vertical line connected to the note head. Its length is approximately equal to a distance of three spaces on the staff. The stem may or may not be used with a white note head, but is almost always used with a black note head.* A vertical line connected to a note head is called a ________. **Black notes without stems are used in the notation of some ecclesiastical music.*
	167. The location of the note head on the staff determines the placement of the stem. When a single note is *above the third line,* the stem points down and is found on the left side of the note head. Place stems correctly on these note heads:

168. When a single note is *below the third line,* the stem points up and is found on the right side of the note head.

Place stems correctly on these note heads:

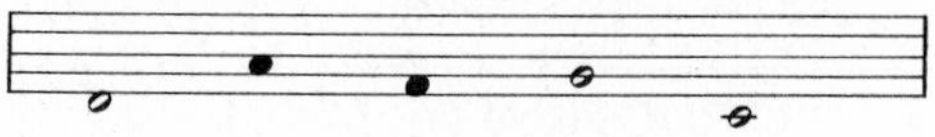

---

169. When a single note is *on the third line,* the stem may point either way.

Either stem direction may be used when the note head is on the ______ line of the staff.

third

---

170. Place stems correctly on these note heads:

(or)

---

171. The *flag* (*hook*) is often added to the stem of a black note (white notes do not have flags). One to three flags are commonly used; four and five more rarely. Flags *always* appear to the *right* of the stem.

one flag | two flags | three flags

Flags are found

a) only on ______ notes.

b) only on the ______ side of the stem.

c) commonly not more than ______ at a time.

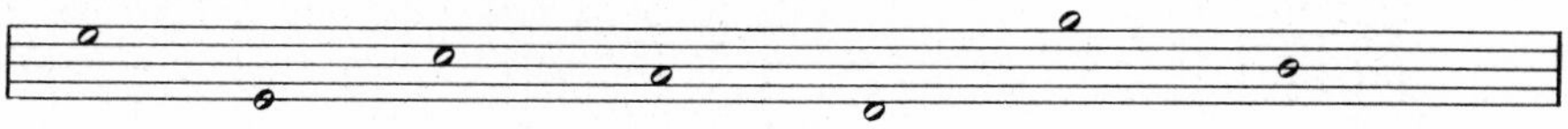

a) black

b) right

c) three

---

172. Place one flag on each of these notes:

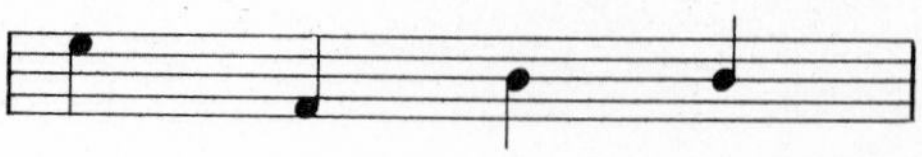

BEAMED NOTES

173. In a group of notes, each using the same number of flags, the stems may be connected by a heavy *straight* line, called a *beam* or a *ligature.* The number of beams is the same as the number of flags replaced.

a) b)

Rewrite these notes, using beams:

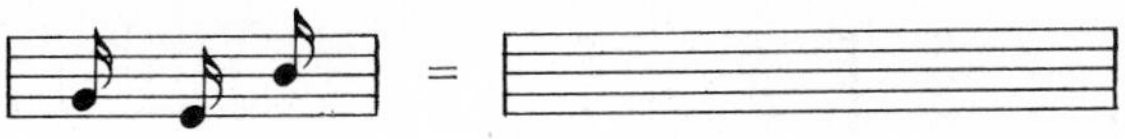

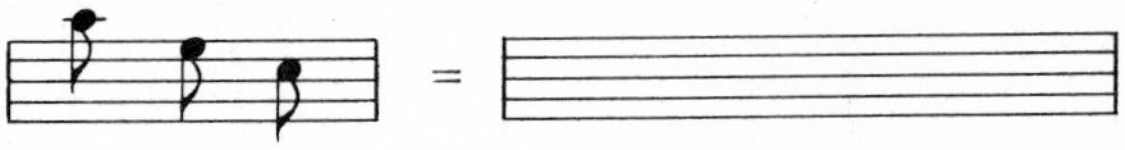

174. When beamed notes are found both above and below the third line, use a stem direction that is correct for a majority of the notes in the group.

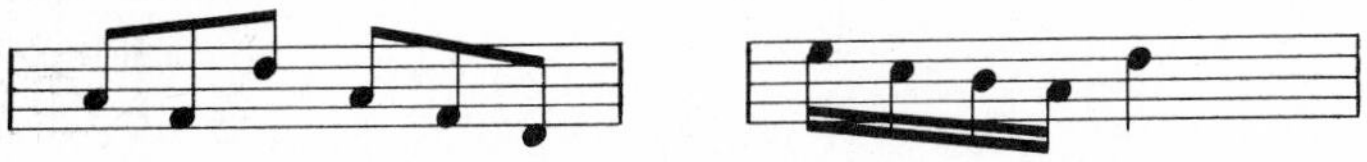

Place stems and a single beam on these notes:

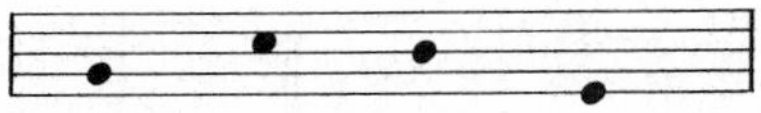

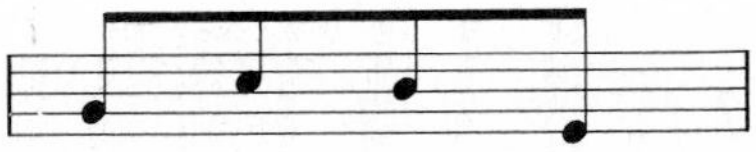

175. Place stems and two beams on this group of notes:

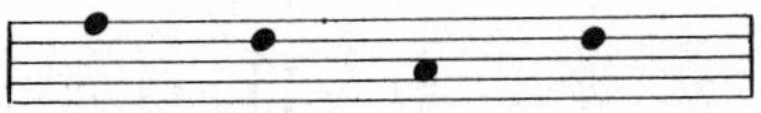

176. If there are an equal number of notes on each side of the middle line, choose a stem direction for the note farthest from the middle line.

Place stems and one beam on these notes:

NAMING NOTE VALUES

177. A note value can be identified by its construction, i.e., its combination of head, stem, and flag, while the name of the note value indicates its relationship to the whole note, which is assigned the value "1."

Note	*Name*	*Value*
𝅝	whole note	1
𝅗𝅥 or 𝅗𝅥	half note	1/2
♩ or ♩	quarter note	1/4
♪ or ♪	eighth note	1/8
𝅘𝅥𝅯 or 𝅘𝅥𝅯	sixteenth note	1/16
𝅘𝅥𝅰 or 𝅘𝅥𝅰	thirty-second note	1/32
𝅘𝅥𝅱 or 𝅘𝅥𝅱	sixty-fourth note*	1/64
𝅘𝅥𝅲 or 𝅘𝅥𝅲	128th note*	1/128
𝅜 or 𝅜 or 𝅜	double whole note*	2

**Not commonly used*

---

178. Study frame 177 and then fill in these blanks:

	Note	*Name*
a) quarter note	a) ♩	______ note
b) whole note	b) 𝅝	______ note
c) sixteenth note	c) 𝅘𝅥𝅯	______ note
d) half note	d) 𝅗𝅥	______ note
e) eighth note	e) ♪	______ note
f) thirty-second note	f) 𝅘𝅥𝅰	______ note

179. Write the notes for the given note names.

Name	Notes: Stem up	Notes: Stem down
a) half note	______	______
b) sixteenth note	______	______
c) quarter note	______	______
d) thirty-second note	______	______
e) eighth note	______	______
f) whole note	______	

a) 𝅗𝅥 𝅗𝅥
b) 𝅘𝅥𝅯 𝅘𝅥𝅯
c) 𝅘𝅥 𝅘𝅥
d) 𝅘𝅥𝅰 𝅘𝅥𝅰
e) 𝅘𝅥𝅮 𝅘𝅥𝅮
f) 𝅝

PLACING NOTES ON THE STAFF

180. After each note, draw others as indicated by arrows.

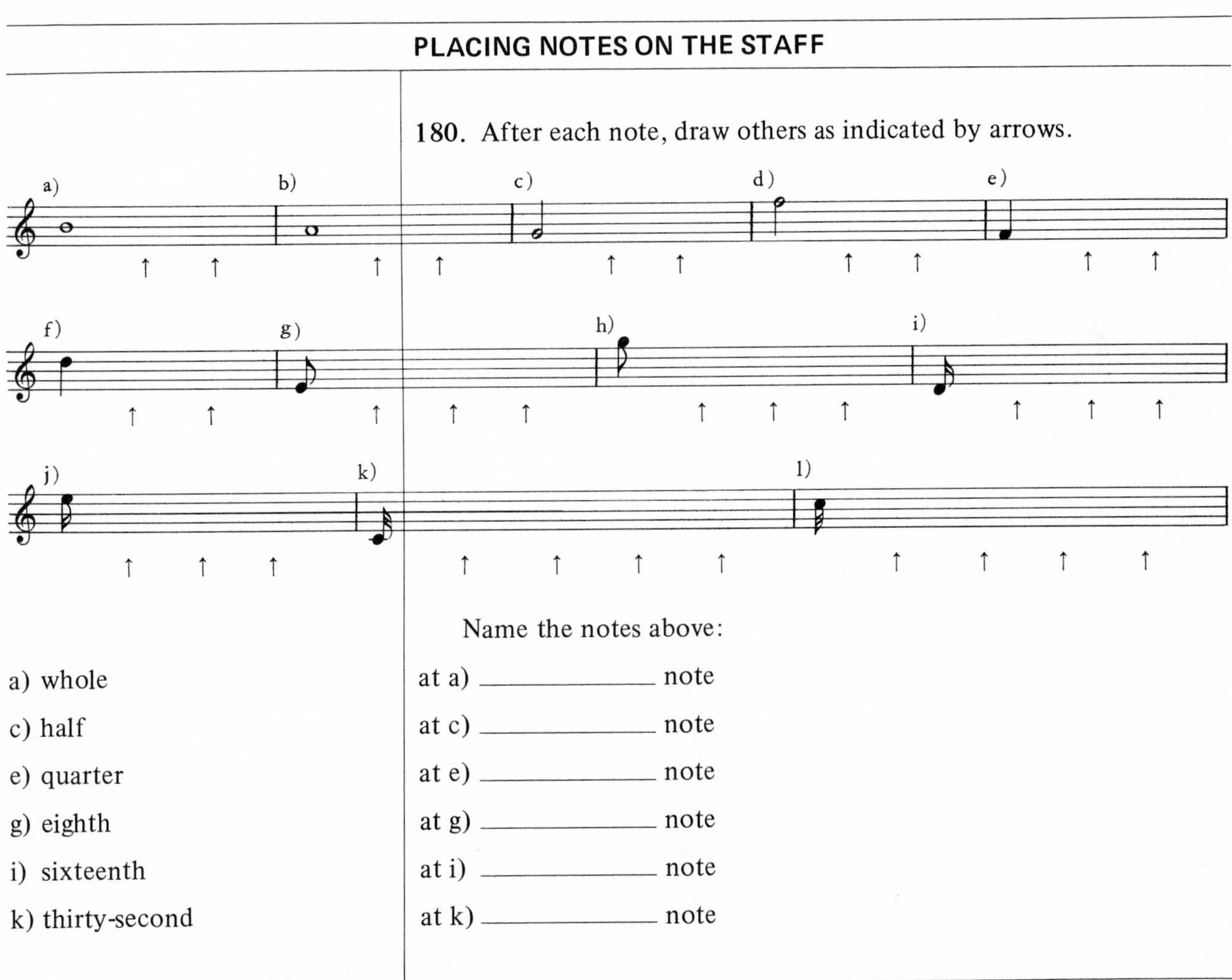

Name the notes above:

at a) ______ note
at c) ______ note
at e) ______ note
at g) ______ note
at i) ______ note
at k) ______ note

a) whole
c) half
e) quarter
g) eighth
i) sixteenth
k) thirty-second

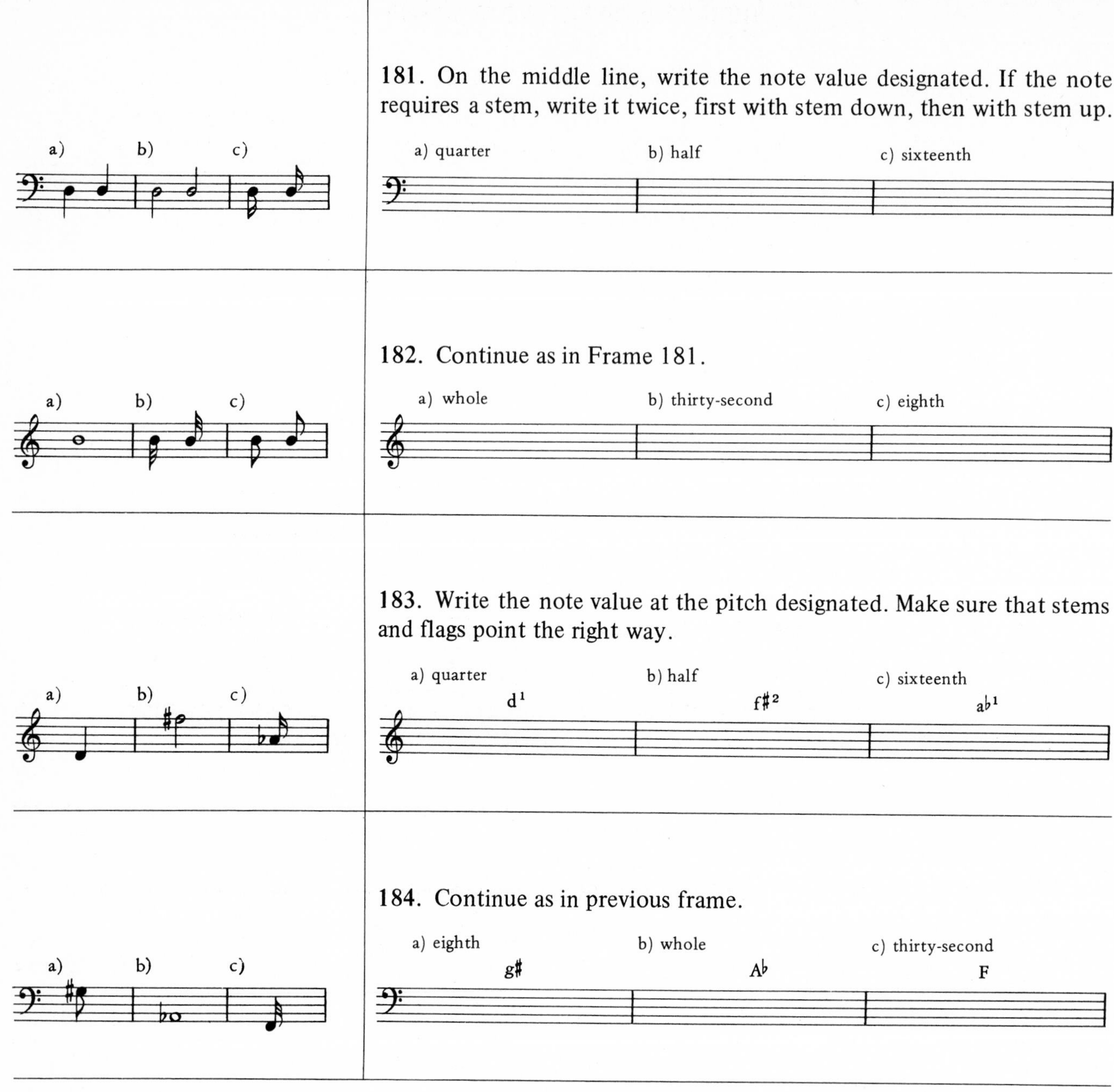
181. On the middle line, write the note value designated. If the note requires a stem, write it twice, first with stem down, then with stem up.
a)
b)
c)
a) quarter
b) half
c) sixteenth
182. Continue as in Frame 181.
a)
b)
c)
a) whole
b) thirty-second
c) eighth
183. Write the note value at the pitch designated. Make sure that stems and flags point the right way.
a)
b)
c)
a) quarter
d¹
b) half
f♯²
c) sixteenth
a♭¹
184. Continue as in previous frame.
a)
b)
c)
a) eighth
g♯
b) whole
A♭
c) thirty-second
F

RELATIONSHIP OF NOTE VALUES

185. Values of the various types of notes are not absolute, but are relative to each other, as indicated by their fractional names. In studying the example below, observe that (1) any note value is equal to two of the next lower note value, e.g., 𝅝 = 𝅗𝅥 𝅗𝅥 , or (2) two note values are equal to one of the next higher note value, e.g. 𝅗𝅥 𝅗𝅥 = 𝅝 .

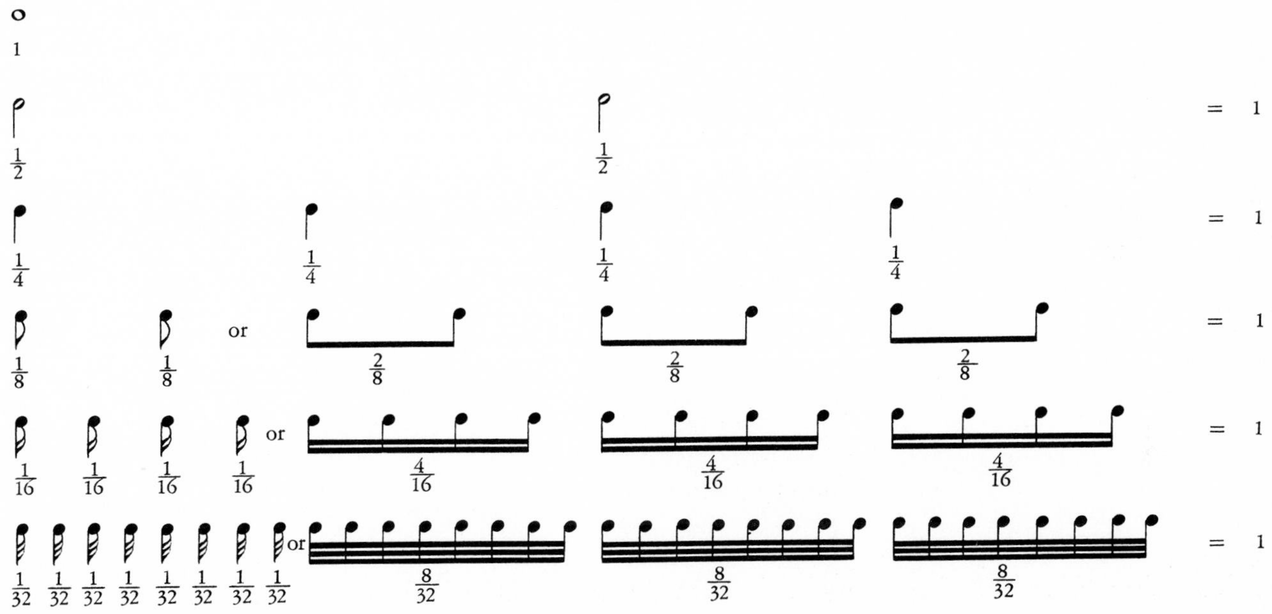

186. Indicate the two note values equal to the given note value, as demonstrated by the whole note.

𝅝 = 𝅗𝅥 𝅗𝅥 ($1 = \frac{1}{2} + \frac{1}{2}$)

𝅗𝅥 = ____ ____ ($\frac{1}{2} =$ ___ + ___)

♩ = ____ ____ ($\frac{1}{4} =$ ___ + ___)

♪ = ____ ____ ($\frac{1}{8} =$ ___ + ___)

𝅘𝅥𝅯 = ____ ____ ($\frac{1}{16} =$ ___ + ___)

𝅘𝅥𝅰 = ____ ____ ($\frac{1}{32} =$ ___ + ___)

𝅝 = 𝅗𝅥 𝅗𝅥 ($1 = \frac{1}{2} + \frac{1}{2}$)

𝅗𝅥 = ♩ ♩ ($\frac{1}{2} = \frac{1}{4} + \frac{1}{4}$)

♩ = ♪ ♪ ($\frac{1}{4} = \frac{1}{8} + \frac{1}{8}$)

♪ = 𝅘𝅥𝅯 𝅘𝅥𝅯 ($\frac{1}{8} = \frac{1}{16} + \frac{1}{16}$)

𝅘𝅥𝅯 = 𝅘𝅥𝅰 𝅘𝅥𝅰 ($\frac{1}{16} = \frac{1}{32} + \frac{1}{32}$)

𝅘𝅥𝅰 = 𝅘𝅥𝅱 𝅘𝅥𝅱 ($\frac{1}{32} = \frac{1}{64} + \frac{1}{64}$)

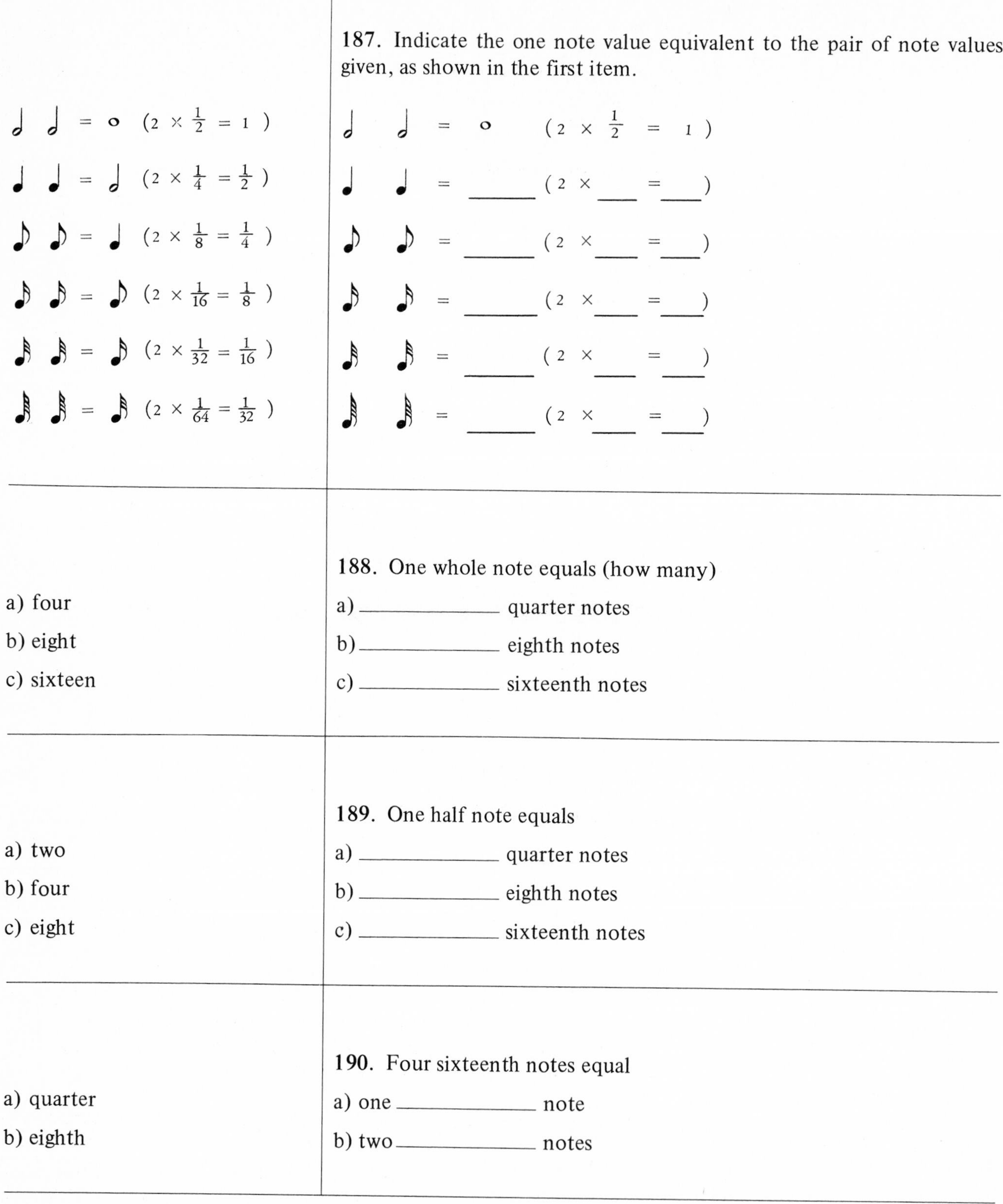

𝅗𝅥 𝅗𝅥 = 𝅝 $(2 \times \frac{1}{2} = 1)$

♩ ♩ = 𝅗𝅥 $(2 \times \frac{1}{4} = \frac{1}{2})$

♪ ♪ = ♩ $(2 \times \frac{1}{8} = \frac{1}{4})$

𝅘𝅥𝅯 𝅘𝅥𝅯 = ♪ $(2 \times \frac{1}{16} = \frac{1}{8})$

𝅘𝅥𝅰 𝅘𝅥𝅰 = 𝅘𝅥𝅯 $(2 \times \frac{1}{32} = \frac{1}{16})$

𝅘𝅥𝅱 𝅘𝅥𝅱 = 𝅘𝅥𝅰 $(2 \times \frac{1}{64} = \frac{1}{32})$

187. Indicate the one note value equivalent to the pair of note values given, as shown in the first item.

𝅗𝅥 𝅗𝅥 = 𝅝 $(2 \times \frac{1}{2} = 1)$

♩ ♩ = _____ (2 × ___ = ___)

♪ ♪ = _____ (2 × ___ = ___)

𝅘𝅥𝅯 𝅘𝅥𝅯 = _____ (2 × ___ = ___)

𝅘𝅥𝅰 𝅘𝅥𝅰 = _____ (2 × ___ = ___)

𝅘𝅥𝅱 𝅘𝅥𝅱 = _____ (2 × ___ = ___)

---

a) four
b) eight
c) sixteen

188. One whole note equals (how many)

a) __________ quarter notes
b) __________ eighth notes
c) __________ sixteenth notes

---

a) two
b) four
c) eight

189. One half note equals

a) __________ quarter notes
b) __________ eighth notes
c) __________ sixteenth notes

---

a) quarter
b) eighth

190. Four sixteenth notes equal

a) one __________ note
b) two __________ notes

a) ♩
b) 𝅗𝅥
c) 𝅝
d) 𝅗𝅥
e) 𝅝

191. Write the single note value equal to the total value of the given group, e.g., ♬♬ = ♩.

a) ♫ = ____________
b) ♫♫ = ____________
c) 𝅘𝅥 𝅘𝅥 𝅘𝅥 𝅘𝅥 = ____________
d) 𝅘𝅥𝅯𝅘𝅥𝅯𝅘𝅥𝅯𝅘𝅥𝅯 𝅘𝅥𝅯𝅘𝅥𝅯𝅘𝅥𝅯𝅘𝅥𝅯 = ____________
e) ♫♫ ♫♫ = ____________

---

a) 2
b) 16
c) 8
d) 32
e) 4

192. How many thirty-second notes are equivalent to each of the notes in the left column?

a) 𝅘𝅥𝅯 = ________ thirty-second notes
b) 𝅗𝅥 = ________ thirty-second notes
c) ♩ = ________ thirty-second notes
d) 𝅝 = ________ thirty-second notes
e) ♪ = ________ thirty-second notes

RESTS

193. Silence in music has duration, and can be represented by symbols called *rests.* For each note value representing sound there is a corresponding rest value for silence. Whether treble or bass clef is used, the position of the rest on the staff is not affected.

whole	half	quarter	8th	16th	32nd	64th	double whole
𝅝	𝅗𝅥	♩	♪	𝅘𝅥𝅯	𝅘𝅥𝅰	𝅘𝅥𝅱	𝅜
𝄻	𝄼	𝄽	𝄾	𝄿	𝅀	𝅁	𝄺

etc.

194. Observe that while symbols for whole and half rests are similar, a black oblong shape, the whole rest is found *beneath* (or suspended from) the fourth line.

Write several whole rests.

etc.

195. The half rest is *upon* (or sits on) the third line. Write several half rests.

etc.

196. There are two symbols for the quarter rest, 𝄽 and 𝄾. The first, 𝄽, is used in most American editions of music, while the symbol 𝄾 is found in many foreign editions. Because of the possible confusion with the eighth rest (𝄾 = quarter, 𝄾 = eighth), the use of 𝄾 as a quarter rest is not recommended. Write several quarter rests (as in Frame 193).

etc.

197. Write several eighth rests (the flag is in the third space).

etc.

198. Write several sixteenth rests (the upper flag is in the third space).

199. Write several thirty-second rests (with three or more flags, the upper flag is found in the fourth space).

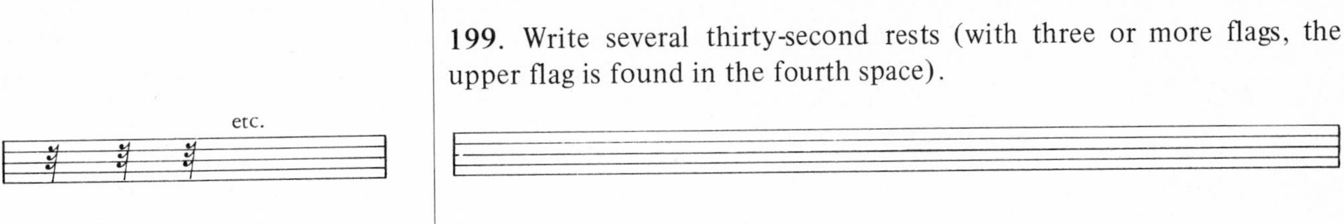

MUSIC EXAMPLES

200. Here is an example from music literature showing many different note values and rests. Answer questions in Frame 201.

Haydn, Sonata in E♭ Major for Piano

*Tremolo, *played as sixteen 32nd notes, alternating contra F and great F.*

(1) sixteenth note

(2) quarter note

(3) eighth note

(4) eighth rest

(5) half rest

(6) half note

(7) thirty-second note

201. In the music example in Frame 200, below each number is a note or rest. State complete name for each. Use two words, e.g., *whole note, whole rest,* etc.

(1) ______________ ______________

(2) ______________ ______________

(3) ______________ ______________

(4) ______________ ______________

(5) ______________ ______________

(6) ______________ ______________

(7) ______________ ______________

202. Answer questions in Frame 203.

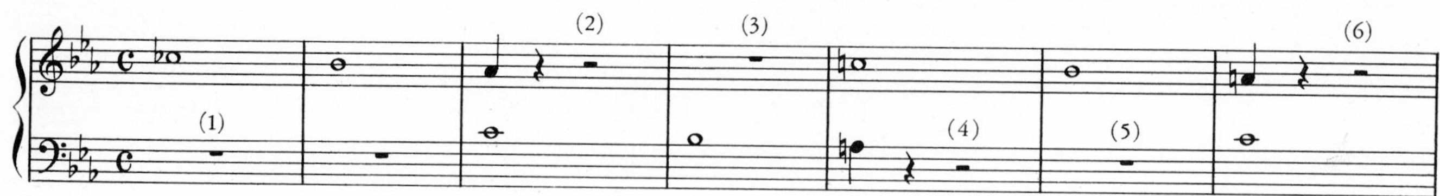

203. From the music excerpt in Frame 202 identify the rest under each number.

(1) ________ rest

(2) ________ rest

(3) ________ rest

(4) ________ rest

(5) ________ rest

(6) ________ rest

(1) whole
(2) half
(3) whole
(4) half
(5) whole
(6) half

THE DOT; THE TIE

204. The duration of a note or rest may be extended by placing a *dot* after the note: 𝅝· , 𝅘𝅥. , 𝄾· , etc. The dot increases the value of the note or rest by one half. These are called "dotted notes," e.g., "dotted whole note," "dotted eighth note," etc., and with rests, "dotted quarter rest," etc.

𝅝·	=	𝅝	+	𝅗𝅥	𝄻·	=	𝄻	+	𝄼
𝅗𝅥.	=	𝅗𝅥	+	𝅘𝅥	𝄼·	=	𝄼	+	𝄽
𝅘𝅥.	=	𝅘𝅥	+	𝅘𝅥𝅮	𝄽·	=	𝄽	+	𝄾
𝅘𝅥𝅮.	=	𝅘𝅥𝅮	+	𝅘𝅥𝅯	𝄾·	=	𝄾	+	𝄿
𝅘𝅥𝅯.	=	𝅘𝅥𝅯	+	𝅘𝅥𝅰	𝄿·	=	𝄿	+	𝅀

To increase the duration of a note or rest by one half, place a ______ after the note.

dot

a)

b)

c)

205. In the blank space, place the note value called for by the dot.

a) = + ____________

b) = + ____________

c) = + ____________

a)

b)

c)

206. In the blank space, place the rest value called for by the dot.

a) = + ____________

b) = + ____________

c) = + ____________

207. On the staff, the dot is always found in a space: (1) immediately after the note head if the note is in a space or (2) in the space above if the note is on a line.

1) 2)

Place a dotted quarter note on the staff for each letter name indicated below.

a1 f2 c1 c2 g1

a1 f2 c1 c2 g1

208. With rests, the dot is always on the third space except for the thirty-second and sixty-fourth rests, where the dot is in the fourth space, opposite the highest flag.

(In printed music, the equivalent of a dotted rest is often indicated by two rest signs, e.g., = , =).

For these rests, , , , , , place the dot in the ____________ space.

third

fourth	209. For these rests, 𝄿, 𝅀, place the dot in the ________ space.
a) ♩.. b) 𝄻.. c) ♪..	210. The *double dot,* found much less frequently than the single dot, will again increase the duration of a note or rest. The second dot receives half the value of the first dot. 𝅝.. = 𝅝 + 𝅗𝅥 + ♩ 𝄻.. = 𝄻 + 𝄼 + 𝄽 𝅗𝅥.. = 𝅗𝅥 + ♩ + ♪ 𝄼.. = 𝄼 + 𝄽 + 𝄾 ♩.. = ♩ + ♪ + 𝅘𝅥𝅯 𝄽.. = 𝄽 + 𝄾 + 𝄿 ♪.. = ♪ + 𝅘𝅥𝅯 + 𝅘𝅥𝅰 𝄾.. = 𝄾 + 𝄿 + 𝅀 Place in the right column a double dotted note equivalent to the total of the notes and rests in each left column: a) ♩ + ♪ + 𝅘𝅥𝅯 = ________ b) 𝄻 + 𝄼 + 𝄽 = ________ c) ♪ + 𝅘𝅥𝅯 + 𝅘𝅥𝅰 = ________
tie	211. The *tie* also can be used to extend the duration of a note. The tie is a curved line connecting two or more note heads on the same line or space of the staff. Two notes on the same line or space can be connected with a ______.
𝅗𝅥	212. The notes connected by a tie (or ties) sound as one note equal in duration to the sum of the values tied (rests, however, are not tied). These two notes tied, ♩‿♩, could also be written as ________.
♪.	213. These two notes tied, ♪‿𝅘𝅥𝅯, could also be written as ________.

214. Frames 214–218 contain music excerpts which illustrate various uses of dots and ties. Questions on these excerpts will be found in Frame 219.

Beethoven, Quartet for Strings, Op. 18, No. 1

215.

Folk Song

216.

Bach, Prelude and Fugue in C Minor (organ)

217.

Schumann, Myrthen, *"Hauptmanns Weib," Op. 25, No. 19*

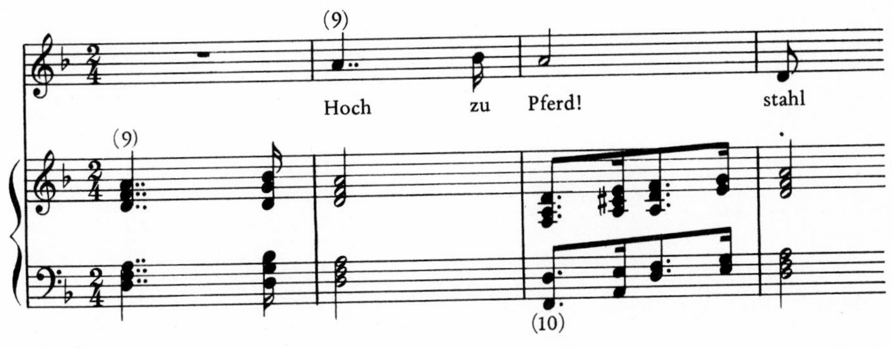

218.

Brahms, Intermezzo, Op. 117, No. 2

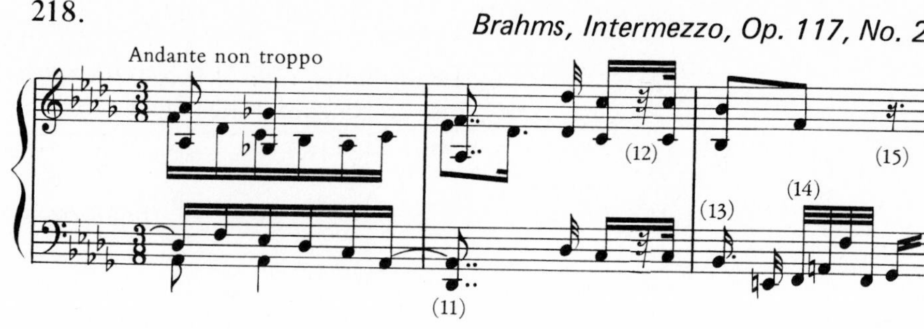

219. From frames 214–218, find an example of each of the items listed below. An example of each item described is numbered in the music. When you have found the example, place its number in the blank space before its description.

a) _____ half note tied to an eighth note

b) _____ dotted half note tied to a quarter note

c) _____ sixteenth note tied to a double dotted note

d) _____ dotted eighth note followed by a sixteenth note

e) _____ thirty-second rest

f) _____ eighth note tied to a longer undotted note

g) _____ doubled dotted quarter note

h) _____ several whole notes tied

i) _____ dotted sixteenth note followed by a thirty-second note

j) _____ eighth note tied to a longer dotted note

k) _____ quarter note tied to a sixteenth note

l) _____ dotted half note (not tied)

m) _____ group of four thirty-second notes

n) _____ dotted quarter note

o) _____ dotted sixteenth rest

a) 6
b) 1
c) 11
d) 10
e) 12
f) 4
g) 9
h) 5
i) 13
j) 2
k) 8
l) 3
m) 14
n) 7
o) 15

SIMPLE AND COMPOUND DIVISION OF NOTES VALUES

220. When a note value is divided into two parts, the division is known as *simple division.* All undotted note values divide naturally into two parts, e.g.,

𝅝 = 𝅗𝅥 𝅗𝅥, 𝅘𝅥𝅮 = 𝅘𝅥𝅯 𝅘𝅥𝅯, etc.

In simple division, a note value is divided into ________ parts

two

---

221. A simple division of a quarter note is ________ ________ notes.

two eighth

---

222. When a note value is divided into three parts, the division is known as *compound division.* All dotted notes divide naturally into three parts, e.g.,

𝅗𝅥. = 𝅘𝅥 𝅘𝅥 𝅘𝅥, 𝅘𝅥𝅮. = 𝅘𝅥𝅯 𝅘𝅥𝅯 𝅘𝅥𝅯, etc.

Division of a note value into three parts is known as ________ division.

compound

---

223. A compound division of a dotted quarter note is ________ ________ notes.

three eighth

---

224. Indicate for each item whether the division is simple or compound.

a) 𝅘𝅥𝅮. = 𝅘𝅥𝅯 𝅘𝅥𝅯 𝅘𝅥𝅯 ________

b) 𝅗𝅥 = 𝅘𝅥 𝅘𝅥 ________

c) 𝅝 = 𝅗𝅥 𝅗𝅥 ________

d) 𝅝. = 𝅗𝅥 𝅗𝅥 𝅗𝅥 ________

a) compound

b) simple

c) simple

d) compound

CHAPTER SUMMARY

1. Duration, the length of time a sound or silence is held, can be represented on the staff by note or rest values.

2. Note and rest values are not absolute, but are relative to each other, as indicated by their fractional names.

3. Note values are differentiated by varying combinations of note head, stem, and flag. Most note values may be found in varying forms according to placement on the staff.

4. *Beams* may replace flags when successive flagged notes are used.

5. The *dot,* placed to the right of a note head, receives one half the value of that note. When the *double dot* is used, the second dot receives half the value of the first dot.

6. The *tie* is a curved line connecting two or more note heads of the same pitch. These sound as one note value equalling the sum of the two or more values.

7. Dividing a note value into two parts is known as *simple division.*

8. Dividing a note value into three parts is known as *compound division.*

PRE–TEST
SIMPLE TIME

1. When beats are grouped in threes, the music is said to be in________ time.

2. When beats are grouped in twos, the music is said to be in ________ time.

3. When beats are grouped in fours, the music is said to be in________ time.

4. The distance from one bar line to the next is called a ____________.

5. A note immediately preceding the first measure is known as a(n) ________________.

6. When a note divisible into two parts is used to represent a beat, the music is said to be in ____________ time.

7. $\frac{4}{2}$ is an example of ____________ ____________ time.

8. $\frac{3}{16}$ is an example of ____________ ____________ time.

9. $\frac{2}{8}$ is an example of ____________ ____________ time.

10. The symbol ______ is commonly used as a substitute for the time signature $\frac{2}{2}$.

ANSWERS

In the right hand column, score 10 for each correct answer. Add this column for your score.

	Score
1. Triple	____
2. Duple	____
3. Quadruple	____
4. Measure	____
5. Anacrusis, *or* upbeat, *or* pickup	____
6. Simple	____
7. Quadruple simple	____
8. Triple simple	____
9. Duple simple	____
10. ¢	____
Total score:	____
Perfect score:	100

If your score is 80 or above, turn now to Chapter 6, page 92. If your score is less than 80, continue with Chapter 5.

SIMPLE TIME

Knowing the symbols used to represent durations of sounds, we must next know how to measure these durations. Measurement of solid objects is easy—we merely hold a ruler or tape measure to the object and read off in feet or inches its dimension in space. Measuring time is not so easy. We do have calendars and clocks for this purpose. These measure time in terms of years, months, days, minutes, and seconds. In music we have a different device for measuring time, one which does not have to represent a specific amount of time, but which may vary according to the needs of various pieces of music. This device is known as the beat. *Fortunately, the beat is a common experience to almost everybody. If, in listening to music, you make a* regular *series of taps with your finger or your foot, you are making beats. Each tap is measuring a small unit of time, and if the taps are regular, each beat measures the same amount of time. In another instance, if you are walking with regular steps (without changing your gait), you are also marking off regular units of time. In either case, you are not consciously measuring specific amounts of time between taps or between footsteps. The important fact is that a* regular succession *of lengths of time has been established. Beats such as these constitute the temporal measuring device of music.*

THE BEAT

beat	225. When time is divided into a regular succession of equal lengths, each of these durations is known, in music, as a *beat.* If you tap your foot with a regular succession of taps, each tap is a ______.
(Respond by singing.) .	226. Beats are best experienced while performing or listening to music. Can you sing "America"? If so, sing or whistle along with these words and make *regular taps* (each one the same length) with your finger. The vertical dash (I) indicates where the tap should occur. My coun - try 'tis of thee →I I I I I I
Sweet land of lib - er - ty →I I I I I I (Did you make a tap between " 'tis" and "of," and between "lib-" and "er-" of "liberty"? Try again if you missed this.)	227. Now, sing it again with the second line of words added. Place the vertical dash (I) at each place you make a tap in the second line. My coun - try 'tis of thee →I I I I I I Sweet land of lib - er - ty →
Hap-py birth - day to you, →I I I I I I Hap-py birth - day to you, →I I I I I I	228. Each mark you made in Frame 227 represents a beat. Try it again with these words. Hap - py birth - day to you, → I I I Hap - py birth - day to you, →

(Sing previous frame.)	229. You sang two syllables on the first tap (beat), as indicated in the answer frame above. Arriving at the word "you," it was necessary to tap twice before you moved to the second line. If this didn't happen, try it again.
same different	230. Did you observe that the beats you are tapping and the lengths of the pitches you are singing are not always the same? *Rhythm* is the name given to the varying changes of time values as shown in these two pieces. Although the beat always measures the (same/different) ________ amount of time, pitches in melody may display (same/different) ________ lengths of time.
beat	231. The regular recurring pulse in music is called the________.
rhythm	232. The pattern of varying lengths of time in a melody is called its ________.

GROUPING OF BEATS

Sweet land of lib - er - ty I I I I I I > >	233. In most music, beats tend to group themselves into patterns of two, three or four. When singing "America," you will notice that every third beat is accented—that is, it seems stronger than the other two (> = accent). Sing the tune and place accent marks in the second line. My coun - try 'tis of thee I I I I I I > > Sweet land of lib - er - ty I I I I I I

Hap-py birth - day to you,

| | | | | |
  >   >

Hap-py birth - day to you,

| | | | | |
  >   >

Sing melody again if you missed the accents.

234. In "Happy Birthday," the first word is *not* the strong accent. Can you tell where the strong accents are? Sing the tune and mark the accents.

Hap - py birth - day to you,

| | | | | |

Hap - py birth day to you,

| | | | | |

---

three

235. In both of these tunes, the accents grouped the beats into similar recurring patterns. In Frame 234, start with an accent (>), and count the beats from that accent up to the next accent. There are (how many?)________ beats in each group.

Joy to the world the

| | | |
>   >

Lord is come

| | | |
>   >

two

236. Sing the first line of "Joy to the World." Place beat marks (ı), then accents (>).

Joy to the world the

| |
>

Lord is come

There are ________ beats in each group.

1

237. In showing beat patterns, a longer line may be used to represent a strong (heavy) beat and a shorter line for a weak (light) beat. We can show a two-beat pattern as:

1 2 1 2 1 2

| ı | ı | ı
>   >   >

and a three-beat pattern as:

1 2 3 1 2 3 1 2 3

| ı ı | ı ı | ı ı
>   >   >

In the two-beat and three-beat patterns, the strong beat is numbered_____.

1 and 3

238. Four-beat patterns also exist. These are more difficult to demonstrate, as both the first and third beats are strong beats (though the third is not quite as strong as the first).

1	2	3	4	1	2	3	4
|	ı	|	ı	|	ı	|	ı

In a four-beat grouping, the strong beats are____ and____ .

two

239. Here is a well-known tune usually written in groupings of four beats:

1	2	3	4	1	2	3	4
Jin - gle	bells,	jin - gle	bells,	jin - gle	all the	way,	
ı >	ı	ı >	ı	ı >	ı	ı >	ı

While singing and tapping this tune, you will notice that you can easily consider it to be in two-beat groupings, each group of four beats sounding like two groups of two beats. Differentiation between two-beat and four-beat groupings will be easier when we have studied the notation of time.

A four-beat grouping often sounds much like (how many?)____ two-beat groupings.

two, three, and four

240. Although other groupings exist, and will be studied later, we have now considered those most often used in music. They are:______-beat, ______-beat, and ______-beat groupings.

a) two
b) three
c) four

241. When beats are in groups of two, the music is said to be in *duple time;* in groups of three, *triple time;* and in groups of four, *quadruple time.* (The word *meter* is often used instead of *time.*)

a) Duple time means ______ beats per group.

b) Triple time means ______ beats per group.

c) Quadruple time means ______ beats per group.

three, triple	242. "America," in Frame 233, shows groups of ________ beats; therefore it is in ________ time.
two, duple	243. "Joy to the World," Frame 235, shows groups of ________ beats; therefore it is in ________ time.
four, quadruple	244. "Jingle Bells," Frame 239, shows groups of ________ beats; therefore it is in ________ time.

RELATION OF NOTE VALUES TO BEATS

note	245. Now that you have heard beats and know their groupings, we must find a way to put this information on the staff. This is easy to do. We merely select a note value from those studied in the previous chapter, and assign this note the value of one beat. To represent a beat in music, any ________ value may be used.
Hap-py birth - day to you ♩ ♩ ♩ ♩ ♩ ♩	246. Although any possible note value (dotted or undotted) may be used to represent a beat, the quarter note is the most commonly used. In Frame 228 you marked the beats for "Happy Birthday." Let us sing "Happy Birthday" again, and write a quarter note (♩) at the place for each beat. Hap - py birth - day to you ♩

quarter	247. When you tap the beats in Frame 246, you are tapping ________ note values.
Hap - py birth - day ♪ ♪ ♩ ♩	248. On the word "Hap-py" you tapped *one* beat, but you sang *two* syllables, equally dividing the beat. This means you must use two note values equal to one quarter note. Place these two note values under "Hap-py." Hap - py birth - day ♩ ♩
two	249. You held the word "you" longer than one beat. How many beats was it held? ________
half	250. Since "you" is held two beats, the two beats are tied together, ♩‿♩, so we need a note value twice as long as a quarter note. Such a note is a ________ note.
Beats: I I I I I I Notes: ♪ ♪ ♩ ♩ ♩ 𝅗𝅥	251. Place the half note in its correct position. Hap - py birth - day to you Beats: I I I I I I Notes: ♪ ♪ ♩ ♩ ♩

252. We will now place all the notes of "Happy Birthday" on the staff, as would be found in a printed edition. Refer to this frame in Frames 253–262.

BAR LINE; MEASURE; ANACRUSIS; DOUBLE BAR

three

253. We have already decided that the beats of "Happy Birthday" are found in groups of ________.

you

254.* To indicate groups of beats on the staff, we place a *bar line* before each strong beat. In the example below, the syllable "birth-" appears on the first strong beat; therefore the first bar line is placed before the syllable "birth-." The next bar line is placed before the word "________."

**Bar line* and *double bar* are discussed here and in Frame 260. For repeat signs, *da capo, dal segno,* and first and second endings, see Appendix 4, page 349.

255. Frame 252 contains the remaining bar lines needed. The distance from one bar line to the next is called a *measure.*

bar lines

A *measure* is the distance between two ____ ________.

---

256. In a given piece of music, all measures are ordinarily alike in that each has the same number of beats as the others. In "Happy Birthday,"

three

each measure has ________beats.

---

257. However, before the first bar line of "Happy Birthday," there are only two eighth notes (= ♩), not a full measure. When the first few notes of a melody do not last the full measure, they are usually simply written ahead of the first bar line. This note, or group of notes is known as an *anacrusis.*

Happy

In Frame 252, the anacrusis is on the word "________."

---

258. When found exactly on the beat preceding the accent, or on a note value shorter than that beat, the anacrusis is also known as an *upbeat* or *pickup,* while the accent is known as a *downbeat.* These terms refer to the actions of the conductor of a music ensemble: a rising hand movement on the beat before the bar line, and a downward movement at the accent.

In Frame 252, the piece begins on an anacrusis, also known as an

upbeat, pickup

____________ or as a ____________.

---

downbeat

259. In Frame 233, the first word occurs on the ____________. (upbeat/downbeat).

260. While the bar line separates each group of beats, the *double bar*

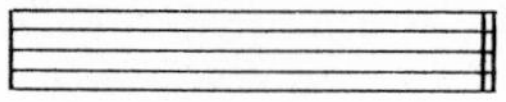

marks the end of a piece of music. This can be seen by looking at the end of any music composition (see Frame 252).

Two bar lines at the end of a piece is known as a __________.

double bar

---

261. When a piece begins with an anacrusis, the last measure before the double bar contains only that number of beats, which, when added to the anacrusis, will equal the number of beats in each of the other measures. If "Happy Birthday" has an anacrusis of one beat, the last measure should include only ________ beats (remembering that there are three beats per measure).

two

---

262. In this example:

a) There are ________ beats in each measure.

b) The anacrusis receives ________ beat.

c) The final measure receives ________ beat.

d) The total of the anacrusis and the final measure is ________ beats.

a) two

b) one

c) one

d) two

SIMPLE TIME SIGNATURES

263. Refer to Frame 252 again. Only the symbol $\frac{3}{4}$ at the beginning has been left unexplained. This is a *time signature* (*meter signature*). This device announces in advance of the music what to expect in terms of number of beats in a measure and the notation to be used to represent the beat.

$\frac{3}{4}$ is an example of a ________ __________.

time signature

264. A time signature is derived by adding together all the beat values of a full measure. Thus in Frame 252, each measure has three beats, each represented by a quarter note.

| ♩ ♩ ♩ |

$\frac{1}{4} + \frac{1}{4} + \frac{1}{4} = \frac{3}{4}$

The sum equals a time signature, in this case $\frac{3}{4}$. Placed at the beginning of the piece, its numerator, 3, tells us in advance that there will be three beats per measure, and its denominator, 4, tells us in advance that a quarter note will represent the beat (4 stands for ¼ or quarter).

When the signature is $\frac{3}{4}$, a ____________ note represents the beat.

quarter

265. When the beat value is represented by an undotted note value (as in the previous frame), the time signature is known as a *simple* time signature. The name derives from the fact that the beat note used is capable of *simple* division, that is, division into two parts.

Circle each note which can be used to represent a beat in simple time.

♩, 𝅗𝅥., ♪, 𝅘𝅥𝅯, ♪.

♩, ♪, 𝅘𝅥𝅯

266. Observe from Example 5.1 that all time signatures with a numerator of 2 indicate *duple simple* time. The numerator in duple simple time means that there are two beats in a measure, and each beat is divisible into two parts (or, two beat-divisions).

In the same way, any numerator of 3 indicates triple simple time, and any numerator of 4 indicates quadruple simple time.

a) Duple simple time is indicated by a numerator of ____.

b) Quadruple simple time is indicated by a numerator of ____.

c) Triple simple time is indicated by a numerator of ____.

a) 2

b) 4

c) 3

Ex. 5.1 *Derivation of Simple Time (Meter) Signatures*

Beat Value	Beat Grouping	Meter (Time) Signature	Meter Name
eighth note $\frac{1}{8}$	one, two: $\frac{1}{8} + \frac{1}{8} =$	$\frac{2}{8}$	DUPLE SIMPLE
quarter note $\frac{1}{4}$	one, two: $\frac{1}{4} + \frac{1}{4} =$	$\frac{2}{4}$	
half note $\frac{1}{2}$	one, two: $\frac{1}{2} + \frac{1}{2} =$	$\frac{2}{2}$ or ¢*	
eighth note $\frac{1}{8}$	one, two, three: $\frac{1}{8} + \frac{1}{8} + \frac{1}{8} =$	$\frac{3}{8}$	TRIPLE SIMPLE
quarter note $\frac{1}{4}$	one, two, three: $\frac{1}{4} + \frac{1}{4} + \frac{1}{4} =$	$\frac{3}{4}$	
half note $\frac{1}{2}$	one, two, three: $\frac{1}{2} + \frac{1}{2} + \frac{1}{2} =$	$\frac{3}{2}$	
eighth note $\frac{1}{8}$	one, two, three, four: $\frac{1}{8} + \frac{1}{8} + \frac{1}{8} + \frac{1}{8} =$	$\frac{4}{8}$	QUADRUPLE SIMPLE
quarter note $\frac{1}{4}$	one, two, three, four: $\frac{1}{4} + \frac{1}{4} + \frac{1}{4} + \frac{1}{4} =$	$\frac{4}{4}$ or C*	
half note $\frac{1}{2}$	one, two, three, four: $\frac{1}{2} + \frac{1}{2} + \frac{1}{2} + \frac{1}{2} =$	$\frac{4}{2}$	

*See Frame 274.

These signatures can also be derived this way: multiply the number of beats per measure by the note value; e.g., 2 (beats per measure) X ¼ (quarter note beat value) = $\frac{2}{4}$.

quadruple simple	267. 4 in the numerator of a time signature indicates ________ ________ time.
duple simple	268. 2 in the numerator of a time signature indicates ________ ________ time.
triple simple	269. 3 in the numerator of a time signature indicates ________ ________ time.
three	270. These time signatures have what in common? $\frac{3}{4}$ $\frac{3}{8}$ $\frac{3}{2}$. They all indicate ________ beats per measure.
eighth	271. The lower number of a simple time signature indicates the simple note value used to represent one beat: 2 means ½, or a half note 4 means ¼, or a quarter note 8 means 1/8, or an eighth note Example, $\frac{3}{4}$: a quarter note receives one beat. With the signature $\frac{3}{8}$, each beat is represented by a(n) ________ note.

Ex. 5.2. *Meaning of Simple Time Signatures*

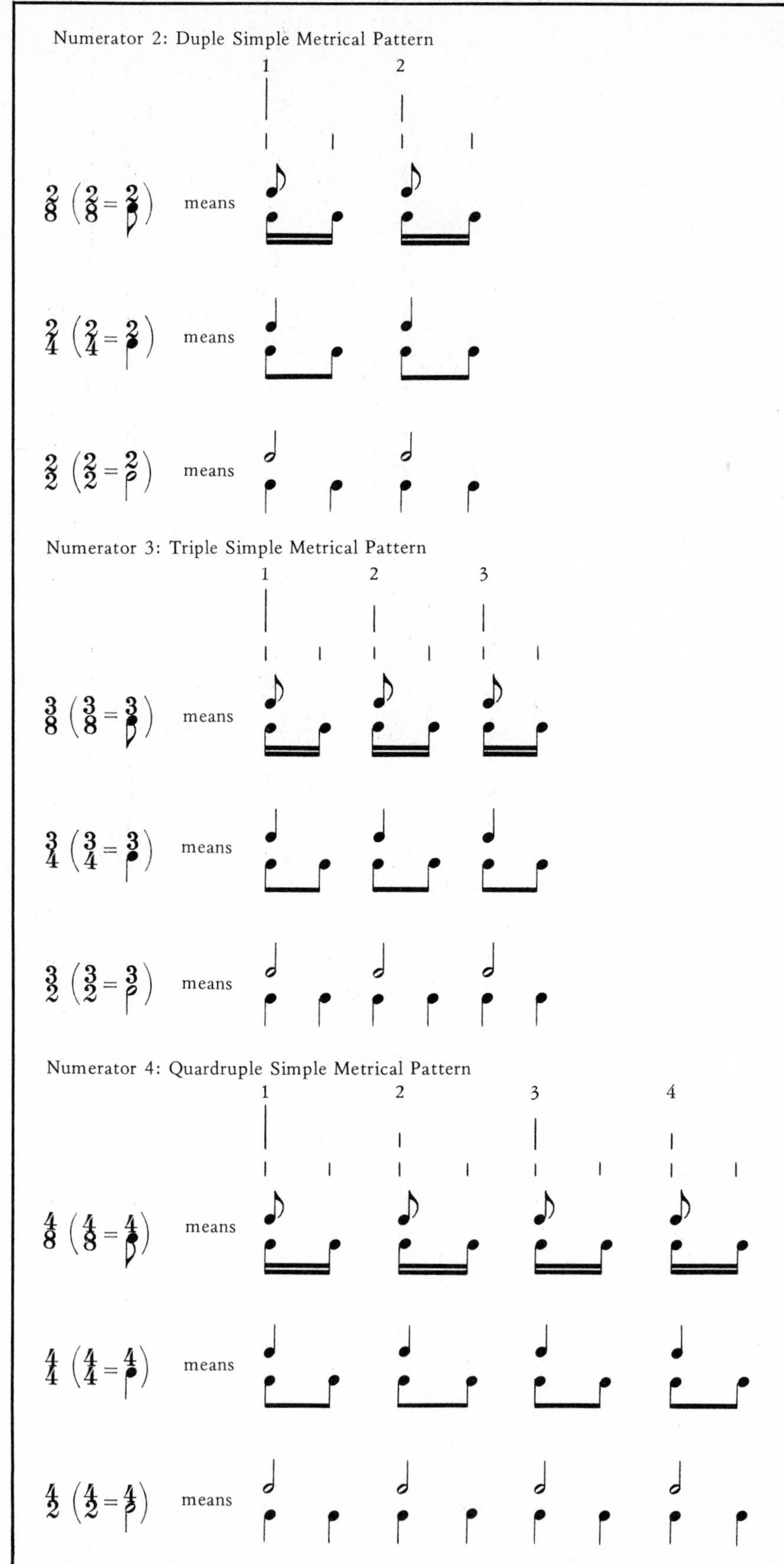

half	272. With the signature $\frac{4}{2}$, each beat is represented by a ________ note.
simple	273. These time signatures have what in common? $\frac{2}{4}$ $\frac{3}{8}$ $\frac{4}{2}$. They all indicate ________ time.
a) **C** b) **¢**	274. Example 5.1 contains two alternate time signatures, **C** and **¢** **C** is called *common time,* and substitutes for $\frac{4}{4}$. **¢** is called *cut time* or *alla breve* and substitutes for $\frac{2}{2}$. a) Instead of $\frac{4}{4}$, use the signature ____. b) Instead of $\frac{2}{2}$, use the signature____. Study now Example 5.2 (page 84).
no response	275. Using the beat note given, convert the given metrical pattern to notation, showing the beats and the beat divisions. Also, supply the time signature and in the blank spaces, name the meter. Example: ♩ = 1 beat Answer: $\frac{2}{4}$ duple simple Follow these directions in Frames 276–279.

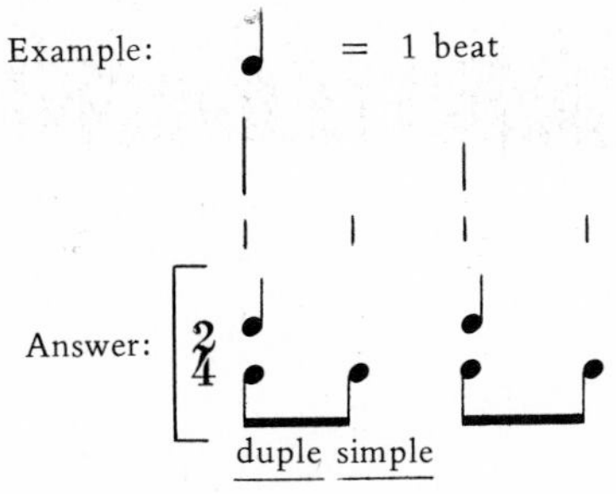

$\frac{2}{8}$ ♪ ♪
duple simple

276. ♪ = 1 beat

$\frac{3}{4}$ ♩ ♩ ♩
triple simple

277. ♩ = 1 beat

$\frac{4}{8}$ ♪ ♪ ♪ ♪
quadruple simple

278. ♪ = 1 beat

$\frac{3}{2}$ 𝅗𝅥 𝅗𝅥 𝅗𝅥
triple simple

279. 𝅗𝅥 = 1 beat

CORRELATING RHYTHMIC PATTERNS WITH METRICAL PATTERNS

280. In this and similar exercises following, a series of numbers, such as 1 2 3 4, indicates the beats in one measure. Place each note of the given rhythmic pattern below the correct beat number.

Example: 4/4 𝅗𝅥 ♩ ♩ Answer: 4/4 1 2 3 4 / 4/4 𝅗𝅥 ♩ ♩

Continue with this example:

4/4 ♩ ♩ ♩ ♩ | ♩ ♩ 𝅗𝅥 ||

4/4 1 2 3 4 | 1 2 3 4 ||
4/4 | ||

Answer:
4/4 1 2 3 4 | 1 2 3 4 ||
4/4 ♩ ♩ ♩ ♩ | ♩ ♩ 𝅗𝅥 ||

281. 4/4 𝅝 | ♩ ♩ 𝅗𝅥 ||

4/4 1 2 3 4 | 1 2 3 4 ||
4/4 | ||

Answer:
4/4 1 2 3 4 | 1 2 3 4 ||
4/4 𝅝 | ♩ ♩ 𝅗𝅥 ||

282. 4/4 𝅗𝅥. ♩ | 𝅗𝅥 𝅗𝅥 ||

4/4 1 2 3 4 | 1 2 3 4 ||
4/4 | ||

Answer:
4/4 1 2 3 4 | 1 2 3 4 ||
4/4 𝅗𝅥. ♩ | 𝅗𝅥 𝅗𝅥 ||

283. 3/4 𝅗𝅥. | ♩ ♩ ♩ ||

3/4 1 2 3 | 1 2 3 ||
3/4 | ||

Answer:
3/4 1 2 3 | 1 2 3 ||
3/4 𝅗𝅥. | ♩ ♩ ♩ ||

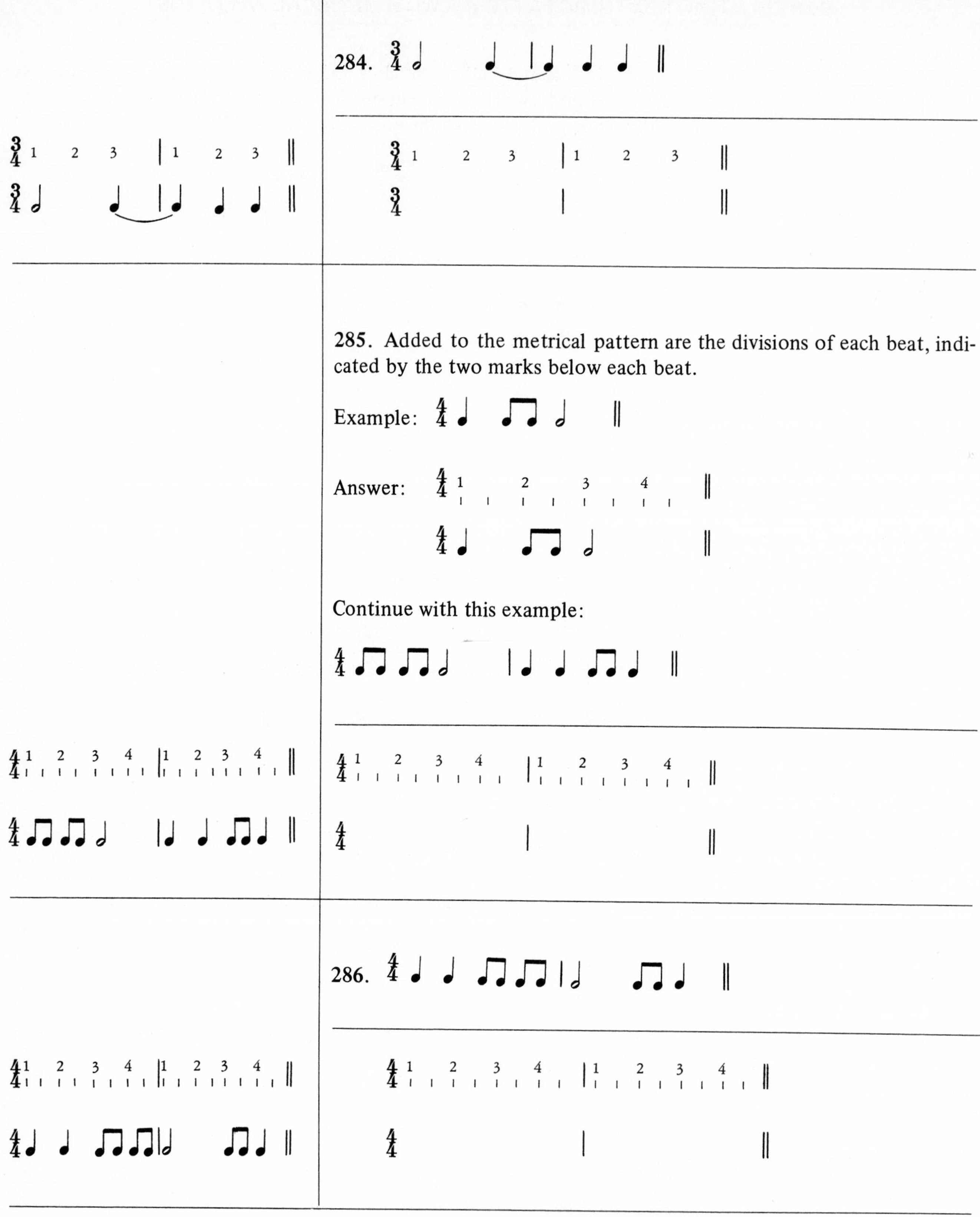
284.
1 2 3 1 2 3
1 2 3 1 2 3
285. Added to the metrical pattern are the divisions of each beat, indicated by the two marks below each beat.
Example:
Answer:
1 2 3 4
Continue with this example:
1 2 3 4 1 2 3 4
1 2 3 4 1 2 3 4
286.
1 2 3 4 1 2 3 4
1 2 3 4 1 2 3 4

287. 4/4

4/4 1 2 3 4 | 1 2 3 4 ||

4/4 | ||

4/4 1 2 3 4 | 1 2 3 4 ||

288. 4/4

4/4 1 2 3 4 | 1 2 3 4 ||

4/4 | ||

4/4 1 2 3 4 | 1 2 3 4 ||

289. In the remaining frames, 2 or 8 is found in the denominator.

Example: 2/2

Answer: 2/2 1 2 | 1 2 ||

no response

290. 4/2

4/2 1 2 3 4 | 1 2 3 4 ||

4/2 | ||

4/2 1 2 3 4 | 1 2 3 4 ||

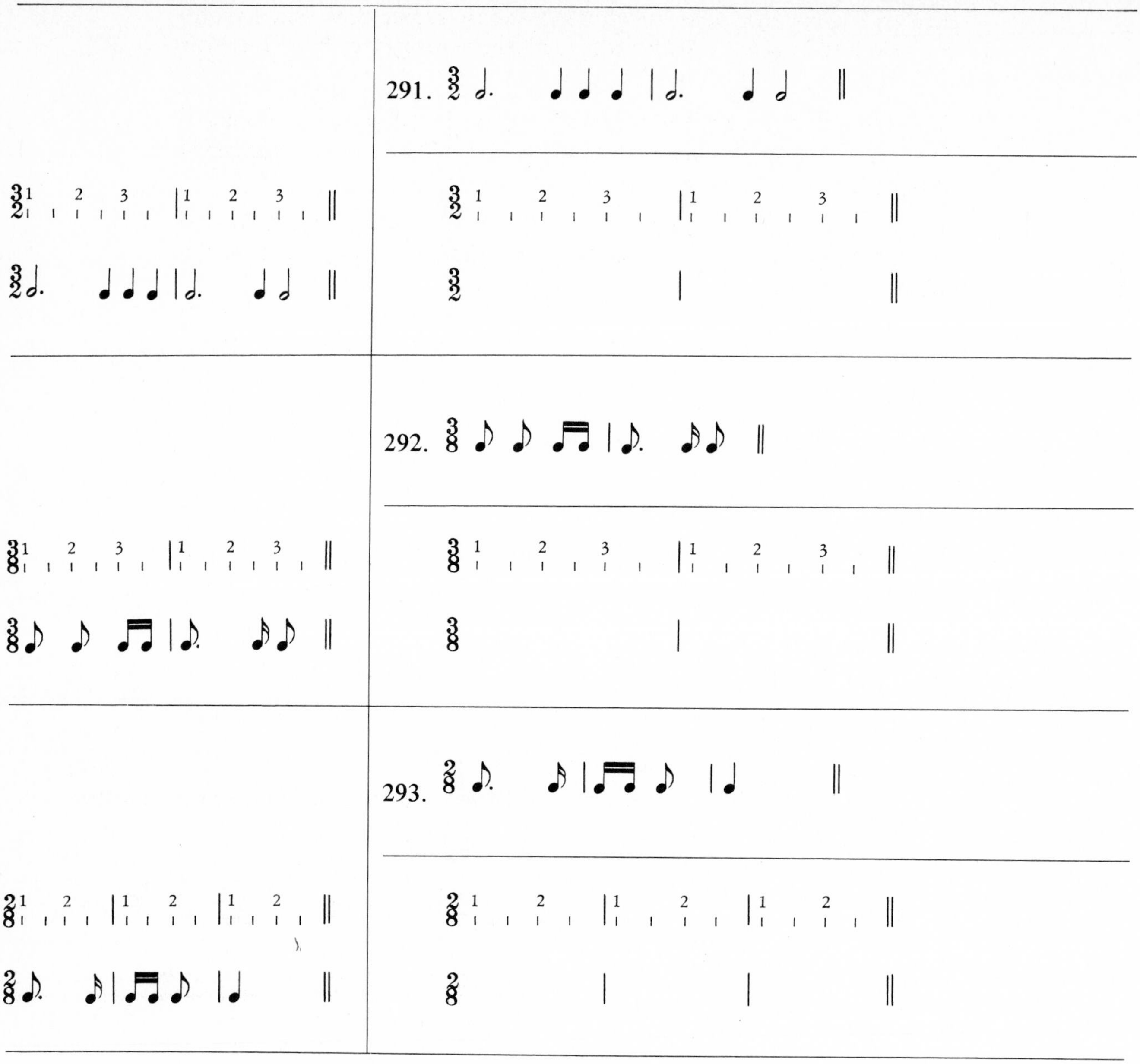

291. 3/2

292. 3/8

293. 2/8

CHAPTER SUMMARY

1. The *beat,* a temporal measuring device in music, indicates a regular succession of lengths of time.

2. Beats tend to group themselves into patterns of two, three, and four. These groupings are referred to as *duple time* (or *meter*), *triple time,* and *quadruple time.*

3. *Bar lines* mark off groups of beats.

4. A *measure* is the distance between two bar lines. Each measure usually encompasses two, three, or four beats.

5. A *time signature* is a device placed at the beginning of a piece of music to indicate the number of beats in a measure and the notation to be used.

6. *Simple time signatures* are those which use simple time values (notes divisible into two parts) as the beat, and can be recognized by numerators of 2, 3, or 4.

7. Combining the concepts of simple time and beat groupings results in three types of simple time signatures: *duple simple, triple simple,* and *quadruple simple.*

8. The *anacrusis* is a single note or a few notes found preceding the first bar line, or before the first accent of a melodic line. When it consists of a single note it is also known as an *upbeat* or *pickup.*

9. **C** (common time) is a substitute for $\frac{4}{4}$; ¢ (cut time) is a substitute for $\frac{2}{2}$.

PRE–TEST
COMPOUND TIME

1. In compound time, the note value representing the beat is divisible into ____________ parts.

2. Compound time may be recognized by time signatures with these numerators:

   a) ____________ b) ____________ c) ____________

3. Write a time signature for each of these specifications:

   a) duple compound time, 𝅗𝅥. = 1 beat ________

   b) quadruple compound time, ♩. = 1 beat ________

   c) triple compound time, ♪. = 1 beat ________

4. Place the correct time signature before each of these rhythm patterns.

   a)____

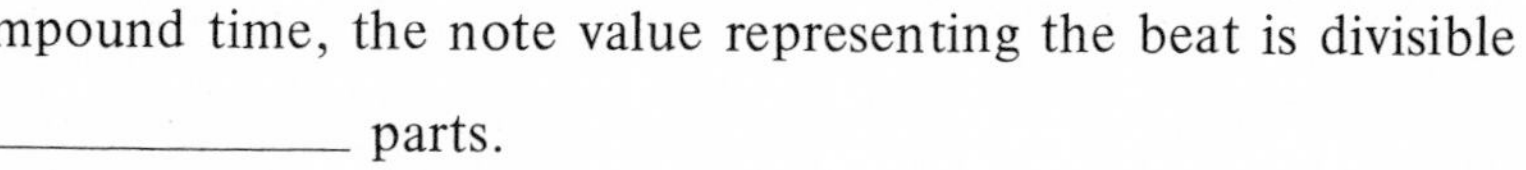

   b)____

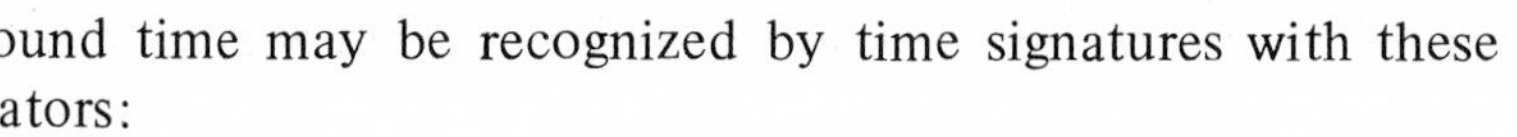

5. The beams in one measure of each of the following are incorrect. Rewrite the measure, using beams correctly.

a) $\frac{6}{8}$

b) $\frac{9}{8}$

c) $\frac{3}{4}$

6. One measure of this example shows incorrect use of rests. Rewrite the measure.

$\frac{6}{8}$

7. If in a piece of music a given beat note, ♪, is to have the duration of one half second, it can be indicated this way:

♪ = M.M. ______

ANSWERS

A score is given in parentheses after each answer. Place score for each correct answer in the right-hand column. Add this column for your score.

Score

1. three (10) ____

2. (any order) ____

a) 6 (5) ____

b) 9 (5) ____

c) 12 (5) ____

3. a) $\frac{6}{4}$ (10) ____

b) $\frac{12}{8}$ (10) ____

c) $\frac{9}{16}$ (10) ____

4. a) $\frac{9}{4}$ (10) ____

b) $\frac{6}{16}$ (10) ____

5. a) second measure: ♪♪♪ ♪♪♪ (5) ____

b) first measure: ♩. ♪♪♪ ♪♪♪ (5) ____

c) second measure: ♫ ♫ ♫ (5) ____

6. fourth measure: 𝄽 𝄾 𝄾 ♫ (5) ____

7. 120 (5) ____

Total score: ____

Perfect score: 100

If your score is 80 or above, turn now to Chapter 7, page 119. If your score is less than 80, continue with Chapter 6.

chapter six

COMPOUND TIME

COMPOUND TIME SIGNATURES

compound	294. Compound time is so called because it uses a compound note value to represent the beat. (Review Chapter 4, Frame 222). In compound time, the beat is represented by a ____________ note value.
compound	295. Compound note values are those notes divisible into three equal parts. If a note is divisible into three parts, it is a ____________ note value.
dotted	296. Only dotted notes have compound division. Therefore, in compound time, a ____________ note will represent a beat.
3/8	297. Most commonly used as a compound beat note is the dotted quarter note. ♩. = ♪ + ♪ + ♪ $\frac{1}{8} + \frac{1}{8} + \frac{1}{8} = \frac{3}{8}$ Therefore a ♩. note has a fractional value of __/__.
♪ ♪ ♪	298. The compound division of a ♩. is notated ____________.
♩ ♩ ♩	299. The compound division of a 𝅗𝅥. note is notated ____________.
3/4	300. A 𝅗𝅥. note has a fractional value of __/__.

3	301. A single dotted note can be represented mathematically only by a fraction with a numerator of ____.
quadruple	302. Compound time, like simple time, is found in beat groupings of two, three, and four. These groupings are called duple compound, triple compound, and ________ compound time.

303. Sing this well-known Christmas song, tapping the beats and accents as indicated.

*The slur *connecting notes of different pitch is used when one word or one syllable is found on two or more different pitches, showing just what notes are used with that word or syllable.*

anacrusis (upbeat, pickup) If you missed this, review Frames 257–258.	304. The first note in Frame 303, an ♪ note, is called the ________.
♩.	305. The first beat of the first complete measure ("came up-") is ♩ ♪. This is equivalent to the single note value ____.
♩.	306. In Frame 303, the second beat of the first complete measure ("-on a") is ♫ ♪. This is equivalent to the single note value ____.

307. Thus, in the first complete measure we have two beats, each a ♩. note.

came up - on a

beat: ♩. ♩.

divisions:

$\frac{3}{8} + \frac{3}{8} = \frac{6}{8}$

The time signature $\frac{6}{8}$ has been derived by taking both beat notes and adding together their fractional values, ________ + ________, which results in a time signature of ________.

$\frac{3}{8} + \frac{3}{8}$, $\frac{6}{8}$

---

308. Observe in the $\frac{6}{8}$ signature that the numerator indicates the number of beat divisions in the measure. In $\frac{6}{8}$ there are ________ beat divisions per measure.

six

---

309. Since three beat divisions equal one beat, six beat divisions equal ________ beats.

two

---

310. Therefore, in compound time, the numerator divided by three indicates the number of ________ per measure.

beats

---

311. In $\frac{6}{8}$ time, the numerator divided by three indicates ________ beats per measure.

two

	312. The denominator in compound time indicates the note value of the beat division. In $\frac{6}{8}$ time, the beat division is a(n)__________ note.
eighth (♪)	313. Therefore, the beat note in compound time is equivalent to three of the notes indicated by the denominator. In $\frac{6}{8}$ time, the denominator indicates __________ notes, three of which equal the beat note, a __________ __________ note.
eighth (♪) dotted quarter (♩.)	314. $\frac{6}{8}$ time is duple compound time because there are (a) __________ beats per measure, each a (b) __________ __________ note, and the beat note is divisible into (c) __________ parts, each a(n) (d) __________ note.
a) two b) dotted quarter (♩.) c) three d) eighth (♪)	

Ex. 6.1. *Derivation of Compound Meter Signatures.*

Beat Value	Beat Grouping	Meter (Time) Signature	Meter Name
$\frac{3}{16}$	one + two: $\frac{3}{16} + \frac{3}{16} =$	$\frac{6}{16}$	DUPLE COMPOUND
$\frac{3}{8}$	one + two: $\frac{3}{8} + \frac{3}{8} =$	$\frac{6}{8}$	
$\frac{3}{4}$	one + two: $\frac{3}{4} + \frac{3}{4} =$	$\frac{6}{4}$	
$\frac{3}{16}$	one + two + three: $\frac{3}{16} + \frac{3}{16} + \frac{3}{16} =$	$\frac{9}{16}$	TRIPLE COMPOUND
$\frac{3}{8}$	one + two + three: $\frac{3}{8} + \frac{3}{8} + \frac{3}{8} =$	$\frac{9}{8}$	
$\frac{3}{4}$	one + two + three: $\frac{3}{4} + \frac{3}{4} + \frac{3}{4} =$	$\frac{9}{4}$	
$\frac{3}{16}$	one + two + three + four: $\frac{3}{16} + \frac{3}{16} + \frac{3}{16} + \frac{3}{16} =$	$\frac{12}{16}$	QUADRUPLE COMPOUND
$\frac{3}{8}$	one + two + three + four: $\frac{3}{8} + \frac{3}{8} + \frac{3}{8} + \frac{3}{8} =$	$\frac{12}{8}$	
$\frac{3}{4}$	one + two + three + four: $\frac{3}{4} + \frac{3}{4} + \frac{3}{4} + \frac{3}{4} =$	$\frac{12}{4}$	

Ex. 6.2. *Meaning of Compound Meter Signatures.*

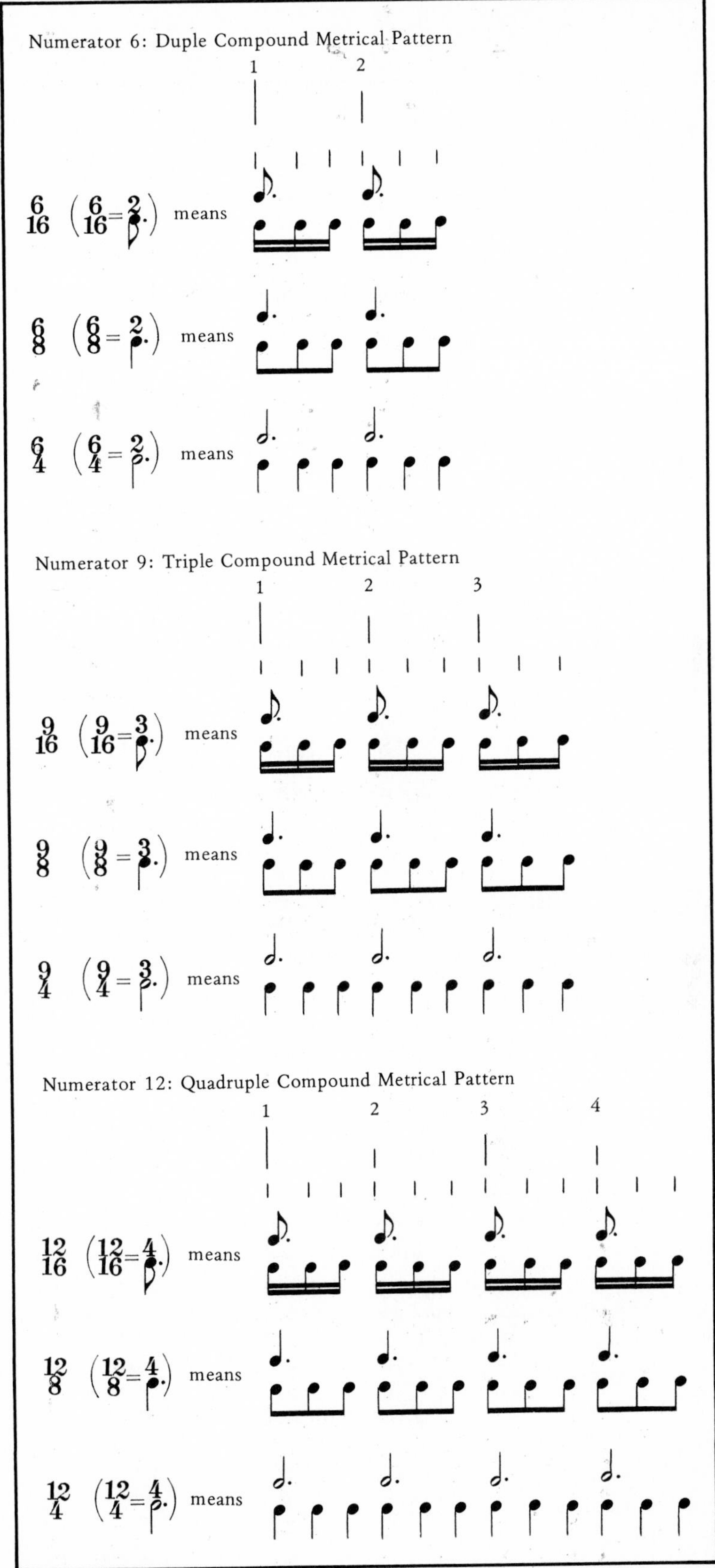

beat divisions	315. While in simple time the numerator tells the number of beats per measure, in compound time the numerator tells the number of ________ ________ per measure.
3	316. To find the number of beats indicated by a compound time signature, divide the numerator by ____.
beat division	317. While in simple time the denominator identifies the value of the beat note, in compound time the denominator identifies the value of the ________ ________.
three	318. To find the note value receiving one beat in compound time, add together (how many) ________ of the note values indicated by the lower number of the time signature.
	Study now Examples 6.1 and 6.2 (pages 100 and 101).
compound	319. A numerator of 6, 9, or 12 always indicates ________ time.
duple compound	320. A numerator of 6 always indicates ________ ________ time.
triple compound	321. A numerator of 9 always indicates ________ ________ time.

quadruple compound

322. A numerator of 12 always indicates ______ ______ time.

323. Using the beat note given, convert the given metrical pattern to notation, showing the value of each beat and its division into three parts. Supply the time signature and name the meter in the blank spaces.

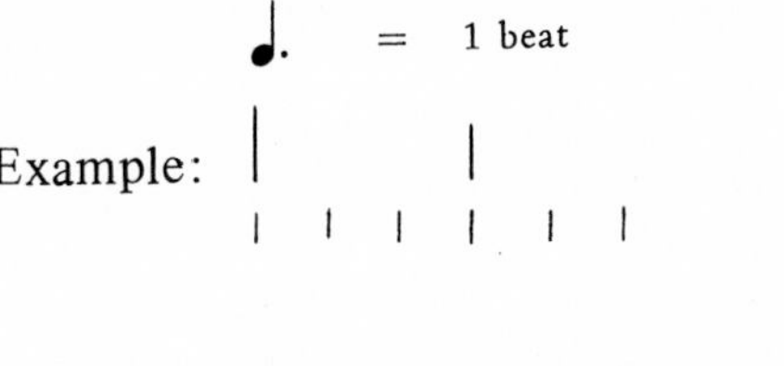

______ ______

Follow these directions in Frames 324–327.

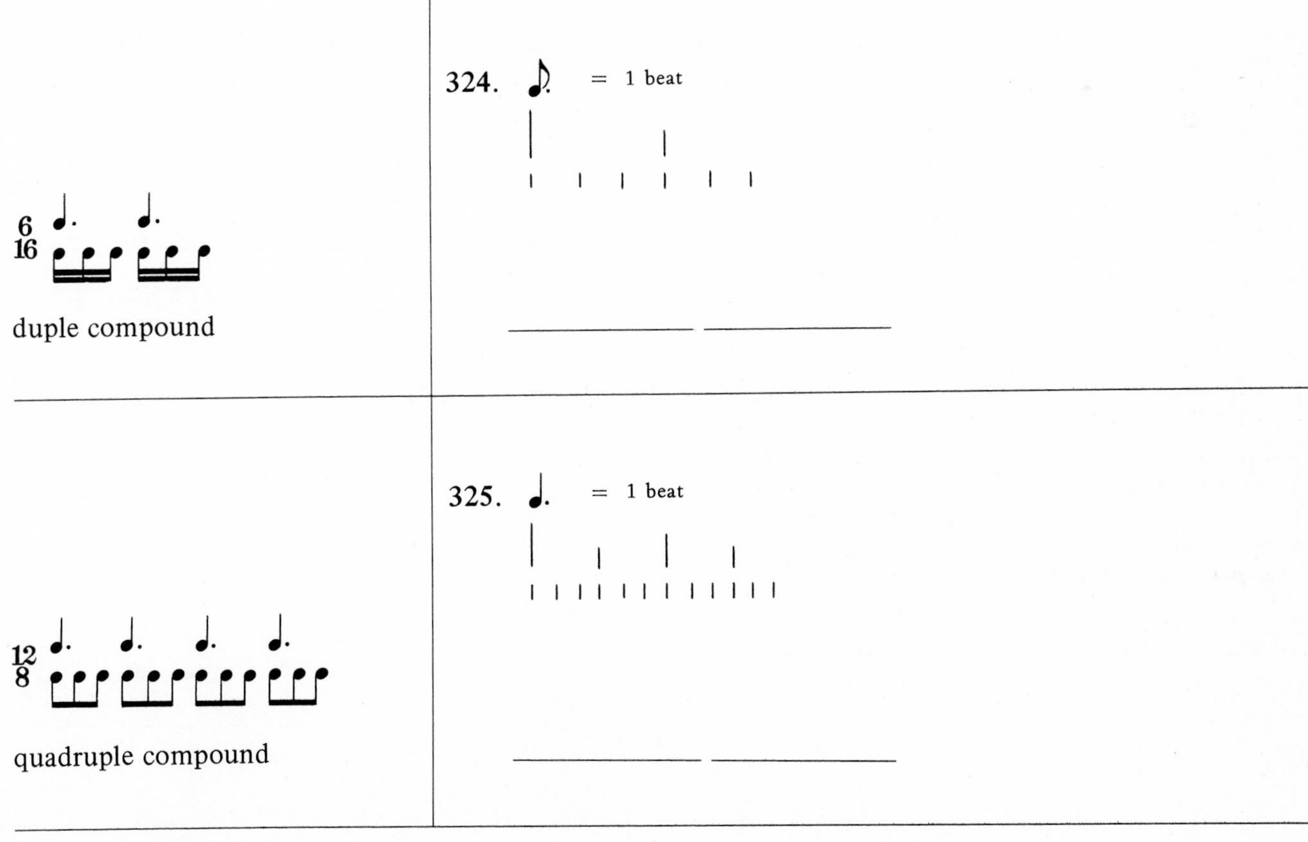

326. 𝅗𝅥. = 1 beat

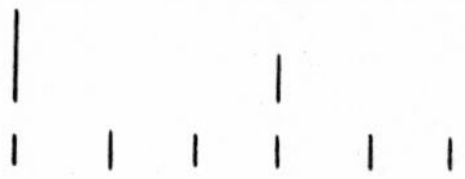

$\frac{6}{4}$ 𝅗𝅥. 𝅗𝅥.

duple compound

327. 𝅗𝅥. = 1 beat

$\frac{9}{4}$ 𝅗𝅥. 𝅗𝅥. 𝅗𝅥.

triple compound

328. After the given time signature, write the metrical pattern and name the meter.

Example: $\frac{6}{8}$

Answer: $\frac{6}{8}$ 𝅘𝅥. 𝅘𝅥.

duple compound

Follow these directions in Frames 329–332.

no response

329. $\frac{12}{4}$

$\frac{12}{4}$ 𝅗𝅥. 𝅗𝅥. 𝅗𝅥. 𝅗𝅥.

quadruple compound

Answer	Frame
 $\frac{9}{8}$ ♩. ♩. ♩. (♪♪♪ ♪♪♪ ♪♪♪) triple compound	330. $\frac{9}{8}$ ________ ________
 $\frac{9}{16}$ ♪. ♪. ♪. (sixteenth notes in groups of three) triple compound	331. $\frac{9}{16}$ ________ ________
 $\frac{6}{4}$ 𝅗𝅥. 𝅗𝅥. (♩♩♩ ♩♩♩) duple compound	332. $\frac{6}{4}$ ________ ________
$\frac{9}{8}$	333. In Example 6.2, observe the equivalency of compound time signatures. For example, $\frac{6}{8}$ = $\frac{2}{♩.}$ means: 2 × ♩. (or ♪♪♪) (or $\frac{3}{8}$) = $\frac{6}{8}$ Would compound time signatures be easier to read if always written this way? $\frac{3}{♩.}$ means 3 × ♩. = ________
$\frac{6}{4}$	334. $\frac{2}{𝅗𝅥.}$ is the same as ____.
$\frac{12}{16}$	335. $\frac{4}{♪.}$ is the same as ____.
$\frac{9}{4}$	336. $\frac{3}{𝅗𝅥.}$ is the same as ____.

CORRELATING RHYTHMIC PATTERNS WITH METRICAL PATTERNS

337. In these exercises, a series of numbers indicates the beats in the measure. The compound divisions of the beat are indicated by the marks below each beat number. Place each note and rest of the given rhythmic pattern below the correct beat number or the beat division.

Example: 6/8

Answer: 6/8 1 2 | 1 2 ||

6/8

no response

338. Continue with this example:

6/8

6/8 1 2 | 1 2 ||

6/8 | ||

6/8 1 2 | 1 2 ||

6/8

339. 6/8

6/8 1 2 | 1 2 ||

6/8 | ||

6/8 1 2 | 1 2 ||

6/8

340. 6/8

6/8 1 2 | 1 2 ||

6/8 | ||

6/8 1 2 | 1 2 ||

6/8

341. 9/8 ♩. ♩. | ♩ ♪♩ ♪♩. ||

9/8 1 2 3 |

342. 12/8 𝄾 𝄾 ♪♩. 𝄾 𝄾 ♪♩. | ♩. ♪ 𝄾 ♪ 𝅗𝅥. ||

12/8 1 2 3 4 |

343. 6/4 𝄽 𝄽 ♩ ♩ 𝄽 𝄽 | ♩ 𝄽 ♩ 𝅗𝅥. ||

6/4 1 2 | 1 2 ||

344. $\frac{9}{4}$

$\frac{9}{4}$ 1 2 3

$\frac{9}{4}$

1 2 3

$\frac{9}{4}$ 1 2 3

$\frac{9}{4}$

1 2 3

345. $\frac{12}{4}$

$\frac{12}{4}$ 1 2 3 4

$\frac{12}{4}$

1 2 3 4

$\frac{12}{4}$ 1 2 3 4

$\frac{12}{4}$

1 2 3 4

346. $\frac{9}{16}$

$\frac{9}{16}$ 1 2 3

$\frac{9}{16}$

1 2 3

$\frac{9}{16}$ 1 2 3

$\frac{9}{16}$

1 2 3

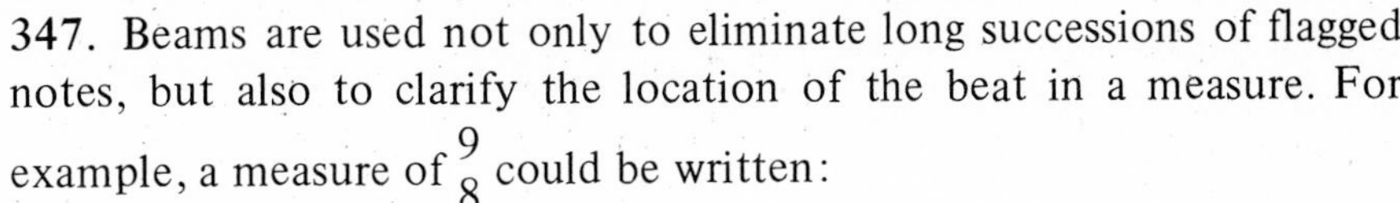

347. Beams are used not only to eliminate long successions of flagged notes, but also to clarify the location of the beat in a measure. For example, a measure of $\frac{9}{8}$ could be written:

but by beaming each group of three eighth notes, the location of the beats is clear:

On the other hand, beaming these notes at random could make it more difficult to read the music, as in this example, where the beams do not coincide with the beats of triple compound meter.

In Frames 348–353, each pattern is correct, but would be improved by beaming. Rewrite each, using beams where feasible. Examples will be in both simple and compound times.

$\frac{2}{4}$

348. $\frac{2}{4}$

$\frac{2}{4}$

$\frac{4}{4}$

Optionally, in simple time, a beam beginning on a strong beat may extend through the following weak beat:

349. $\frac{4}{4}$

$\frac{4}{4}$

$\frac{3}{8}$

350. $\frac{3}{8}$

$\frac{3}{8}$

(In Frames 351–352, the same notation pattern is beamed in two ways to show the two different meters.)

351.

352.

353.

354. In Frames 354–358, each example shows one or more incorrect uses of beams. Rewrite each example.

355.

356.

357. 9/8

358. 4/8

RESTS IN NOTATION

359. Dotted rests. Although dotted rests are possible, and are occasionally used, more frequently the value of the dot is expressed as a rest value of its own, e.g. 𝄽· = 𝄽 𝄾 .

Rewrite each of these dotted rests using two rest signs:

a) =

b) =

c) =

d) =

360. When a complete measure is silent, a whole rest may be written, regardless of the time signature or the number of beats involved.

3/4

Place a single rest sign in measure two of this example.

9/16

361. When, on a single staff, two or more successive measures are silent, the number of measures silent may be expressed by placing that number over the staff, together with a special sign:

This symbol, as used above, indicates four measures (12 beats) of rest.

Indicate two measures of rest in the blank measure:

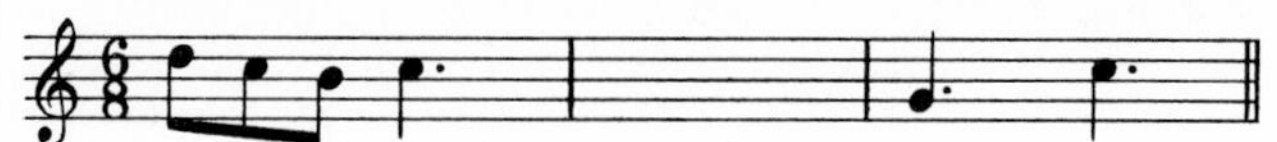

362. Rest values on successive beats may be combined, e.g.,

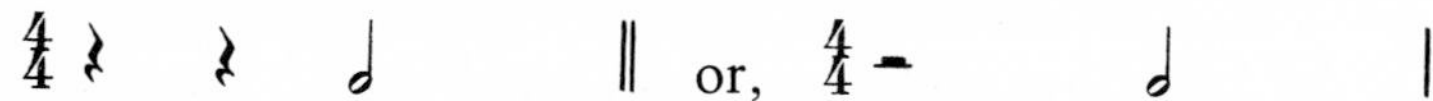

A combined rest, however, should not obscure the location of the strong beat:

1 2 3 4 not 1 2 3 4

1 2 not 1 (2)

In compound meter, separate rests are ordinarily used for the second and third divisions of the beat:

not

Also review Frame 359 for use of dotted rests.

Rewrite exercises in Frames 363–368, showing clearer use of rest signs.

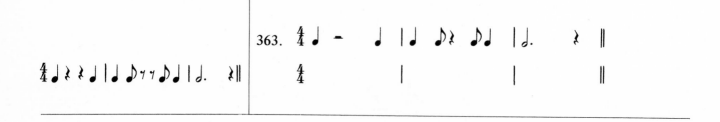

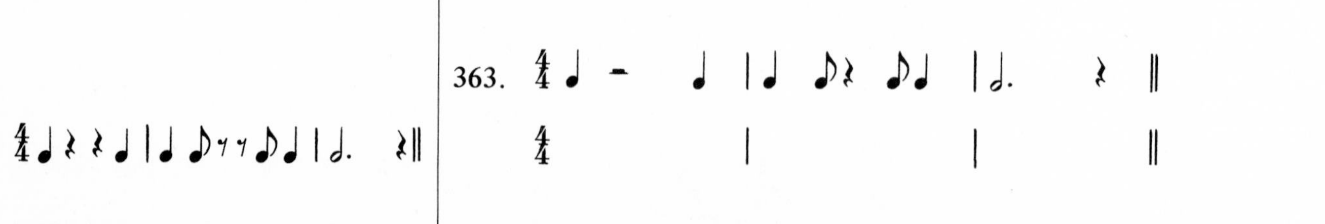

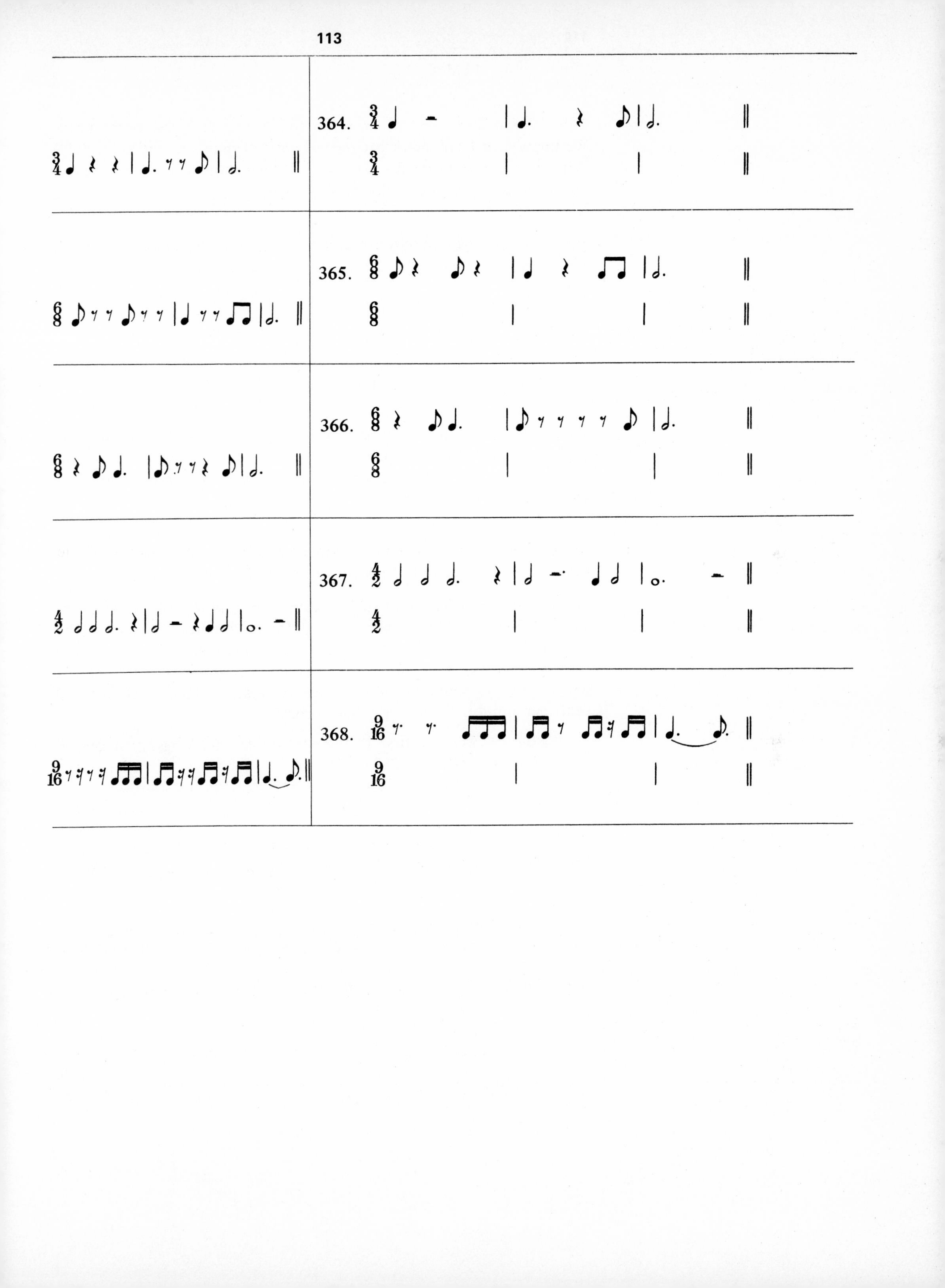

364. 3/4

365. 6/8

366. 6/8

367. 4/2

368. 9/16

TEMPO

369. *Tempo* is a word which refers to the rate of speed of the beats. We know that beats mark off regular units of time, but the notation of beats does not indicate for how long or how short a time each beat is held. There are two ways of indicating tempo:

(1) A language direction may be found at the beginning of a piece. These words, most often in Italian, indicate only approximate tempo, such as:

allegro: fast
adagio: slow
presto: very fast

With only these directions the performer must still choose an exact tempo, based on his musical sensitivity and his understanding of the music. A list of words used to express tempo, dynamics, and other performance information is found in Appendix 3.

(2) The *metronome* is an instrument which indicates specific lengths of beats. Reference to this instrument may often be found at the beginning of a piece of music in such a way: ♩ = M.M. 100. M.M. means Mälzel's Metronome, named in 1812 for its supposed inventor. The metronome is calibrated, and can be set to sound a series of ticks (beats) ranging from 40 to 208 beats per minute. When it is set at 60, 60 beats per minute are sounded, or one each second. At 120, there are 120 beats per minute, or one every half second.

Beethoven was the first to use metronome markings, as shown in the excerpts in Frames 370–372.

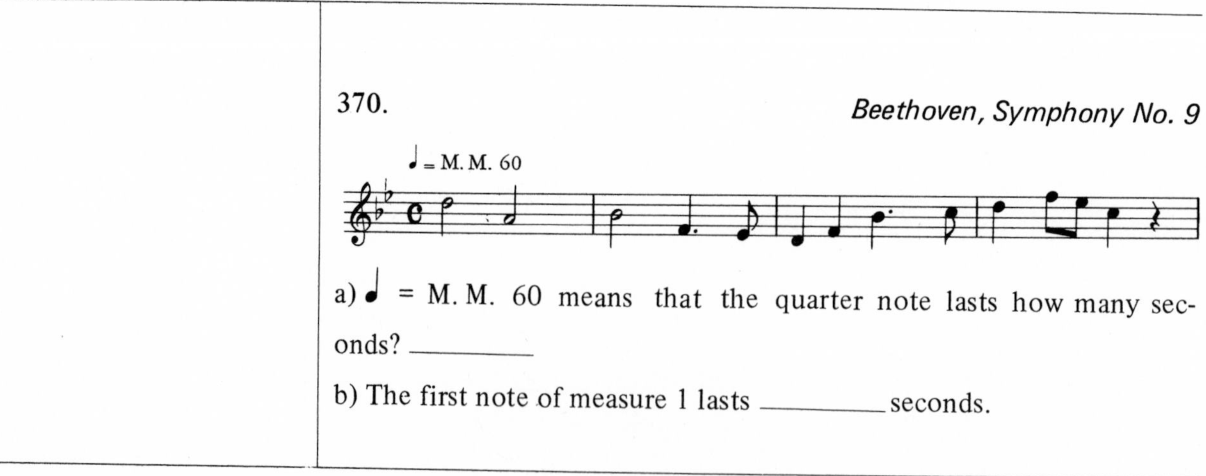

a) one
b) two

370. *Beethoven, Symphony No. 9*

a) ♩ = M. M. 60 means that the quarter note lasts how many seconds? ________

b) The first note of measure 1 lasts ________ seconds.

371. *Beethoven, Symphony No. 1*

♪ = M.M. 120

a) ♪ = M. M. 120 means that the beat note lasts how long? A ________ ________

b) The first complete measure lasts ________ seconds.

a) half (½) second
b) one and a half

---

372. *Beethoven, Symphony No. 6*

♩. = M.M. 50

a) With this metronome marking, the tempo is slower or faster than M.M. 60? ________

b) The beat note lasts slightly longer or shorter than one second? ________ ________

a) slower
b) longer

373. *Rhythmic transcription* is the rewriting of a piece using a meter signature with the same numerator but a different denominator. This will produce a notation which looks different from the original, but in performance will sound identical to the original. When, for example, you hear a rhythmic pattern in quadruple simple time, there is no way of knowing what the notation will be until you are told, or decide for yourself, the bottom number of the meter signature. A pattern in quadruple simple time can be written with a half note, a quarter note, or an eighth note as the beat unit, and although the notation looks different, each one will sound exactly like the others, assuming all have the same tempo indication. In the example below, the beat note in each line of music is M.M. 60. Therefore each rhythm pattern will sound the same as the others.

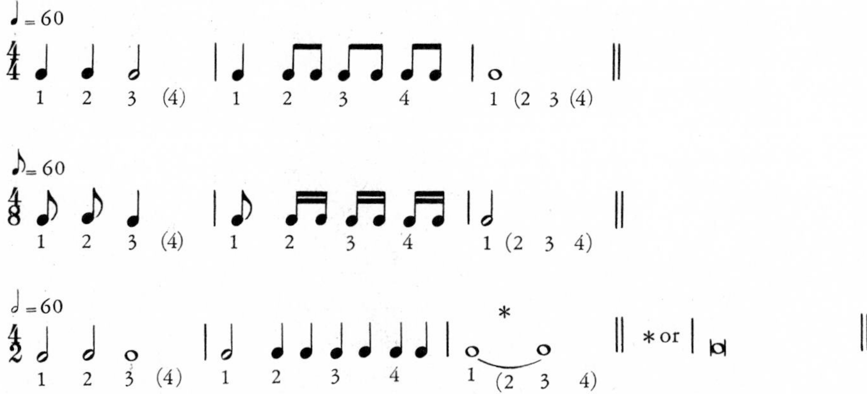

In the following frames, rewrite the given material with the new time signature.

1 2 3 1 (2) 3 1 (2 3) 1 (2 3)

376.

1 (2 3) 1 2. 3 1 (2 3)

377.

1 2 1 2 (2) 1

378.

1 2 3 1 (2) 3 1 (2 3)

379.

1 2 3 1 (2) 3 1 (2 3)

380.

1 2 3 4 1 (2) 3 (4)

381.

1 2 3 4 1 2 3 (4)

382.

CHAPTER SUMMARY

1. Compound time is so called because it uses a compound note value (a note value divisible into three parts) to represent the beat. Such notes are dotted notes.

2. Like simple time, compound time is found in beat groupings of two, three, and four, known as duple compound time, triple compound time, and quadruple compound time.

3. Unlike simple time, the numerators of time signatures in compound time are 6, 9, and 12, indicating the number of beat divisions in a measure. Since three beat divisions equal one beat, 6 indicates two beats in a measure—duple compound time—9 indicates triple compound time, and 12 indicates quadruple compound time.

4. Unlike simple time, the denominator in compound time indicates the note value receiving a beat division, three of which equal one beat.

5. As an example, in $\frac{6}{8}$, the 6 indicates duple compound time (two beats per measure, each divisible by three), while 8 indicates the beat division to be an eighth note, three of which equal the beat note, a dotted quarter note. Therefore, in $\frac{6}{8}$, there are two beats per measure, each a dotted quarter note.

6. *Beams* are used not only to replace flags in notation, but also to clarify the location of beats in a measure.

7. *Dotted rests* are possible, but use of a rest sign instead of the dot is more common, e.g., 𝄾 𝄿 instead of 𝄾.

8. *Rests* should be written so as not to obscure the location of the beat, e.g., $\frac{4}{4}$ ♩ 𝄽 𝄽 ♩, not ♩ 𝄼 ♩.

9. *Tempo,* the rate of speed in music, can be indicated in a general way by words, most often in Italian, or specifically by assigning a note value a number on the *metronome,* e.g., ♩ = M.M. 100 (M.M. = Mälzel's Metronome), or simply ♩ = 100.

PRE–TEST
ADDITIONAL CONCEPTS IN TIME

1. When a quarter note receives one beat, a triplet division of the beat is written: ____________

2. 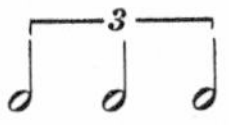 (three half notes, triplet) receives the same time value as what single note value?

____

3. What is the time signature for this measure of music? (eighth, eighth, sixteenth-note triplet, sixteenth-note triplet)

____

4. When a (dotted eighth note) receives one beat, a duplet division of the beat is written: ____________

5.  (two quarter notes, duplet) receives the same time value as what single note value?

____

6. What is the time signature for this measure of music? (half note, quarter rest, quarter-note duplet, eighth-note quadruplet)

____

7. The figure (four eighth notes, quadruplet) of the preceding question is called a: ____________

8. Using a dotted barline, divide this measure in one of the two ways it might commonly be found. 5/4 ♩ ♩ ♩ ♩ ♩

9. What single time signature at the beginning of this piece could be used to replace the time signatures shown?

3/4 ♩ ♩ ♩ | 4/4 ♩ ♩ ♩ ♩ | 3/4 ♩ ♩ ♩ | 4/4 ♩ ♩ ♩ ♩ | ____________

10. Copy this measure, placing an > mark on that note within the measure receiving an accent. 7/16 ♪ ♪ ♪ ♪ ♪ ♪ ♪ | ______________

____

ANSWERS

For each correct answer, place a score of 10 in the column at the right. Add this column for your score.

Score

1.  (triplet figures) (any one) ____

2. o (whole note) ____

3. 3/8 ____

4.  (duplet figures) (any one) ____

5. ♩. (dotted quarter) ____

6. 9/4 ____

7. Quadruplet ____

8. 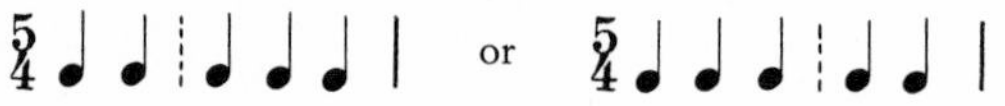 5/4 ♩ ♩ ┆ ♩ ♩ ♩ | or 5/4 ♩ ♩ ♩ ┆ ♩ ♩ | ____

9. 7/4 ____

10.  7/16 ♪ ♪ ♪ ♪ ♪ ♪ ♪ | ____

Total score: ____

Perfect score: 100

If your score is 80 or above, turn now to Chapter 8, page 139. If your score is less than 80, continue with Chapter 7.

CHAPTER SEVEN

ADDITIONAL CONCEPTS IN TIME

TRIPLET DIVISION OF UNDOTTED NOTE VALUES

383. Undotted note values, which normally divide into two parts (e.g. ), may also quite commonly be found with three divisions, e.g., 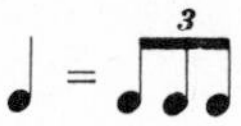. This group of notes is called a *triplet,* equally dividing the given note into three parts.

To divide an undotted note into three parts a ____________ is used.

triplet

---

384. The triplet does not mathematically divide the given note into three parts. Actually, it is an artificial division, indicated by placing a 3 in proximity to the three notes. There are two ways to do this. The first is to place the 3 next to the beam, , , or to enclose it in a bracket if there is no beam, 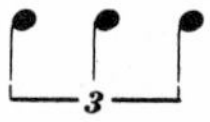.

Place a 3 so as to make a triplet of each of these groups:

 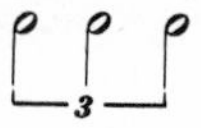

---

385. In the second method of indicating a triplet, the 3 is placed next to the note heads: alone, with a slur, or with a bracket, 

Place a 3 in three different ways on these groups:

(any order)

386. The method shown in Frame 384 reflects common practice by recent composers and in recent publications, whether of new or traditional music. The method in Frame 385 is favored in traditional practice. There is no consistency, however: scores using either or both in the same piece may be found from almost any historical period.

Write "traditional" or "recent" after each group.

a) ♩♩♩ (3) ________

b) 𝅘𝅥𝅯𝅘𝅥𝅯𝅘𝅥𝅯 (3) ________

c) 𝅗𝅥𝅗𝅥𝅗𝅥 (3) ________

a) traditional

b) recent

c) recent

---

387. When an undotted note is divided into three parts (triplet), the same note value is used for the division of three as would be used for the division of two.* ♩ = ♫, therefore ♩ = ♪♪♪ (3).

The principle is the same for other note values. Fill in the blanks.

𝅝 = 𝅗𝅥 𝅗𝅥 ; 𝅝 = 𝅗𝅥𝅗𝅥𝅗𝅥 (3)

𝅗𝅥 = ________ ; 𝅗𝅥 = ________

♪ = ________ ; ♪ = ________

𝅘𝅥𝅯 = ________ ; 𝅘𝅥𝅯 = ________

*In the music of a few composers (Hindemith, for example), the triplet is equal to three of the note value being divided, e.g., ♩ = ♩♩♩ (3).

𝅝 = 𝅗𝅥 𝅗𝅥 ; 𝅝 = 𝅗𝅥𝅗𝅥𝅗𝅥 (3)

𝅗𝅥 = ♩♩ ; 𝅗𝅥 = ♩♩♩ (3)

♪ = 𝅘𝅥𝅯𝅘𝅥𝅯 ; ♪ = 𝅘𝅥𝅯𝅘𝅥𝅯𝅘𝅥𝅯 (3)

𝅘𝅥𝅯 = 𝅘𝅥𝅰𝅘𝅥𝅰 ; 𝅘𝅥𝅯 = 𝅘𝅥𝅰𝅘𝅥𝅰𝅘𝅥𝅰 (3)

---

388. Indicate the single note value to which each triplet is equivalent.

𝅗𝅥𝅗𝅥𝅗𝅥 (3) = 𝅝 ________ 𝅘𝅥𝅰𝅘𝅥𝅰𝅘𝅥𝅰 (3) = ________

♩♩♩ (3) = ________ 𝅘𝅥𝅱𝅘𝅥𝅱𝅘𝅥𝅱 (3) = ________

♪♪♪ (3) = ________

𝅗𝅥𝅗𝅥𝅗𝅥 (3) = 𝅝 𝅘𝅥𝅰𝅘𝅥𝅰𝅘𝅥𝅰 (3) = 𝅘𝅥𝅯

♩♩♩ (3) = 𝅗𝅥 𝅘𝅥𝅱𝅘𝅥𝅱𝅘𝅥𝅱 (3) = 𝅘𝅥𝅰

♪♪♪ (3) = ♩

389. Rewrite this example, substituting a division of three (triplet) for each circled note.

390. Continue through Frame 392 in the same way as above.

391.

392.

DUPLET DIVISION OF DOTTED NOTE VALUES

393. A dotted note, which normally divides into three parts (e.g., ♩. = ♪♪♪), may be divided into two parts, called *duplet,* by two dotted notes of the next smaller note value.

♩. = ♪. ♪.

$\frac{6}{16} = \frac{3}{16} + \frac{3}{16}$

Fill in the duplet division of these notes:

𝅗𝅥. = ________

♪. = ________

𝅘𝅥𝅯. = ________

Answers: 𝅗𝅥. = ♩. ♩. ; ♪. = 𝅘𝅥𝅯. 𝅘𝅥𝅯. or 𝅘𝅥𝅯. 𝅘𝅥𝅯. (beamed) ; 𝅘𝅥𝅯. = 𝅘𝅥𝅰. 𝅘𝅥𝅰. or 𝅘𝅥𝅰. 𝅘𝅥𝅰. (beamed)

394. Indicate the single note value equal to each of these duplets.

= ________

= ________

= ________

= ________

395. Although the duplet division just described is mathematically accurate, another system is more widely used, probably because it is easier to read. Instead of dots, the notation 2 or └2┘ is used.*

Fill in these duplet divisions:

= ________

= ________

= ________

= ________

= ________

*The variants described in Frames 384 and 385 also apply here.

396. Indicate the single note value to which each duplet is equivalent.

= ________

= ________

= ________

= ________

397. Rewrite the examples in Frames 397–399, substituting a division of two by using a duplet for each circled note.
398.
399.
400. Replace the circled note with a duplet. At a) use a 2 or ⌞2⌟ ; at b) use dotted notes.
a)
b)
401. Continue as above.
a)
b)

(any order)

402. In compound time, a dotted note of two beats duration is, of course, divided into two dotted notes, as each of these will represent the beat.

A dotted note representing three beats in simple time may be divided as a duplet using either system.

Replace the circled note with a duplet using both systems.

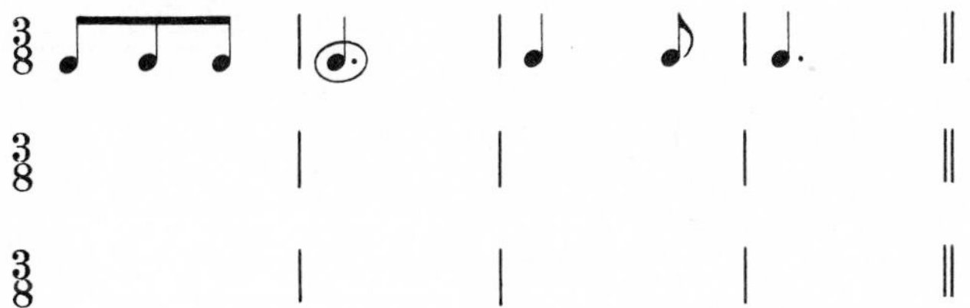

(no response)

403. These additional practices are also common:

a) Two successive duplets may be combined as one *quadruplet.*

b) In a series of like divisions, the number may be omitted after the first group or the first several groups.

etc.

c) Groupings may encompass more than two or three notes, such as

etc.

404. Frames 404–414 show some of the more common uses of duplets and triplets as studied in this chapter. Most of the excerpts are taken from Chapter 18 of Ottman, *Music for Sight Singing,* 2nd edition, Prentice-Hall, Inc., 1967, where additional and more complex uses of these notational devices may be found.

Answer questions in Frames 415–426.

Grieg, To Spring

405. *Schumann,* Jemand, *Op. 25, No. 4*

406. *Couperin,* Brunette

407. *Tchaikovsky, Symphony No. 5*

408. *Brückler,* Als ich zum erstenmal

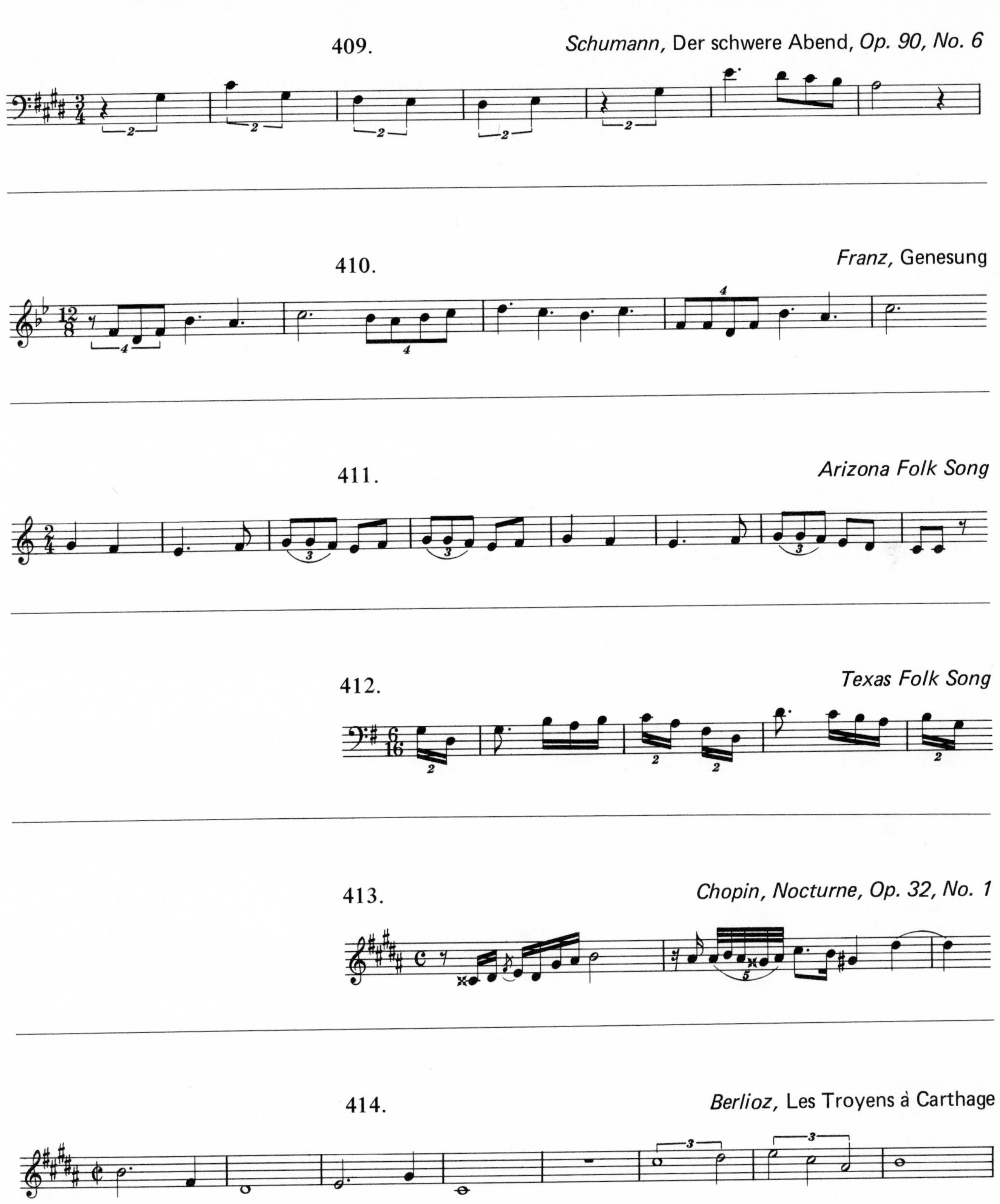
409.
Schumann, Der schwere Abend, Op. 90, No. 6
410.
Franz, Genesung
411.
Arizona Folk Song
412.
Texas Folk Song
413.
Chopin, Nocturne, Op. 32, No. 1
414.
Berlioz, Les Troyens à Carthage

411 ♩, ♫	415. An example of ♫³ is in Frame ____. This triplet is equal to the single note value ____ and its normal division, ____.
405 𝅗𝅥, ♩ ♩	416. An example of ♩♩♩ (3) is in Frame ____. This triplet is equal to the single note value ____ and its normal division, ____.
406 ♪, ♬	417. An example of ♬³ is in Frame ____. This triplet is equal to the single note value ____ and its normal division, ____.
414 𝅝, 𝅗𝅥 𝅗𝅥	418. An example of 𝅗𝅥𝅗𝅥𝅗𝅥 (3) is in Frame ____. This triplet is equal to the single note value ____ and its normal division, ____.
406 ♪, 𝅘𝅥𝅰𝅘𝅥𝅰	419. An example of 𝅘𝅥𝅰𝅘𝅥𝅰𝅘𝅥𝅰³ is in Frame ____. This triplet is equal to the single note value ____ and its normal division, ____.
407 ♩., ♪♪♪	420. An example of ♫² is in Frame ____. This duplet is equal to the single note value ____ and its normal division, ____.
412 ♪., ♬♬♬	421. An example of ♬² is in Frame ____. This duplet is equal to the single note value ____ and its normal division, ____.
404	422. Examples of the duplet ♩ ♩ (2) can be seen in three different frames above. In Frame ____, it is equal in value to a 𝅗𝅥. note in compound time.

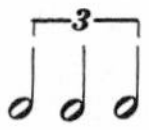

408	423. This same duplet is equal in value to a ♩. in compound time, as shown in Frame ____.
409	424. In its third appearance, it is equivalent to a 𝅗𝅥. in simple time. It is in Frame ____.
410 	425. Two successive duplets,  ♪♪ ♪♪ (2, 2) may also be written _____. An example is in Frame ____.
413 	426. A grouping other than two or three is seen in Frame ____. The grouping is ____.

TIME SIGNATURES WITH A NUMERATOR OF 5

5 and 7	427. Most time signatures have as numerators the numbers 2, 3, 4, 6, 9, or 12, as we learned in Chapters 5 and 6. Numerators of 5 and 7 are used to a limited extent, while other numerators are used quite sparingly. Other than the common time signatures already studied, we can occasionally expect signatures with numerators of ____ and ____.
five	428. The numerator 5 usually indicates an alternation of groups of two and three beats. Rather than change the time signature every measure  $\frac{2}{4}$ ♩ ♩ | $\frac{3}{4}$ ♩ ♩ ♩ | $\frac{2}{4}$ ♩ ♩ | $\frac{3}{4}$ ♩ ♩ ♩ | etc. we use the single time signature 5 to indicate this.  $\frac{5}{4}$ ♩ ♩ ♩ ♩ ♩ | ♩ ♩ ♩ ♩ ♩ | etc. Alternation of measures of two and three beats can be indicated by single measures of _____ beats.

429. The alternation may be 3 + 2 or 2 + 3. Several notational devices will indicate which. In these examples, 2 + 3 is indicated.

a) A dotted bar line within the regular bar lines

b) Slurs to indicate each group

c) Beams for each group (♪ notes and smaller)

d) A longer note value to indicate the new division

430. After each example, indicate the order of groups by 2 + 3 or 3 + 2.

a) __________

b) __________

c) __________

d) __________

a) 2 + 3

b) 3 + 2

c) 3 + 2

d) 2 + 3

MUSIC EXAMPLES

431. Questions in Frames 435–438 refer to the music examples in the four following frames 431–434.

Berlioz, La Prise de Troie

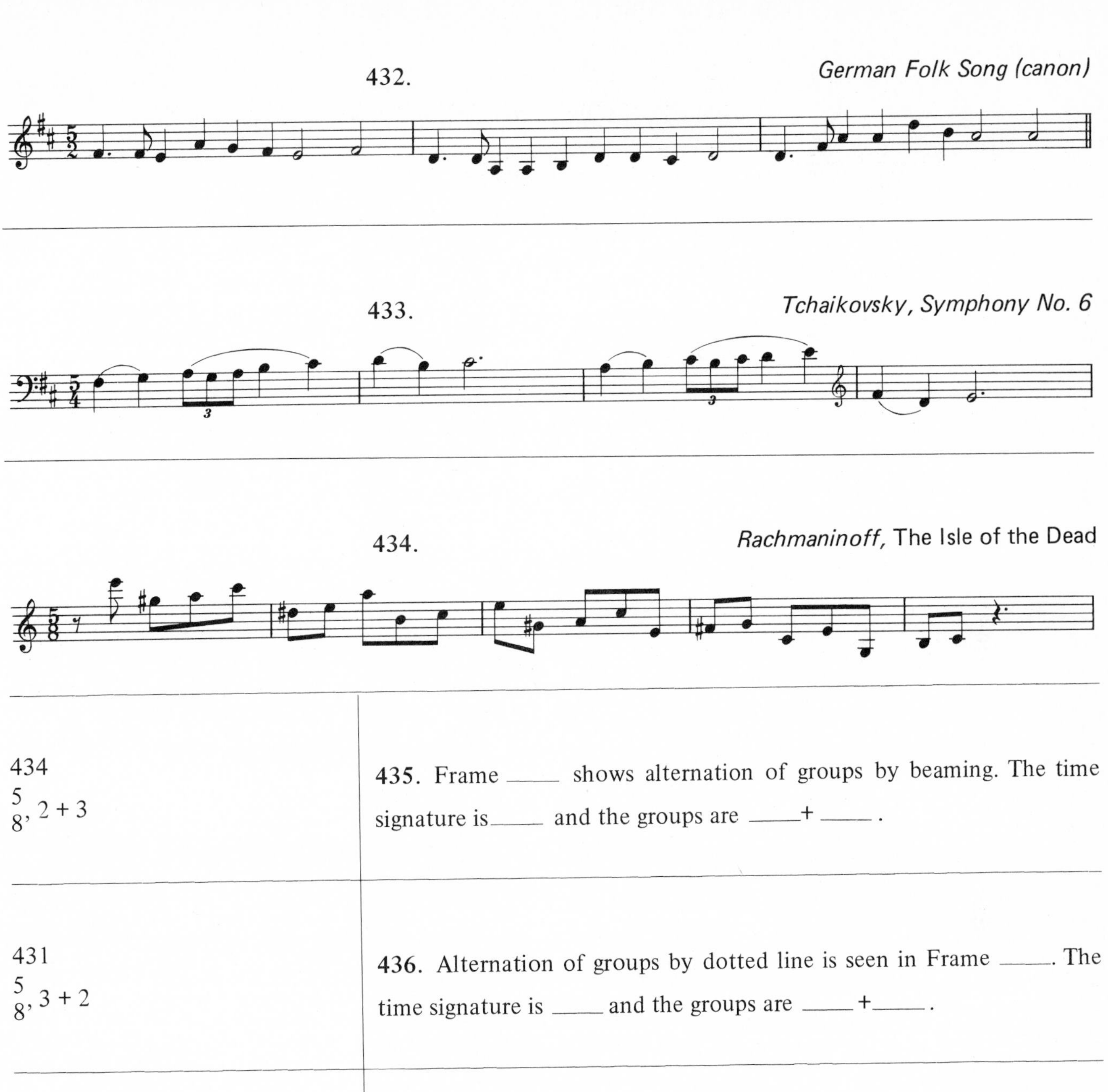

434 $\frac{5}{8}$, 2 + 3	**435.** Frame ____ shows alternation of groups by beaming. The time signature is____ and the groups are ____+ ____ .
431 $\frac{5}{8}$, 3 + 2	**436.** Alternation of groups by dotted line is seen in Frame ____. The time signature is ____ and the groups are ____ +____ .
433 $\frac{5}{4}$, 2 + 3	**437.** The slur as a means of indicating groups is seen in Frame ____ . The time signature is____ and the groups are ____+____.
432 $\frac{5}{2}$, 3 + 2	**438.** Groupings made obvious by the long note in the measure is seen in Frame ____ . The time signature is ____ and the grouping is ____ + ____ .

TIME SIGNATURES WITH A NUMERATOR OF 7

439. Time signatures with a numerator of 7 are even less frequent than those with 5. When found, the grouping is usually 3 + 4,

though the reverse, 4 + 3, can occasionally be found.

In this pattern, the alternation is ____ + ____.

3 + 4

440. In this pattern, the alternation is ____ + ____.

4 + 3

MUSIC EXAMPLES

441. Answer questions in Frames 444–447 based on music examples in Frames 441–443.

Greek Folk Song

442.

Croatian Folk Song

443.

Bulgarian Folk Song

444. In which example(s) are the beats grouped 4 + 3?

443

441 and 442	445. In which example(s) are the beats grouped 3 + 4?
$\frac{7}{4}$	446. By using slurs, show the beat groups of number 442, measure 1. $\frac{7}{4}$
$\frac{7}{16}$	447. Using a dotted bar line, show the beat groups of measures 1–3 of Frame 443. $\frac{7}{16}$

CHAPTER SUMMARY

1. A simple time value (undotted note) may be divided into three parts with the indication 3 over three notes of the next lower value, e.g., 3.

2. This figure of three notes, called *triplet,* receives the same duration as two of the same note value, e.g., 3 = =

3. Although writing the triplet as 3 is accepted current practice, it is also commonly found as 3 or 3.

4. A compound time value (dotted note) may be divided into two parts with the indication 2 over two notes of the next lower value, e.g., = 2, or by two dotted notes of the same value, e.g., = . The latter is mathematically accurate, but the former is more commonly used.

5. This figure of two notes, called a *duplet,* receives the same duration as three notes of the same time value, e.g., 2 = = .

6. As with the triplet (see 3 above), 2 may be written 2 or 2.

7. For duplets and triplets, a few composers use note values the same as the note being divided, e.g., = 3, = 2

8. Time signatures with numerators other than 2, 3, 4, 6, 9, or 12 are uncommon. Those with 5 of 7 usually indicate an alternation of 2 and 3, 3 and 2, 3 and 4, or 4 and 3, e.g., $\frac{5}{4}$ = $\frac{2}{4}$ | $\frac{3}{4}$ | or $\frac{3}{4}$ | $\frac{2}{4}$ |.

9. The division of a measure into 5 or 7 may be indicated in several ways: (a) dotted bar lines, $\frac{5}{4}$ | b) beaming, $\frac{5}{8}$ c) slurs, $\frac{7}{4}$, or d) implied accent at a longer note value, $\frac{7}{8}$ (>) .

PRE-TEST
MAJOR SCALES

1. Half steps in the scale below occur between numbers ____________ .
   1 2 3 4 5 6 7 8
   E F G A B C D E

2. In the music of Western civilization since the seventeenth century two scales most used are ____________ and ____________ .

3. Spell the following major scales, as indicated.

   (a) D♭ (ascending): ____________
   (b) E (ascending): ____________
   (c) F♯ (ascending): ____________
   (d) G♭ (descending): ____________

4. Notate the following major scales, ascending for one octave:

   (a) E♭:
   (c) A♭:
   (b) B:
   (d) C♯:

5. Names of the first two scale degrees are given. Name the remaining scale degrees in order.

(1) tonic ______

(2) supertonic ______

(3) ______

(4) ______

(5) ______

(6) ______

(7) ______

(8) ______

ANSWERS

A score is given at the end of each answer. If your answer is correct, place that score in the column at the right. Add this column for your score.

Score

1. 1–2 5–6 (4 each pair) ——

2. major minor (4 each) ——

3. The complete answer must be correct:

(a) D♭ E♭ F G♭ A♭ B♭ C D♭ (9) ——

(b) E F♯ G♯ A B C♯ D♯ E (9) ——

(c) F♯ G♯ A♯ B C♯ D♯ E♯ F♯ (9) ——

(d) G♭ F E♭ D♭ C♭ B♭ A♭ G♭ (9) ——

4. The complete answer must be correct:

(a) E♭ : (9) ——

(b) B: (or octave higher) (9) ——

(c) A♭ : (9) ——

(d) C♯ : (9) ——

5. (3) mediant (2) ____

(4) subdominant (2) ____

(5) dominant (2) ____

(6) submediant (2) ____

(7) leading tone or subtonic (2) ____

(8) tonic (2) ____

Total score: ____

Perfect score: 100

If your score is 80 or above, turn now to Chapter 9, page 160. If your score is less than 80, continue with Chapter 8.

CHAPTER EIGHT

MAJOR SCALES

Like rhythm, the resources of pitch in music can be organized into well-defined patterns. A pattern commonly used to express organization of pitch is the scale (Latin, scala, *ladder). A scale is an orderly graduated arrangement of ascending or descending pitches. There are many kinds of scales used in music depending on historical period or geographical culture. Most scales in Western music, including those which we will study here, ascend and descend through a series consisting of half steps and whole steps with each pitch named by a successive letter of the musical alphabet. Because our scale study is based on half steps, whole steps, and accidentals, review Chapter 2 so that your knowledge of these elements will be secure and ready for application.*

448. For purposes of study, a scale is revealed in a series of eight notes encompassing the interval of an octave. The first and last notes of the series (scale) have identical letter names.

A scale beginning on A, either ascending or descending, will end on ___.

A

---

449. All scales are alike in that each uses successive letter names of the musical alphabet. Beginning on A, for example, and writing successive letter names until the next A is reached will produce a scale:

1	2	3	4	5	6	7	8
A	B	C	D	E	F	G	A

A series of successive letter names beginning and ending with the same letter produces a ______.

scale

---

450. Write the letter names for an ascending scale beginning on C.

1	2	3	4	5	6	7	8
C	_	_	_	_	_	_	C

C D E F G A B C

---

451. Write (spell) a descending scale beginning on C.

8	7	6	5	4	3	2	1
C	B	_	_	_	_	_	_

C B A G F E D C

---

452. When writing successive natural letter names of the musical alphabet, the interval between any two adjacent letter names is either a whole step or a half step. In our study of the keyboard (Chapter 2) we learned that half steps occur naturally between B–C and E–F.

In Frame 449, with a scale starting on A, the half step B–C occurs under the numbers ___-___, and the half step E–F under the numbers ___-___.

2–3
5–6

3–4
7–8

453. In Frame 450, with a scale starting on C, the half step E–F occurs under the numbers _____ - _____, and the half step B–C under the numbers _____ - _____.

half

454. The scales written above are alike in that each uses successive letter names, but they are unlike in that starting on different letter names (A and C), the half steps B–C and E–F occur in different places (under different numbers).

Scales are different because of differing locations for the ________ steps.

1 2 3 4 5 6 7 8
A [B C] D [E F] G A

1 2 3 4 5 6 7 8
[B C] D [E F] G A B

1 2 3 4 5 6 7 8
C D [E F] G A [B C]

1 2 3 4 5 6 7 8
D [E F] G A [B C] D

1 2 3 4 5 6 7 8
[E F] G A [B C] D E

1 2 3 4 5 6 7 8
F G A [B C] D [E F]

1 2 3 4 5 6 7 8
G A [B C] D [E F] G

455. Seven distinct scales* are spelled below beginning on each of the seven letters of the musical alphabet. To dramatize the different locations of half-steps, mark with a bracket the locations of B–C and E–F in each scale. Scales beginning on A and C are marked.

1 2 3 4 5 6 7 8
A [B C] D [E F] G A

1 2 3 4 5 6 7 8
B C D E F G A B

1 2 3 4 5 6 7 8
C D [E F] G A [B C]

1 2 3 4 5 6 7 8
D E F G A B C D

1 2 3 4 5 6 7 8
E F G A B C D E

1 2 3 4 5 6 7 8
F G A B C D E F

1 2 3 4 5 6 7 8
G A B C D E F G

**Later in this text you will be directed to Appendix 2, where these same scales are discussed and named. This information is not necessary to the development of skills presented in this chapter.*

456. We have demonstrated that many different scale forms can exist because of the various possible locations for the half steps. In the music of Western civilization since the seventeenth century two scales have been most used. These scales are called *major* and *minor* and will be the subjects of our first study of scales.

Two scales most used in Western music are ________ and ________.

major minor

SPELLING MAJOR SCALES

457. We will first study the major scale, a series of eight pitches, called scale degrees, with certain placement of half steps and whole steps within the octave. The intervals between successive pitches are, in ascending order: whole step; whole step; half step; whole step; whole step; whole step; and half step. In the following illustration whole steps are represented by 1 and half steps are represented by 1/2.

Structure of the Major Scale

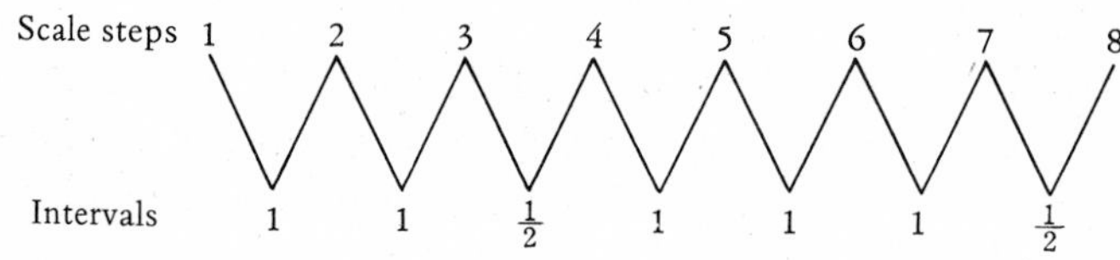

The major scale consists of whole steps except for half steps between scale numbers ____-____ and ____-____.

3-4 7-8

---

458. Whether the form of the scale is ascending or descending, the pitches of the major scale are the same. In descending 8-7-6-5-4-3-2-1, observe that half steps occur in order between 8-7 and 4-3.

In the ascending major scale the half steps occur in order between 3-4 and 7-8; in descending the half steps occur in order between ____-____ and ____-____.

8-7 4-3

459. A scale may be shown on the staff by placing eight notes on successive lines and spaces. The scale is identified by the name of the first note and by the relative location of whole steps and half steps.

The C Major Scale.

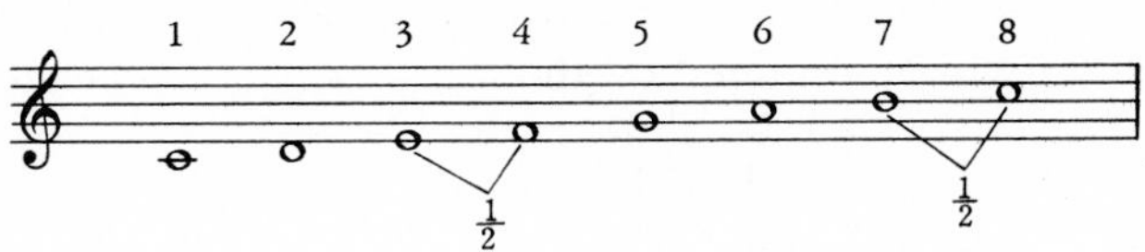

C major

Beginning eight successive notes with C as 1, and with half steps found between 3–4 and 7–8, the resultant scale is called ____ ______.

C D E F G A B C

460. Using successive letters of the complete musical alphabet, the C major scale is spelled ____ ____ ____ ____ ____ ____ ____ ____.

---

461. Using your knowledge of the keyboard, notice that the major scale starting on C involves only white keys because the half steps 3–4 and 7–8 coincide with the white keys E–F and B–C.

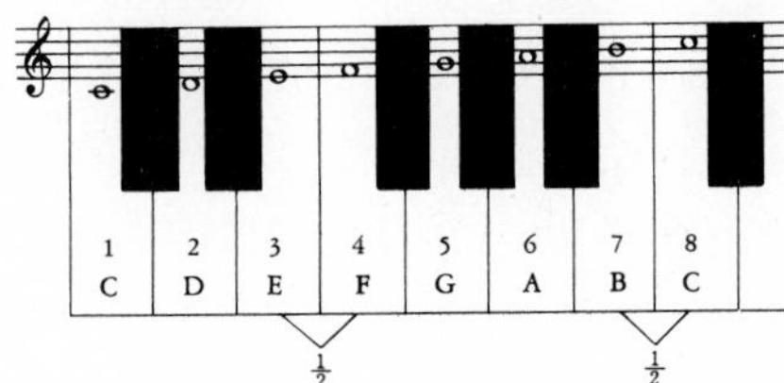

C

The major scale consisting entirely of white keys begins on the pitch____.

462. The major scale of C is the only major scale consisting entirely of white keys. But the sound of the major scale is not restricted to that beginning on C. A major scale can be produced beginning on any pitch name or any key of the piano by using the structure of the major scale shown in Frame 457.

The characteristic sound or structure of the major scale is determined by these intervals between successive scale degrees:

	between degrees	answer: whole or half
whole	1 - 2	____________ step
whole	2 - 3	____________ step
half	3 - 4	____________ step
whole	4 - 5	____________ step
whole	5 - 6	____________ step
whole	6 - 7	____________ step
half	7 - 8	____________ step

---

463. When starting a major scale on a pitch other than C, we must employ one or more accidentals to maintain the characteristic whole-step and half-step arrangement demonstrated in Frame 462.

To construct a major scale starting on a pitch other than C, we must employ one or more ____________.

accidentals

---

464. Spell the major scale starting on G by using your knowledge of intervals, accidentals, and scale structure.

G ___ ___ ___ ___ ___ ___ G
1 2 3 4 5 6 7 8

1 1 $\frac{1}{2}$ 1 1 1 $\frac{1}{2}$

G A B C D E F♯ G

---

465. The G major scale requires one accidental, F♯, which is needed to produce a whole step between ____ and F♯, and a half step between F♯ and ____.

E

G

466. Care should be taken that incorrect spellings of pitches by enharmonics are not used. Remember that in spelling the scale the complete musical alphabet must be employed, also that when notating the scale the notes must be placed on consecutive lines and spaces (adjacent staff degrees). In the following illustration the major scale sounds correct but it contains an error in notation.

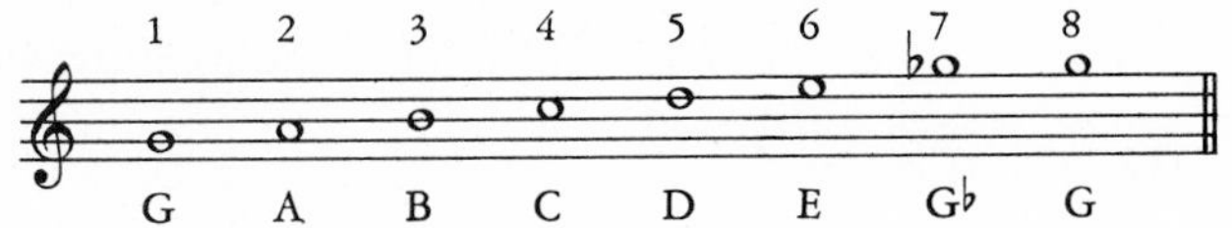

G-flat (G♭)

The wrong note in the G major scale above is ________ ________.

F-sharp (F♯)

467. The seventh degree of the G major scale should be spelled and notated ________ ________.

D E F♯ G A B C♯ D

468. Spell the major scale starting on D.

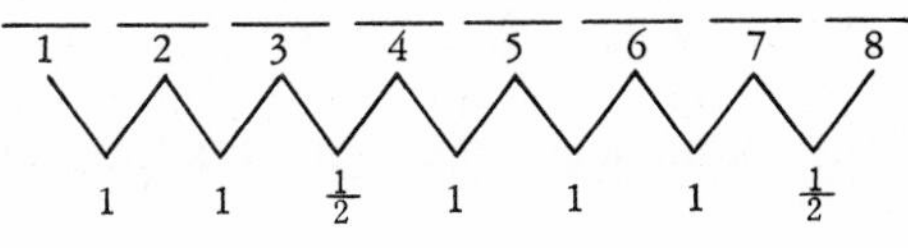

A B C♯ D E F♯ G♯ A

469. Continue spelling major scales.
A major:

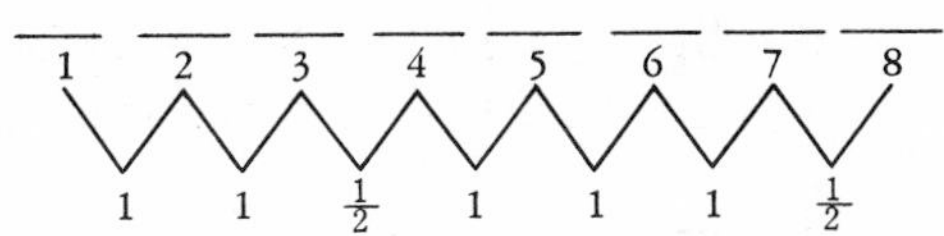

E F♯ G♯ A B C♯ D♯ E

470. E major:

___ ___ ___ ___ ___ ___ ___ ___
1 2 3 4 5 6 7 8

B C♯ D♯ E F♯ G♯ A♯ B	471. B major: ____ ____ ____ ____ ____ ____ ____ ____
F♯ G♯ A♯ B C♯ D♯ E♯ F♯	472. Major scales may begin on letter names containing an accidental or on black keys. Spell the major scale starting on F♯. ____ ____ ____ ____ ____ ____ ____ ____ 1 2 3 4 5 6 7 8 1 1 $\frac{1}{2}$ 1 1 1 $\frac{1}{2}$
C♯ D♯ E♯ F♯ G♯ A♯ B♯ C♯	473. Spell the C♯ major scale. ____ ____ ____ ____ ____ ____ ____ ____ 1 2 3 4 5 6 7 8
seven	474. The complete alphabet is sharped in the C♯ major scale. Compare the scale of C♯ with C. The major scale of C contains no accidentals; the major scale of C contains (number) ________ sharps.
F G A B♭ C D E F	475. Spell the major scale starting on F. ____ ____ ____ ____ ____ ____ ____ ____ 1 2 3 4 5 6 7 8 1 1 $\frac{1}{2}$ 1 1 1 $\frac{1}{2}$
A C	476. The F major scale contains one accidental, B♭, which is needed to produce a half step between____ and B-flat, and a whole step between B-flat and____.

A♯	477. The following scale sounds correct but it contains an error in notation. 1 2 3 4 5 6 7 8 F G A A♯ C D E F The wrong note in the F major scale above is ____.
B♭	478. The fourth degree in the scale of F major should be spelled and notated ____.
B♭ C D E♭ F G A B♭	479. Spell the major scale starting on B♭. ___ ___ ___ ___ ___ ___ ___ ___ 1 2 3 4 5 6 7 8 1 1 $\frac{1}{2}$ 1 1 1 $\frac{1}{2}$
E♭ F G A♭ B♭ C D E♭	480. Continue writing major scales. E♭ major: ___ ___ ___ ___ ___ ___ ___ ___ 1 2 3 4 5 6 7 8
A♭ B♭ C D♭ E♭ F G A♭	481. A♭ major: ___ ___ ___ ___ ___ ___ ___ ___
D♭ E♭ F G♭ A♭ B♭ C D♭	482. D♭ major: ___ ___ ___ ___ ___ ___ ___ ___

Gb Ab Bb Cb Db Eb F Gb

483. Gb major:

____ ____ ____ ____ ____ ____ ____ ____

Cb Db Eb Fb Gb Ab Bb Cb

484. Cb major:

____ ____ ____ ____ ____ ____ ____ ____

seven

485. The complete alphabet is flatted in the Cb major scale. Compare the scale of Cb with C. The major scale of C contains no accidentals; the major scale of C contains (number) ________ flats.

NOTATING MAJOR SCALES

486. Having *spelled* all major scales, we shall proceed to *notate* them on the great staff. The C major scale is given as a model for you to follow. Write the assigned scales ascending for one octave and show locations of the half steps. Remember that the descending form of a major scale if notated or played would be the same as the ascending. Be accurate in writing the appropriate accidentals. Place each accidental carefully on the line or space and immediately before the note to be affected. Be sure that treble and bass notes are properly (vertically) aligned.

C Major

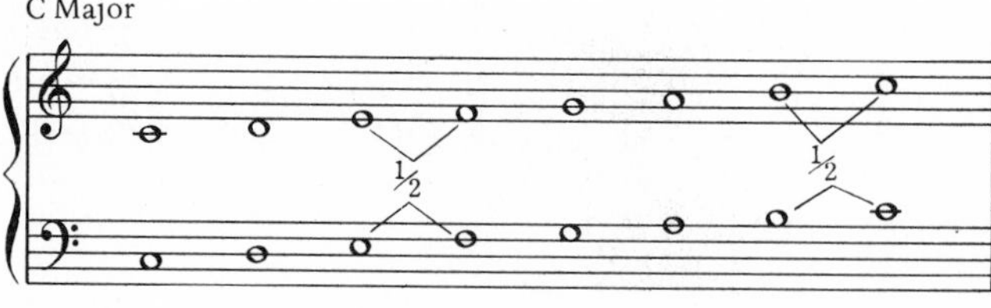

G Major

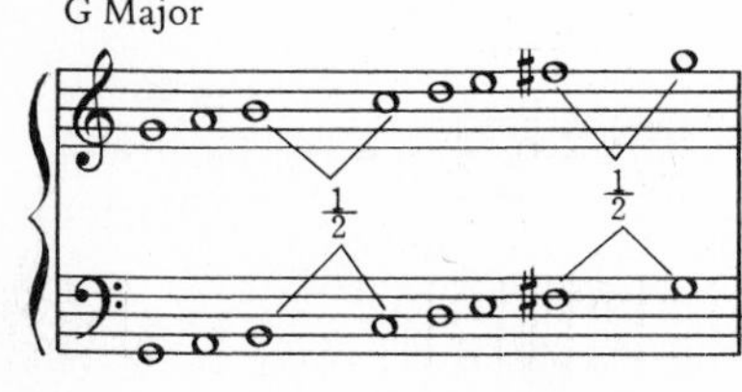

487.

G Major

D Major
½
½
488.
D Major
A Major
½
½
489.
A Major
E Major
½
½
490.
E Major
B Major
½
½
491.
B Major
F♯ Major
½
½
492.
F♯ Major

C♯ Major
½
½
493.
C♯ Major
F Major
1/2
1/2
494.
F Major
B♭ Major
½
½
495.
B♭ Major
E♭ Major
1/2
1/2
496.
E♭ Major

A♭ Major
½
½
497.
A♭ Major
D♭ Major
½
½
498.
D♭ Major
G♭ Major
½
½
499.
G♭ Major
C♭ Major
½
½
500.
C♭ Major

NAMES OF SCALE DEGREES

501. The scale has been shown to be composed of eight successive pitches, each known as a scale degree. The terms *scale tone* and *scale step* are often used synonymously with *scale degree.* For example, in the scale of C major, the fifth degree, G, may be called the fifth scale tone or fifth scale step. In addition to these general designations, each tone, step, or degree of the scale can be identified by a specific name of its own. These names and the significance of each are presented in the following frames.

---

tonic

502. The name of the first scale degree is *tonic* (Greek, *tonos;* Latin, *tonus*). It is the main tone, the tone which gives the scale its identity.

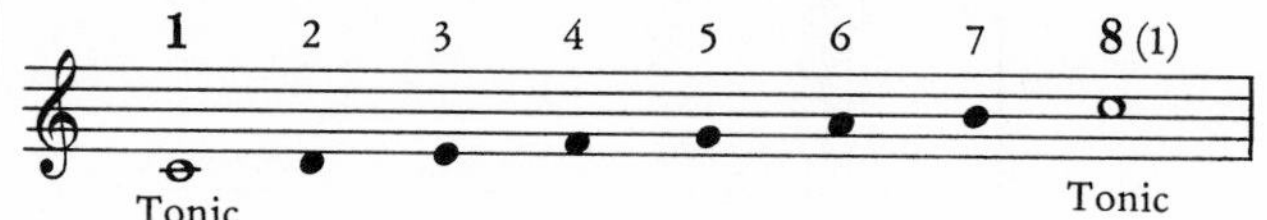

The name of the first scale degree is ________.

---

dominant

503. Since the tonic is the most important tone, all other scale degrees are signified by their relationship to it. In rank of importance after the tonic is the fifth scale tone, which is called *dominant.* It dominates or is dominant to all other scale tones except tonic.

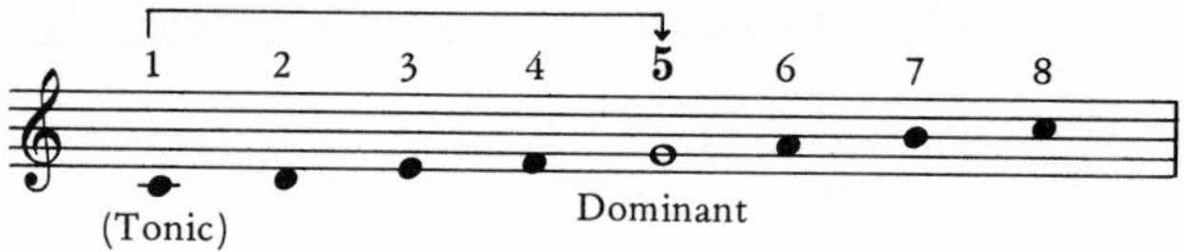

The name of the fifth degree above tonic is ________.

---

subdominant

504. The scale tone five steps below the tonic and ranking next in importance to the dominant is called *subdominant.* While the dominant is five steps above tonic, the subdominant is five steps below tonic on the fourth scale degree (coincidentally one step below the dominant). The prefix *sub* means, in this instance, under or below the tonic.

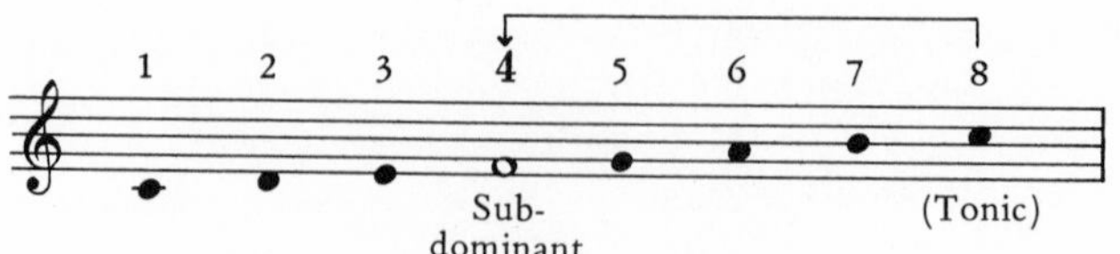

The name of the fourth scale degree is ________.

mediant

505. The third scale tone, the middle or median tone between the tonic and dominant, is called *mediant.*

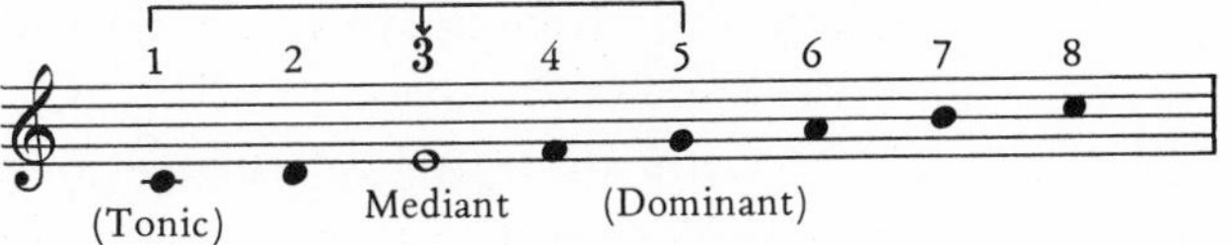

The name of the third scale degree is ______________.

submediant

506. The sixth scale tone, the middle or median tone between tonic and subdominant is called *submediant.* While the mediant is three steps above tonic, the submediant is three steps below tonic on the sixth scale degree.

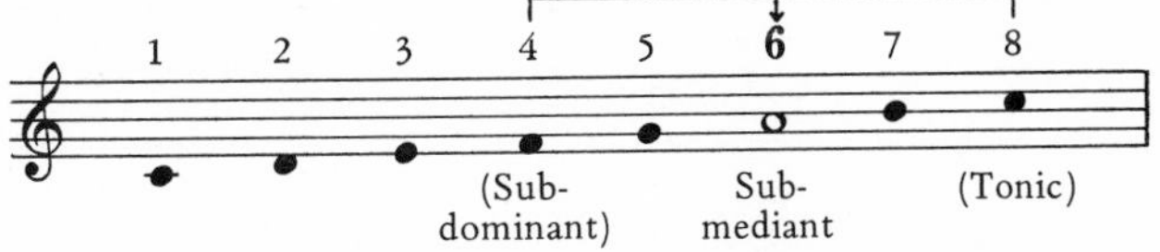

The name of the sixth scale degree is ______________.

leading tone

507. The seventh tone in the major scale is called *leading tone*, because of its strong tendency to ascend or lead upward to tonic. It is also referred to, though less commonly, as *subtonic* since it is immediately below tonic.

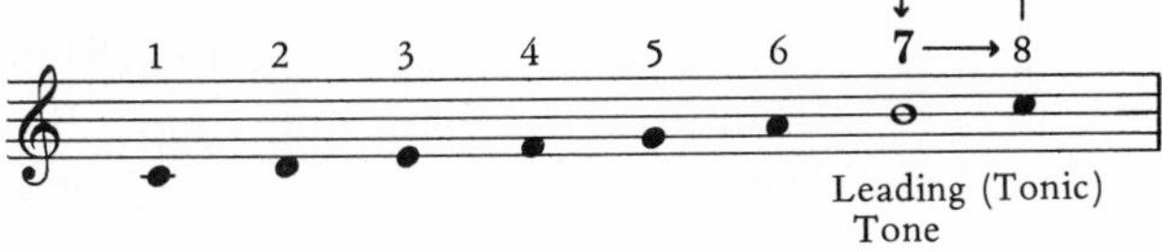

The name of the seventh scale degree is ______________ __________.

supertonic

508. The second scale tone, the scale degree immediately above tonic, is called *supertonic.*

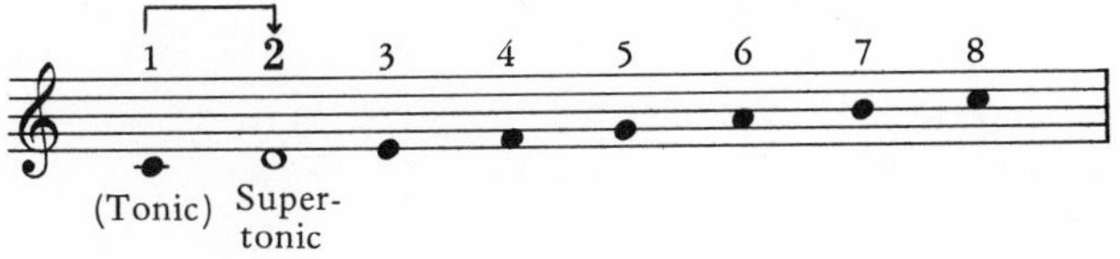

The name of the second scale degree is ______________.

509. In ascending order the names of the scale tones are (1) tonic, (2) supertonic, (3) mediant, (4) subdominant, (5) dominant, (6) submediant, (7) leading tone.

Write the name of each scale degree. The first note is tonic of the major scale of C.

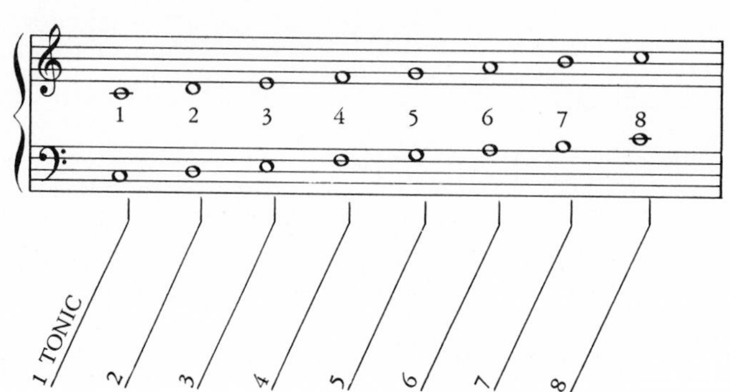

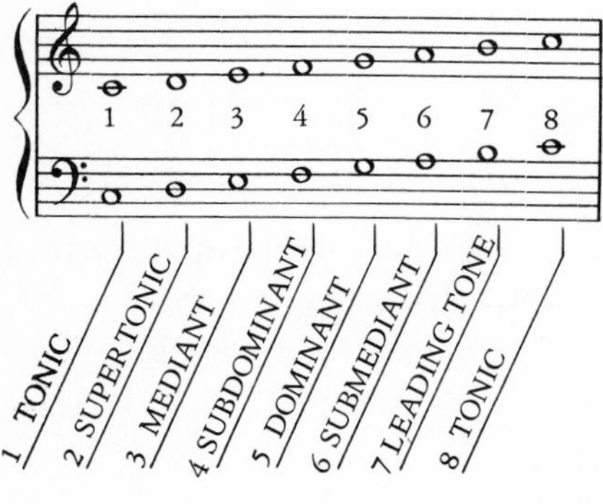

510. Using information from Frame 509, write the pitch name for each scale degree randomly listed. Tonic is C.

dominant____ supertonic ____ subdominant ____

submediant ____ leading tone ____ mediant ____

G D F

A B E

511. Scale tone names are applied in similar manner for all major scales. Using information from Frame 509, write the name of each scale degree. The first note is tonic in the major scale of G.

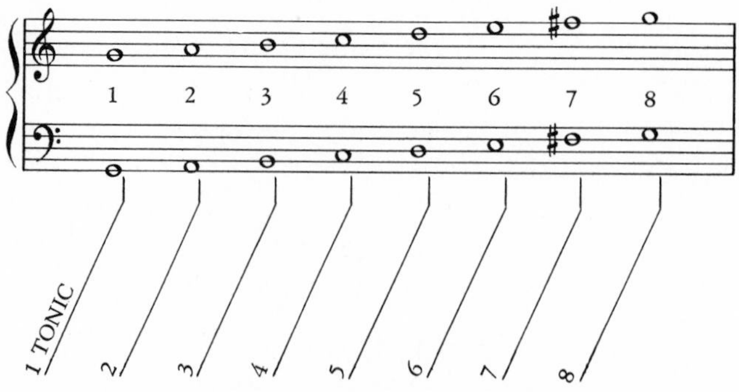

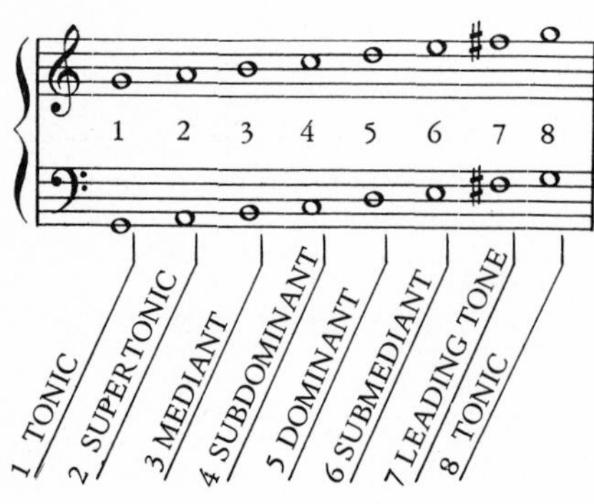

Answers	Frames
	512. Using information from Frame 511, write the pitch name for each scale degree randomly listed. Tonic is G.
E C B	submediant ____ subdominant ____ mediant____
F♯ D A	leading tone____ dominant____supertonic ____
1 2 3 4 5 6 7 8 1 TONIC, 2 SUPERTONIC, 3 MEDIANT, 4 SUBDOMINANT, 5 DOMINANT, 6 SUBMEDIANT, 7 LEADING TONE, 8 TONIC	**513.** Using information from Frame 509, write the name of each scale degree. The first note is tonic in the major scale of F. 1 2 3 4 5 6 7 8 1 TONIC, 2, 3, 4, 5, 6, 7, 8
	514. Using information from Frame 513, write the pitch name for each scale degree randomly listed. Tonic is F.
E B♭ D	leading tone____ subdominant____ submediant____
C A G	dominant____mediant____ supertonic____
C♯	**515.** When D is supertonic, C is tonic. When D♯ is supertonic, ____ is tonic.
G	**516.** When B♭ is mediant, G♭ is tonic. When B is mediant, ____ is tonic.

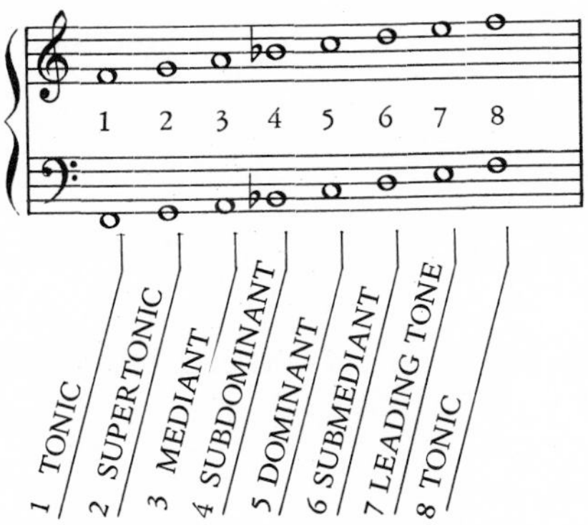

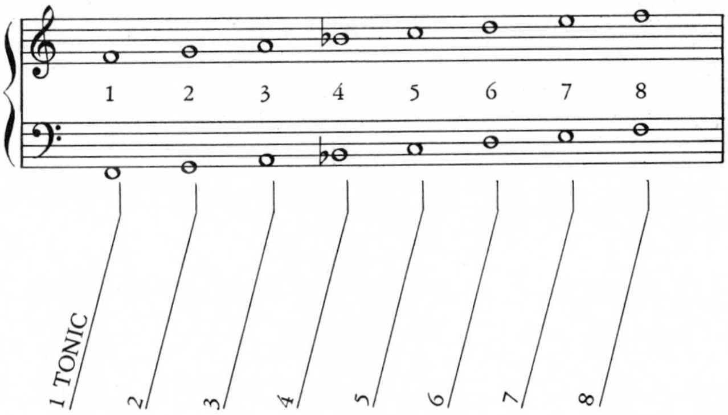

D	517. When G♭ is subdominant, D♭ is tonic. When G is subdominant, ____ is tonic.
F	518. When C♯ is dominant, F♯ is tonic. When C is dominant, ____ is tonic.
C	519. When A♭ is submediant, C♭ is tonic. When A is submediant, ____ is tonic.
B	520. When A is leading tone, B♭ is tonic. When A♯ is leading tone, ____ is tonic.

CHAPTER SUMMARY

1. A scale is an orderly graduated arrangement of ascending or descending pitches.

2. There are many different scales. The two most used in our music are *major* and *minor.* These scales are spelled with successive letter names or notated on consecutive lines and spaces of the staff.

3. The major scale is characterized by the location of half steps between degrees 3–4 and 7–8. All other intervals are whole steps. Whether ascending or descending, the major scale is the same.

4. The major scale can be written/played beginning on fifteen different pitch locations. C contains no accidentals. Scales starting on other pitches require one or more accidentals. Seven scales require sharps and seven scales require flats.

5. Each scale degree has a special name according to its relation to the first degree, called tonic. Ascending from (1) tonic are (2) supertonic, (3) mediant, (4) subdominant, (5) dominant, (6) submediant, and (7) leading tone.

PRE-TEST
MAJOR KEY SIGNATURES

1. This melody (incomplete) is based on the scale of ____.

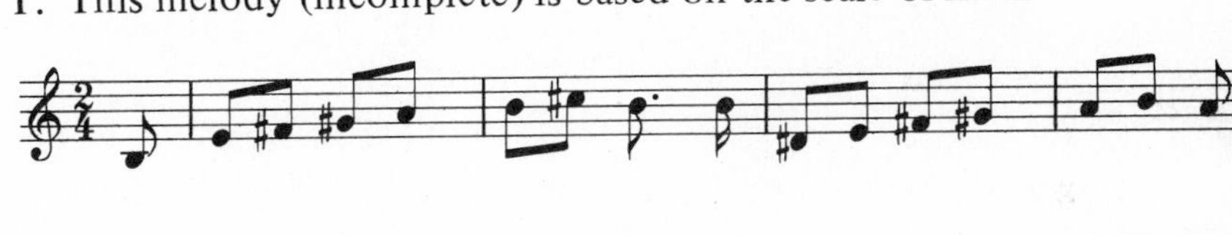

2. Spell the circle of fifths, ascending, beginning on C: __C__ ____ ____ ____ ____ ____ ____ ____.

3. Spell the circle of fifths, descending, beginning on C: __C__ ____ ____ ____ ____ ____ ____ ____.

4. The accidentals of key signatures are written in a certain order.
   (a) Name each of the seven sharps in order: ____ ____ ____ ____ ____ ____ ____.
   (b) Name each of the seven flats in order: ____ ____ ____ ____ ____ ____ ____.

5. Write key signatures on the great staff.

(a)
E♭ major

(c)
C♭ major

(b)
B major

(d)
C♯ major

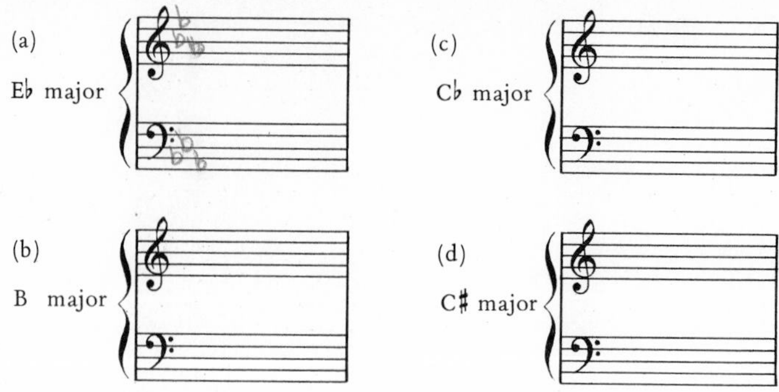

ANSWERS

A score is given at the end of each answer. If your answer is correct, place that score in the column at the right. Add this column for your score.

Score

1. E, or E major (12) ____

2. The complete answer must be correct.

   (C) G D A E B F♯ C♯ (10) ____

3. The complete answer must be correct.

   (C) F B♭ E♭ A♭ D♭ G♭ C♭ (10) ____

4. The complete answer must be correct.

   (a) f c g d a e b (10) ____

   (b) b e a d g c f (10) ____

5. There is no alternative in order, and no alternative of line/space for each accidental.

   (a)
   E♭ major
   (6) ____
   (6) ____

   (b)
   B major
   (6) ____
   (6) ____

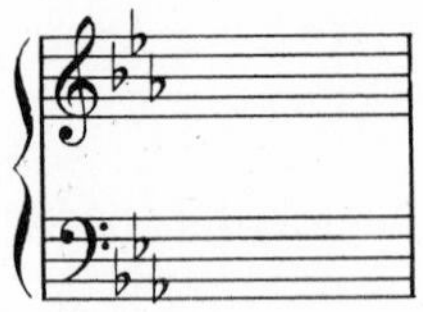

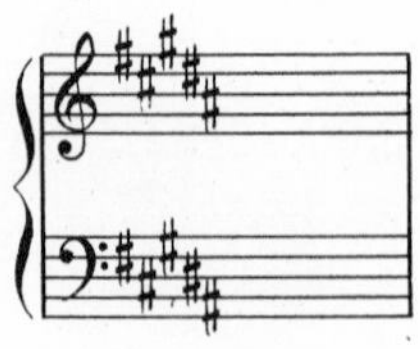

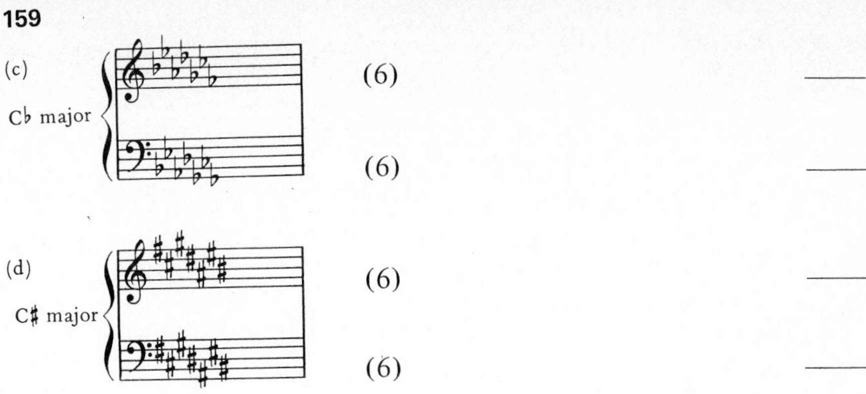

Total score: ____

Perfect score: 100

If your score is 80 or above, turn now to Chapter 10, page 187. If your score is less than 80, continue with Chapter 9.

MAJOR KEY SIGNATURES

The major scale, with its characteristic locations of half steps and whole steps, constitutes a musical pattern having its own unique aural quality. In Chapter 8 we constructed the major scale with fifteen different locations as tonic: C plus seven scales containing sharps and seven scales containing flats.

Ex. 9.1. *Major Scales and Numbers of Accidentals.*

Scale	C	G	D	A	E	B	F♯	C♯
Accidentals	none	1♯	2♯	3♯	4♯	5♯	6♯	7♯
Scale		F	B♭	E♭	A♭	D♭	G♭	C♭
Accidentals		1♭	2♭	3♭	4♭	5♭	6♭	7♭

Since all major scales have the same characteristic sound, there are not really fifteen different scales; there is simply one major scale structure which can be written or played at fifteen different locations.

Melodies based on major scales are shown in Frames 521–530. Questions on these melodies are found in Frames 531–545. Turn now to Frame 531.

MAJOR MELODIES

521. *Bach,* O Ewigkeit, du Donnerwort, *Chorale No. 26*

522. *Beethoven, Trio, Op. 97* (Archduke)

523. *Handel, "Joy to the World"*

524. *Elgar, Suite No. 1, Op. Ia,* The Wand of Youth, *"Sun Dance"*

525. *Meyer,* Es Ist Kein Tag

526. *Rendle, Vesper Hymn*

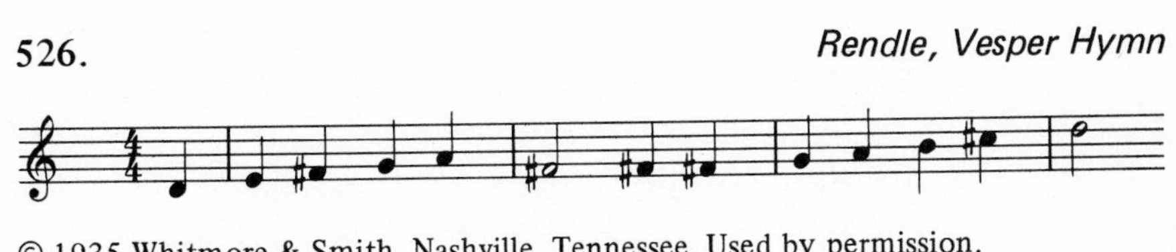

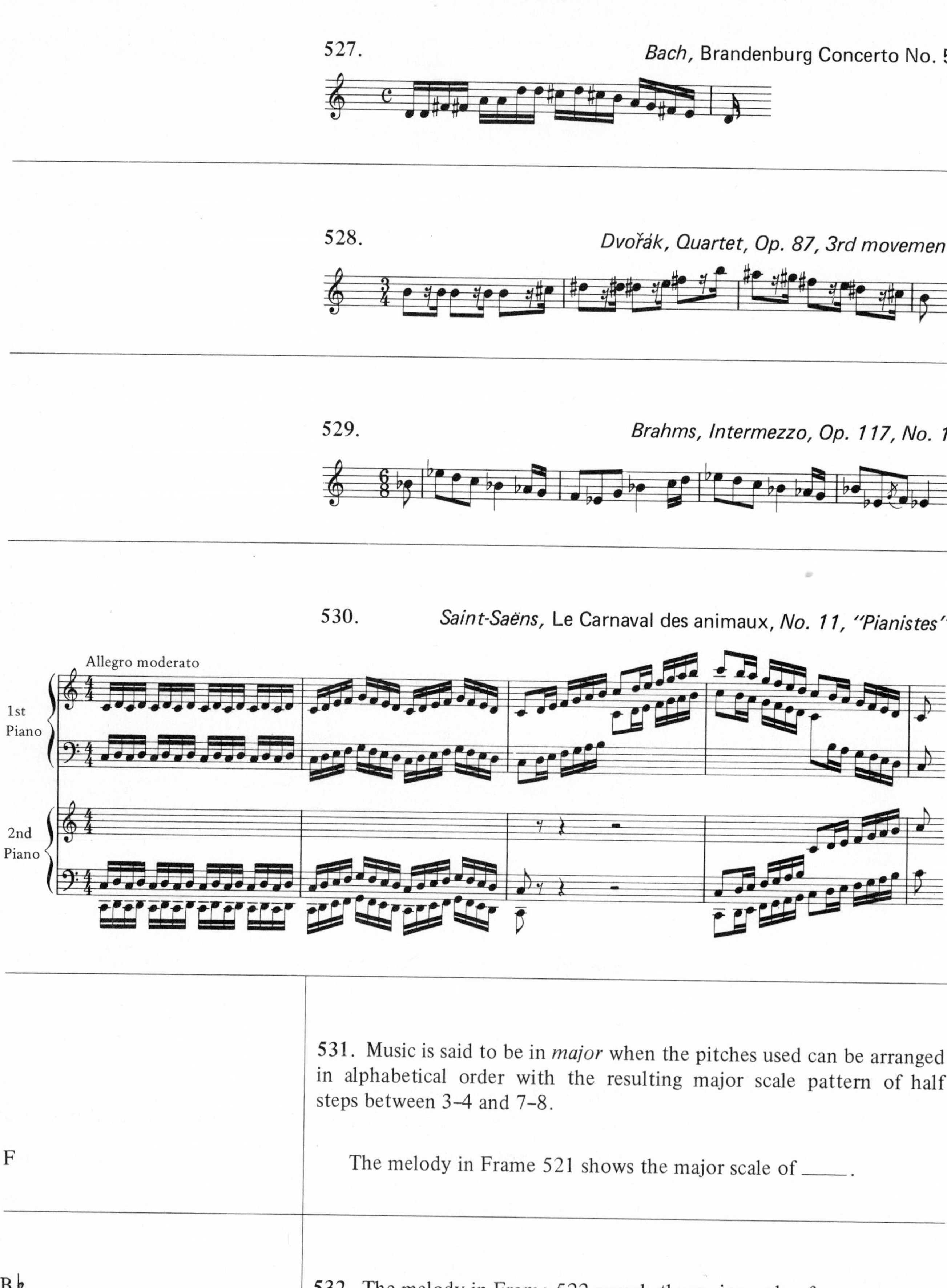

531. Music is said to be in *major* when the pitches used can be arranged in alphabetical order with the resulting major scale pattern of half steps between 3–4 and 7–8.

F

The melody in Frame 521 shows the major scale of ____.

B♭

532. The melody in Frame 522 reveals the major scale of ____.

D	533. The melody in Frame 523 is identical to the descending major scale of ____.
C	534. The pitches of the melody in Frame 524, though not completely in scale order, can be rearranged in alphabetical order with half steps between E–F (3–4) and B–C (7–8), resulting in the major scale of ____.
D	535. The pitches of the melody in Frame 525 can be arranged in alphabetical order resulting in the major scale of ____.
D	536. The melody of Frame 526 is based on the major scale of ____.
D	537. The melody in Frame 527 reveals the major scale of ____.
B	538. The melody in Frame 528 is composed with notes of the major scale of ____.
E♭	539. The melody in Frame 529 is based on the major scale of ____.
C	540. In Frame 530 the composer has amusingly employed the scale in different octave registers. This excerpt ranges from great C to c^3 and shows the major scale of ____.

KEY

key	541. We could identify a piece of music by saying it uses a certain scale, but instead, we say the music is in a certain *key*. We could identify the music in Frame 521 by saying it uses the major scale of F, but instead, we ordinarily say the music is in the key of F major. The music in Frame 522 reveals the major scale of B♭. Accordingly, we say the music is in the ________ of B♭ major.
key D	542. The music in Frame 523 is in the ________ of ______ major.
D	543. The term *key* refers to the letter name of the tonic (first degree) of that scale upon which the composition is based. In the music of Frame 524, the key is C major and the tonic is C. In Frame 525, the tonic is _____.
D	544. The letter name of the tonic is also called *keynote*. In Frame 526, D is the tonic and keynote. In Frame 527, the keynote is _____.
C major	545. The first note of a scale, the tonic, and the keynote are identical. This note alone, however, does not reveal the nature of the scale (e.g., whether major or minor). To identify the particular aural quality of the music in Frame 530, we say it is in the key of _____ ________.

546. Music could be written with the correct accidentals placed before each note when needed, as in Frames 521–523 and 525–529, but this is obviously cumbersome and makes the music appear unduly complicated. To facilitate the notation of accidentals we use a device called *key signature,* found on the staff at the beginning of a composition. The key signature consists of the accidentals used in the scale of the composition. The illustrations below show random examples of key signatures.

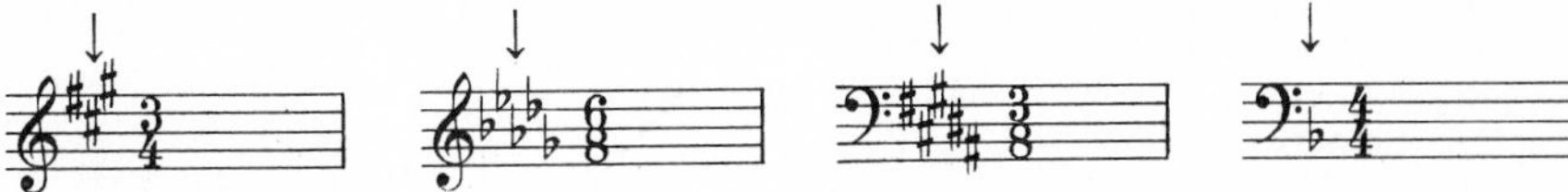

The accidentals used in the scale of a composition are grouped together to form the ________ ____________.

key signature

547. In the composition below (a) the scale is E major. In (b), by extracting the four sharps of the scale and arranging them in a certain order on the staff between the clef and time signature we produce the key signature of E major.

Verdi, Rigoletto, *"Caro nome"*

There are fifteen major keys (including C with no sharps and no flats), just as there are fifteen locations of the major scale.

We can find the number and names of sharps or flats for each major key signature by extracting the accidentals from each major ________.

scale

548. The key signature is placed (before/after) ____________ the time signature.

before

549. By extracting the accidentals from the fifteen major scales, we can list fifteen corresponding keys, the number of accidentals needed for each key signature, and the name of each accidental in turn. Do not attempt to memorize this table, but use it freely as a reference.

Number and Names of Accidentals for Major Key Signatures.

Name of key (Name of tonic or keynote)	Number of ♯'s or ♭'s in key signature	Names of ♯'s or ♭'s
C	none	
G	1♯	f♯
D	2♯	f♯ c♯
A	3♯	f♯ c♯ g♯
E	4♯	f♯ c♯ g♯ d♯
B	5♯	f♯ c♯ g♯ d♯ a♯
F♯	6♯	f♯ c♯ g♯ d♯ a♯ e♯
C♯	7♯	f♯ c♯ g♯ d♯ a♯ e♯ b♯
(C)	(none)	
F	1♭	b♭
B♭	2♭	b♭ e♭
E♭	3♭	b♭ e♭ a♭
A♭	4♭	b♭ e♭ a♭ d♭
D♭	5♭	b♭ e♭ a♭ d♭ g♭
G♭	6♭	b♭ e♭ a♭ d♭ g♭ c♭
C♭	7♭	b♭ e♭ a♭ d♭ g♭ c♭ f♭

CIRCLE OF FIFTHS

550. To remember all the keys and the order of their accidentals may appear to be a formidable task. It can be made easy, however, by learning the principle of the *circle of fifths.* In addition to solving key signatures, the relationships of fifths have many other uses in music which you will find in future studies in harmony, composition, and musical analysis. To understand the circle of fifths, you must first be able to measure the interval of a *perfect fifth.** A perfect fifth spans five staff degrees and is comprised of three whole steps and one half step, or seven half steps. However, rather than counting steps, we can calculate

a perfect fifth more quickly by using as a tool information already learned in connection with the scale. Consider the note from which the measurement is to be made as tonic. From a tonic note up to its dominant note is an ascending perfect fifth. When C is tonic, G is dominant. Therefore, a perfect fifth above C is G. See the following illustrations:

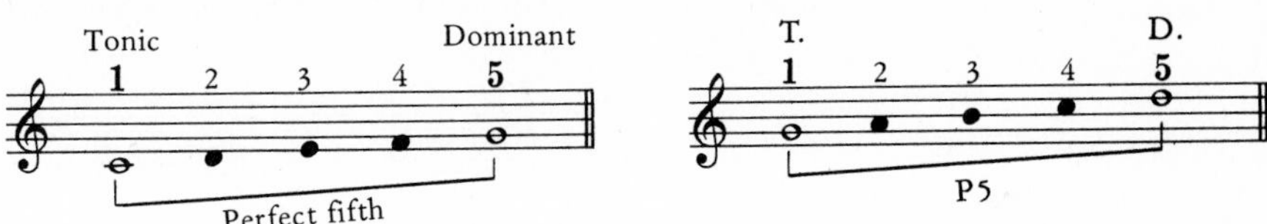

D

A perfect fifth above G is ____.

*Interval names, including other kinds of fifths, will be studied in Chapters 13 and 14.

551.

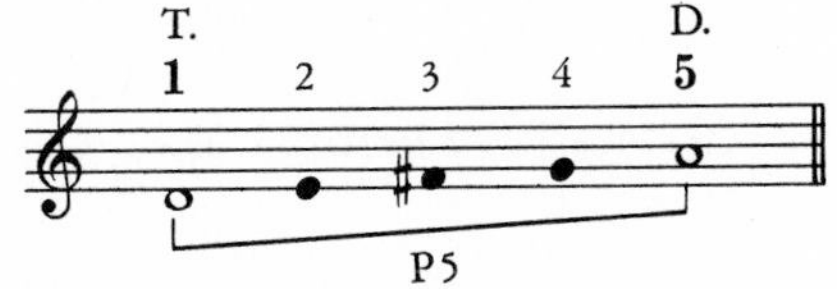

A

A perfect fifth above D is ____.

E

552. A perfect fifth above A is ____.

B

553. A perfect fifth above E is ____.

F♯

554. The dominant or perfect fifth above B is the pitch ____.

C♯

555. The dominant or perfect fifth above F♯ is the pitch ____.

556. As well as determining ascending perfect fifths, it is necessary to calculate *descending* perfect fifths. From a tonic note down to its subdominant note is a descending perfect fifth.

Tonic 8 7 6 5 Sub-dominant 4

Perfect fifth

When C is tonic, F is subdominant. Therefore, a perfect fifth below C is ____.

F

557.

T. 8 7 6 5 Sd. 4

P5

A perfect fifth below F is ____.

B♭

558.

T. 8 7 6 5 Sd. 4

P5

A perfect fifth below B♭ is ____.

E♭

A♭

559. A perfect fifth below E♭ is ____.

D♭

560. A perfect fifth below A♭ is ____.

G♭

561. A perfect fifth below D♭ is ____.

C♭

562. A perfect fifth below G♭ is ____.

563. It is through the interval of the perfect fifth that keys are related to each other. Using the tool of tonic-dominant analysis to determine ascending perfect fifths, proceed from C up a perfect fifth to find the keynote G for the scale with *one* sharp; calculate a perfect fifth above G to find the keynote D for the scale with *two* sharps, and so on until reaching C♯ with *seven* sharps. The complete process is illustrated below.

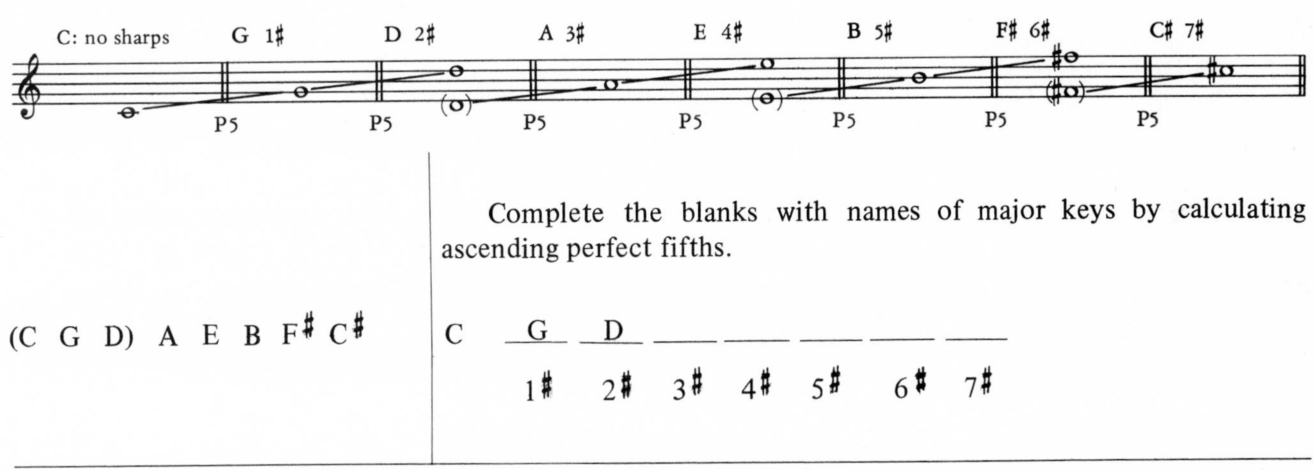

Complete the blanks with names of major keys by calculating ascending perfect fifths.

(C G D) A E B F♯ C♯

C __G__ __D__ ____ ____ ____ ____ ____

1♯ 2♯ 3♯ 4♯ 5♯ 6♯ 7♯

564. The flat keys are related in a similar manner. Using the tool of tonic-subdominant analysis to determine descending perfect fifths, proceed *down* a perfect fifth to find the keynote F for the scale with *one* flat; calculate a perfect fifth below F to find the keynote B♭ for the scale with *two* flats, and so on until reaching C♭ with *seven* flats. The complete process is illustrated below.

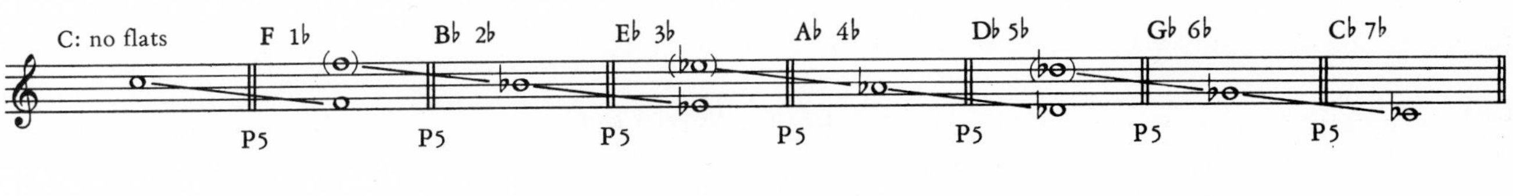

Complete the blanks with names of major keys by calculating *descending* perfect fifths:

(C F B♭) E♭ A♭ D♭ G♭ C♭

C __F__ __B♭__ ____ ____ ____ ____ ____

1♭ 2♭ 3♭ 4♭ 5♭ 6♭ 7♭

565. The information shown in Frames 563 and 564 is diagrammed below, where it can be seen that each progression up a fifth adds one new sharp, and each progression down a fifth adds one new flat.

Progressions by Fifths from C.

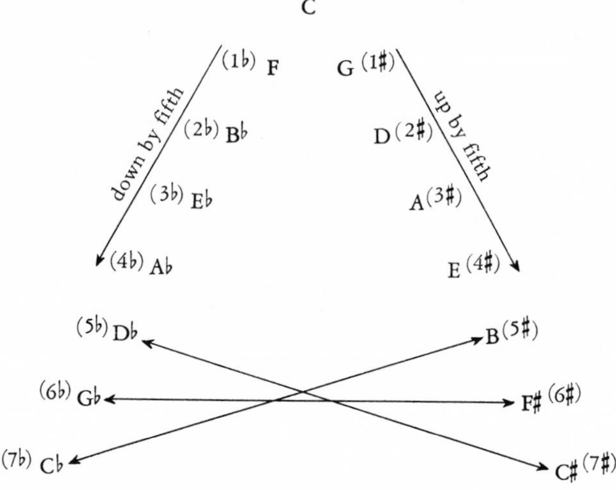

sharp

Each progression up a fifth adds one new (sharp/flat) __________.

---

flat

566. In Frame 565, the illustration shows that each progression down a fifth adds one new (sharp/flat) __________.

---

567. Further observation of the illustration in Frame 565 shows that key names used for five, six, and seven sharps have enharmonic equivalents in the names for keys of five, six, and seven flats: B (five sharps) and C♭ (seven flats); F♯ (six sharps) and G♭ (six flats); C♯ (seven sharps) and D♭ (five flats).

C♭

The enharmonic key to B is ____.

G♭

568. The enharmonic key to F♯ is ____.

C♯

569. The enharmonic key to D♭ is ____.

570. By reconstructing the illustration in Frame 565 so that the enharmonic keys coincide, the *circle of fifths* for major keys is produced.

Circle of Fifths for Major Keys.

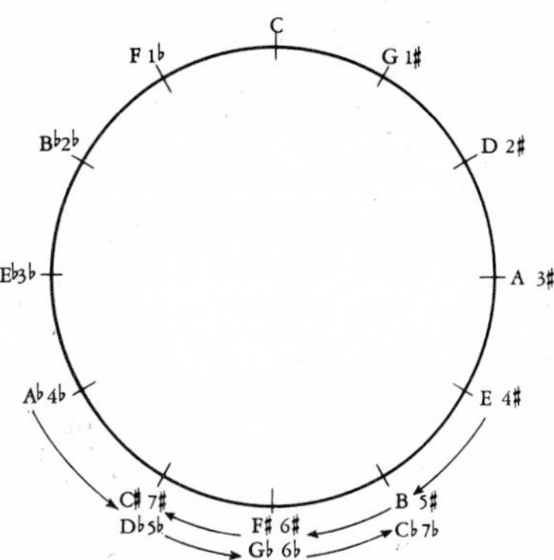

This circle includes all the major key names with the sharp keys reading clockwise from C, and the flat keys reading counterclockwise from C. The circle is joined by the three enharmonic keys.

Sharp keys are found on the circle of fifths by reading (clockwise/ counterclockwise) ________________.

clockwise

---

571. Flat keys are found on the circle of fifths by reading (clockwise/ counterclockwise) ________________.

counterclockwise

---

572. On the circle, the number of sharps or flats for each key can be determined by counting the number of fifths away from C. For example, A has three sharps because it is the third key *clockwise* from C; D♭ has five flats because it is five keys *counterclockwise* from C.

The fourth key clockwise from C is ____with (no.)____ sharps.

E four

---

573. The sixth key counterclockwise from C is____ with (no.) ____ flats.

G♭ six

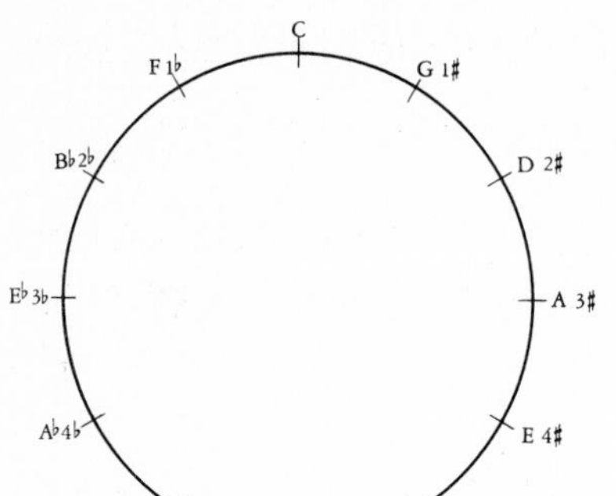

574. On the circle of fifths below, the key names are given. Beside each key name write the correct number of sharps or flats. The answer for G major is given.

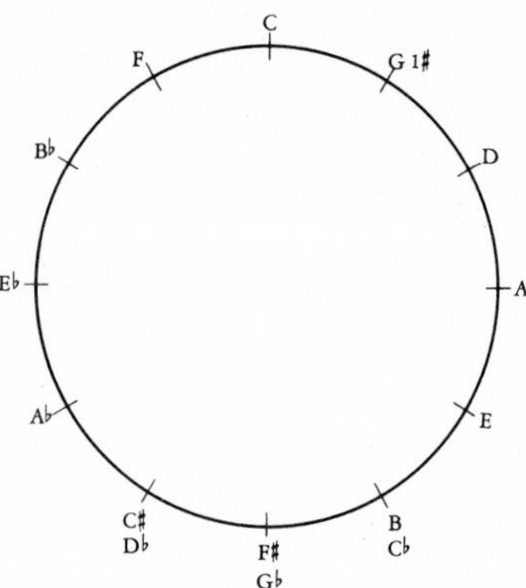

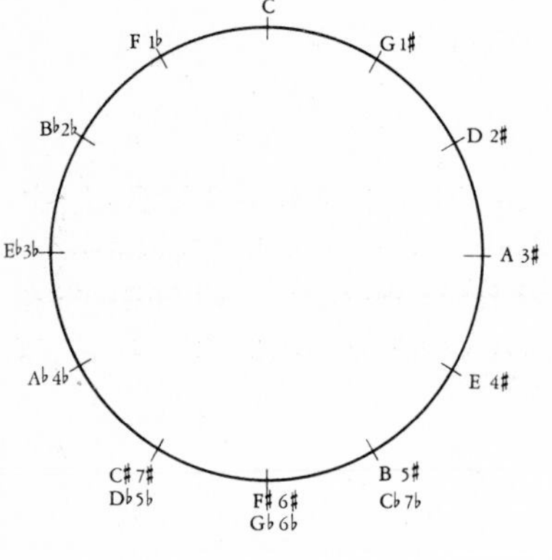

575. On the circle of fifths below, the key signatures are given. Beside each, give the name of the major key. The answer for one flat is given.

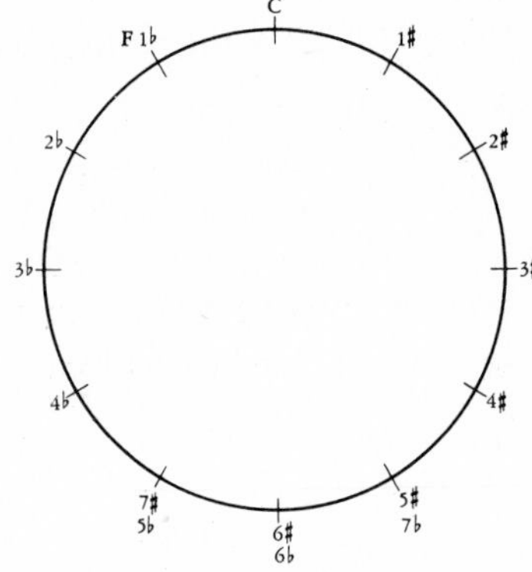

576. The Circle of Fifths for Major Keys, shown in Frame 570, may be referred to when needed. Similar circle-of-fifth illustrations can be found in many other theory textbooks. However, when a reference book is not accessible to you, it is a simple matter to construct this illustration for yourself by following procedures outlined in the following frames.

Draw a circle and mark twelve points like the face of a clock. This provides places for all fifteen keys including three enharmonic keys.

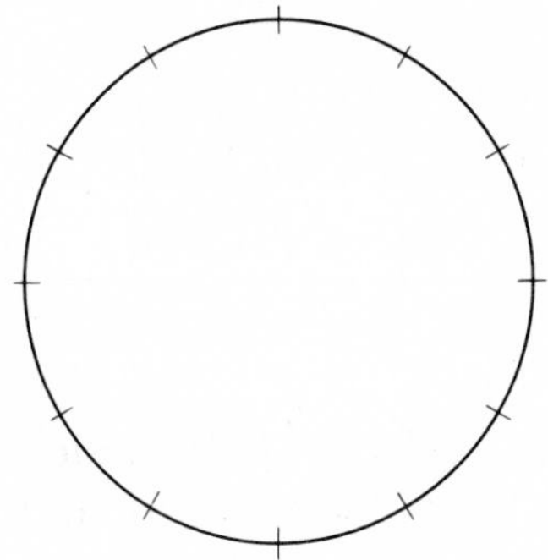

577. Draw the circle with twelve points and place C at the top of the circle as if for 12 o'clock. Proceeding clockwise, at 1 o'clock place the letter name of the key a fifth above C, which is G with one sharp; continue clockwise in fifths and add sharps through the key of C♯, seven sharps.

↓

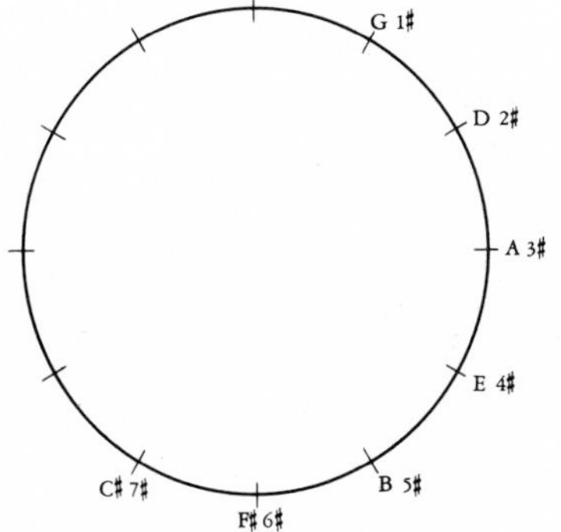

578. Draw the circle with twelve points and place C at 12 o'clock. Proceeding counterclockwise, at 11 o'clock place the letter name of the key a fifth below C, which is F with one flat; continue counterclockwise in fifths and add flats through the key of C♭, seven flats.

↓

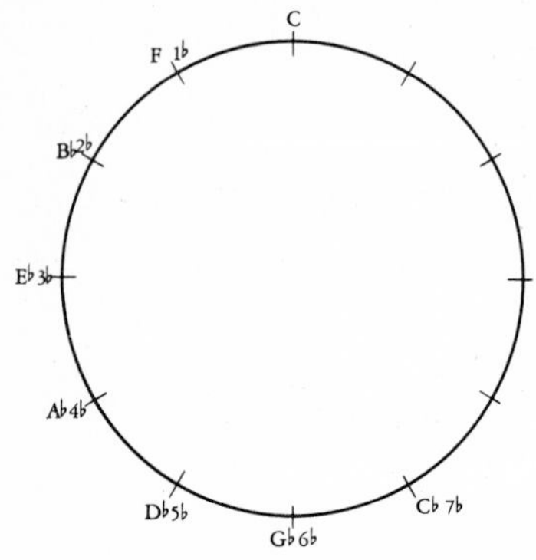

579. Having demonstrated sharp and flat keys on separate circles, now combine all major keys on one circle. Draw the circle with twelve points. Proceeding clockwise from C, place the sharp keys on the circle. Then, proceeding counterclockwise from C, place the flat keys on the circle. If your work is correct you will see the three enharmonic keys at the bottom of the circle.

↓

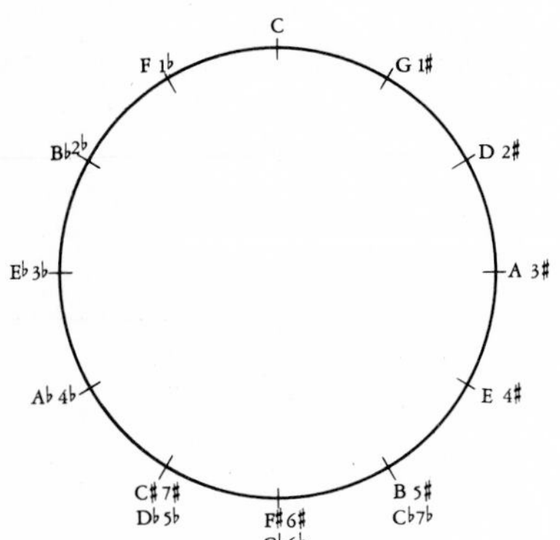

With practice, students can construct this illustration in a minute's time. Using scrap paper, practice until you can achieve this goal.

ORDER OF SHARPS AND FLATS ON THE STAFF

580. Accidentals of key signatures are written in a certain order. Refer to Frame 549. Names of sharps are easily remembered in turn because they are in an order of *ascending* fifths beginning with the first sharp, f.

Names of Sharps

f c g d a e b

Do not confuse with names of keys; this series of fifths relates to *names of sharps.*

Sharps in key signatures occur in this order:

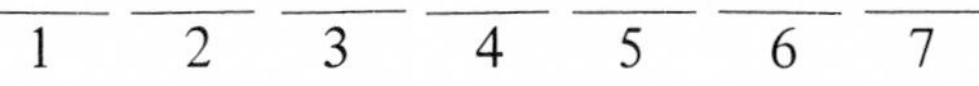

f c g d a e b

581. For sharp keys the first sharp appears on the staff at the location of f^2 (treble clef) and on small f (bass clef).

This sharp applies to any F in the musical composition whether on the same lines or on any other locations, and this same principle is observed for any other sharps (or flats) of the key signature.

Place the key signature for G major on the staff.

582. Name the pitches:

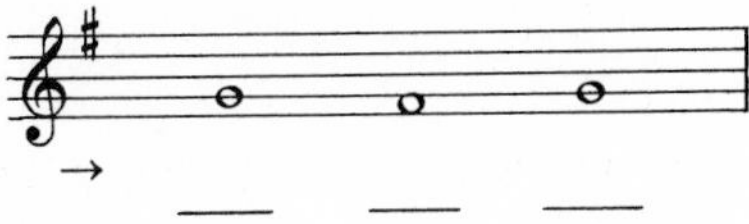

G F♯ G

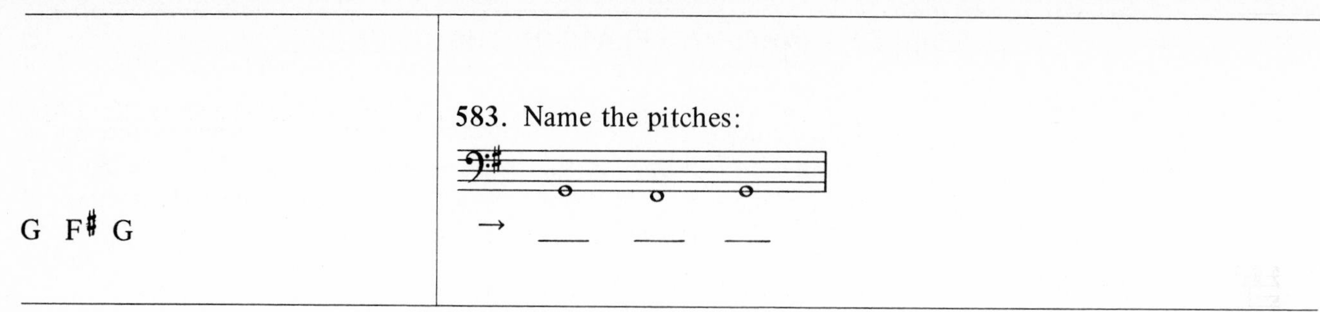

583. Name the pitches:

→ ___ ___ ___

G F♯ G

584. By tradition, all sharps are placed as shown below.

C Major and Sharp Key Signatures.

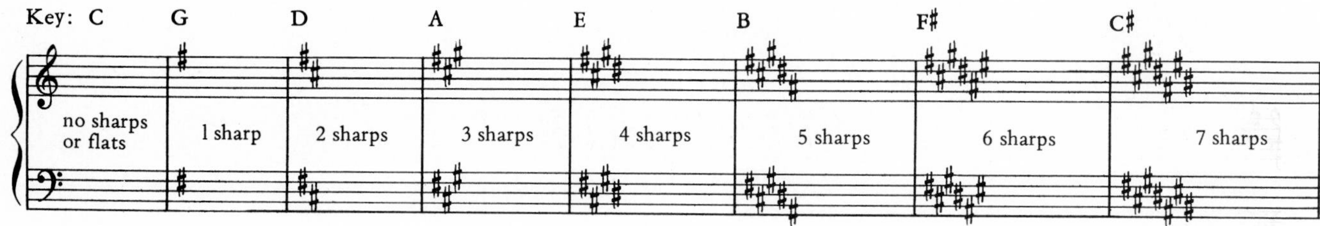

Notice that the sharps progress from left to right in an orderly arrangement and that the *pattern* of accidentals in key signatures is the same for treble and bass, the up-and-down contour changed only at sharps 4 and 5.

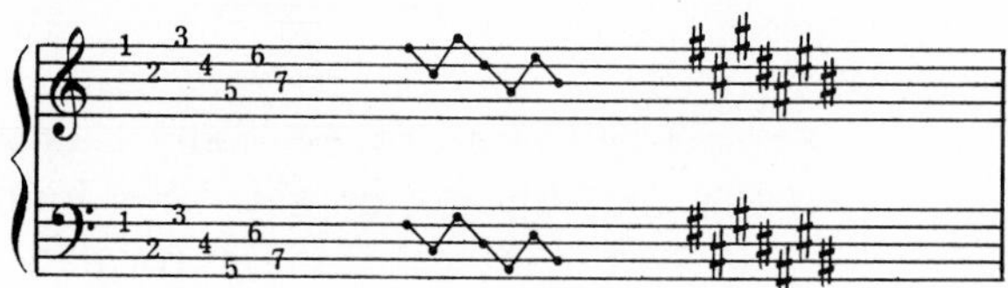

Refer to these illustrations in answering Frames 585–590.

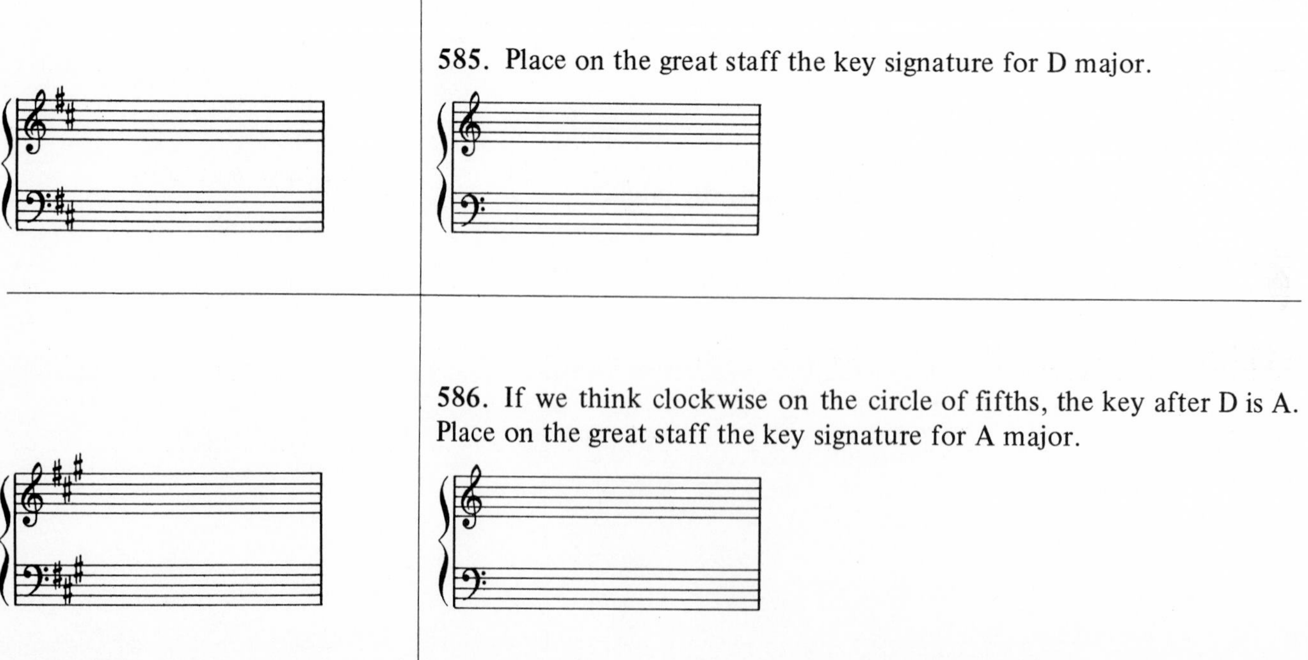

585. Place on the great staff the key signature for D major.

586. If we think clockwise on the circle of fifths, the key after D is A. Place on the great staff the key signature for A major.

587. The key signature for E major contains four sharps in the order f♯, c♯, g♯, d♯.

Place these sharps on the great staff.

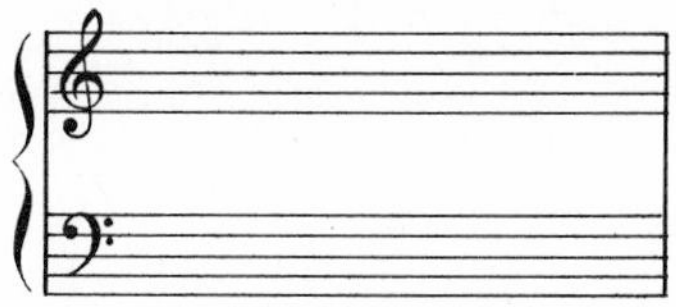

B

588. Write the key signature comprised of five sharps.

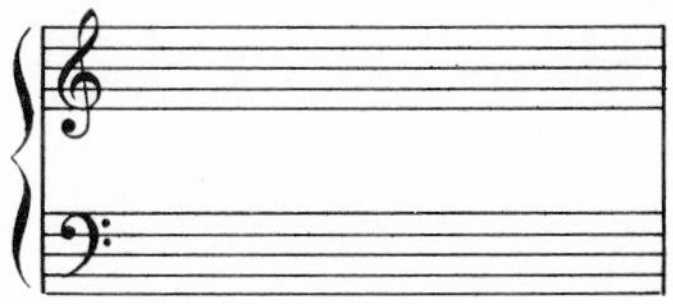

The key is ____ major.

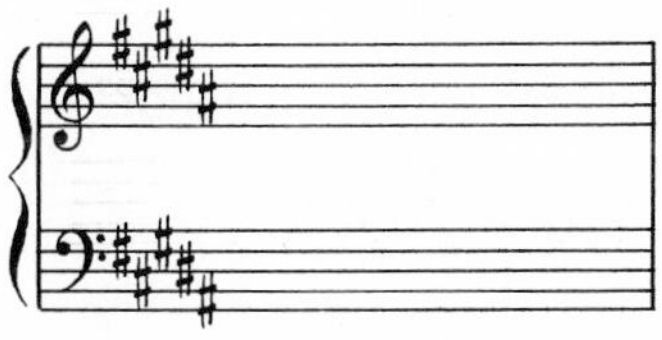

589. The scale of F♯ major contains six sharps. When the accidentals are extracted from the scale to form the key signature, they must, by tradition, be placed on the staff in this manner:

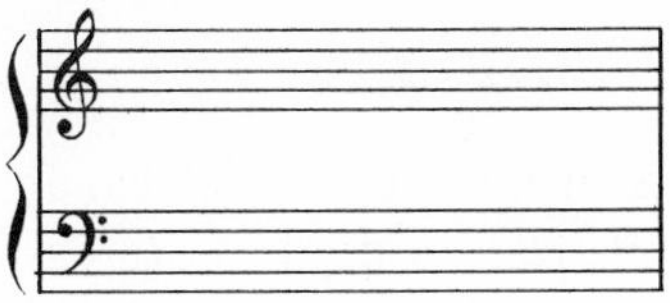

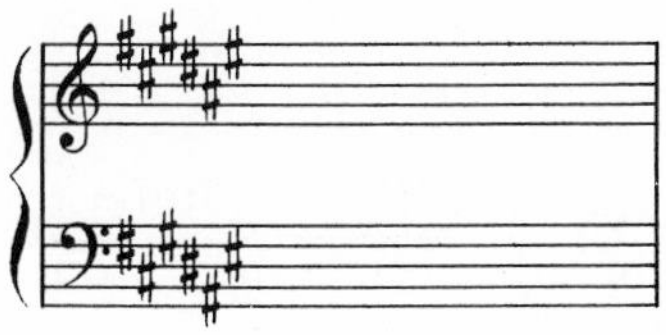

590. The last sharp key on the circle contains all seven sharps.
Write the key signature for C♯ major.

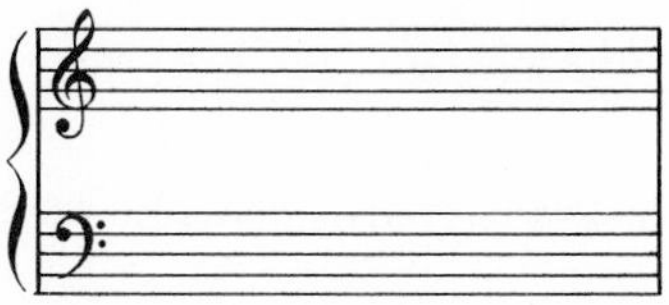

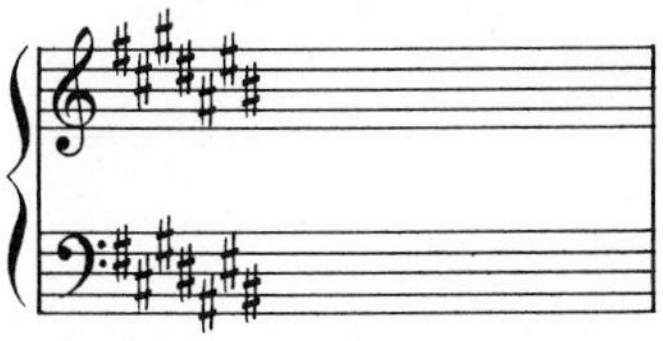

591. For quick identification of a major key signature of one or more sharps, notice that the keynote occupies that staff degree immediately above the last sharp.

Key of D major   Key of F♯ major

E

shows the key signature for ____ major.

*Called F sharp because the sign ♯ is already on the fifth line.

B

592. 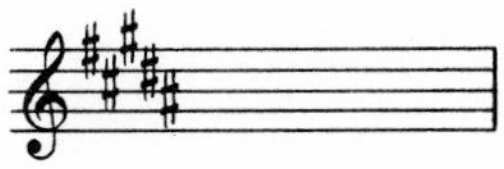 shows the key signature for ____ major.

G

593.  shows the key signature for ____ major.

A

594.  shows the key signature for ____ major.

595. Flats in key signatures also are written in a certain order. Refer to Frame 549. Names of flats are easily remembered because they are in an order of *descending* fifths beginning with the first flat, b.

Names of Flats

b e a d g c f

Do not confuse with names of keys; this series of fifths relates to *names of flats.*

Flats in key signatures occur in this order:

b e a d g c f

____	____	____	____	____	____	____
1	2	3	4	5	6	7

596. For flat keys the first flat appears on the staff at the location of b[1] (treble clef) and on great B (bass clef).

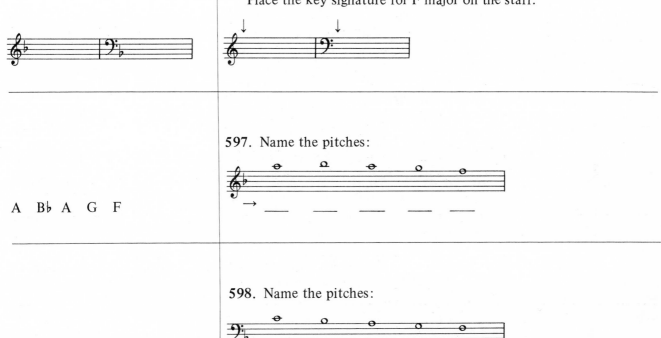

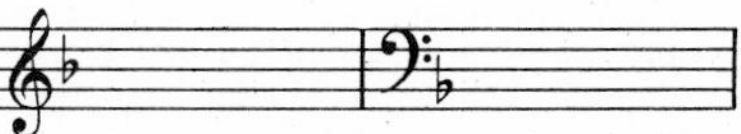

This flat applies to any B in the musical composition whether on the same lines or in other octave registers, and this same principle is observed for any other flats (or sharps) of the key signature.

Place the key signature for F major on the staff.

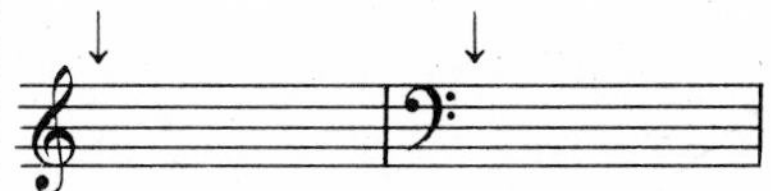

597. Name the pitches:

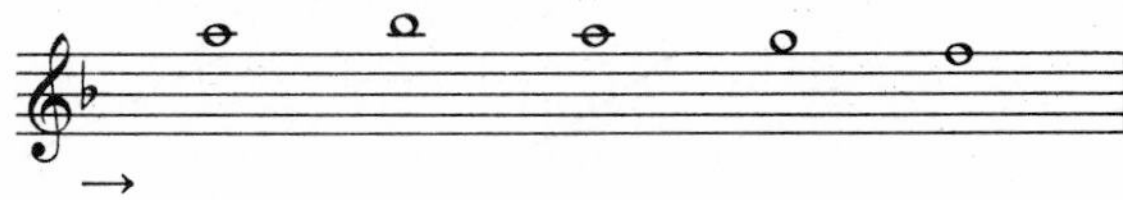

A B♭ A G F

598. Name the pitches:

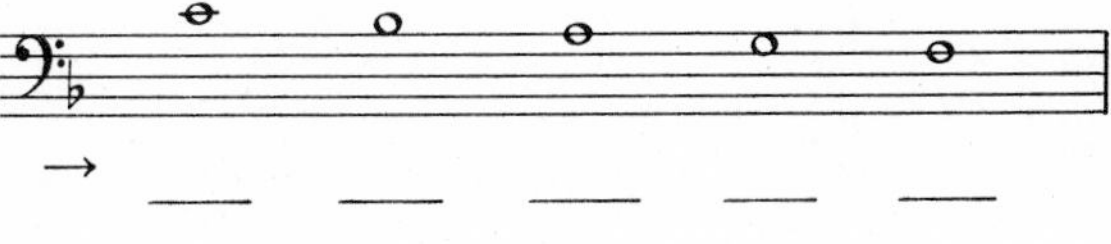

C B♭ A G F

599. By tradition, all flats are placed as shown below.

C Major and Flat Key Signatures.

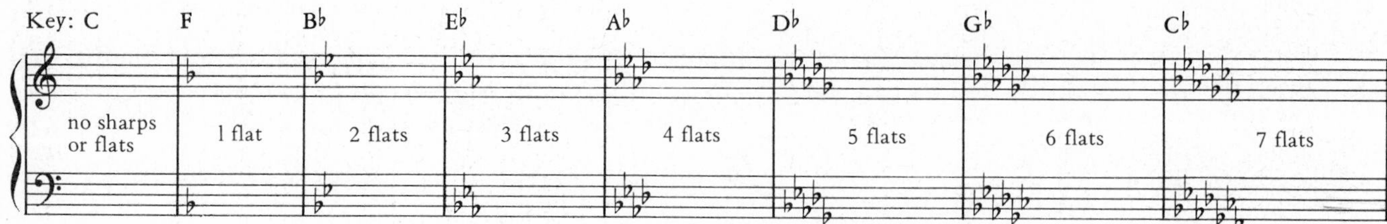

Notice that the flats progress from left to right in an orderly and regular arrangement and that the *pattern* of accidentals in key signatures is the same for treble and bass.

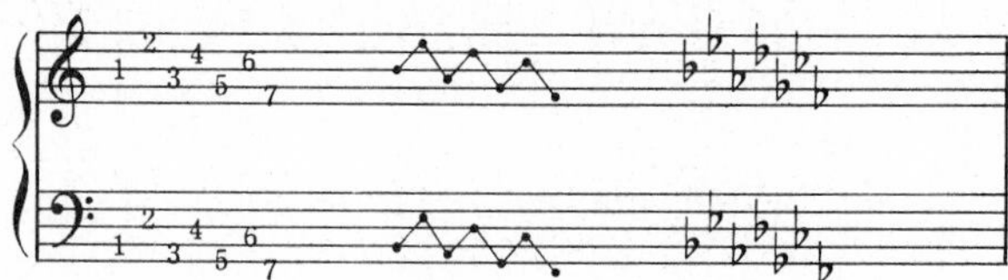

Refer to these illustrations in answering Frames 600–605.

600. Place on the great staff the key signature for B♭ major.

601. If we think counterclockwise on the circle of fifths, the key after B♭ is E♭.

Place on the great staff the key signature for E♭ major.

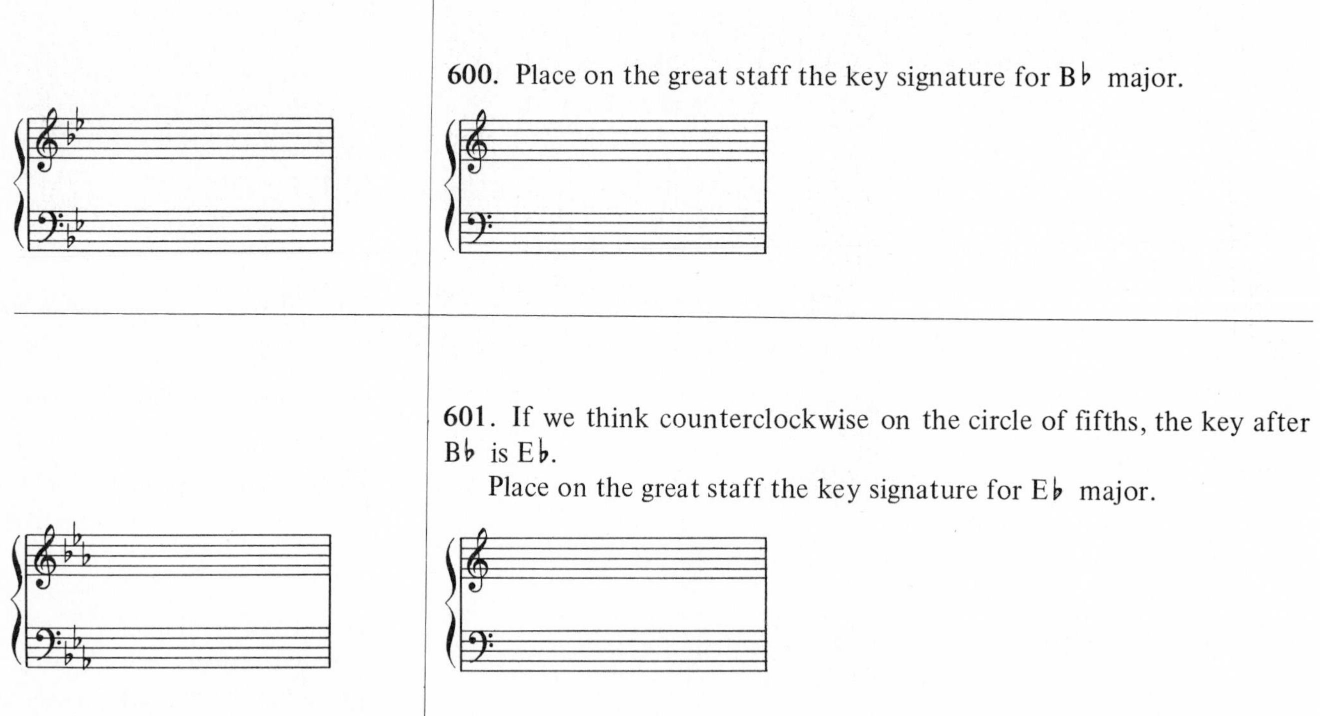

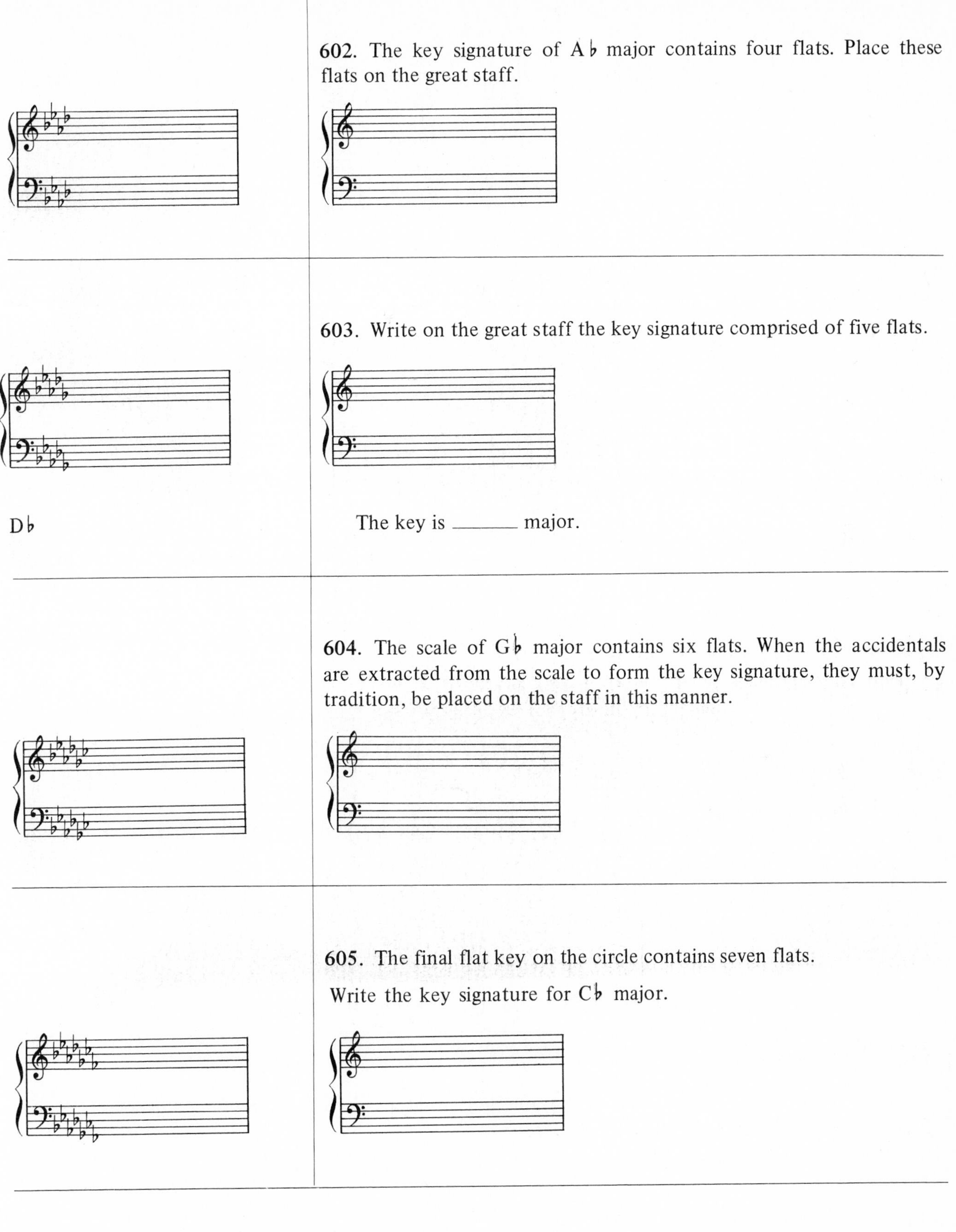

602. The key signature of A♭ major contains four flats. Place these flats on the great staff.

D♭

603. Write on the great staff the key signature comprised of five flats.

The key is ______ major.

604. The scale of G♭ major contains six flats. When the accidentals are extracted from the scale to form the key signature, they must, by tradition, be placed on the staff in this manner.

605. The final flat key on the circle contains seven flats.
Write the key signature for C♭ major.

606. For quick identification of a major key signature of two or more flats, notice that the keynote is identical with the penultimate (next-to-last) flat. (F major, one flat, must be remembered separately.)

Key of B♭ major Key of G♭ major

shows the key signature for ______ major.

A♭

607. shows the key signature for ______ major.

D♭

608. shows the key signature for ______ major.

E♭

609. shows the key signature for ______ major.

C♭

610. Supply the key signature for F major and compare with Frame 521.

Bach, O Ewigkeit, du Donnerwort

611. Supply the key signature for B♭ major and compare with Frame 522.

Beethoven, Trio, Op. 97 (Archduke)

612. Supply the key signature for D major and compare with Frame 523.

Handel, Joy to the World

C major

613. This melody is also found in Frame 524.

Elgar, "Sun Dance"

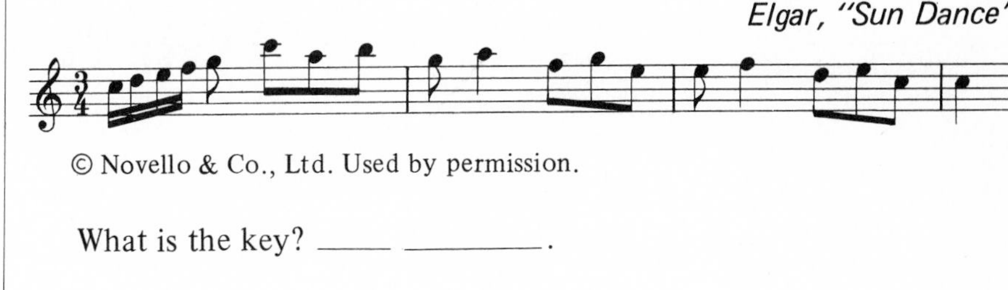

What is the key? _____ __________.

CHAPTER SUMMARY

1. Major melodies are based on major scales.

2. *Key* refers to the tonic of that scale upon which a composition is based. The first note of a scale, the tonic, and the *keynote* are the same.

3. Accidentals used in the scale of a composition are grouped together to form the *key signature.*

4. There are fifteen major keys, just as there are fifteen major scales.

5. The *circle of fifths* enables us to organize knowledge of keys, including relationships of keys, number of accidentals required for each key signature, and enharmonic keys.

6. The order for major keys is (beginning with C, no sharps or flats):

	G	D	A	E	B	F♯	C♯
	1♯	2♯	3♯	4♯	5♯	6♯	7♯
C							
	F	B♭	E♭	A♭	D♭	G♭	C♭
	1♭	2♭	3♭	4♭	5♭	6♭	7♭

7. The accidentals of key signatures are written in a prescribed order. Names of sharps are: f c g d a e b. Names of flats are: b e a d g c f.

8. Accidentals of the key signature are placed by tradition on lines and spaces of the staff as shown:

PRE-TEST
MINOR SCALES

1. Spell the scales:

    (a) C♯ minor, natural (pure) form

    (b) E♭ minor, melodic form

    (c) G♯ minor, harmonic form

2. Notate the following scales (octave range)

    (a) D♯ minor, melodic form

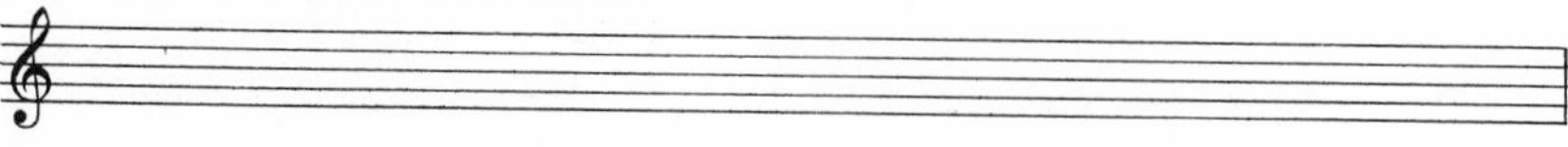

    (b) G minor, harmonic form

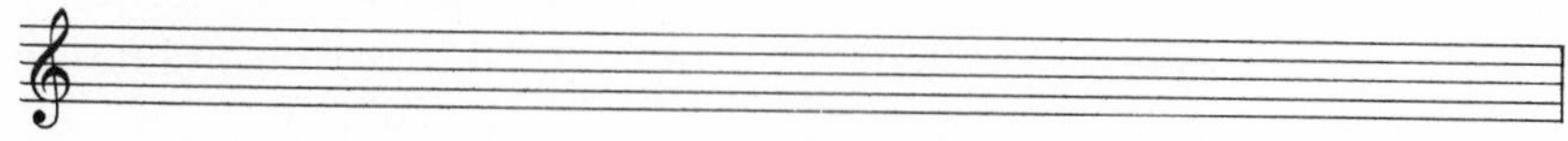

    (c) B♭ minor, natural form

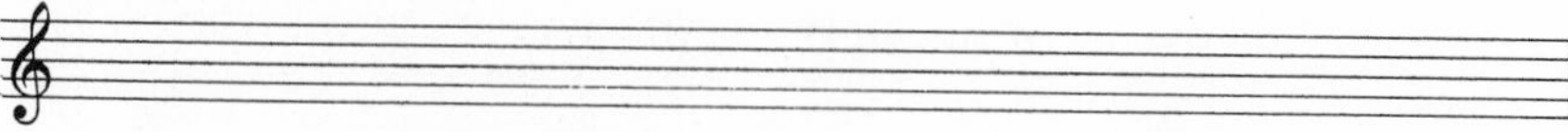

    (d) F♯ minor, natural form

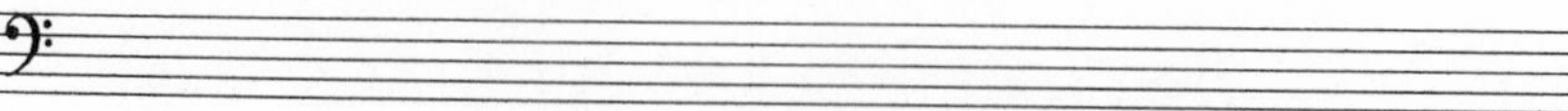

(e) D minor, melodic form

(f) A♯ minor, harmonic form

3. Give the scale-step names for these notes in minor with C as tonic:

(a) B♭ ____________

(b) A♮ ____________

(c) B♮ ____________

(d) A♭ ____________

ANSWERS

A score is given at the end of each answer. If your answer is correct, place that score in the column at the right. Add this column for your score.

Score

1. The complete answer must be correct.

(a) C♯ D♯ E F♯ G♯ A B C♯ (10) ____

(b) (*asc.*) E♭ F G♭ A♭ B♭ C(♮) D(♮) E♭
(*desc.*) E♭ D♭ C♭ B♭ A♭ G♭ F E♭ (12) ____

(c) G♯ A♯ B C♯ D♯ E F𝄪 G♯ (10) ____

2. The complete answer must be correct.

(e) (10) ____

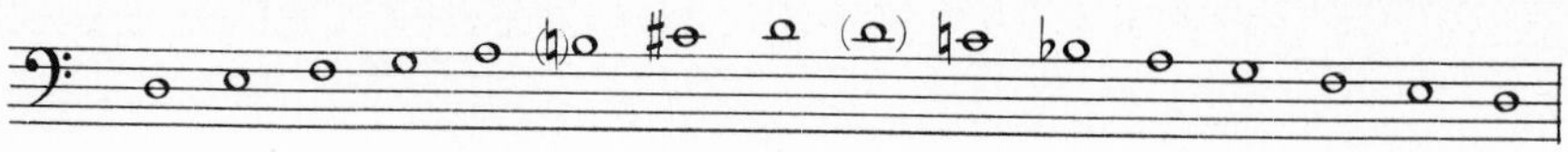

(f) (10) ____

3. (a) subtonic (2) ____

(b) raised submediant (2) ____

(c) leading tone (2) ____

(d) submediant (2) ____

Total score: ____

Perfect score: 100

If your score is 80 or above, turn now to Chapter 11, page 219. If your score is less than 80, continue with Chapter 10.

MINOR SCALES

We have learned that the sound of a scale is determined by the location of half steps and whole steps in the scale. Therefore, we can expect that the minor scale, which sounds different from the major scale, will have a different arrangement of half steps and whole steps. Not only is this true, but there are three different forms of the minor scale. When you have learned the construction of each form and have completed the writing of all scales, it will be suggested that you turn to Appendix 2 for a brief history of the derivation of major and minor scales. The information in this appendix, though not necessary for the development of skills presented in this chapter, will help clarify particular musical practices often found puzzling to students.

Writing certain minor scales requires the use of accidentals other than sharps and flats found in major scales. Therefore, we will first study the remaining accidentals: the double sharp, double flat*, *and* natural sign, *all previously introduced in Chapter 2. The double sharp and double flat are never used in key signatures but may appear in the music for a variety of reasons which you will discover later.*

*Though not found in major or minor scale spelling, the double flat is included here to complete the study of accidentals.

ACCIDENTALS: DOUBLE SHARP, DOUBLE FLAT, AND NATURAL SIGN

614. The *double sharp,* 𝄪, raises the pitch of a note two half steps or one whole step.

Insert the required accidentals:

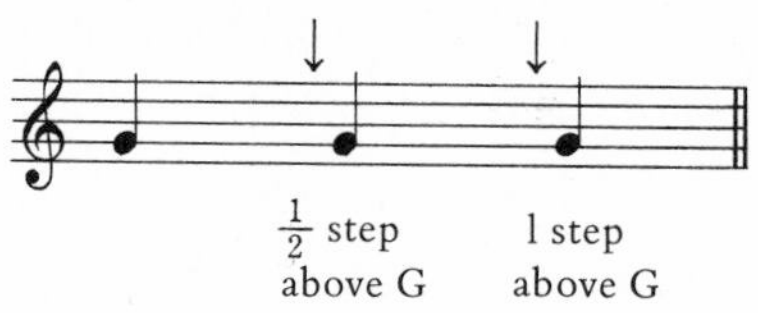

615. Insert the required double sharps:

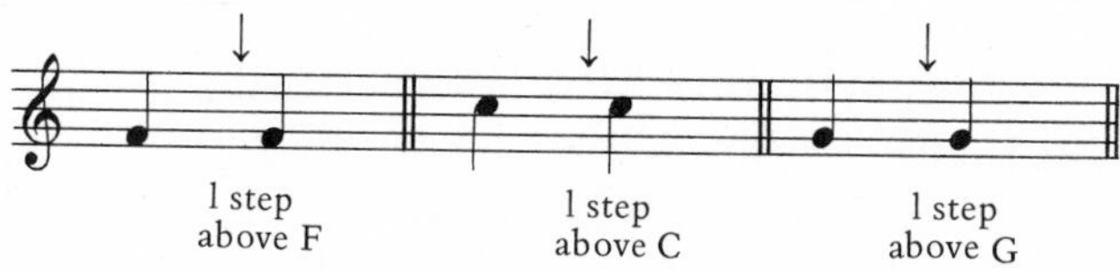

616. It can be seen, most obviously on the keyboard, that a note carrying a double sharp will always be enharmonic with another pitch name. For example, F𝄪 is enharmonic with the pitch G.

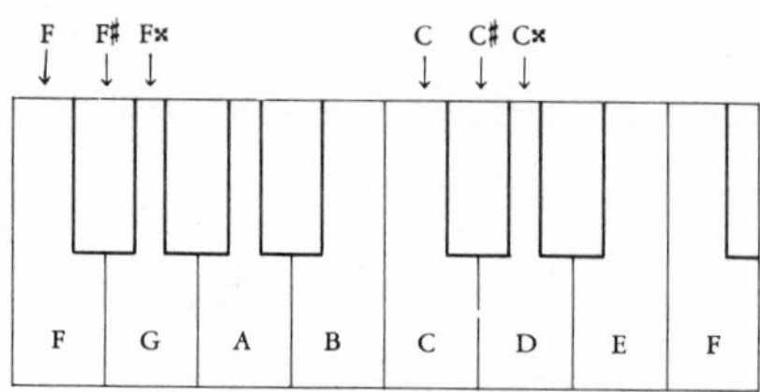

D

C𝄪 is enharmonic with the pitch ____.

A

617. G𝄪 is enharmonic with ____.

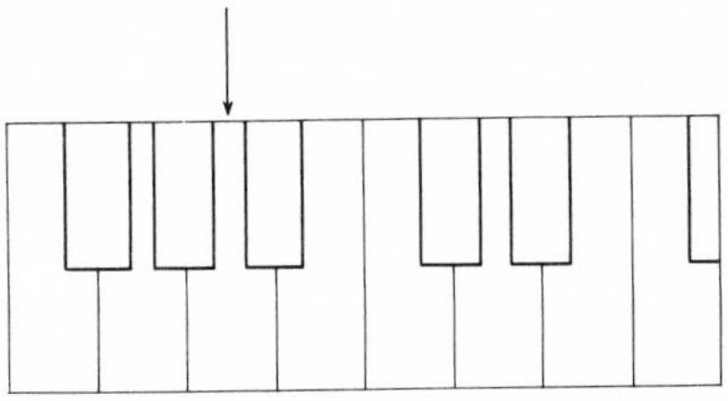

618. Draw an arrow pointing to G𝄪 on the keyboard:

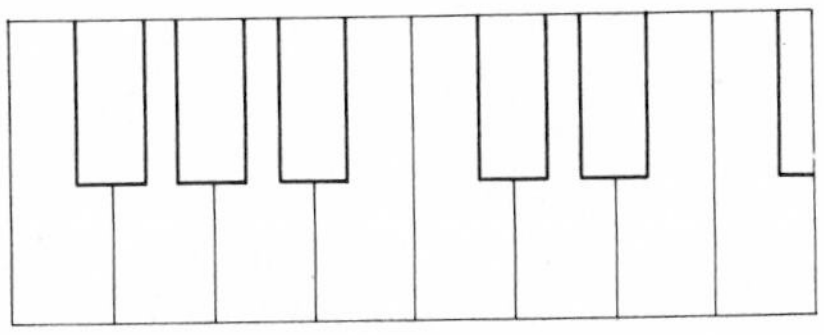

619. The *double flat,* 𝄫, lowers the pitch of a note two half steps or one whole step.

½ step below G | 1 step below G | ½ step below C | 1 step below C

Insert the required accidentals:

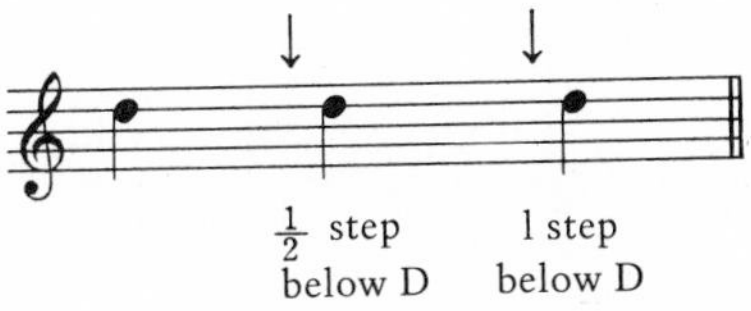

½ step below D | 1 step below D

620. Insert the required double flats:

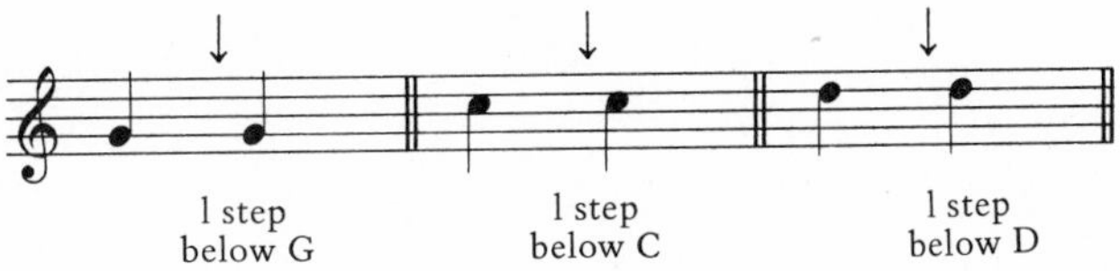

1 step below G | 1 step below C | 1 step below D

621. A double flat will always be enharmonic with another pitch name. For example, G𝄫 is enharmonic with the pitch F.

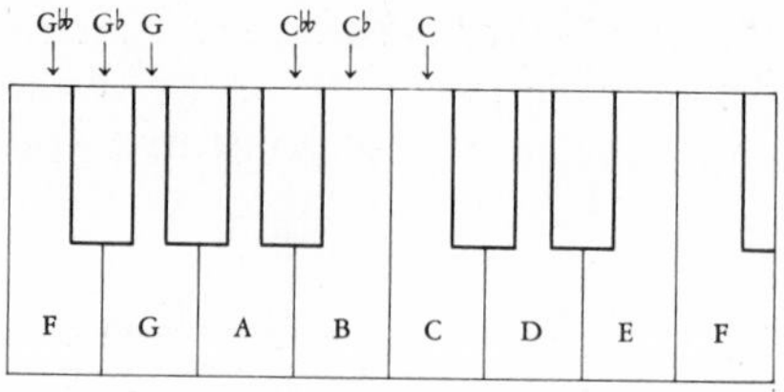

G𝄫 G♭ G C𝄫 C♭ C

F G A B C D E F

C𝄫 is enharmonic with ____ flat.

B♭

---

622. D𝄫 is enharmonic with ____.

C

---

623. Draw an arrow pointing to D𝄫 on the keyboard:

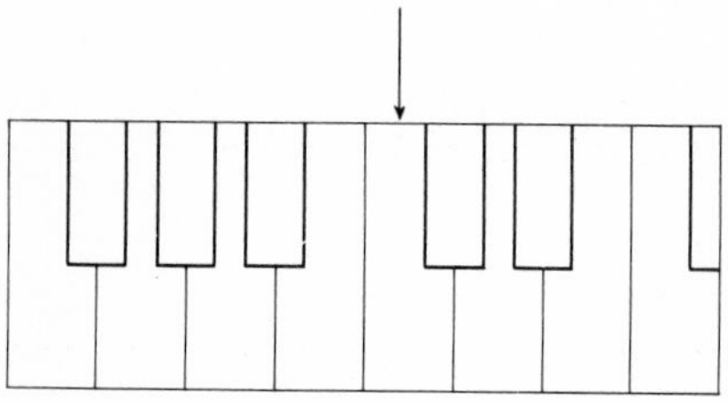

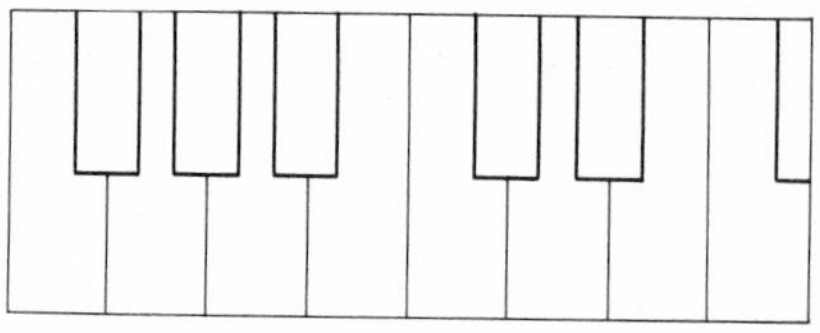

---

624. The *natural sign,* ♮, cancels a previously used accidental. It also cancels the effect of the accidental in the key signature, for that line or space only, and for that measure only. Give the pitch names:

D ___ ___ ___ | ___ ___ ___ ___ | ___

D C♯ C♮ B |
A♯ B A♮ G | F♯

625. Give the pitch names:

___ ___ ___ | ___ ___ | ___ ___ ___ | ___

A♭ G F | E♮ F |
G♭ F G♮ | A♭

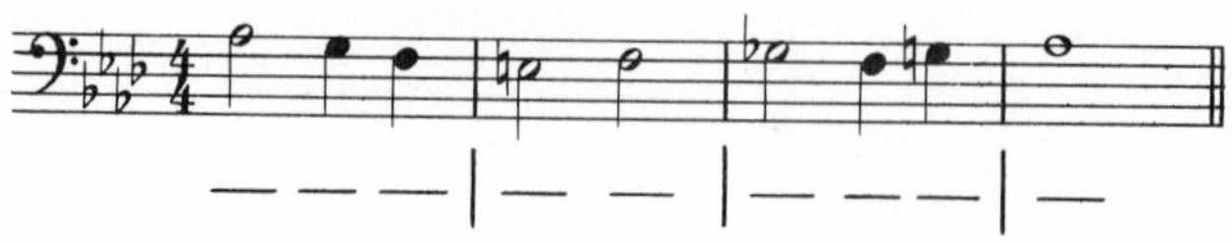

CONSIDERATIONS IN USING ACCIDENTALS

D A G♯ A B A G♯

A | F♯

626. An accidental placed before a note applies to that pitch throughout the measure, or until cancelled in the measure.

D F♯ A F♯ A F♯ A F♯ A F♯ A F♯ A G F♮ E♭ | D

Give the pitch names:

__ __ __ __ __ __ __ __ | __

E♭ D C A♭ E♮ F

E♭ D C E♮ F

627. Any accidental placed before a note affects the pitch on that line or space only.

D C♮ C♯ D

Give the pitch names:

__ __ __ __ __ __ __ __ __ __ __

C C♯ D E♭ |

C D E♭

628. The effect of an accidental lasts only until the next bar line.

D C♮. B C♮ D C♯ B C♯ D

Give the pitch names:

__ __ __ __ | __ __ __

D E♮ F♯ |

G F E♭ | D

629. Give the pitch names:

__ __ __ | __ __ __ | __

630. An accidental may be used optionally as a reminder. The following illustration, similar to that in Frame 629, shows reminders in the second measure. The sign ♭ before E does not imply double flat.

Most present-day editors of music use accidentals as reminders. This practice helps the performer to be more confident and accurate when playing or singing the pitches, especially when reading the music for the first time (sight reading).

Place the reminder in the second measure:

631. Place reminders in the second measure:

632. Although the symbol for double flat is 𝄫, the symbol for double sharp is never ♯♯, but is _____.

𝄪

633. When it is necessary that a note carry a double sharp or a double flat, the symbol 𝄪 or 𝄫 is always used, even if there is already a sharp or flat in the signature.

Notate the designated pitches:

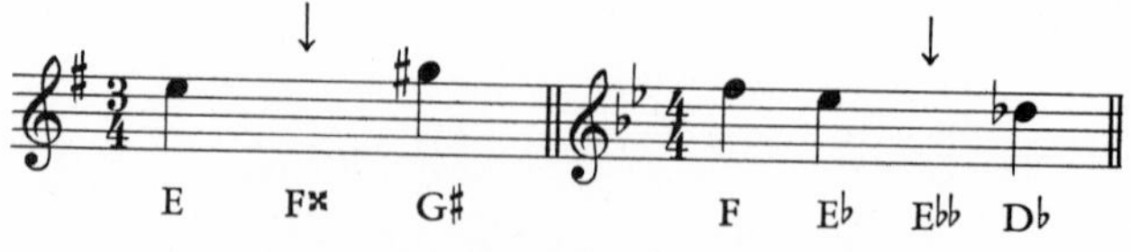

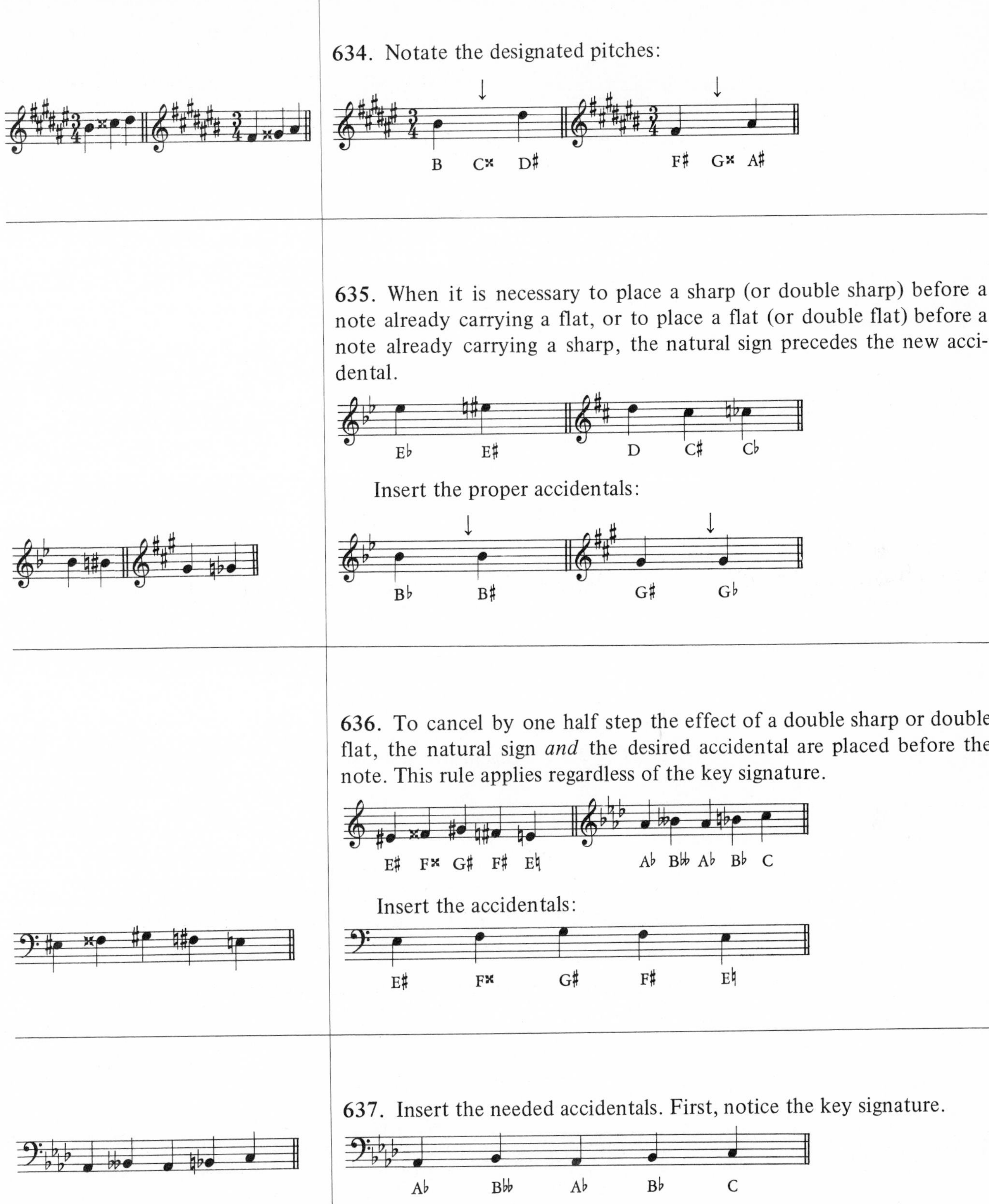

634. Notate the designated pitches:

B C× D♯ F♯ G× A♯

635. When it is necessary to place a sharp (or double sharp) before a note already carrying a flat, or to place a flat (or double flat) before a note already carrying a sharp, the natural sign precedes the new accidental.

E♭ E♯ D C♯ C♭

Insert the proper accidentals:

B♭ B♯ G♯ G♭

636. To cancel by one half step the effect of a double sharp or double flat, the natural sign *and* the desired accidental are placed before the note. This rule applies regardless of the key signature.

E♯ F× G♯ F♯ E♮ A♭ B𝄫 A♭ B♭ C

Insert the accidentals:

E♯ F× G♯ F♯ E♮

637. Insert the needed accidentals. First, notice the key signature.

A♭ B𝄫 A♭ B♭ C

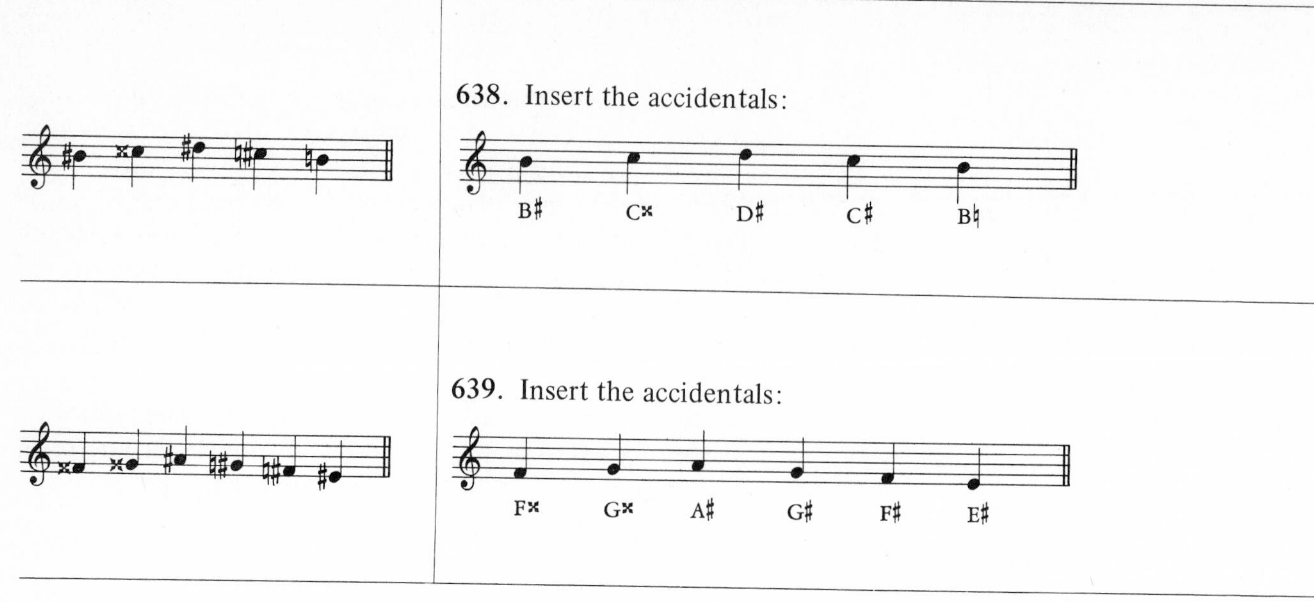

638. Insert the accidentals:

639. Insert the accidentals:

THE NATURAL (PURE) FORM OF THE MINOR SCALE

640. Now that we are informed in the use of accidentals, we are ready to proceed to the study of the minor scale and its three forms: (1) *natural,* also called *pure;* (2) *harmonic;* and (3) *melodic.* In this textbook, we will ordinarily use the name *natural* instead of *pure,* although both names are equally acceptable.

The three forms of the minor scale are

(1) ____________, (2) ____________, and (3) ____________.

(1) natural (2) harmonic (3) melodic

641. Another name for the natural minor scale is the ____________ minor scale.

pure

642. We have learned that the unique aural quality of the major scale is due to its arrangement of half steps and whole steps, the half steps occurring between scale degrees 3–4 and 7–8. The aural quality of the natural minor scale, different from major, is also determined by a particular arrangement of half steps and whole steps. The intervals between ascending pitches are whole step, half step, whole step, whole step, half step, whole step, whole step. Whether the natural minor scale is ascending or descending, the pitches are the same.

Structure of the Natural (Pure) Minor Scale.

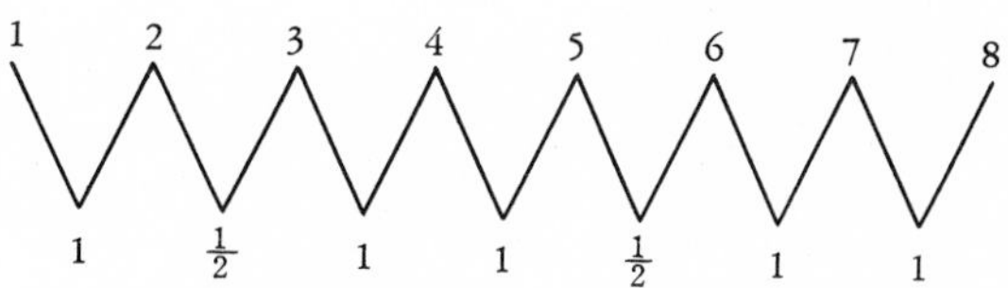

The natural minor scale consists of whole steps except for half steps between scale degrees ____-____ and ____-____.

2–3 5–6

SPELLING NATURAL MINOR SCALES

643. The A minor scale, natural form, is shown below:

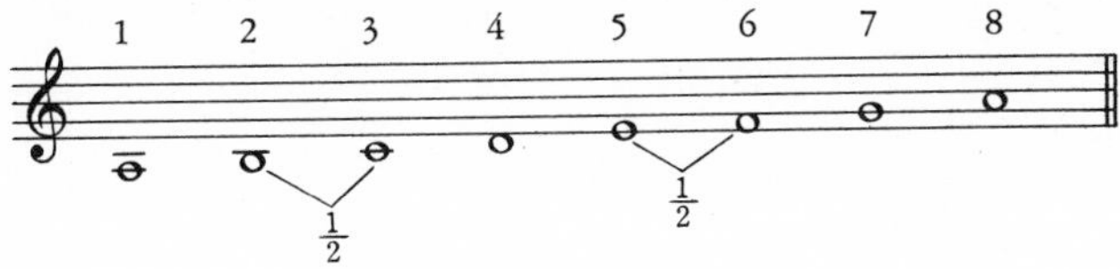

Where are the half steps?

Half step Numbers	*Half step Pitch Names*
___-___	___-___
___-___	___-___

2–3 B–C
5–6 E–F

644. The scale may be named by different arrangements of the terminology, such as "A minor, natural form," or "A natural minor." Using successive letters of the complete musical alphabet, the A natural minor scale is spelled

___ ___ ___ ___ ___ ___ ___ ___

A B C D E F G A

645. On the keyboard the natural minor scale starting on A involves only white keys because the half steps 2–3 and 5–6 coincide with the white keys B–C and E–F.

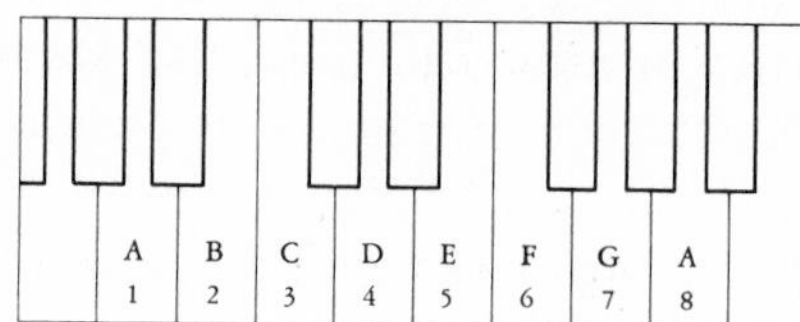

The natural minor scale consisting entirely of white keys begins on the pitch ____.

A

646. All natural minor scales starting on pitches other than A require one or more accidentals in order to maintain the characteristic half step and whole step arrangement.

The characteristic sound or structure of the natural minor scale is determined by these intervals between successive scale degrees:

Answer key	Between degrees	Answer: whole or half
whole	1 - 2	____ step
half	2 - 3	____ step
whole	3 - 4	____ step
whole	4 - 5	____ step
half	5 - 6	____ step
whole	6 - 7	____ step
whole	7 - 8	____ step

647. Spell the natural minor scale starting on E by using your knowledge of intervals, accidentals and scale structure.

E F♯ G A B C D E

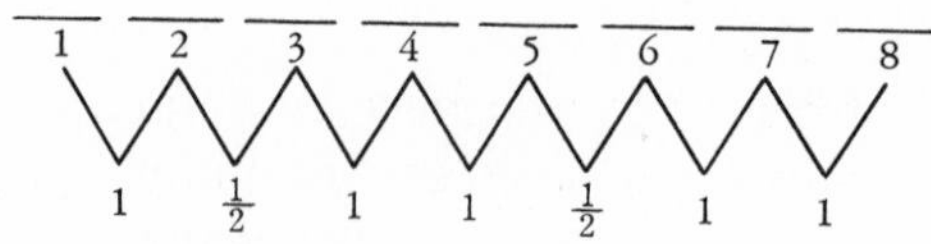

E G	648. The E natural minor scale requires one accidental, F♯, which is needed to produce a whole step between ___ and F♯ and a half step between F♯ and ___.
G♭ F♯	649. As previously learned in writing major scales, care should be taken that incorrect spellings of pitches by enharmonics are not used. Remember that in spelling the scale, the complete musical alphabet must be employed; also when notating the scale the notes must be placed on consecutive lines and spaces. In the following illustration the descending natural minor scale sounds correct but it contains an error in notation. 8 7 6 5 4 3 2 1 The wrong note in the *e* minor scale above is ___; it should be notated ___.
B C♯ D E F♯ G A B	650. Spell the natural minor scale starting on B. ___ ___ ___ ___ ___ ___ ___ ___ 1 2 3 4 5 6 7 8 1 ½ 1 1 ½ 1 1
F♯ G♯ A B C♯ D E F♯	651. Continue spelling minor scales. F♯ minor, natural form: ___ ___ ___ ___ ___ ___ ___ ___ 1 2 3 4 5 6 7 8 1 ½ 1 1 ½ 1 1

C♯ D♯ E F♯ G♯ A B C♯	652. C♯ minor, natural form: ___ ___ ___ ___ ___ ___ ___ ___ 1 2 3 4 5 6 7 8 (2–3: 1/2; 5–6: 1/2)
G♯ A♯ B C♯ D♯ E F♯ G♯	653. G♯ minor, natural form: ___ ___ ___ ___ ___ ___ ___ ___ 1 2 3 4 5 6 7 8
D♯ E♯ F♯ G♯ A♯ B C♯ D♯	654. D♯ minor, natural form: ___ ___ ___ ___ ___ ___ ___ ___
A♯ B♯ C♯ D♯ E♯ F♯ G♯ A♯	655. A♯ minor, natural form: ___ ___ ___ ___ ___ ___ ___ ___
seven	656. Compare the natural minor scale of A♯ with A. The natural minor scale of A contains no accidentals; the natural minor scale of A♯, with the complete alphabet sharped, contains (no.) ____ sharps.
D E F G A B♭ C D	657. Spell the natural minor scale starting on D. ___ ___ ___ ___ ___ ___ ___ ___ 1 2 3 4 5 6 7 8 1 1/2 1 1 1/2 1 1

A C	**658.** The D natural minor scale requires one accidental, B♭, which is needed to produce a half step between ____ and B♭, and a whole step between B♭ and ____ .
G A B♭ C D E♭ F G	**659.** Spell the natural minor scale of G: __ __ __ __ __ __ __ __ 1 2 3 4 5 6 7 8 (2–3: ½; 5–6: ½)
C D E♭ F G A♭ B♭ C	**660.** Continue spelling minor scales. C minor, natural form: __ __ __ __ __ __ __ __ 1 2 3 4 5 6 7 8
F G A♭ B♭ C D♭ E♭ F	**661.** F minor, natural form: __ __ __ __ __ __ __ __
B♭ C D♭ E♭ F G♭ A♭ B♭	**662.** B♭ minor, natural form: __ __ __ __ __ __ __ __
E♭ F G♭ A♭ B♭ C♭ D♭ E♭	**663.** E♭ minor, natural form: __ __ __ __ __ __ __ __

A♭ B♭ C♭ D♭

E♭ F♭ G♭ A♭

664. A♭ minor, natural form:

____ ____ ____ ____ ____ ____ ____ ____

---

seven

665. Compare the natural minor scale of A♭ with A. The natural minor scale of A contains no accidentals; the natural minor scale of A♭, with the complete alphabet flatted, contains (no.) ____ flats.

HARMONIC FORM OF THE MINOR SCALE, SPELLING

666. The *harmonic* form of the minor scale is derived from the natural form. It is like the natural form but with the *seventh degree raised one half step.* You have spelled the natural form of the minor scale at all fifteen pitch locations. To spell any harmonic minor scale, raise the seventh degree of the spelling for the natural form by an appropriate accidental.

Change the spelling of the A minor scale, natural form, to the harmonic form by inserting the needed accidental:

A	B	C	D	E	F	G	A
1	2	3	4	5	6	7	8

A B C D E F G♯ A

---

667. The interval between the sixth and seventh degrees of the natural minor scale is a whole step. By raising the seventh, the interval between 6 and 7 becomes a step and a half* (three half steps). Also as a result, the interval between 7 and 8, originally a whole step in the natural form, becomes a half step.

The A Minor Scale, Harmonic Form.

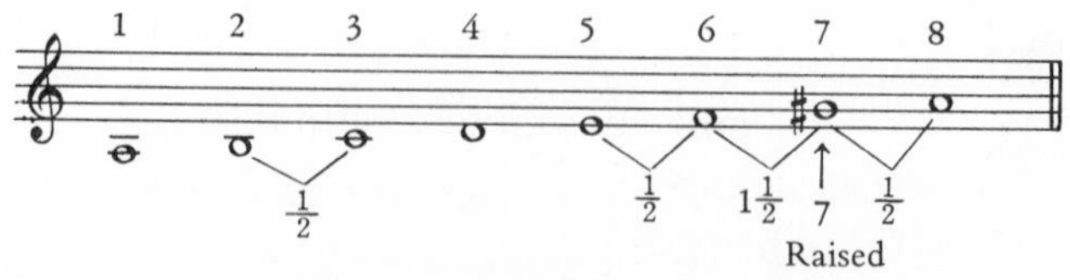

A unique characteristic of the harmonic form of the minor scale is the interval of a step and a half occurring between scale degrees____ and____.

*Called augmented second; *included in the study of intervals in Chapter 14.*

6 7

Answers	Frames
E F♯ G A B C D♯ E	**668.** Spell the harmonic minor scale of E. ___ ___ ___ ___ ___ ___ ___ ___ 1 2 3 4 5 6 7 8 (2–3: ½; 5–6: ½; 6–7: 1½; 7–8: ½)
G♯ A♯ B C♯ D♯ E F𝄪 G♯	**669.** Spell the scale of G♯ minor, harmonic form. (The natural form was spelled in Frame 653.) Remember that a pitch already carrying a sharp is raised another half step by use of the double sharp. ___ ___ ___ ___ ___ ___ ___ ___ 7 (raised)
D E F G A B♭ C♯ D	**670.** In spelling scales up to this point, the accidentals employed in each scale have been either all sharps (including double sharps) or all flats. Notice below in spelling the harmonic form of the D minor scale that both flat and sharp are needed. Change the spelling of the D minor scale, natural form, to the harmonic form by inserting the needed accidental. D E F G A B♭ C D 1 2 3 4 5 6 7 8
C D E♭ F G A♭ B♮ C	**671.** Spell the scale of C minor, harmonic form. ___ ___ ___ ___ ___ ___ ___ ___ 7 (raised) Did you spell the seventh degree B♮ or simply B? Either is correct, but B♮ is more logical because it indicates *raising* the seventh degree of the natural form, B♭ to B♮.

MELODIC FORM OF THE MINOR SCALE

672. The *melodic form* of the minor scale is derived from the natural form. Unlike all other major and minor scales, its ascending and descending forms are different. The ascending form of the melodic minor scale is the natural form but with *raised sixth and raised seventh* degrees. The descending form is the same as the natural form; the *seventh and sixth degrees are lowered* from their ascending form.

The A Minor Scale, Melodic Form.

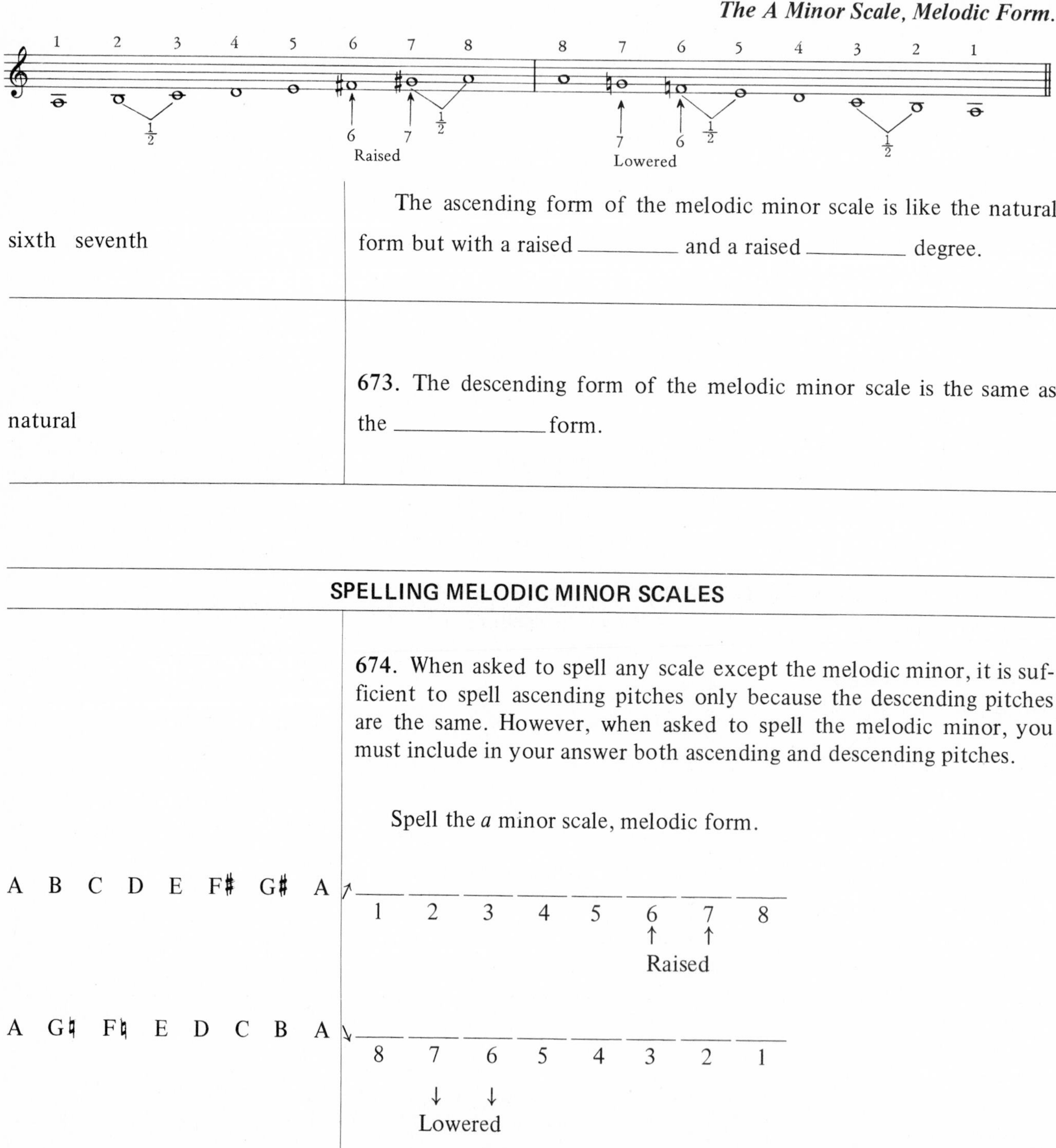

The ascending form of the melodic minor scale is like the natural form but with a raised ________ and a raised ________ degree.

sixth seventh

---

673. The descending form of the melodic minor scale is the same as the ________ form.

natural

SPELLING MELODIC MINOR SCALES

674. When asked to spell any scale except the melodic minor, it is sufficient to spell ascending pitches only because the descending pitches are the same. However, when asked to spell the melodic minor, you must include in your answer both ascending and descending pitches.

Spell the *a* minor scale, melodic form.

↗ ___ ___ ___ ___ ___ ___ ___ ___
1 2 3 4 5 6 7 8
6 ↑ 7 ↑ Raised

↘ ___ ___ ___ ___ ___ ___ ___ ___
8 7 6 5 4 3 2 1
7 ↓ 6 ↓ Lowered

A B C D E F♯ G♯ A

A G♮ F♮ E D C B A

D♯ E♯ F♯ G♯

A♯ B♯ C𝄪 D♯

D♯ C♯ B A♯ G♯

F♯ E♯ D♯

675. Spell the D♯ melodic minor scale. (The natural form was spelled in Frame 654.)

↗ ____ ____ ____ ____ ____ ____ ____ ____

↘ ____ ____ ____ ____ ____ ____ ____ ____

A♭ B♭ C♭ D♭

E♭ F G A♭

A♭ G♭ F♭ E♭

D♭ C♭ B♭ A♭

676. Spell the melodic form of the A♭ minor scale.

↗ ____ ____ ____ ____ ____ ____ ____ ____

↘ ____ ____ ____ ____ ____ ____ ____ ____

NOTATING MINOR SCALES

(1) 2–3 5–6

(2) raised seventh

(3) sixth seventh
seventh sixth

677. Significant points in writing minor scales are:

(1) The natural form has half steps between scale degrees ____ – ____ and ____ – ____.

(2) The harmonic form is like natural minor but with a __________ __________ degree.

(3) The melodic form is like natural but with raised __________ and __________ when ascending, and lowered* __________ and __________ when descending.

**In relation to the ascending form.*

678. We shall proceed to notate all fifteen minor scales, each in three forms, on the great staff. The A minor scale is given as a model for you to follow. In the *natural form* indicate the locations of half steps. In the *harmonic form* indicate "raised 7." In the *melodic form* indicate "raised 6 – 7" and "lowered 7 – 6."

Model for Writing Minor Scales

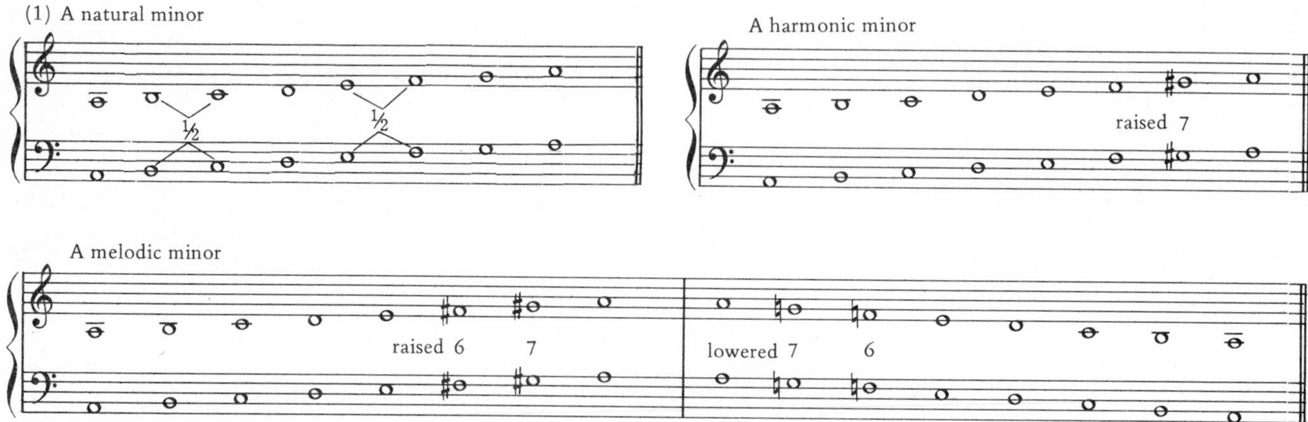

679. Notate minor scales in the following frames.

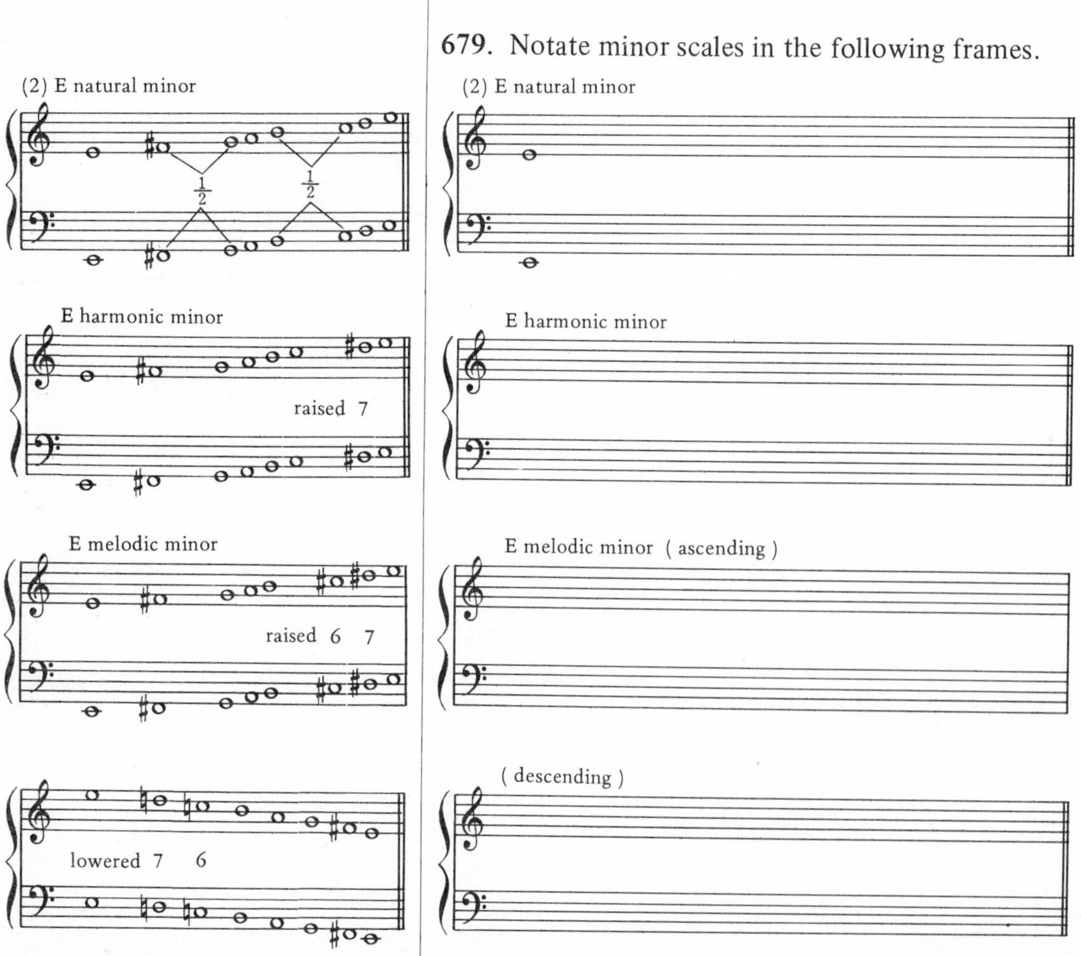

(3) B natural minor
½
½
B harmonic minor
raised 7
B melodic minor
raised 6 7
lowered 7 6
680.
(3) B natural minor
B harmonic minor
B melodic minor (ascending)
(descending)
(4) F♯ natural minor
½
½
F♯ harmonic minor
raised 7
F♯ melodic minor
raised 6 7
lowered 7 6
681.
(4) F♯ natural minor
F♯ harmonic minor
F♯ melodic minor

(5) C♯ natural minor
½
½
C♯ harmonic minor
raised 7
C♯ melodic minor
raised 6 7
lowered 7 6
682.
(5) C♯ natural minor
C♯ harmonic minor
C♯ melodic minor
(6) G♯ natural minor
1/2
1/2
G♯ harmonic minor
raised 7
G♯ melodic minor
raised 6 7
lowered 7 6
683.
(6) G♯ natural minor
G♯ harmonic minor
G♯ melodic minor

(7) D♯ natural minor
½
½
D♯ harmonic minor
raised 7
D♯ melodic minor
raised 6 7
lowered 7 6
684.
(7) D♯ natural minor
D♯ harmonic minor
D♯ melodic minor
(8) A♯ natural minor
½
½
A♯ harmonic minor
raised 7
A♯ melodic minor
raised 6 7
lowered 7 6
685.
(8) A♯ natural minor
A♯ harmonic minor
A♯ melodic minor

(9) D natural minor
½
½
D harmonic minor
raised 7
D melodic minor
raised 6 7
lowered 7 6
686.
(9) D natural minor
D harmonic minor
D melodic minor
(10) G natural minor
½
½
G harmonic minor
raised 7
G melodic minor
raised 6 7
lowered 7 6
687.
(10) G natural minor
G harmonic minor
G melodic minor

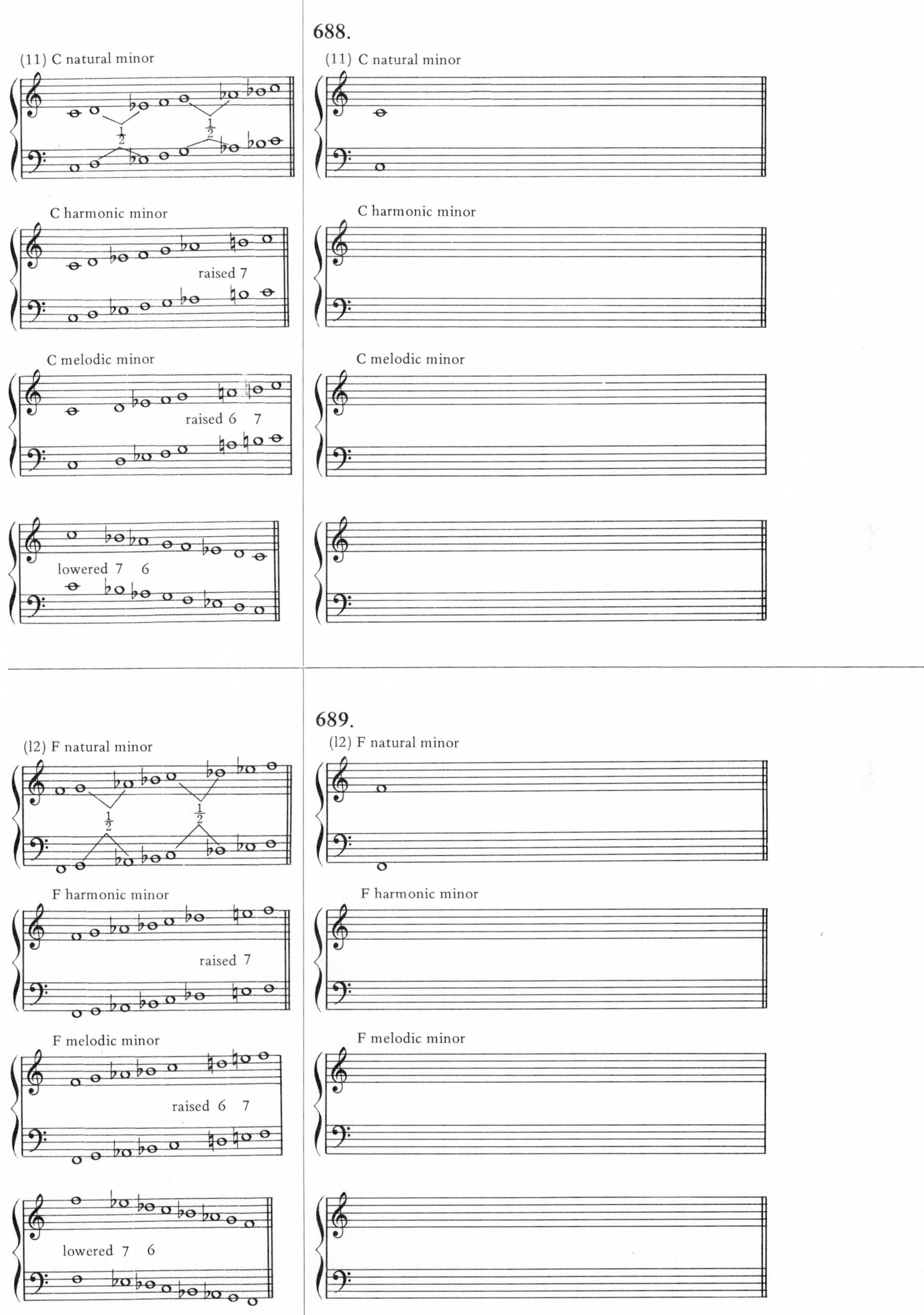
(11) C natural minor
1/2
1/2
C harmonic minor
raised 7
C melodic minor
raised 6 7
lowered 7 6
688.
(11) C natural minor
C harmonic minor
C melodic minor
(12) F natural minor
1/2
1/2
F harmonic minor
raised 7
F melodic minor
raised 6 7
lowered 7 6
689.
(12) F natural minor
F harmonic minor
F melodic minor

690.

691.

(13) B♭ natural minor
½
½
B♭ harmonic minor
raised 7
B♭ melodic minor
raised 6 7
lowered 7 6
(13) B♭ natural minor
B♭ harmonic minor
B♭ melodic minor
(14) E♭ natural minor
½
½
E♭ harmonic minor
raised 7
E♭ melodic minor
raised 6 7
lowered 7 6
(14) E♭ natural minor
E♭ harmonic minor
E♭ melodic minor

692.

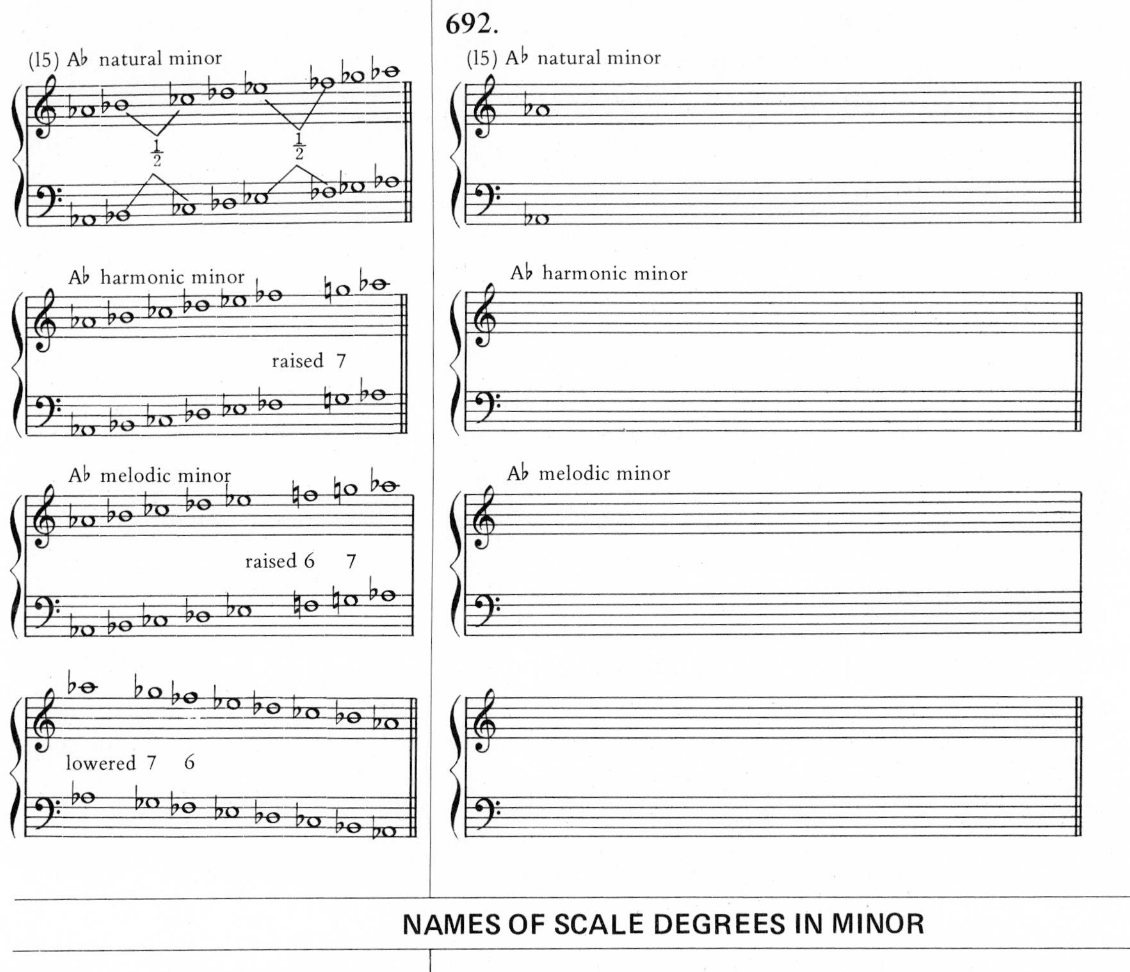

NAMES OF SCALE DEGREES IN MINOR

693. Scale degrees in minor utilize the same names as those for the major scale but because of the alteration of the sixth and seventh steps additional terminology is required. The term *leading tone* in minor refers to the tone one half step below tonic, just as in major. In both the harmonic and melodic forms of the minor scale the raised seventh appears as a tone one half step below tonic.

The raised seventh degree in minor, in either harmonic or melodic forms, is named ______________ __________ .

leading tone

694. When the seventh scale degree is not raised, the interval between 7 and 8 is a whole step as found in the natural form of the scale. It is only when a half step exists between 7 and 8 that the seventh degree exhibits a compelling tendency to ascend—to lead upward. Therefore, when the interval between 7 and 8 is a whole step, instead of the inappropriate term *leading tone,* the name *subtonic* is used for the seventh degree.

In the natural form of the minor scale, the seventh degree is named ______________ .

subtonic

Answers	Frames
leading tone subtonic	**695.** When the interval between 7 and 8 of a scale is a half step, the name of the seventh degree is ______ ______; when the interval between 7 and 8 is a whole step, the name of the seventh degree is ______.
raised submediant	**696.** Submediant in minor refers to the sixth scale step as found in the natural form of the scale. When the sixth scale step is raised, as in the melodic form, it is named *raised submediant.* The scale name for the raised sixth degree in the melodic form of the minor scale is ______ ______.
tonic supertonic mediant subdominant dominant submediant *subtonic* tonic	**697.** In the natural form of the C minor scale below, supply the scale name for the seventh degree. 1 2 3 4 5 6 7 8 TONIC SUPERTONIC MEDIANT SUBDOMINANT DOMINANT SUBMEDIANT ______ TONIC
tonic supertonic mediant subdominant dominant submediant leading tone tonic	**698.** In the harmonic form of the C minor scale below, supply names for all scale degrees. 1 2 3 4 5 6 7 8 TONIC SUPERTONIC ______ ______ ______ ______ ______ ______

tonic
supertonic
mediant
subdominant
dominant
raised submediant
leading tone
tonic

699. In the ascending melodic minor scale below, supply names for all scale degrees.

1 2 3 4 5 6 7 8

tonic
subtonic
submediant
dominant
subdominant
mediant
supertonic
tonic

700. In the descending melodic minor scale below, supply names for all scale degrees.

8 7 6 5 4 3 2 1

C G
B♮ D
B♭ A♭
E♭ A♮
F

701. Using information from Frames 697-700, write the pitch names for each scale degree of C minor randomly listed. Both varieties of the sixth and seventh scale degrees are included.

tonic	____	dominant	____
leading tone	____	supertonic	____
subtonic	____	submediant	____
mediant	____	raised submediant	____
subdominant	____		

F	702. Scale tone names are applied in similar manner for all minor scales. When G♯ is supertonic, F♯ is tonic. When G is supertonic, ____ is tonic.
D	703. When F♯ is mediant of a minor scale, D♯ is tonic. When F is mediant, ____ is tonic.
B♭	704. When E is subdominant, B is tonic. When E♭ is subdominant, ____ is tonic.
A	705. When E♭ is dominant, A♭ is tonic. When E is dominant, ____ is tonic.
E♭	706. When C is submediant of a minor scale, E is tonic. When C♭ is submediant, ____ is tonic.
A♯	707. When F♯ is raised submediant of a minor scale, A is tonic. When F𝄪 is raised submediant, ____ is tonic.

C♯	708. When B♭ is subtonic of a minor scale, C is tonic. When B is subtonic, ____ is tonic.
G	709. When F𝄪 is leading tone, G♯ is tonic. When F♯ is leading tone, ____ is tonic.

Now that you have gained understanding of the construction of major and minor scales, your natural curiosity may evoke questions concerning their evolution and how the different forms of minor are used in musical practice. See Appendix 2, Historical Derivation of Major and Minor Scales.

CHAPTER SUMMARY

1. Accidentals used in writing minor scales are ♯, ♭, ♮, and 𝄪.

2. The *natural (pure) form* of the minor scale has half steps between degrees 2–3 and 5–6. All other intervals are whole steps. Whether ascending or descending, the pitches are the same.

3. The minor scale can be written/played beginning on fifteen different pitch locations. The natural form of A minor contains no accidentals. Scales starting on other pitches require one or more accidentals.

4. The *harmonic form* of the minor scale is like the natural form but with the *seventh degree raised* one half step. This scale is characterized by the interval of a step and a half between the sixth and seventh degrees.

5. The *melodic form* of the minor scale, unlike all other major and minor scales, has different ascending and descending pitches. The ascending scale is the natural form but with *raised sixth* and *raised seventh degrees.* The descending scale is the same as the natural form—that is, the seventh and sixth degrees are lowered from their ascending form.

6. Names of scale degrees in minor are the same as those for the major scale but additional terminology is required for the sixth and seventh degrees. In the natural form of the minor scale the interval between 7 and 8 is a whole step. In this case the seventh degree is called *subtonic.* In both harmonic and melodic (ascending) forms the interval between 7 and 8 is a half step and the seventh degree is called *leading tone,* just as in major. In the ascending form of the minor scale the sixth degree is called *raised submediant.*

PRE-TEST
MINOR KEY SIGNATURES

1. Spell the circle of fifths, ascending, beginning on A: A ____ ____ ____ ____ ____ ____ ____.

2. Spell the circle of fifths, descending, beginning on A: A ____ ____ ____ ____ ____ ____ ____.

3. Write key signatures on the staff.

   (a) B minor

   (b) A♭ minor

   (c) C minor

   (d) D♯ minor

4. Name each key and the form of the minor scale used as a basis for the melody.

ANSWERS

A score is given at the end of each answer. If your answer is correct, place that score in the column at the right. Add this column for your score.

Score

1. The complete answer must be correct.

(A) E B F♯ C♯ G♯ D♯ A♯ (10) ____

2. The complete answer must be correct.

(A) D G C F B♭ E♭ A♭ (10) ____

3. There is no alternative in order, and no alternative of line/space for each accidental.

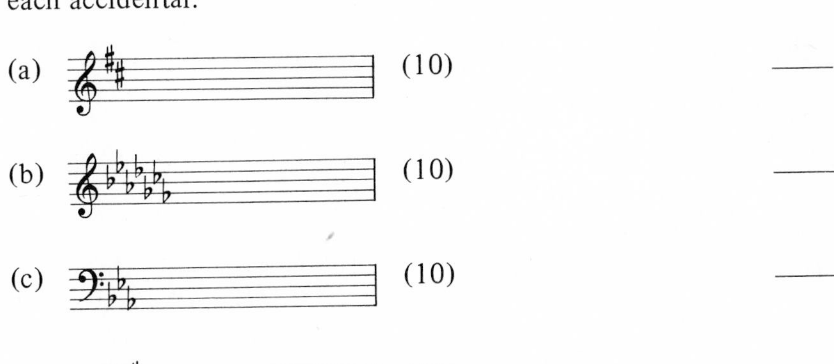

4. (a) Gm melodic (10) ____

   (b) Em harmonic (10) ____

   (c) Am natural (pure) (10) ____

   (d) Fm melodic (10) ____

Total score: ____

Perfect score: 100

If your score is 80 or above, turn now to Chapter 12, page 236. If your score is less than 80, continue with Chapter 11.

MINOR KEY SIGNATURES

710. The function of the key signature is the same in minor as it is in major. We have learned that key signature is determined by accidentals in the scale. The three forms of the minor scale (natural, harmonic, and melodic) use a variety of accidentals, but the minor key signature is determined solely by those sharps or flats in the natural form of the scale.

Table of Minor Scales and Numbers of Accidentals for the Natural Form.

Scale	Am*	Em	Bm	F♯m	C♯m	G♯m	D♯m	A♯m
Accidentals	none	1♯	2♯	3♯	4♯	5♯	6♯	7♯
Scale		Dm	Gm	Cm	Fm	B♭m	E♭m	A♭m
Accidentals		1♭	2♭	3♭	4♭	5♭	6♭	7♭

**The lower case "m" is an abbreviation for "minor."*

The minor key signature uses those accidentals found in the ____________ form of the scale.

natural (pure)

711. The table below shows the number of accidentals needed for each minor key signature, and the name of each accidental in turn. Do not attempt to memorize this table, but use it freely as a reference.

Number and Names of Accidentals for Minor Key Signatures.

Name of minor key	Number of ♯'s or ♭'s in key signature	Names of ♯'s or ♭'s
A minor	none	
E minor	1♯	f♯
B minor	2♯	f♯ c♯
F♯ minor	3♯	f♯ c♯ g♯
C♯ minor	4♯	f♯ c♯ g♯ d♯
G♯ minor	5♯	f♯ c♯ g♯ d♯ a♯
D♯ minor	6♯	f♯ c♯ g♯ d♯ a♯ e♯
A♯ minor	7♯	f♯ c♯ g♯ d♯ a♯ e♯ b♯
(A minor)	(none)	
D minor	1♭	b♭
G minor	2♭	b♭ e♭
C minor	3♭	b♭ e♭ a♭
F minor	4♭	b♭ e♭ a♭ d♭
B♭ minor	5♭	b♭ e♭ a♭ d♭ g♭
E♭ minor	6♭	b♭ e♭ a♭ d♭ g♭ c♭
A♭ minor	7♭	b♭ e♭ a♭ d♭ g♭ c♭ f♭

712. In Frame 711, starting with A minor we progressed up a perfect fifth to each new sharp key, and down a perfect fifth to each new flat key. This order is illustrated on the circle of fifths for minor keys. To construct the circle we must first determine the order of fifths. Just as in major, use the tools of tonic-dominant and tonic-subdominant analysis.

dominant

subdominant

An ascending perfect fifth is calculated by tonic-__________ analysis; a descending perfect fifth is calculated by tonic-__________ analysis.

---

713. Proceed from A up a perfect fifth to find the keynote E for the minor scale with *one* sharp; calculate a perfect fifth above E to find the keynote B for the minor scale with *two* sharps, and so on until reaching A♯ minor with *seven* sharps. The complete process is illustrated below.

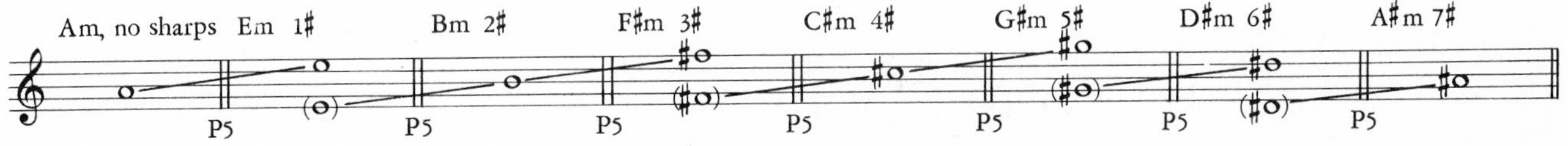

Complete the blanks with names of minor keys by calculating ascending perfect fifths.

(Am Em) Bm F♯m C♯m G♯m D♯m A♯m

Am Em ____ ____ ____ ____ ____ ____
1♯ 2♯ 3♯ 4♯ 5♯ 6♯ 7♯

---

714. Proceed from A down a perfect fifth to find the keynote D for the minor scale with *one* flat, and so on until reaching A♭ minor with *seven* flats. The complete process is demonstrated below.

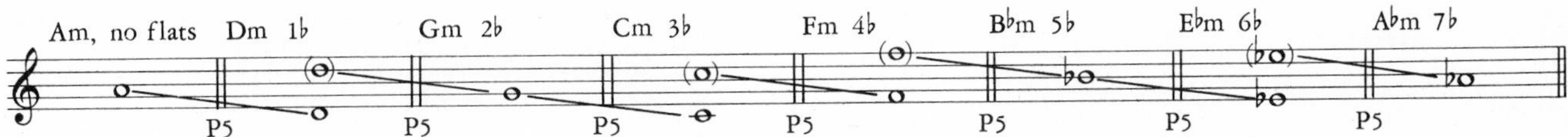

Complete the blanks with names of minor keys by calculating descending perfect fifths.

(Am Dm) Gm Cm Fm B♭m E♭m A♭m

Am Dm ____ ____ ____ ____ ____ ____
1♭ 2♭ 3♭ 4♭ 5♭ 6♭ 7♭

715. The circle of fifths for minor keys is built exactly as its counterpart for major except that the starting point of no sharps or flats at 12 o'clock begins with Am instead of C.

The Circle of Fifths for Minor Keys.

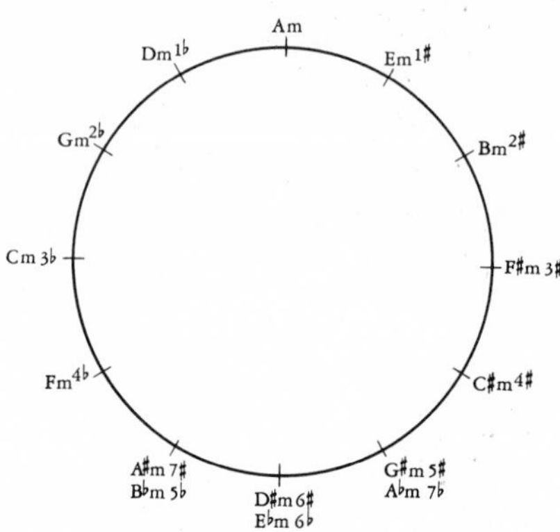

Appearing at the top of the circle (12 o'clock) is the key of ______ ______________

A minor

---

716. This circle includes all the minor key names with sharp keys reading clockwise from A minor and flat keys reading counterclockwise. Observe enharmonic keys at the bottom positions of the circle.

G♯ minor is enharmonic to ____ minor.

E♭ minor is enharmonic to ____ minor.

A♯ minor is enharmonic to____ minor.

A♭

D♯

B♭

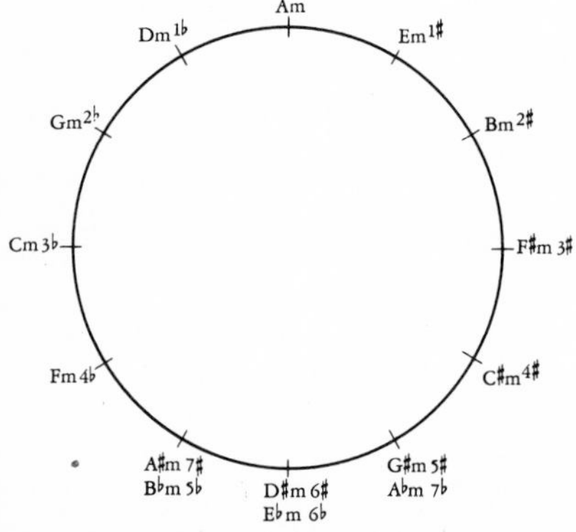

717. On the circle of fifths below, minor key names are given. Beside each name write the number of sharps or flats. The answer for E minor is given.

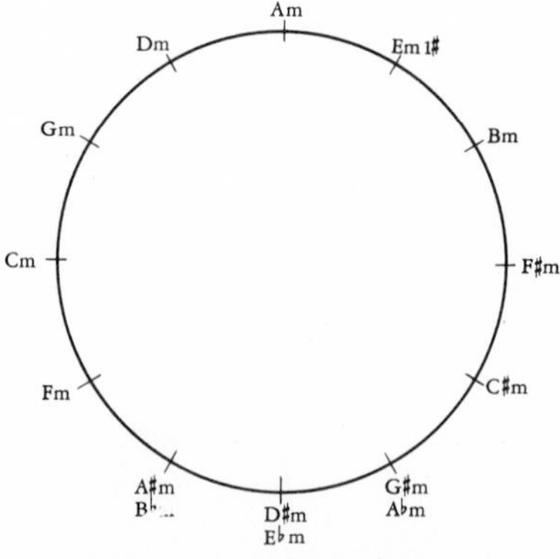

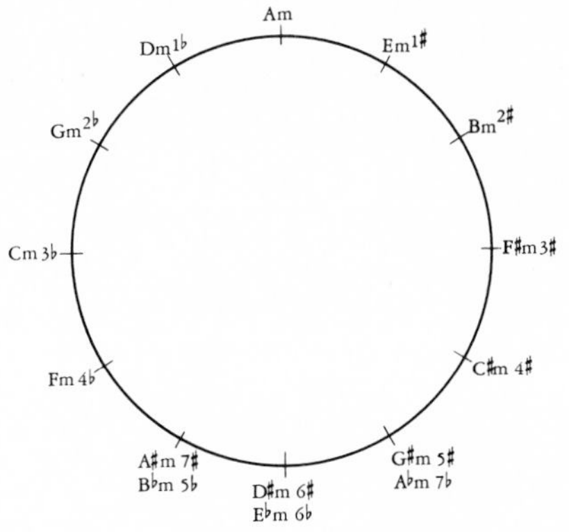

718. On the circle of fifths below, minor key signatures are given. Beside each, give the name of the minor key. The answer for one flat is given.

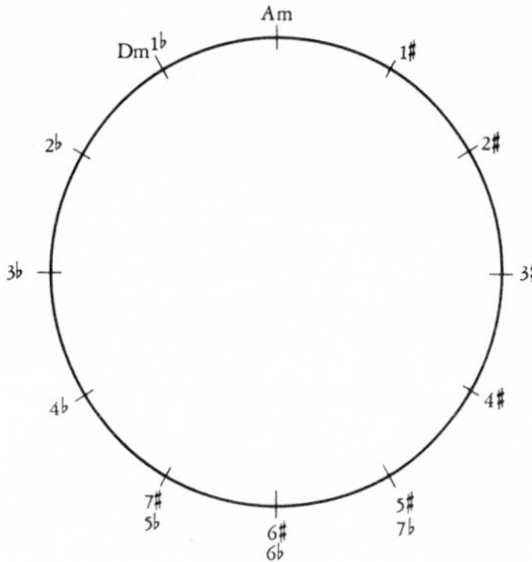

Am
Em1♯
Bm2♯
F♯m 3♯
C♯m 4♯
G♯m 5♯
A♭m 7♭
D♯m 6♯
E♭m 6♭
A♯m 7♯
B♭m 5♭
Fm 4♭
Cm 3♭
Gm2♭
Dm1♭

719. Illustrate the circle of fifths for minor keys. (1) Draw a circle and mark twelve points like the face of a clock. Place Am at the top. (2) Proceeding clockwise, place the letter name and number of accidentals for each key containing sharps. (3) Proceeding counterclockwise from Am, place the letter name and number of accidentals for each key containing flats. Three enharmonic keys will appear at the bottom of the circle.

Using scrap paper, practice until you can produce this illustration in a minute's time.

MINOR KEY SIGNATURES ON THE STAFF

720. The order of accidentals of the key signature on the staff is the same for minor as for major.

Minor Key Signatures

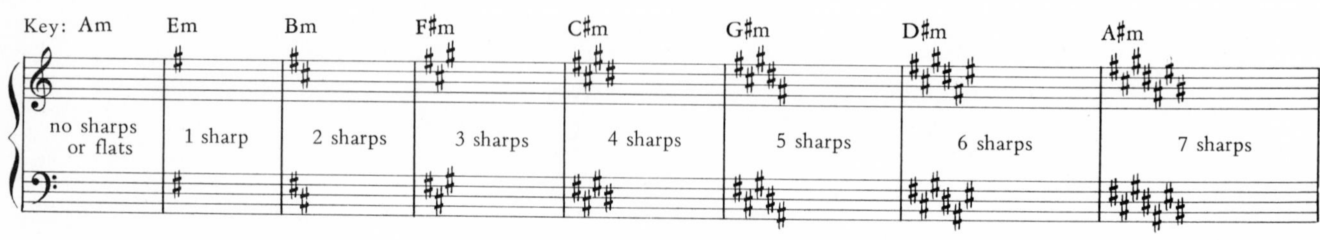

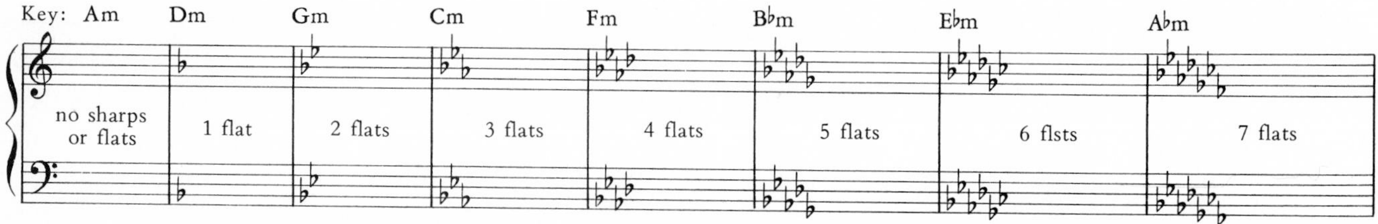

Refer to this illustration in answering Frames 721–734.

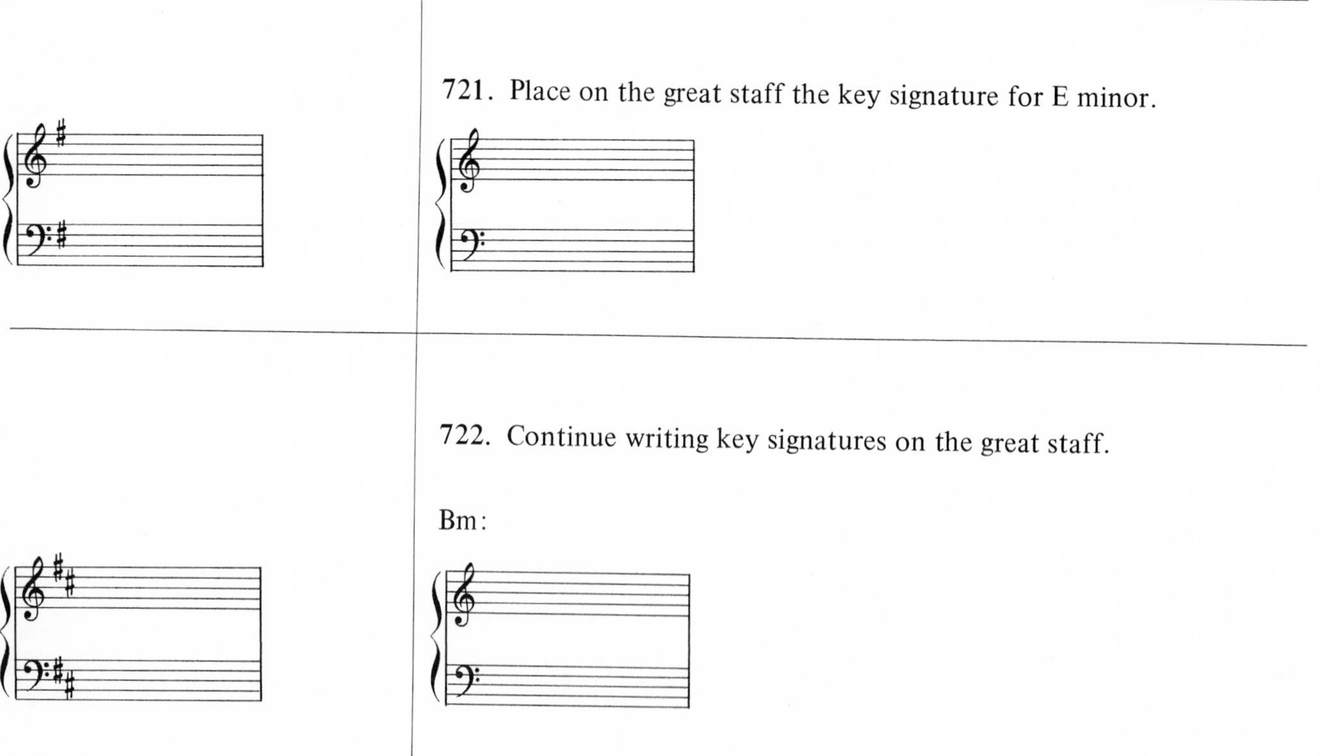

721. Place on the great staff the key signature for E minor.

722. Continue writing key signatures on the great staff.

Bm:

723. F♯m:

724. C♯m:

725. G♯m:

726. D♯m:

727. A♯m:

728. Dm:
729. Gm:
730. Cm:
731. Fm:
732. B♭m

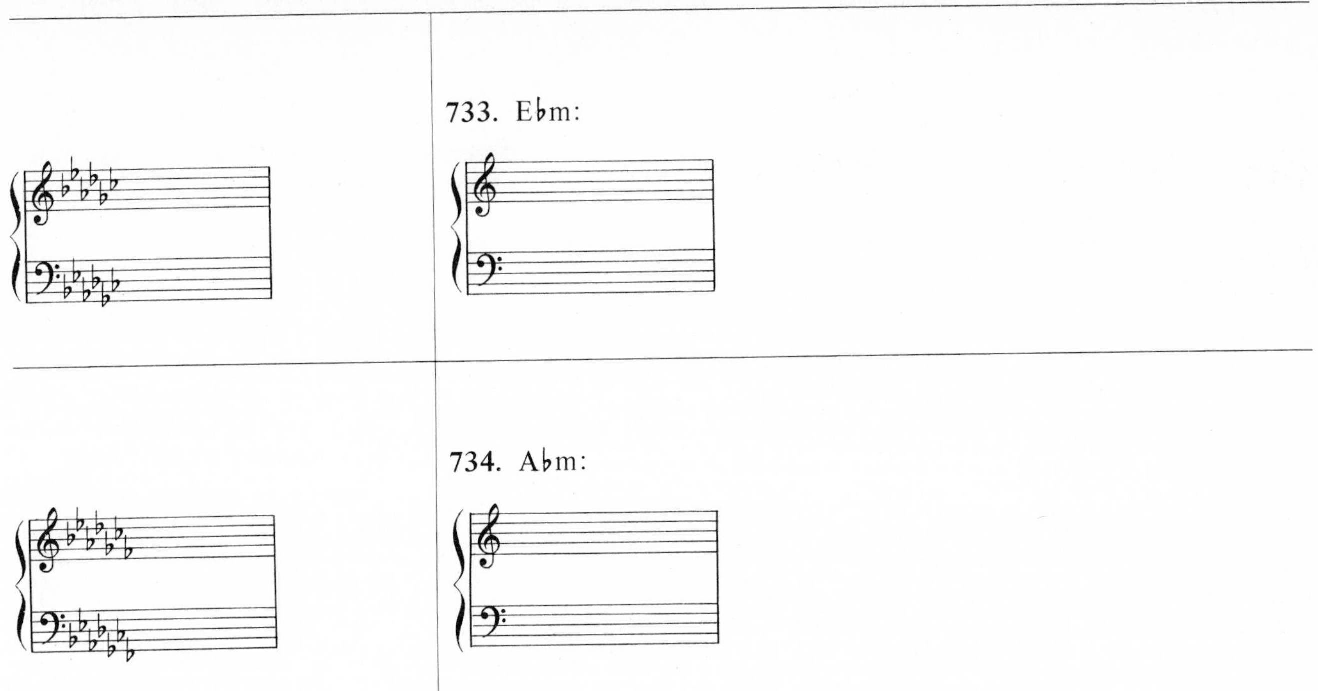

IDENTIFYING KEYS AND SCALE FORMS OF MINOR MELODIES

735. Minor melodies are shown in the following frames. You will be asked to identify the key signature and scale form used for each melody. The form of the minor scale can be identified by analysis of the use of the sixth scale degree (submediant/raised submediant) and seventh scale degree (subtonic/leading tone). Melodies may or may not contain all scale tones. For example, the raised sixth and seventh degrees may appear as for ascending melodic minor but the descending form of the scale may not be in evidence. The burden of evidence in this case would be sufficient to conclude the form to be *melodic minor.*

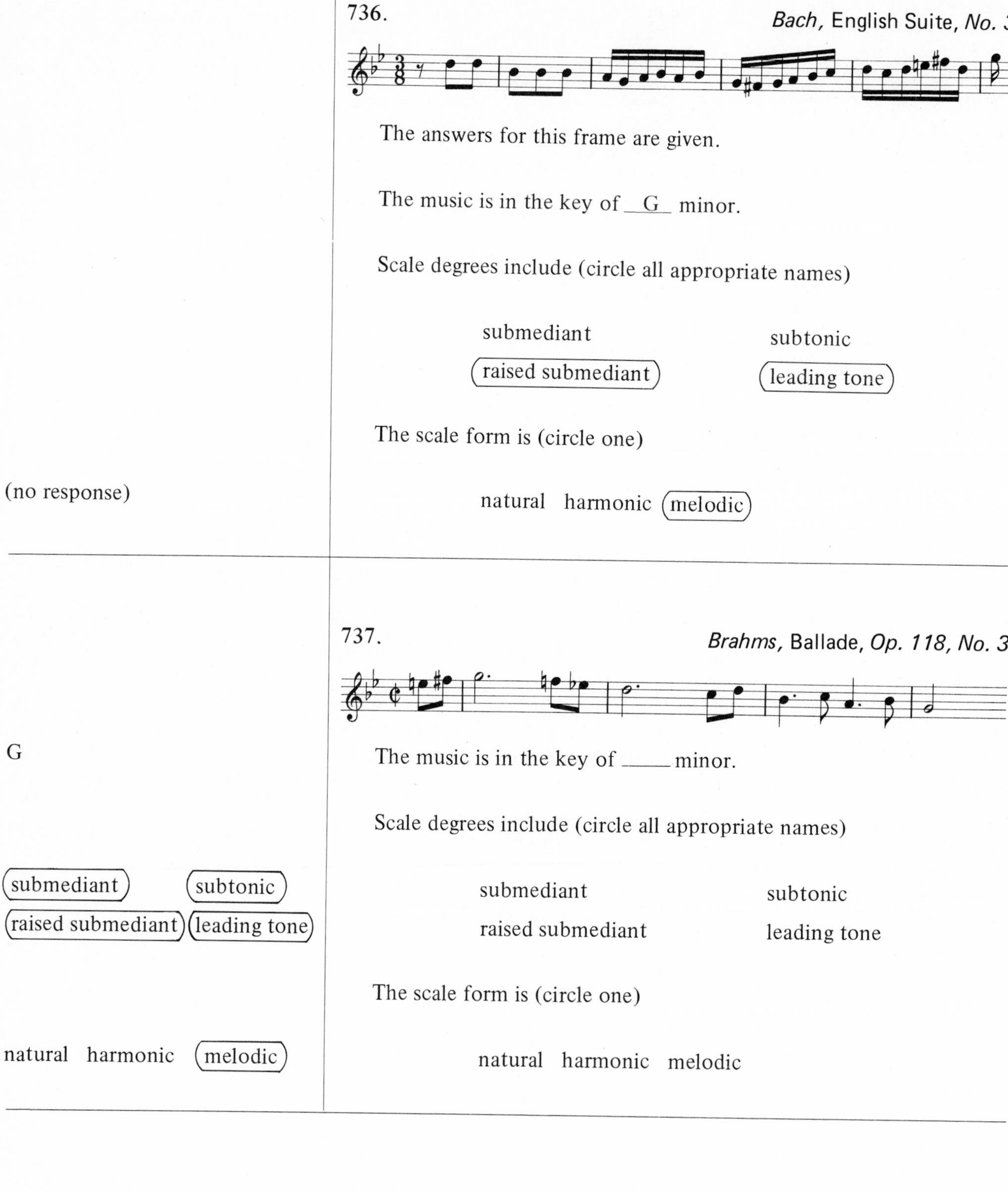

736. *Bach,* English Suite, *No. 3*

The answers for this frame are given.

The music is in the key of __G__ minor.

Scale degrees include (circle all appropriate names)

submediant | subtonic
(raised submediant) | (leading tone)

The scale form is (circle one)

natural harmonic (melodic)

(no response)

---

737. *Brahms,* Ballade, *Op. 118, No. 3*

The music is in the key of _____ minor.

Scale degrees include (circle all appropriate names)

submediant | subtonic
raised submediant | leading tone

The scale form is (circle one)

natural harmonic melodic

G

(submediant) (subtonic)
(raised submediant) (leading tone)

natural harmonic (melodic)

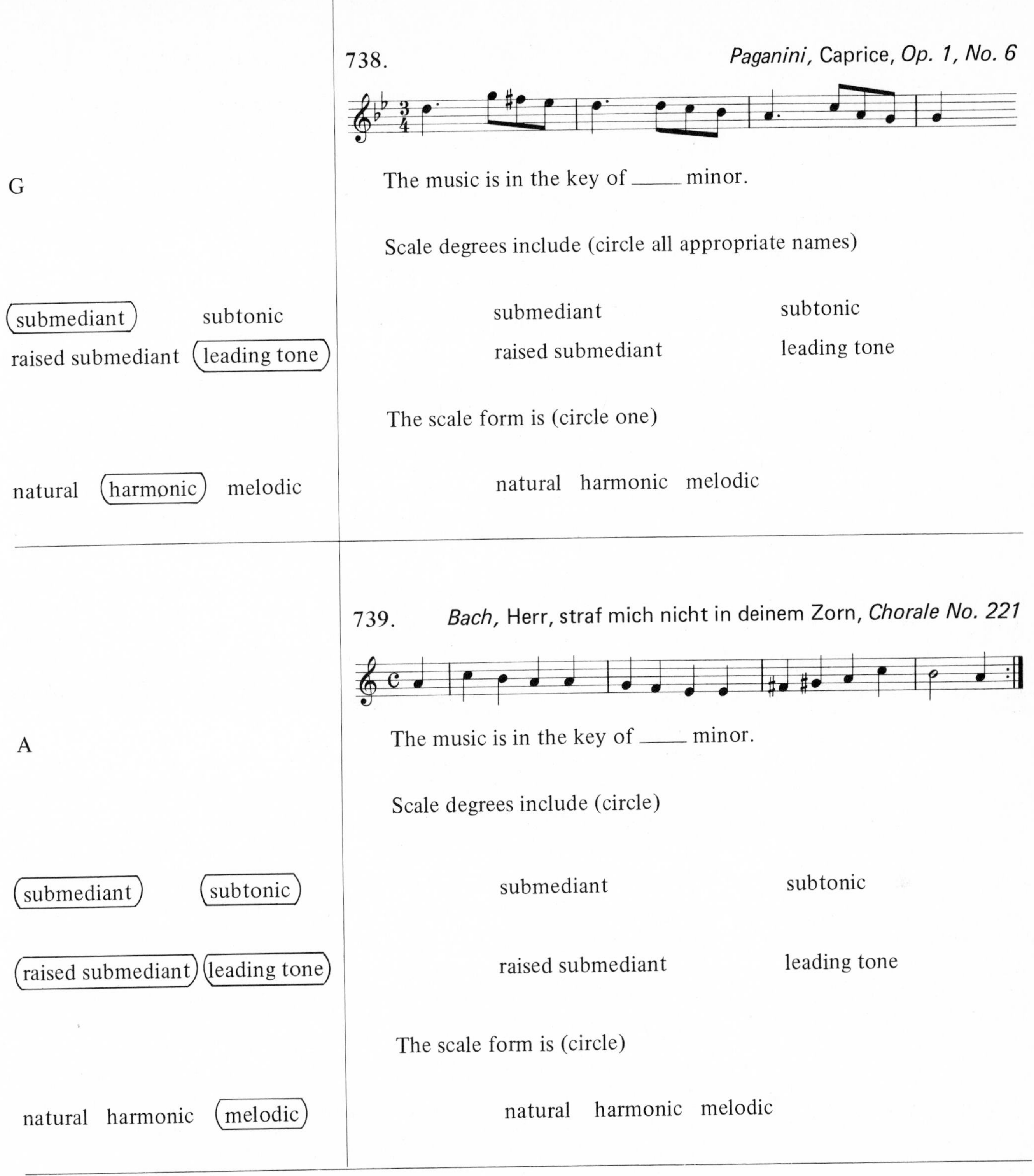

738. *Paganini*, Caprice, *Op. 1, No. 6*

The music is in the key of ____ minor.

Scale degrees include (circle all appropriate names)

submediant   subtonic

raised submediant   leading tone

The scale form is (circle one)

natural   harmonic   melodic

G

(submediant)   subtonic

raised submediant   (leading tone)

natural   (harmonic)   melodic

---

739. *Bach,* Herr, straf mich nicht in deinem Zorn, *Chorale No. 221*

The music is in the key of ____ minor.

Scale degrees include (circle)

submediant   subtonic

raised submediant   leading tone

The scale form is (circle)

natural   harmonic   melodic

A

(submediant)   (subtonic)

(raised submediant)   (leading tone)

natural   harmonic   (melodic)

F

(submediant) (subtonic)
raised submediant leading tone

(natural) harmonic melodic

740. *English Folk Song*

The music is in the key of ____ minor.

Scale degrees include (circle)

submediant subtonic
raised submediant leading tone

The scale form is (circle)

natural harmonic melodic

E♭

(submediant) (subtonic)
raised submediant leading tone

(natural) harmonic melodic

741. *English Folk Song*

The music is in the key of ____ minor.

Scale degrees include (circle)

submediant subtonic
raised submediant leading tone

The scale form is (circle)

natural harmonic melodic

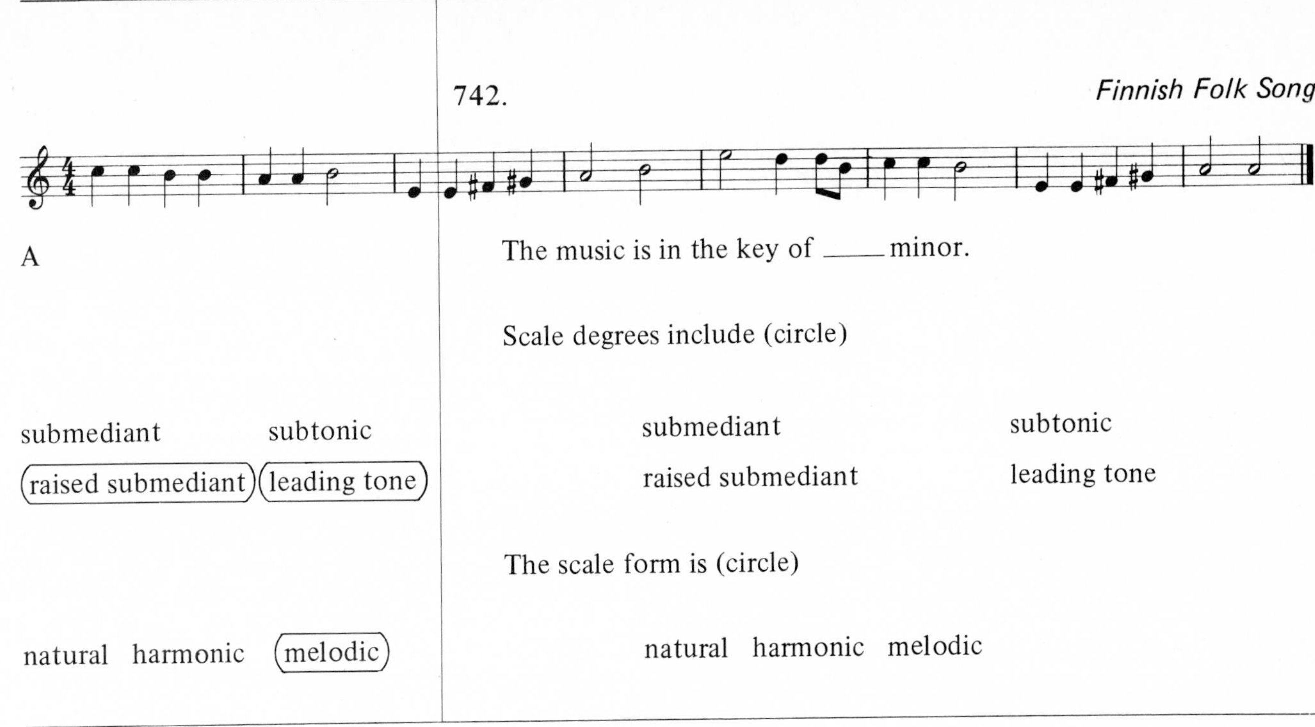

742. *Finnish Folk Song*

A

submediant subtonic

(raised submediant) (leading tone)

natural harmonic (melodic)

The music is in the key of ____ minor.

Scale degrees include (circle)

submediant subtonic

raised submediant leading tone

The scale form is (circle)

natural harmonic melodic

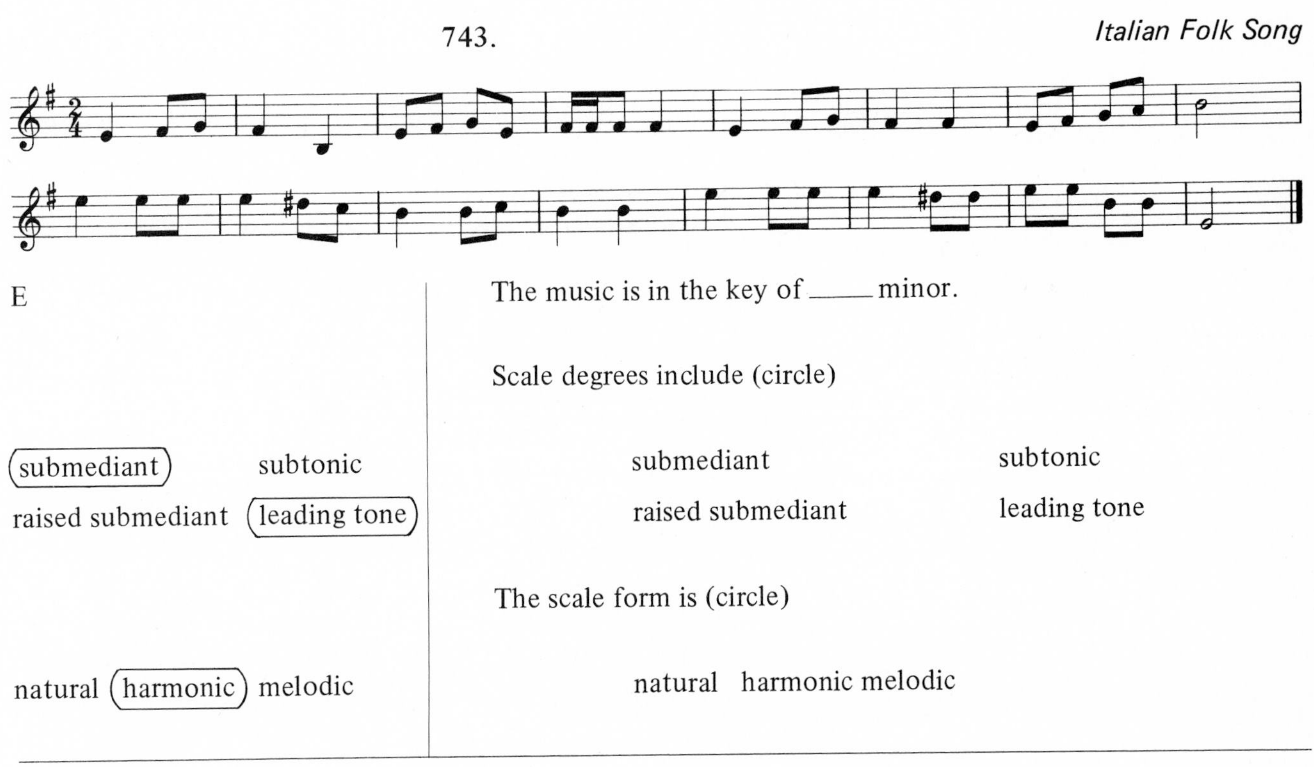

743. *Italian Folk Song*

E

(submediant) subtonic

raised submediant (leading tone)

natural (harmonic) melodic

The music is in the key of ____ minor.

Scale degrees include (circle)

submediant subtonic

raised submediant leading tone

The scale form is (circle)

natural harmonic melodic

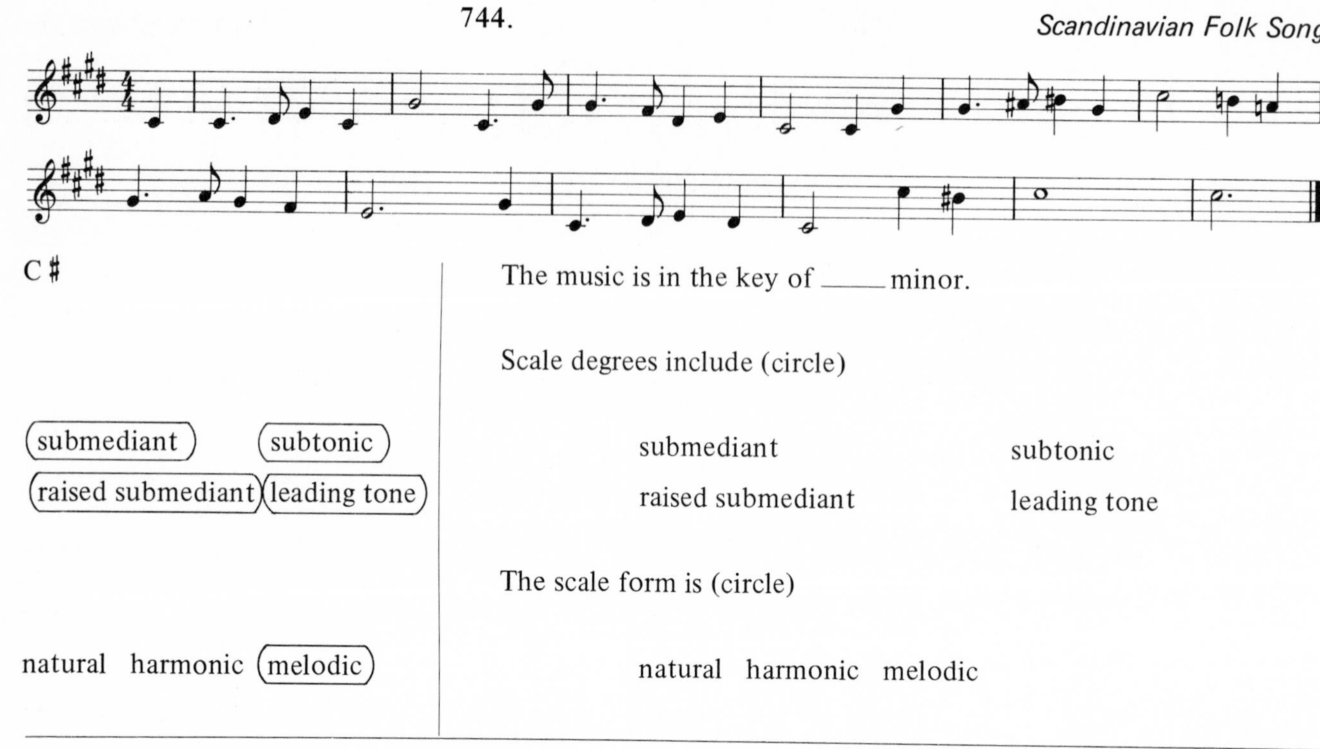

744. *Scandinavian Folk Song*

C♯

The music is in the key of ____ minor.

Scale degrees include (circle)

submediant subtonic

raised submediant leading tone

The scale form is (circle)

natural harmonic melodic

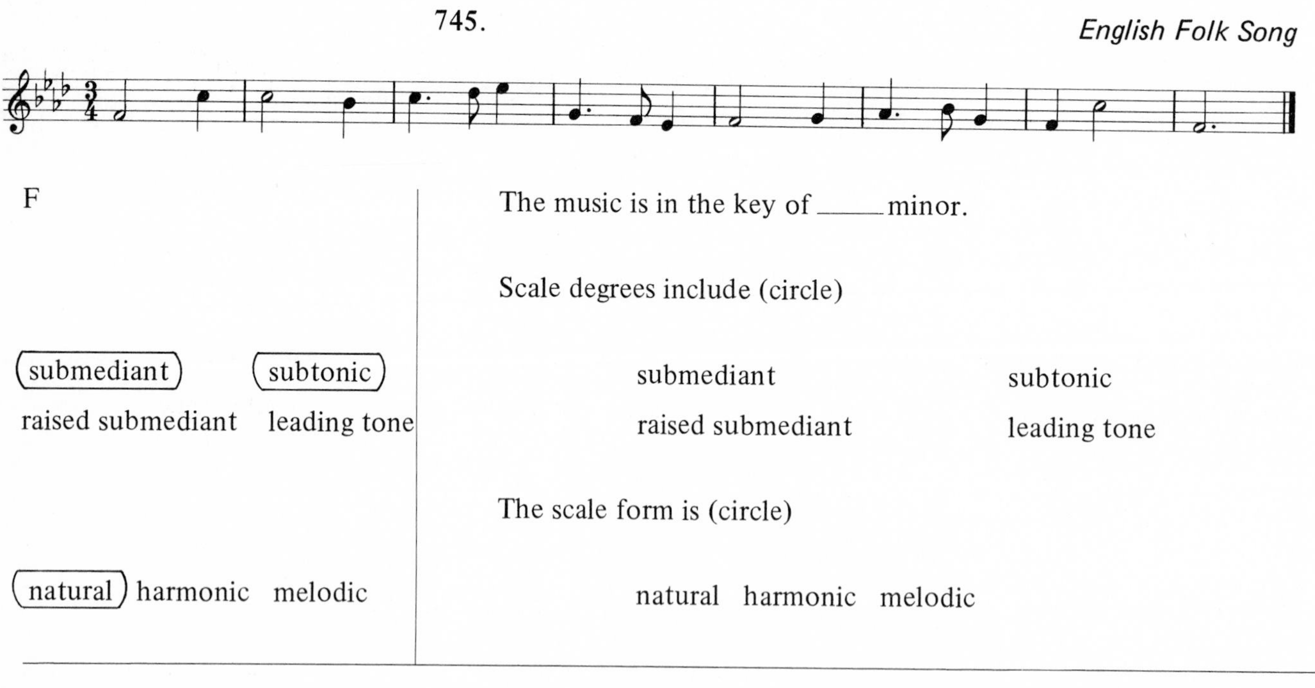

745. *English Folk Song*

F

The music is in the key of ____ minor.

Scale degrees include (circle)

submediant subtonic

raised submediant leading tone

The scale form is (circle)

natural harmonic melodic

746. *Bach, Suite for Lute*

The music is in the key of ____ minor.

Scale degrees include (circle)

submediant subtonic

raised submediant leading tone

The scale form is (circle)

natural harmonic melodic

Answers: E — (submediant) (subtonic) (raised submediant) (leading tone) — natural harmonic (melodic)

747. *English Folk Song*

The music is in the key of ____ minor.

Scale degrees include (circle)

submediant subtonic

raised submediant leading tone

The scale form is (circle)

natural harmonic melodic

Answers: F♯ — (submediant) (subtonic) raised submediant leading tone — (natural) harmonic melodic

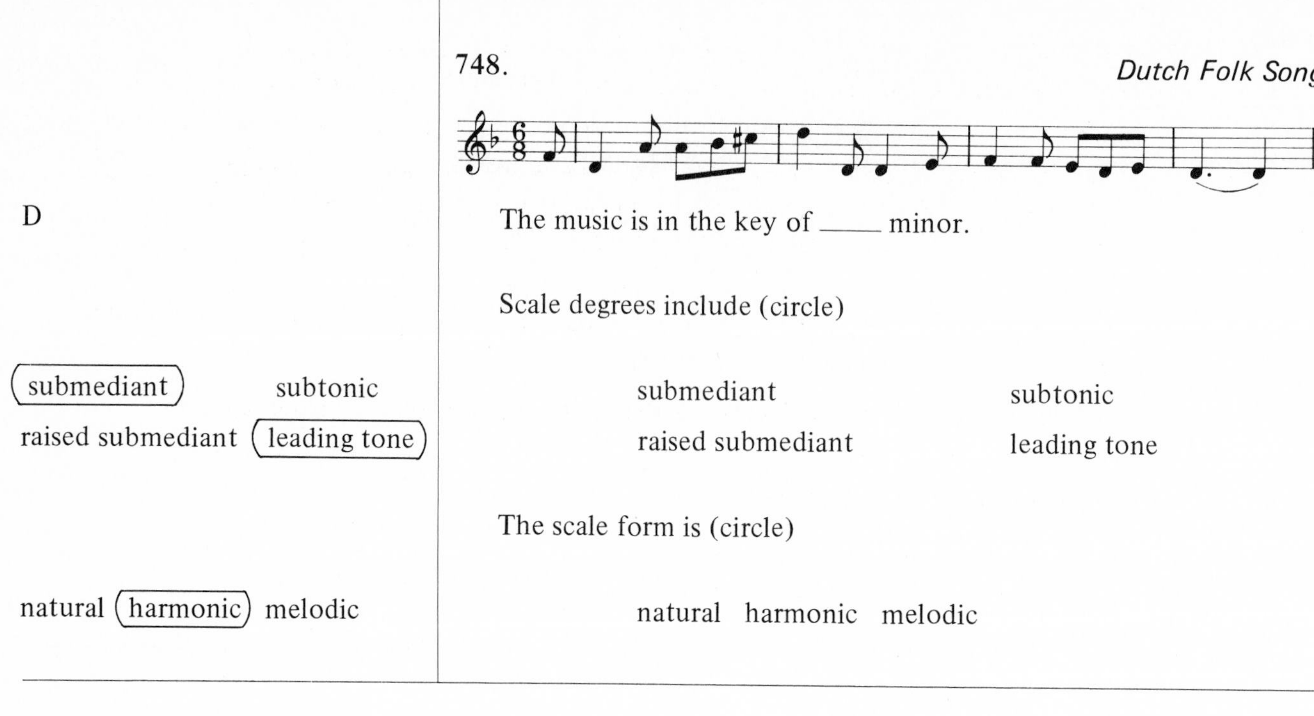

748. *Dutch Folk Song*

D

The music is in the key of ____ minor.

Scale degrees include (circle)

(submediant) subtonic
raised submediant (leading tone)

submediant subtonic
raised submediant leading tone

The scale form is (circle)

natural (harmonic) melodic

natural harmonic melodic

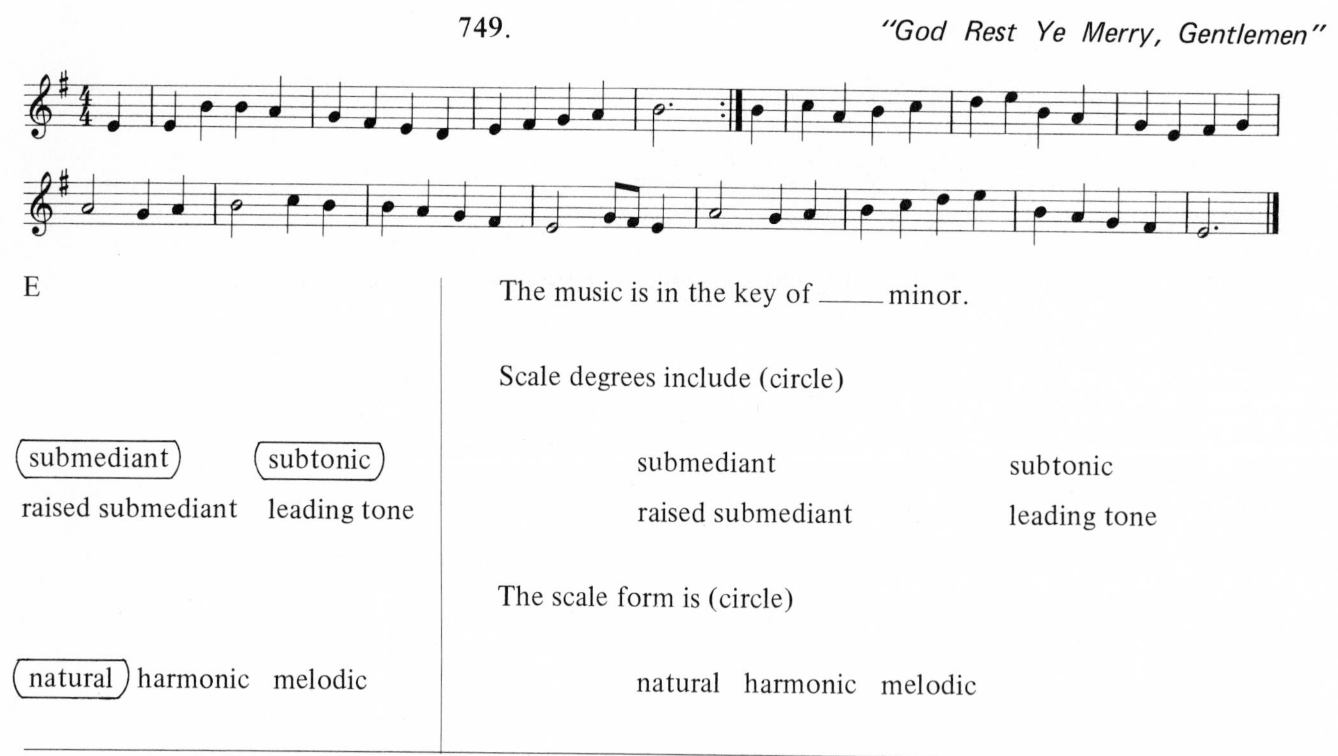

749. *"God Rest Ye Merry, Gentlemen"*

E

The music is in the key of ____ minor.

Scale degrees include (circle)

(submediant) (subtonic)
raised submediant leading tone

submediant subtonic
raised submediant leading tone

The scale form is (circle)

(natural) harmonic melodic

natural harmonic melodic

CHAPTER SUMMARY

1. The function of the key signature is the same in minor as it is in major. As in major, the terms *keynote* and *tonic* refer to the first note of the scale.

2. The three forms of the minor scale (natural, harmonic, and melodic) use a variety of accidentals, but the minor key signature is determined solely by those sharps or flats in the natural (pure) form of the scale.

3. The circle of fifths for minor keys enables us to organize knowledge of keys, including relationships of keys, number of accidentals required for each signature, and enharmonic keys.

4. The circle of fifths for minor keys is built exactly as that for major except the starting point of no sharps or flats is Am instead of C.

5. The order for minor keys is:

Am	Em 1♯	Bm 2♯	F♯m 3♯	C♯m 4♯	G♯m 5♯	D♯m 6♯	A♯m 7♯
Am	Dm 1♭	Gm 2♭	Cm 3♭	Fm 4♭	B♭m 5♭	E♭m 6♭	A♭m 7♭

6. The order of accidentals of the key signature and their position on the staff are the same whether major or minor.

7. The minor key is identified by accidentals of the key signature, but the form of the scale used in the music must be identified by additional analysis. A minor melody containing raised submediant and leading tone is based on the *melodic* form of the scale. A melody with submediant moving to leading tone or vice versa is based on the *harmonic* form. A melody with subtonic but no leading tone is based on the *natural* (*pure*) form.

PRE–TEST
MAJOR AND MINOR KEY RELATIONSHIPS. TERMINOLOGY

1. The relative key of C major is ____ ____________.

2. The relative key of B major is ____ ____________.

3. The relative key of A minor is ____ ____________.

4. The relative key of E♭ minor is ____ ____________.

5. The parallel key to F major is ____ ____________.

6. The parallel key to C minor is ____ ____________.

7. A melody based on a major scale is said to be in *major mode.* (T/F) ____

8. Diatonic is the antonym (opposite) of tonic. (T/F) ____

9. The key is B major. Circle the altered tones.

   F♯ E C C♯ A𝄪 G D♯ E♯ A B

10. A scale consisting entirely of half steps is called a ________ scale.

ANSWERS

A score is given at the end of each answer. If your answer is correct, place that score in the column at the right. Add this column for your score.

Score

For 1–6 each complete answer must be correct.

1. A minor (10) ____
2. G♯ minor (10) ____
3. C major (10) ____
4. G♭ major (10) ____
5. F minor (10) ____
6. C♯ major (10) ____
7. T (true) (10) ____
8. F (false) (10) ____
9. F♯ E (C) C♯ (A𝄪) (G) D♯ (E♯) (A) B (2 each) ____
10. Chromatic (10) ____

Total score: ____

Perfect score: 100

If your score is 80 or above, turn now to Chapter 13, page 250. If your score is below 80, continue with Chapter 12.

MAJOR AND MINOR KEY RELATIONSHIPS. TERMINOLOGY

Although major and minor keys have been covered in two separate presentations, certain relationships exist between the two systems. The fact that there are seven sharp keys, seven flat keys, and one key without accidentals in each of major and minor is evidence that such relationships exist. This evidence can be demonstrated graphically through further study of the circle of fifths.

THE CIRCLE OF FIFTHS FOR MAJOR AND MINOR KEYS TOGETHER

750. This illustration shows major and minor keys on the same circle, with major keys outside the circle and minor keys inside.

The Circle of Fifths for Major and Minor Keys Together.

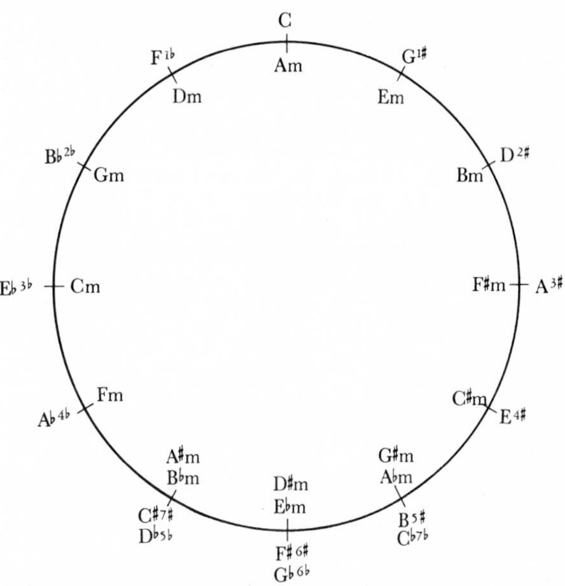

Major keys are placed (outside/inside) the circle. ________

outside

---

751. At each point on the circle are two keys, or two pairs of enharmonic keys. At 12 o'clock on the circle, the position for no sharps or flats, are C major and A minor.

At the point for three sharps the keys are ____ major and ________ minor.

A F♯

---

752. Where two pairs of enharmonic keys appear on one point in the circle, each of the pairs will be on one side of the circle, outside for major and inside for minor.

Are F♯ major and D♯ minor enharmonic keys? (yes/no) ____ .

no

---

753. Are A♭ minor and G♯ minor enharmonic keys? (yes/no) ____.

yes

CONSTRUCTING THE CIRCLE

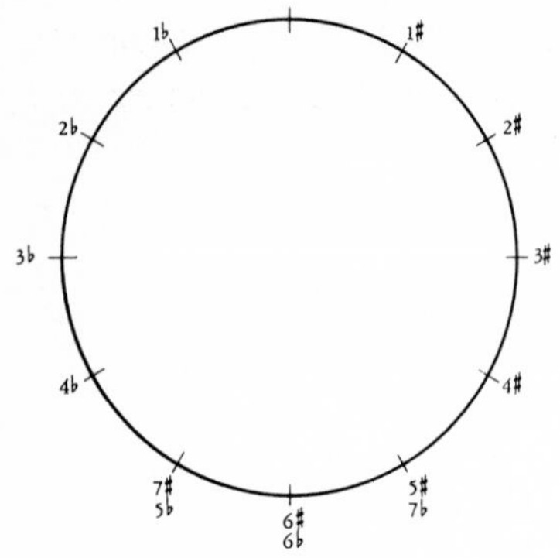

754. A feature of this circle is that at any given point the *number* of accidentals serves both the major and minor key. At each position on the circle below, place the number of accidentals, first sharps then flats.

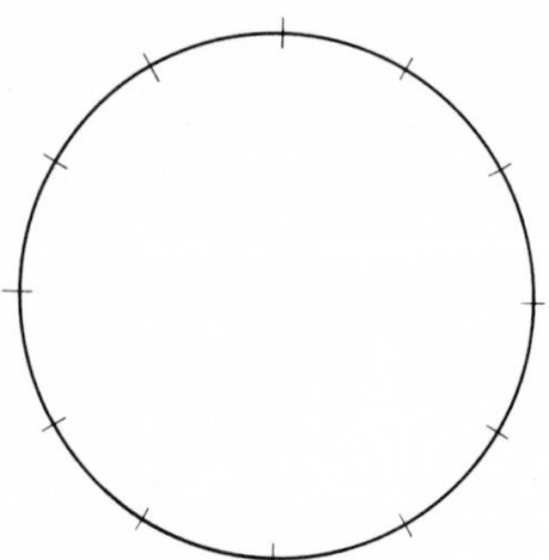

C
Am
F 1♭
Dm
G 1♯
Em
B♭ 2♭
Gm
D 2♯
Bm
E♭ 3♭
Cm
F♯m
A 3♯
Fm
A♭ 4♭
C♯m
E 4♯
A♯m
B♭m
D♯m
E♭m
G♯m
A♭m
C♯ 7♯
D♭ 5♭
F♯ 6♯
G♭ 6♭
B 5♯
C♭ 7♭

755. Add names of all keys. Write major keys in order of sharps, then flats; minor keys in order of sharps, then flats. The answer for one sharp, major key, is given.

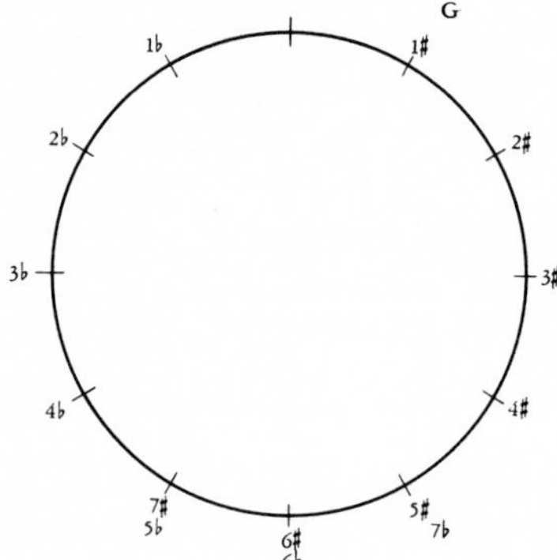

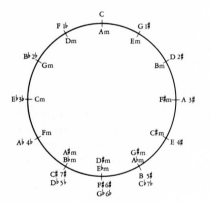

An average student can compose this illustration in less than two minutes. Practice on scrap paper until you can achieve this goal.

RELATIVE KEYS

relative keys

756. Two keys, one major and one minor, having the same accidentals for key signature are known as *relative keys.* G major and E minor with the same key signature of one sharp are ______________ __________.

F♯ D♯	757. The circle of fifths (Frame 750) readily shows all the relative keys because at any one point on the circle the two keys have the same accidentals. The two relative keys having the same accidentals of six sharps are ____ major and ____ minor.
F♯ minor three	758. The relative key of A major is ____ ________. The signature for both keys has (no.)________ sharps.
E♭ major three	759. The relative key of C minor is ____ ________. The signature for both keys has (no.)________ flats.
G major E minor	760. Music written in C major or A minor will have no key signature. To determine whether the key is C or A minor, the tonic must be known. (No sharps or flats) C major tonic — A minor tonic Name the keys: ____ ______ tonic — ____ ______ tonic
D major — B minor	761. Write key signatures of two sharps, notate tonics, and name the keys. ______ major — ______ minor

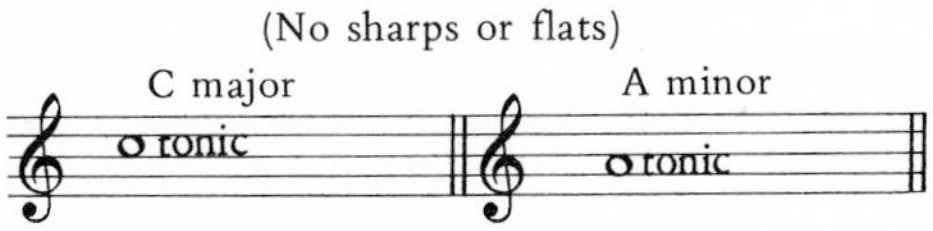

762. In the preceding frames and on the circle of fifths, we have shown each key and its relative key bearing the same signature. Knowing the key name for a given signature enables us to name any key and its relative key. This is the direct way to verify relative keys and is recommended because it supports a concept of parity between major and minor, as minor is not subservient to major.

Two other procedures commonly taught are covered briefly in following frames.

The relative minor key can be found by counting *down* three half steps* (to a pitch name three letter names down) from the tonic of a major key. The relative major key can be found by counting *up* three half steps (to a pitch name three letter names up) from the tonic of the minor key.

**These three half steps equal the interval of a* minor third, *so called because the interval encompasses three letter names, for example, C down to A. The interval previously identified as an augmented second also contains three half steps, but encompasses only two letter names. Intervals will be studied in Chapters 13 and 14.*

Locating Tonic Notes of Relative Keys

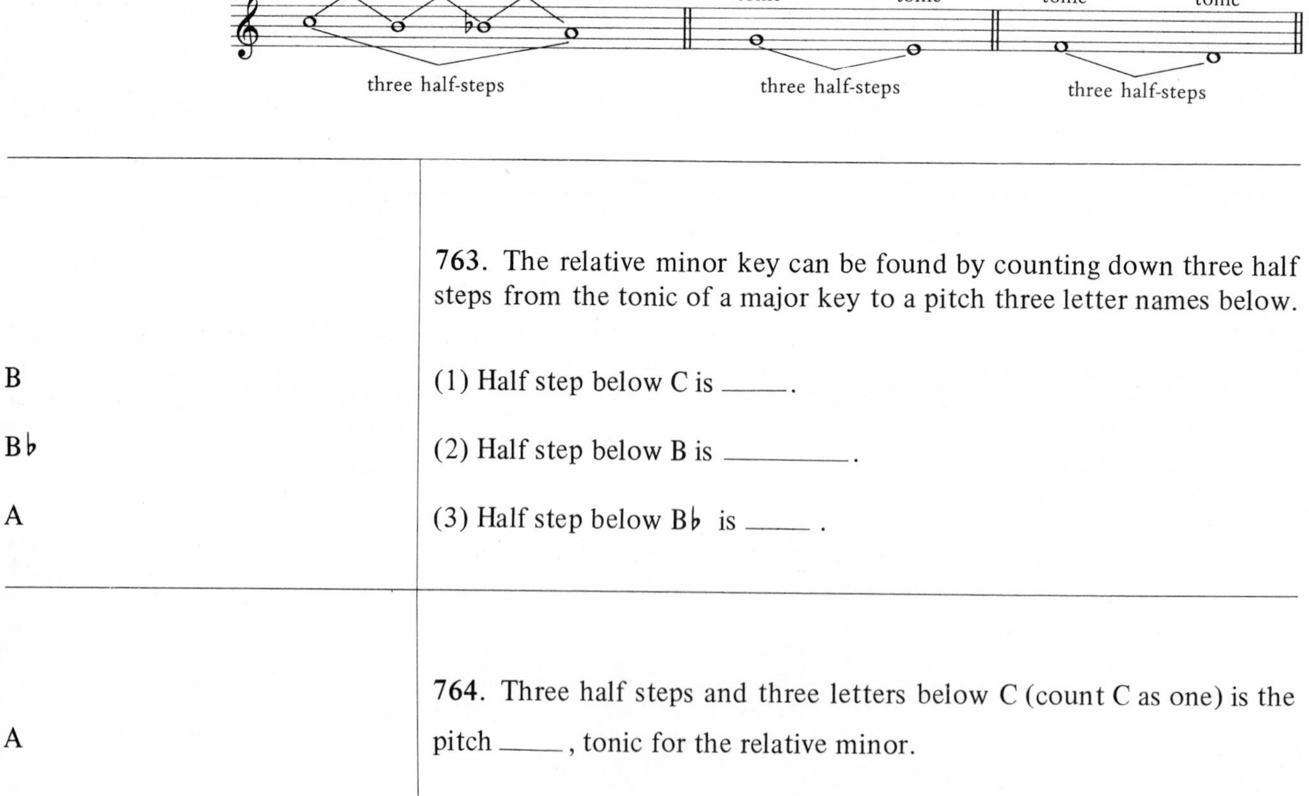

---

763. The relative minor key can be found by counting down three half steps from the tonic of a major key to a pitch three letter names below.

B — (1) Half step below C is ____.

B♭ — (2) Half step below B is ________.

A — (3) Half step below B♭ is ____ .

---

764. Three half steps and three letters below C (count C as one) is the

A — pitch ____, tonic for the relative minor.

	765. The relative minor key may not be found merely by counting down three half steps.
	(1) Half step below B is B♭.
	(2) Half step below B♭ is A.
	(3) Half step below A is A♭.
no	Is the key of A♭ minor relative to B major? (yes/no) _____.
	766. In addition to the three half steps, the tonic of the relative minor key must have the third letter name below the major key.
	(1) Half step below B is B♭.
	(2) Half step below B♭ is A.
	(3) Half step below A is A♭ or G♯.
G♯ (m)	The relative minor key to B major is ________.
F	767. Three half steps and the third letter above the tonic of the key of D minor is the pitch _____, tonic for the relative major.

768. Still another procedure for determining relative keys employs scale-name relationships. The submediant tone of a major scale will be tonic of the relative minor key, and the mediant of a minor scale will be tonic of the relative major key.

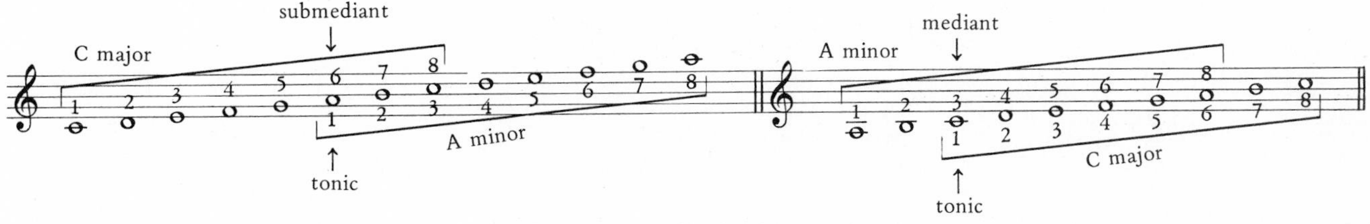

submediant	The tonic of a minor key is the same pitch as the ____________ scale step of the relative major.

C♯ C♯	769. In E major the submediant tone is ________. The relative key to E major is ________ minor.
mediant	770. The tonic of a major key is the same pitch as the ________ scale step of the relative minor.
B♭ B♭	771. In G minor the mediant tone is ________. The relative key to G minor is ________ major.

PARALLEL KEYS

parallel	772. *Parallel keys* are keys with the same tonic pitch, but with completely different key signatures. C major and C minor, each with C as tonic, are ________ keys.
tonic	773. The keys of D major (two sharps) and D minor (one flat) are parallel keys because they have the same ________.
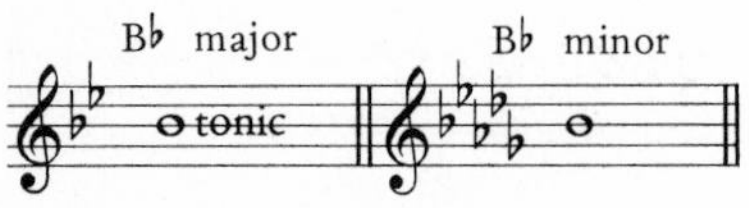 B♭ major (tonic) B♭ minor	774. (1) Name the parallel key to B♭ major, (2) notate the tonic, and (3) write the key signature:  B♭ major (tonic) ____ ________

parallel	775. Two keys having the same tonic are called ________ keys.
relative	Two keys having the same key signature are called ________ keys.

TERMINOLOGY

	776. *Tonality* is a broad term embracing those elements of theory and composition which make a piece *sound* as it does. The single most important aspect of tonality is the presence of tonic and the fact that all other tones relate to it. For this reason the tonic is frequently called *key center* or *tonal center.*
tonic	The most important aspect of tonality is the presence of ________.
	777. When the tonality of a piece is major or minor, musicians sometimes say the piece is in major *mode* or minor *mode.* The word *mode* has other applications, particularly in the study of Medieval and Renaissance music, where it is used in two ways: (1) to refer to scale,* and (2) to identify rhythmic patterns.
mode	Instead of saying a piece is in a major key or in major tonality, we can say it is in major ________.
	**See Appendix 2, Historical Derivation of Major and Minor Scales.*
	778. Music generally is composed with pitches from the scale and with occasional pitches not belonging to the scale. Those pitches found in the scale are *diatonic* pitches.
diatonic	A melody composed entirely of scale tones may be called a ________ melody.

yes	779. In the key of B♭ major, is E♭ a diatonic tone? (yes/no) _______.
	780. Various terms used to specify a non-diatonic tone include *non-scale tone, foreign tone, altered tone.* Circle the altered tones: *Strauss,* Till Eulenspiegels lustige Streiche
A♯ A♭	781. Another term, *chromatic,* is used to signify an altered tone having a special half step relation to an adjunct diatonic tone. A chromatic tone occurs with the half-step alteration of the *same* letter, such as C–C♯, B–B♭, or F♯–F♮. Notation shows both notes on the *same* line or *same* space of the staff. Name the chromatic tone above A:_____ ; below A:_____.
B♭–B♮	782. In Frame 780, the music shows the chromatic progression G–G♯ three times. List below any other chromatic progression occurring in the music:
chromatic	783. If each of the whole steps of a major scale is divided into half steps by chromatic progression, the following arrangement results: original half-step original half-step This orderly arrangement of twelve different pitches within the octave is called a *chromatic scale* (ascending in this case). A scale consisting entirely of half steps is called a __________ scale.

784. Descending from C, the division of whole steps by chromatic progression requires flats.

Complete the addition of flats in the notation of this descending chromatic scale.

CHAPTER SUMMARY

1. Major and minor systems can be combined on one circle of fifths. This device enables us to organize knowledge of keys, including relationships of major and minor keys, number of accidentals for each key signature, and enharmonic keys.

2. At the top of the circle both C major and A minor occupy the position for no sharps or flats. A feature of this circle is that at any given point the number of accidentals serves both the major and minor key.

3. *Relative keys* share the same signature, e.g., G major and E minor (one sharp).

4. The circle of fifths (combined) readily shows relative keys occupying the same point on the circle. Another method to determine relative key is to count down three half steps from a major tonic to find the relative minor tonic, or vice versa. Still another method is to consider that the submediant of a major scale is identical to the tonic of the relative minor, or vice versa.

5. *Parallel keys* are keys with the same tonic but with different key signatures, e.g., C major and C minor.

6. *Tonality* is a broad term embracing elements of theory and composition which make a piece sound as it does. The most important aspect of tonality is the presence of tonic and the fact that all other tones relate to it. The tonic may be called *key center* or *tonal center.*

7. When the tonality of a piece is major or minor, we may say the piece is in major *mode* or minor *mode.*

8. *Diatonic* pitches are scale tones.

9. Non-diatonic tones which may occur in a piece are called *non-scale tones, foreign tones,* or *altered tones.*

10. A *chromatic progression* is the half-step alteration of the same letter, e.g., C–C♯.

11. A *chromatic scale* is comprised entirely of half steps, twelve within the octave.

PRE–TEST INTERVALS: MAJOR AND PERFECT

1. Circle two incorrect interval names.

   M3 P1 M5 M2 P6 P8 M7

2. Name each interval. Use abbreviations.

   (a) A up to F♯____

   (b) E♭ up to G____

   (c) A♭ down to D♭____

   (d) B♯ down to C♯____

3. Name each interval (abbr.).

____ ____ ____ ____

4. Give compound interval names (abbr.)

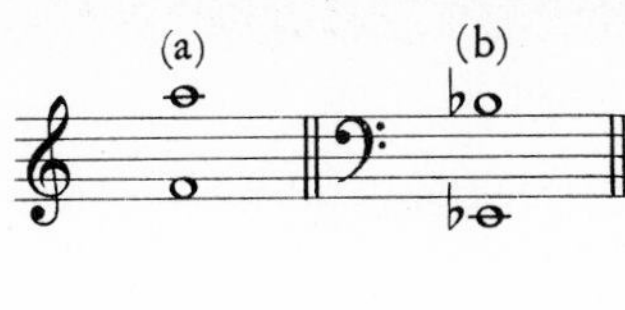

____ ____

ANSWERS

A score is given at the end of each answer. If your answer is correct, place that score in the column at the right. Add this column for your score.

	Score
1. M3 P1 (M5) M2 (P6) P8 M7 (5 each)	____
2. (a) M6 (10)	____
(b) M3 (10)	____
(c) P5 (10)	____
(d) M7 (10)	____
3. (a) (b) (c) (d) (10 each)	____
M2 P4 P5 M6	
4. (a) (b) (5 each)	____
M10 P12	
Total score:	____
Perfect score:	100

If your score is 80 or above, turn now to Chapter 14, page 263. If your score is less than 80, continue with Chapter 13.

INTERVALS: MAJOR AND PERFECT

At various times in the preceding chapters we have referred to intervals. *We have used intervals of the half step and whole step in constructing scales, and we have used the interval of the perfect fifth to help us understand the circle of fifths. The octave was studied in detail in Chapter 3.*

There are two different approaches to the study of intervals. One approach deals with intervals as found above the tonic of the major scale—the approach commonly used in public school music. A second approach deals with intervals as found in chords. The second approach is the more mature and meaningful one because it considers the interval in a truly musical situation, for example, in an actual composition. Nevertheless, in order to expedite our mastery of fundamentals, it is necessary that we thoroughly understand the first approach: intervals found above tonic of the major scale.*

*A *chord* is the simultaneous sounding of more than two notes. Chords are introduced in Chapter 16.

MAJOR AND PERFECT INTERVALS

785. An interval is the distance or difference between two pitches. A *harmonic interval* is the sounding of two pitches simultaneously; a *melodic interval* is the sounding of two pitches consecutively.

Identify below:

c — Harmonic interval (a/b/c)____

a — Melodic interval, ascending (a/b/c)____

b — Melodic interval, descending (a/b/c)____

786. The terms *harmonic* and *melodic* describe only the graphic aspects of intervals. To describe the difference (distance) between two pitches, other terminology is used.* The name of an interval consists of an adjective expressing *quality* and a noun representing *quantity*. Most obvious is the quantity, which is seen by the *number* of staff degrees spanned by the interval. The interval G up to B has the quantity of a *third* because three staff degrees, G–A–B, are spanned.

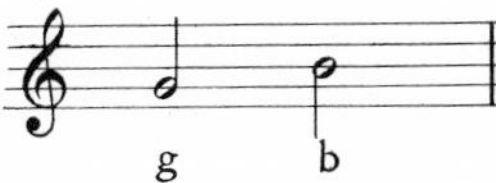

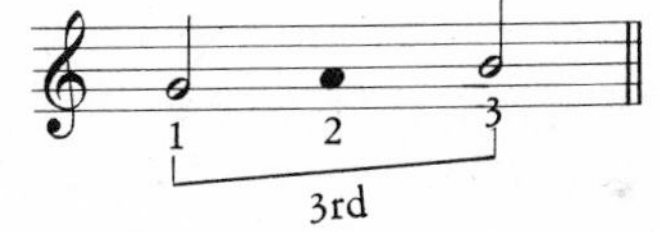

number — Quantity of an interval is determined by the ________ of staff degrees spanned.

**Intervals are treated as ratios of frequencies in Appendix 1, Acoustics.*

787. The interval G up to C

fourth — has the quantity of a ________.

	788. *Quality* of intervals between tonic and other degrees of the major scale is expressed by the adjectives *major* or *perfect.** (Other adjectives to be studied later are *minor, diminished,* and *augmented.*) In the major scale, *only* major and perfect intervals occur above (from) the tonic. The study of this chapter is confined to these intervals.
major/perfect	To describe quality of intervals from tonic up to other degrees of the major scale, the two adjectives used are________and________.
	**Perfect intervals are so named for acoustical reasons (see* Grove's Dictionary of Music and Musicians, *"Intervals"). The terms* major *(this chapter) and* minor *(next chapter) when applied to intervals mean simply larger (greater) or smaller (lesser).*
	789. *Major* modifies or specifies the quantities 2, 3, 6, and 7; *perfect* modifies 4, 5, and 8.
major	The quantities 2, 3, 6, and 7 are modified by the qualitative adjective ____________.
perfect	790. The quantities 4, 5, and 8 are modified by the qualitative adjective ____________.
(2), 3, 6, 7 (4), 5, 8	791. Major intervals are 2,______,______ and______; perfect intervals are 4, _____ and _____ .
	792. There are no interval names such as major fourth or perfect third.
	Circle incorrect names.
Major seventh (Perfect sixth) Perfect octave (Major fifth)	Major seventh Perfect sixth Perfect octave Major fifth

793. The name given to two notes of the same pitch is *perfect prime* (P1).

While not an interval by previous definition, it is included in tables of intervals. It is commonly known by the name *unison.*

The two notes g^1 and g^1 constitute a perfect ________. The abbreviation is ____.

prime

P1

---

794. In a major scale, the distance from the tonic note up to each of the other scale tones provides seven different intervals. Standard abbreviations are capital M for major and P for perfect.

In the following table complete the column "Abbreviated."

	From scale degree	*Up to scale degree*	*Interval name*	*Abbreviated*
(M2)	1	2	Major second	M2
M3	1	3	Major third	____
P4	1	4	Perfect fourth	____
P5	1	5	Perfect fifth	____
M6	1	6	Major sixth	____
M7	1	7	Major seventh	____
P8	1	8	Perfect octave	____
P1	1	1	Perfect prime	____

795. In an interval name, the number of the scale tone above tonic and the number of staff degrees spanned are the same.

Intervals in the C Major Scale.

These intervals are found in the same order in any major scale, for example, D major.

Intervals in the D Major Scale.

---

	796. In the scale of E♭ major, spell each interval above tonic.
F	M2 E♭- ____
G	M3 E♭- ____
A♭	P4 E♭- ____
B♭	P5 E♭- ____
C	M6 E♭- ____
D	M7 E♭- ____
E♭	P8 E♭- ____
M2	797. From 1 to 2 of a major scale is a whole step. Another name for the interval of a whole step is (abbr.) ____.

ANALYSIS OF INTERVALS

798. In analyzing an interval, whether it be ascending melodic, descending melodic, or harmonic, assume the *lower note* to be 1 (tonic) and count the scale degrees to the upper note. The number of scale degrees will determine the name of the interval. For example, D up to A:

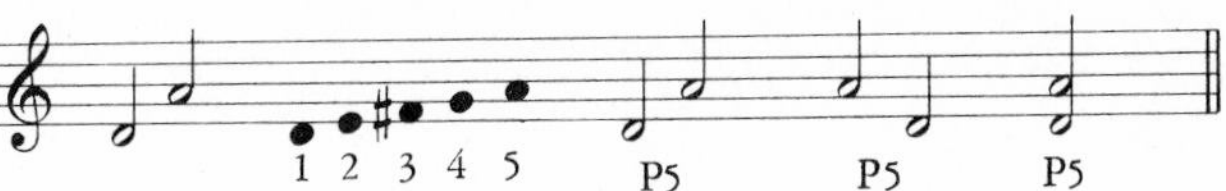

A appears as the fifth degree in the D major scale; therefore, D up to A, or A down to D, or D and A sounded together are perfect fifths.

P5

799. Name the following intervals. (Use abbreviations.)

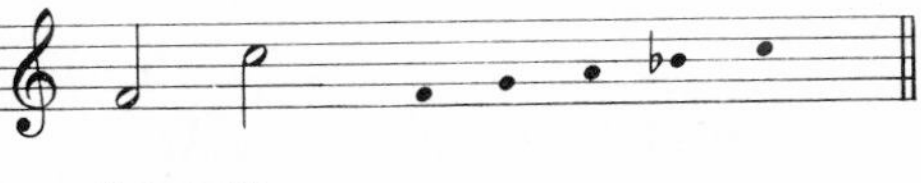

______

M6

800.

______

P4

801.

______

M3

802.

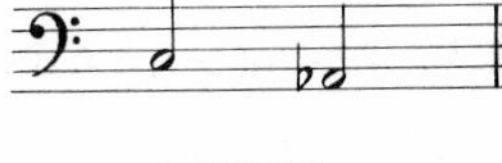

______

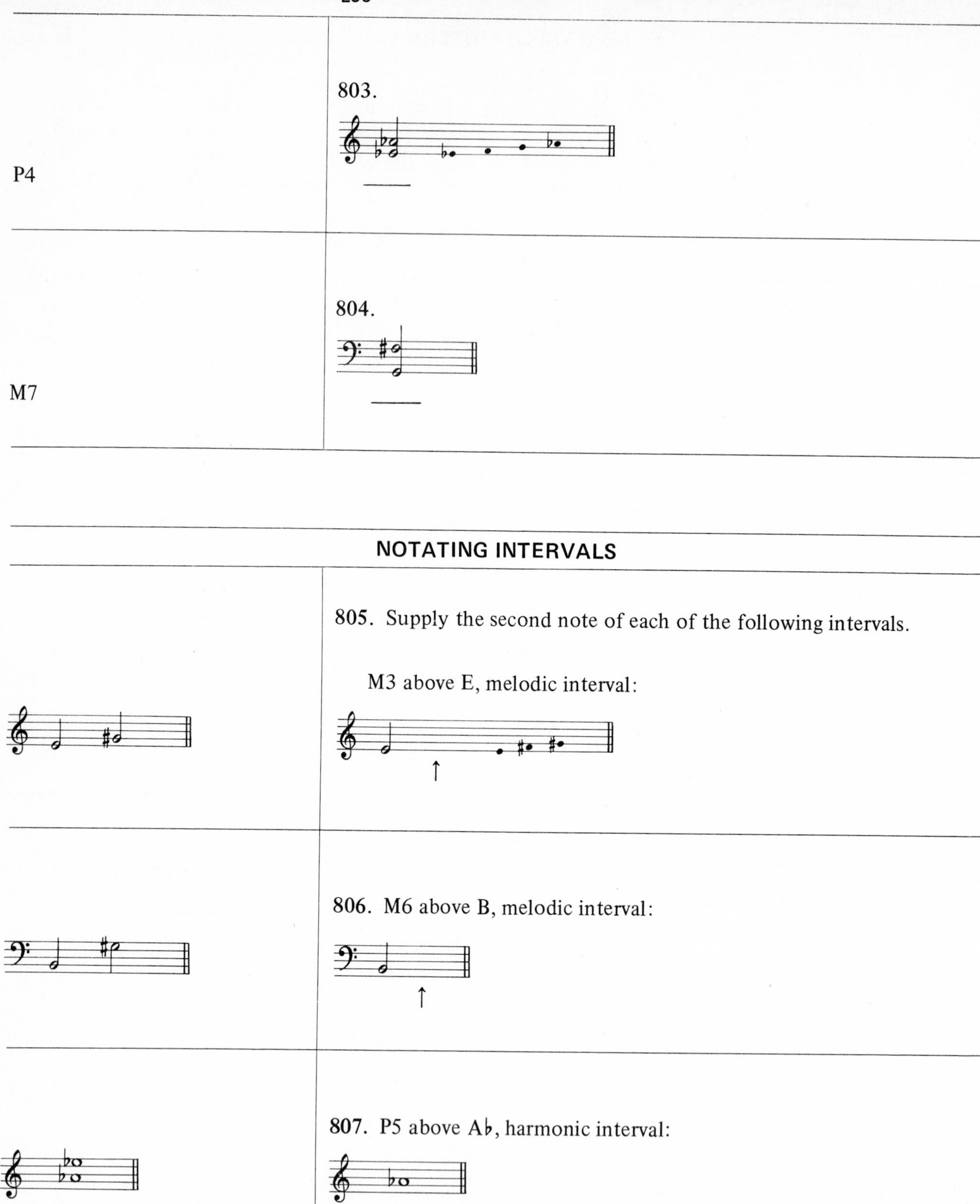
803.
P4
804.
M7
NOTATING INTERVALS
805. Supply the second note of each of the following intervals.
M3 above E, melodic interval:
806. M6 above B, melodic interval:
807. P5 above A♭, harmonic interval:

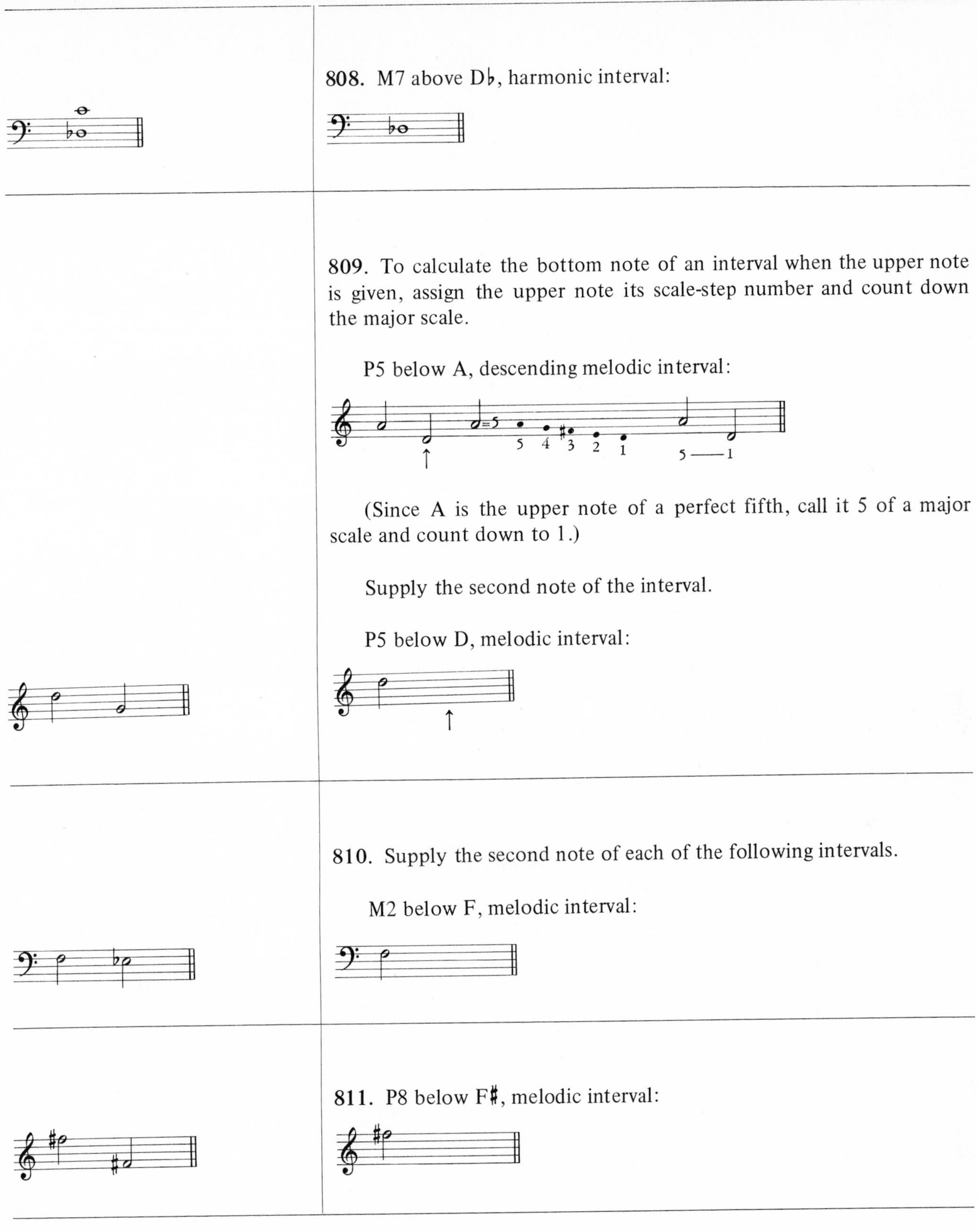

808. M7 above D♭, harmonic interval:

809. To calculate the bottom note of an interval when the upper note is given, assign the upper note its scale-step number and count down the major scale.

P5 below A, descending melodic interval:

(Since A is the upper note of a perfect fifth, call it 5 of a major scale and count down to 1.)

Supply the second note of the interval.

P5 below D, melodic interval:

810. Supply the second note of each of the following intervals.

M2 below F, melodic interval:

811. P8 below F♯, melodic interval:

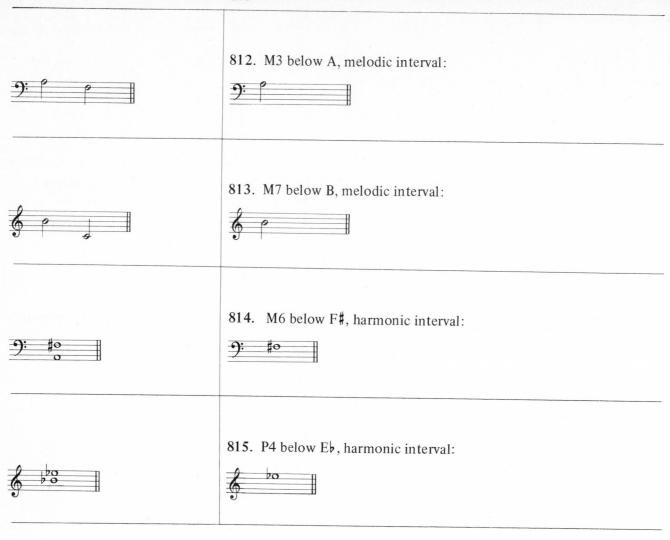

812. M3 below A, melodic interval:

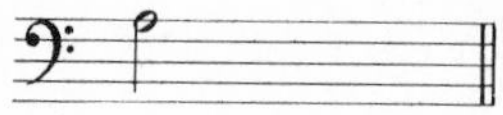

813. M7 below B, melodic interval:

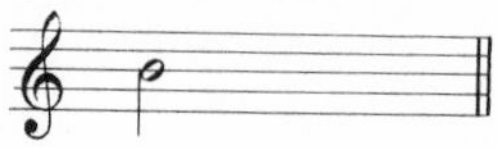

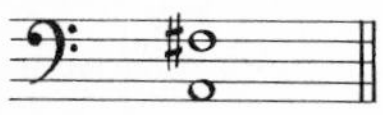

814. M6 below F♯, harmonic interval:

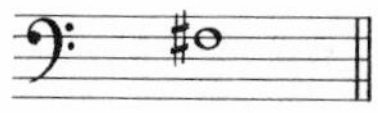

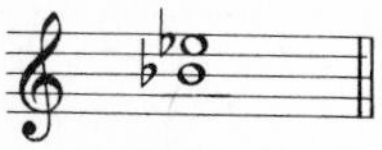

815. P4 below E♭, harmonic interval:

SIMPLE AND COMPOUND INTERVALS

816. Intervals encompassing a perfect octave or less are known as *simple* intervals. Intervals larger than a perfect octave are called *compound* intervals, meaning an octave plus a simple interval already named. Like simple intervals, compound intervals are designated by the number of scale degrees spanned.

Simple and Compound Intervals in the C Major Scale.

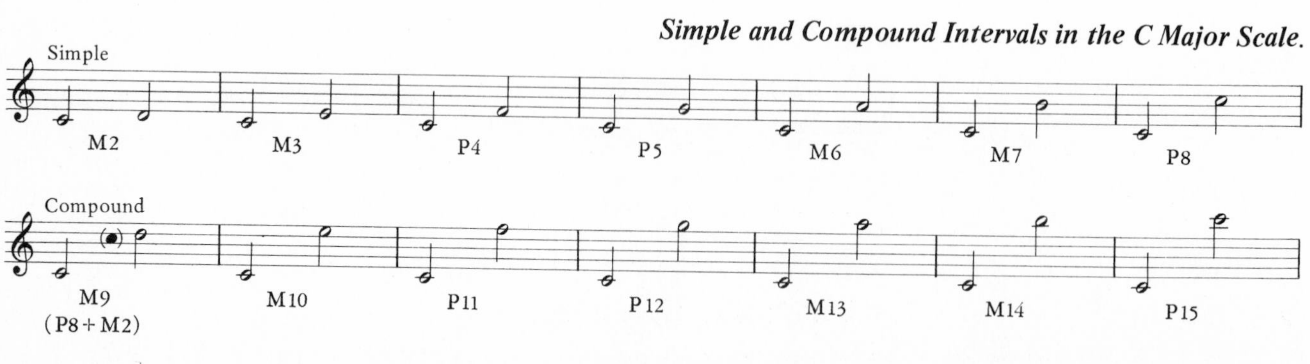

greater	817. A compound interval is (smaller/greater) ______ than a perfect octave.
M9	818. An octave plus a simple interval has an intervallic sum one number less than the arithmetical sum. The intervals added together have one note in common. This note is counted once rather than twice. A perfect octave (8) plus a major second (2) have the intervallic sum of a (abbr.) M ___.
M10	819. M3 plus P8 equals M___.
P11	820. P8 plus P4 equals P ___.
P12	821. P5 plus P8 equals P___.
M13	822. The qualitative adjective for a compound interval is the same as for the simple portion. M6 plus P8 equals___ ___.
M14	823. P8 plus M7 equals ___ ___.
P15	824. P8 plus P8 equals ___ ___.

M10

825. From c^1 to e^1 is a M3; c^1 to e^2 is a____ ____.

P12

826. From small f to c^1 is a P5; f to c^2 is a____ ____.

M3

827. In musical analysis, compound intervals are frequently reduced to simple terminology. For example, although the interval c^1 to g^2 is a perfect twelfth, it may be called a perfect fifth.

P12
sometimes called
P5

This interval may be called a M10 or a____.

CHAPTER SUMMARY

1. An interval is the difference or distance between two pitches.

2. A *harmonic interval* is the sounding of two pitches simultaneously; a *melodic interval* is sounding two pitches consecutively.

3. An interval is named by *quality* and *quantity*. *Major* and *perfect* are terms of quality; quantity is determined by the *number* of staff degrees spanned by the interval.

4. Major and perfect intervals occur between tonic and other degrees of the major scale.

5. Because scales are constructed on consecutive staff degrees and intervals are named by number of staff degrees spanned, the scale-step number and the quantity number of an interval are the same.

6. *Major* modifies numbers 2, 3, 6, and 7; *perfect* modifies 4, 5, 8 (and 1).

7. The intervals from tonic up to each of the major scale tones are: M2, M3, P4, P5, M6, M7, and P8.

8. In analyzing an interval, assume the *lower note* to be 1 (tonic) and count the scale degrees to the upper note.

9. *Simple* intervals encompass a perfect octave or less; larger intervals are called *compound* intervals, meaning an octave plus a simple interval. In musical analysis, compound intervals are frequently reduced to simple terminology.

PRE–TEST
INTERVALS: MINOR, DIMINISHED, AUGMENTED

1. A major interval reduced by one half step becomes ______________.

2. A major interval reduced by one whole step becomes ______________.

3. A perfect interval reduced by one half step becomes ______________.

4. A major or perfect interval increased by one half step becomes ______________.

5. Name each interval (abbr.)

   (a) B♭ up to F ________

   (b) C♯ down to D♯ ________

   (c) F♯ up to G𝄪 ________

   (d) B𝄫 down to B♭ ________

   (e) E♭ up to C♯ ________

   (f) F♯ down to D♯ ________

6. Invert the following intervals. Name each interval (abbr.)

(a) ↓ (b) ↓

___ ___ ___ ___

ANSWERS

A score is given at the end of each answer. If your answer is correct, place that score in the column at the right. Add this column for your score.

Score

1. Minor (5) ___

2. Diminished (5) ___

3. Diminished (5) ___

4. Augmented (5) ___

5. (a) P5 (10) ___
   (b) m7 (10) ___
   (c) aug 2 (10) ___
   (d) dim 8 (10) ___
   (e) aug 6 (10) ___
   (f) m3 (10) ___

6. All parts of the answer for (a) must be correct (10) ___
   All parts of the answer for (b) must be correct (10) ___

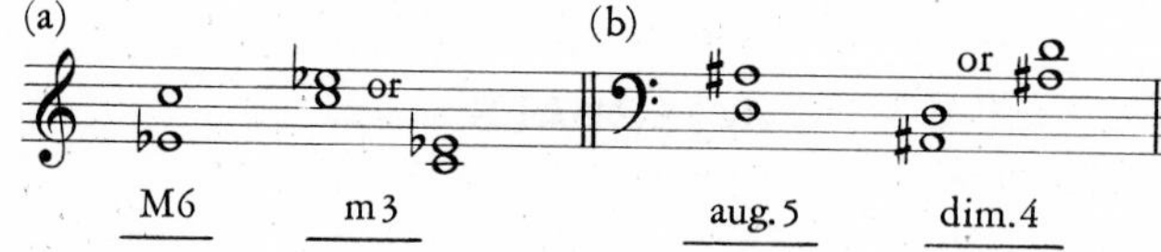

Total score: ___

Perfect score: 100

If your score is 80 or above, turn now to Chapter 15, page 280. If your score is less than 80, continue with Chapter 14.

INTERVALS: MINOR, DIMINISHED, AND AUGMENTED

In addition to major and perfect, three other types (qualities) of intervals exist in music; none of these is found as an interval above the tonic of a major scale. These intervals are minor, diminished, *and* augmented. *Each will be compared to major and perfect intervals already studied.*

MINOR INTERVALS

828. A *minor* interval is one half step smaller than a major interval. To emphasize this distinction, the word *small* is sometimes used in place of *minor* and the word *large* in place of *major*. For example, a *small* third is a *minor* third; a *large* third is a *major* third.

minor — A small sixth is a ________ sixth.

major — A large sixth is a ________ sixth.

---

829. This text uses the terms *major* and *minor* instead of large and small.

minor — A major interval decreased by a half step becomes a ________ interval.

---

830. The adjective *minor* can be applied only to those same quantities which can be modified by *major*: 2, 3, 6, and 7. *Minor* never modifies 4, 5, 8 or 1.

(2), 3, 6, and 7 — *Minor* may modify the numbers 2, ____, ____ and ____.

---

831. Abbreviations for minor are *m* or *min*. This text uses m.

Complete the column of minor intervals. Write the name (abbr.) of each interval and place the second note on the staff.

Answer	*Major interval*	*Decreased by ½ step*	*Becomes minor interval*
m2	 M2	–½=	m2 
m3  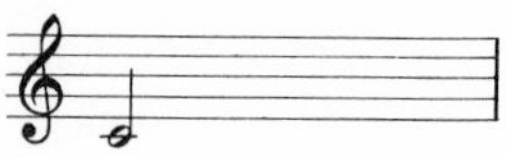	M3	–½=	____
m6	M6	 –½=	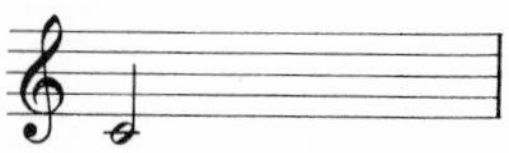 ____
m7 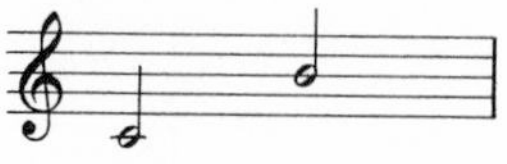 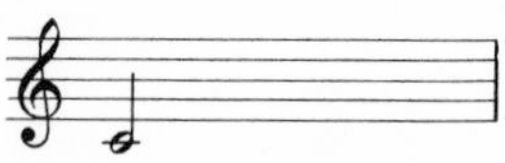	M7	–½=	____

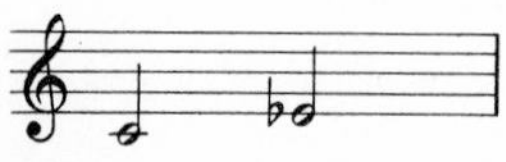

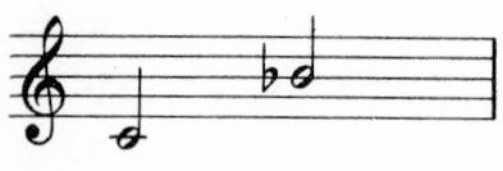

DIMINISHED INTERVALS

832. A *diminished* interval is one half step smaller than a minor or perfect interval. Abbreviation for diminished is *dim.* or sometimes °.

Fill in the column of diminished intervals with the name (abbr.) and the second note for each interval.

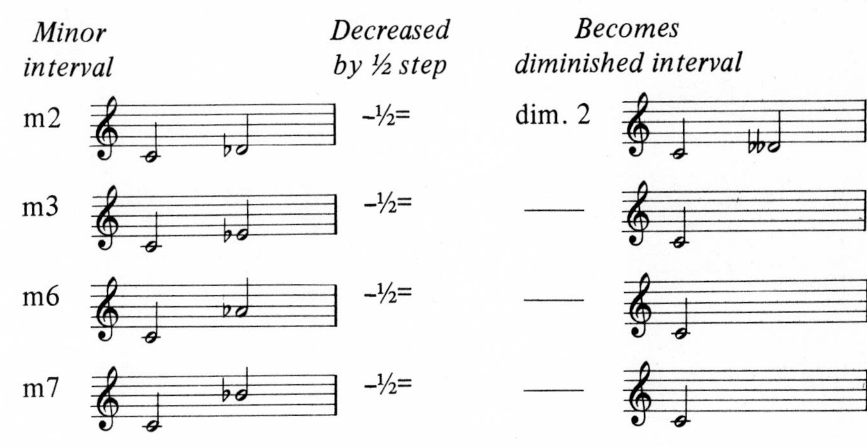

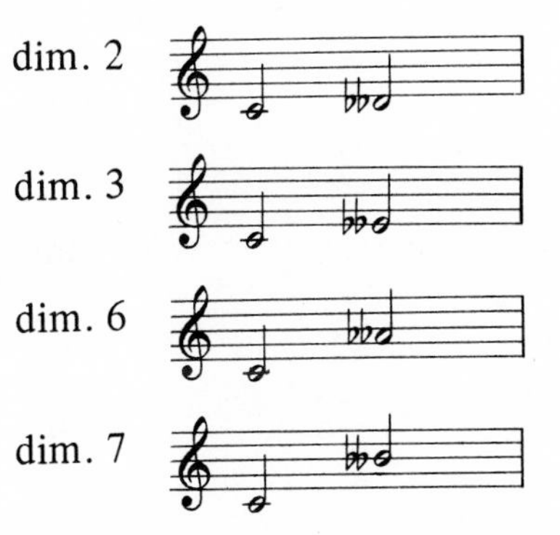

833. If a diminished interval is compared to a major interval, it is two half steps (one whole step) smaller.

A major interval smaller by one half step is a __________ interval.

A minor interval smaller by one half step is a __________ interval.

A major interval smaller by one whole step is a __________ interval.

minor

diminished

diminished

834. Perfect intervals, having no major or minor forms, become directly diminished when decreased by one half step.

Fill in the column of diminished intervals with the name and the second note for each interval.

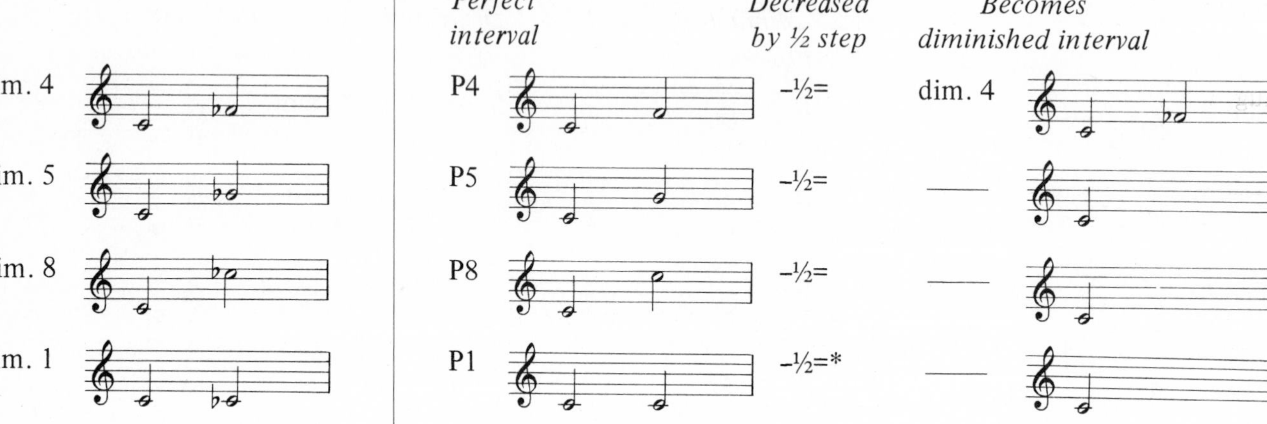

The second note of a diminished prime is lower than the first note. It is not recognized as an interval by most theorists.

AUGMENTED INTERVALS

835. An *augmented* interval is one half step larger than a major or perfect interval.

Abbreviation for augmented is *aug.* or sometimes +.

Complete the column of augmented intervals with the name (abbr.) and the second note for each interval.

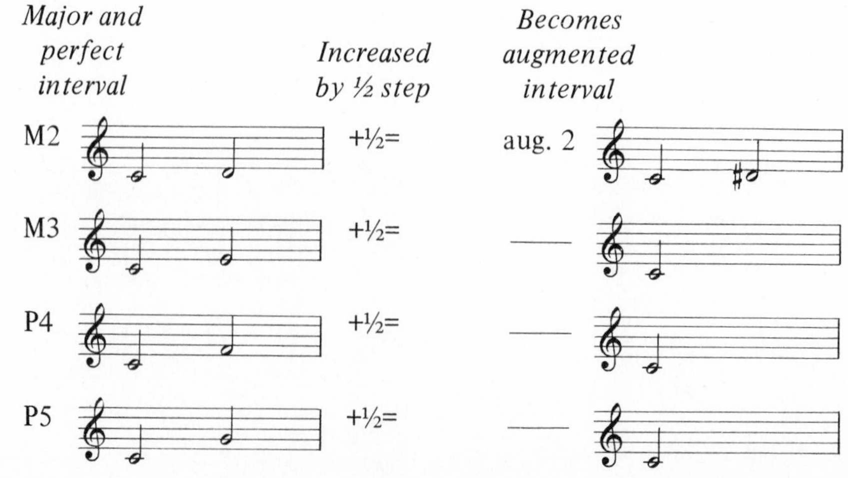

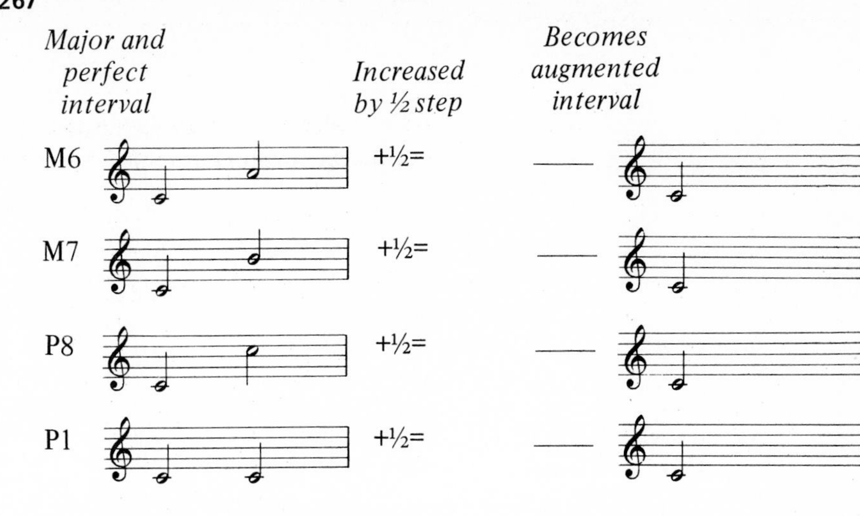

MODIFICATION OF INTERVALS

836. Any type of interval (M, m, P, dim., or aug.) is a modification by one half step of some other type of interval.

Modification of Intervals

Type of interval before	*Modification*		*Type of interval after*
M	– ½ step	=	m
m	– ½ step	=	dim.
P	– ½ step	=	dim.
dim.	– ½ step	=	(doubly dim.*)
aug.	– ½ step	=	P or M
M	+ ½ step	=	aug.
m	+ ½ step	=	M
P	+ ½ step	=	aug.
dim.	+ ½ step	=	P or m
aug.	+ ½ step	=	(doubly aug.*)

**Doubly diminished and doubly augmented intervals are uncommon in musical practice and will not be considered in this text.*

Refer to this example in working the following frames.

837. Below are various intervals and their modifications. Fill in the blanks with interval names. Use abbreviations.

m3

838.

P5

839.

dim. 7

840.

aug. 4

841.

P8

842. An interval can be modified by applying the alteration to *either* the upper *or* lower note. For example, a P5 becomes a dim. 5 by either lowering the upper note one half step, or raising the lower note one half step. In either case the distance between the two pitches is *decreased* by a half step. For example,

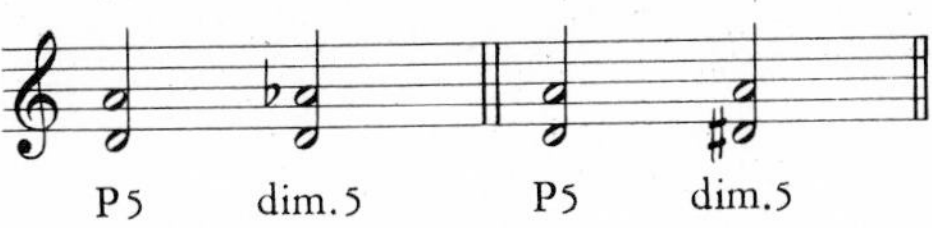

Name the following intervals.

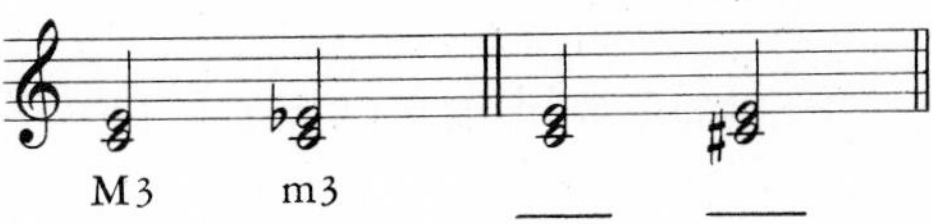

M3 m3

843.

m7 M7 m7

844. A perfect or major interval becomes augmented by either raising the upper note one half step or lowering the bottom note one half step. In either case the distance between the two pitches is increased by a half step.

For example,

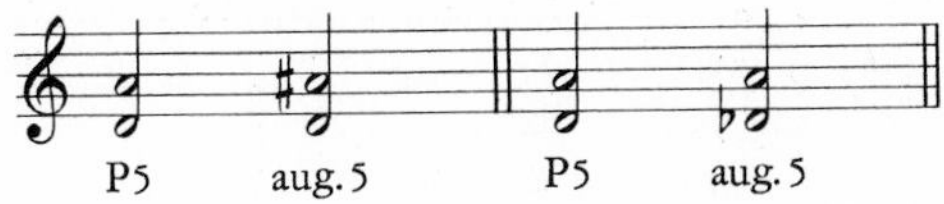

Name the following intervals.

M6 aug. 6

845.

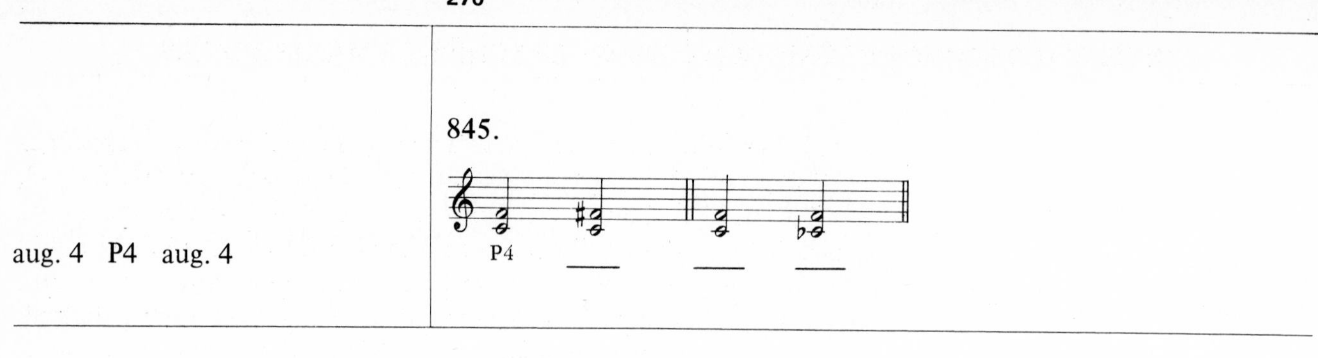

aug. 4 P4 aug. 4

INTERVALS ABOVE TONIC NOTES OTHER THAN C

846. Each of the intervals below can be analyzed as a modification of the interval already known.

Name the intervals.

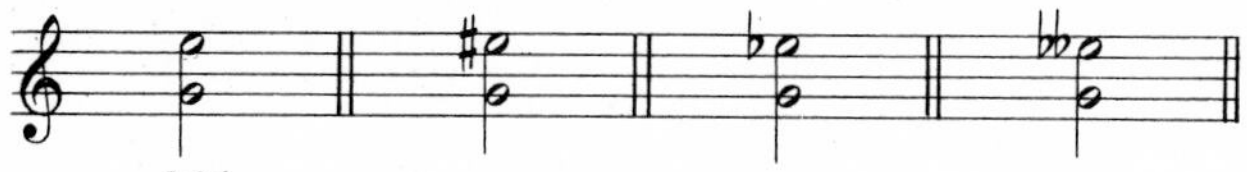

M6 ____ ____ ____

aug. 6 m6 dim. 6

847.

P4 ____ ____

dim. 4 aug. 4

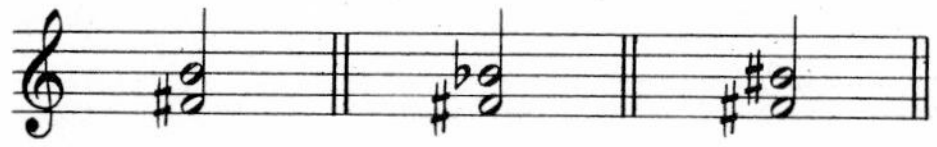

848.

M3 ____ ____ ____

aug. 3 m3 dim. 3

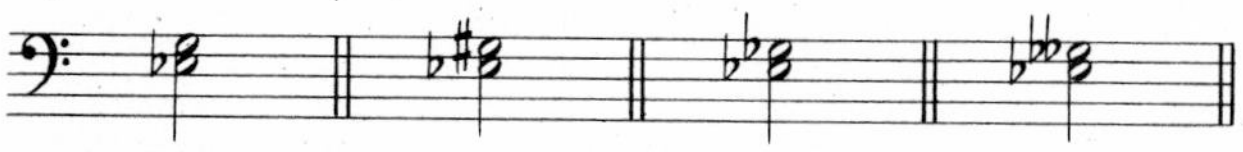

849.

M7 ____ ____ ____

m7 dim. 7 aug. 7

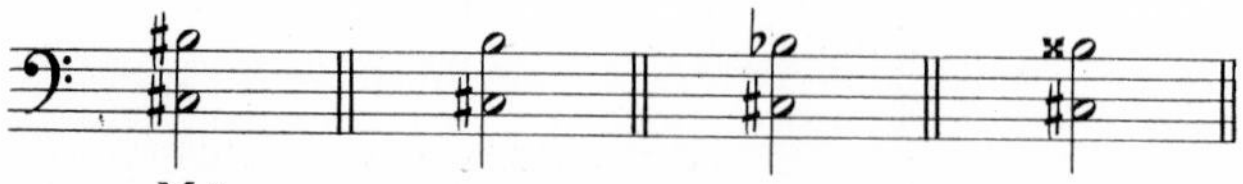

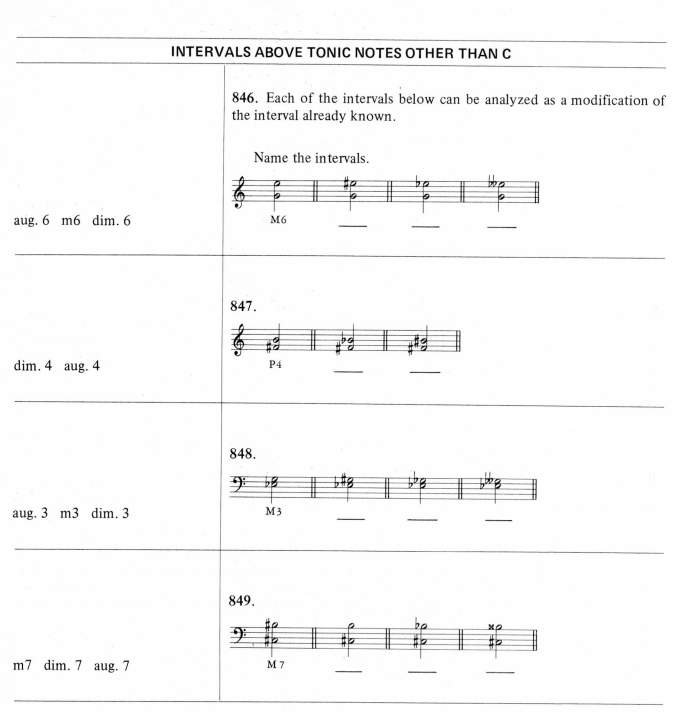

INTERVALS ABOVE NOTES WHICH CANNOT BE TONICS OF MAJOR SCALES

850. Notes other than the fifteen major-scale tonics can also appear as the lower notes of intervals. Included in these notes are D♯, E♯, G♯, A♯, B♯ and F♭ (double-sharped notes and double-flatted notes are studied later in this chapter). To determine intervals above these notes, (1) when the given bottom note is sharped, temporarily lower both notes of the interval one half step, or, if the bottom note is flatted, raised both notes one half step. The bottom note will then appear as one of the regular major-scale tonics. Analyze the resultant interval. (2) replace the original accidentals. The interval name is the same as determined in step (1). For example,

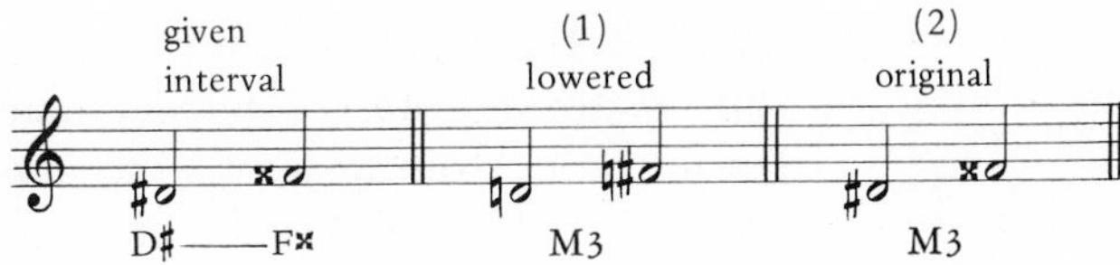

P5 P5

851. Continue to name intervals.

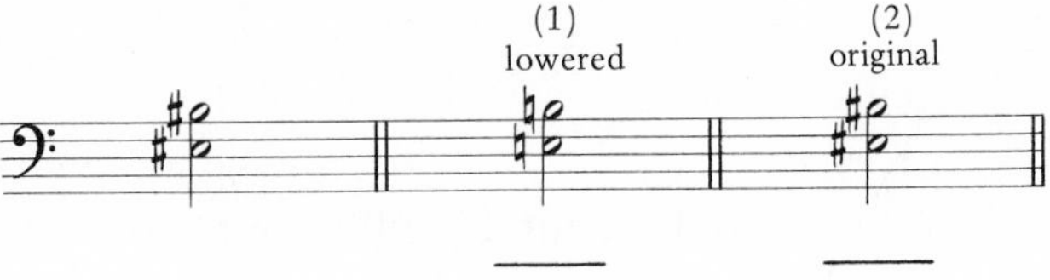

aug. 4

852.

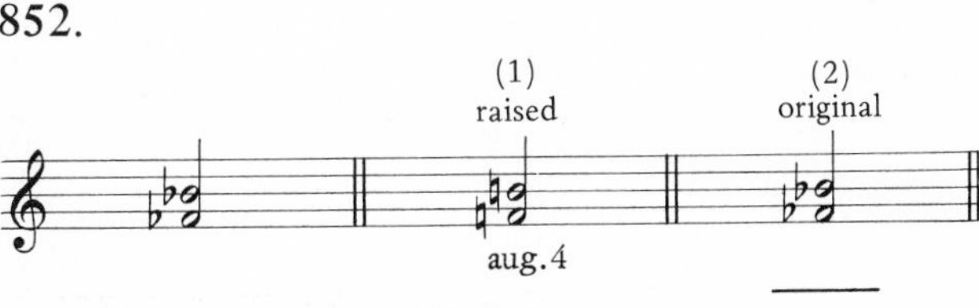

P4

853. When the lower note of an interval carries a double sharp or double flat, the lowering or raising of the interval by a half step may produce a known major-scale tonic on the bottom note. In this case, follow the same procedure (shown in Frame 850) to determine the interval.

Continue naming intervals (fill in blanks).

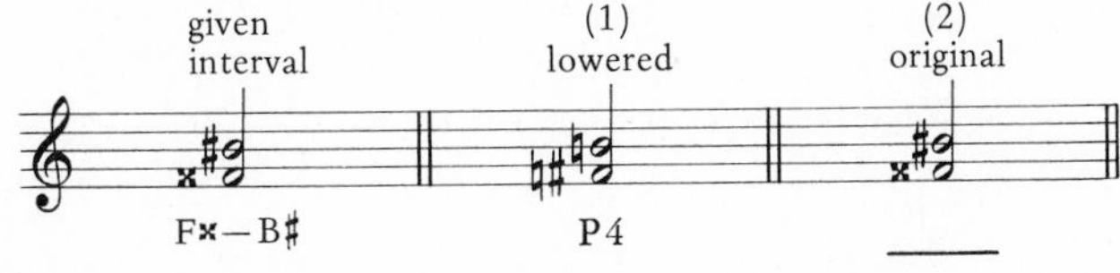

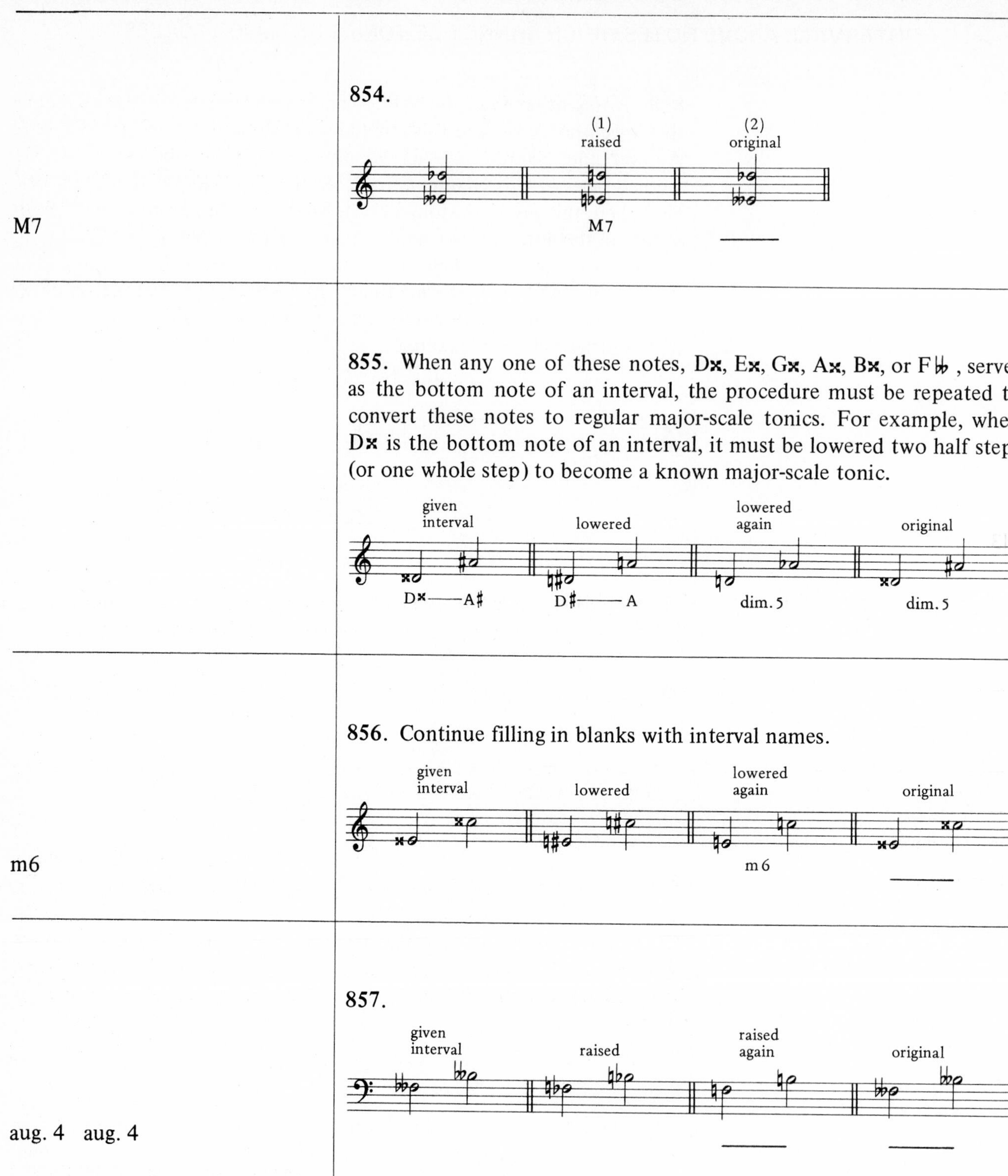

854.

M7

855. When any one of these notes, D𝄪, E𝄪, G𝄪, A𝄪, B𝄪, or F𝄫, serves as the bottom note of an interval, the procedure must be repeated to convert these notes to regular major-scale tonics. For example, when D𝄪 is the bottom note of an interval, it must be lowered two half steps (or one whole step) to become a known major-scale tonic.

856. Continue filling in blanks with interval names.

m6

857.

aug. 4 aug. 4

858. The procedures studied provide a theory for analysis of any type of interval above any pitch notation. The student's power of reasoning and musical insight, however, might provide more direct solutions for complex interval analysis. For example, we can see that any perfect octave occupies a line and space and both notes carry the same accidental, if any.

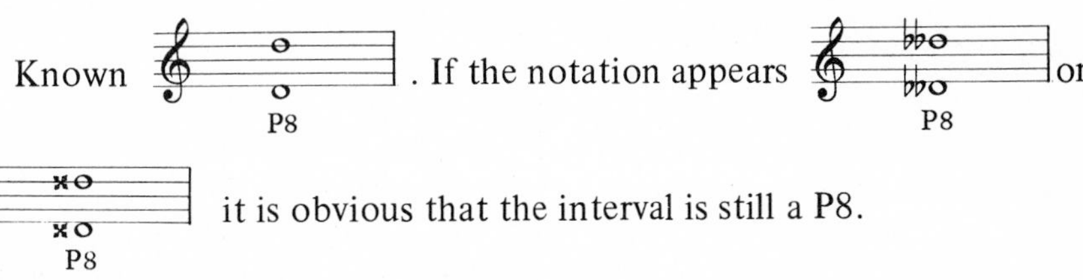

Known . If the notation appears or it is obvious that the interval is still a P8.

Name the intervals.

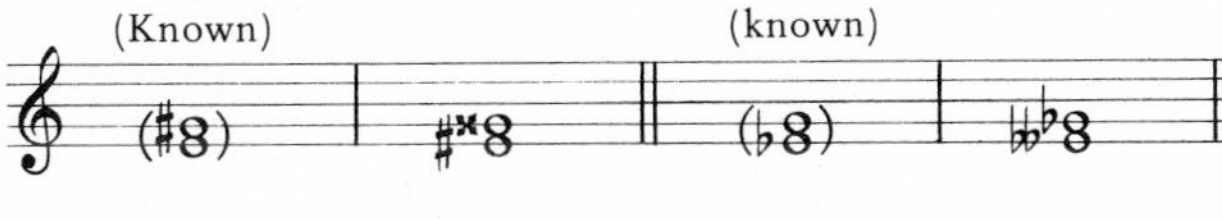

M3 M3

In your subsequent study of harmony, you will find another approach to interval study based on the context of intervals in chords.

ENHARMONIC INTERVALS

859. Enharmonic intervals are frequently obvious, especially when related to the keyboard. In fact, any diminished or augmented interval is enharmonic with some other type of interval (major, minor, or perfect). (Exceptions are the diminished fifth and augmented fourth,* which are enharmonic with each other.) For example, C up to G is an aug. 5 and C up to A♭ is a m6; G♯ and A♭ are enharmonic and are the same key on the keyboard.

Caution is due in this respect: proper spellings must be maintained according to the designation of the interval. It is wrong to say that C up to G♯ is a m6 or that C up to A♭ is an aug. 5 even though the intervals are enharmonic.

**Another name given to the augmented fourth is* tritone, *meaning "three whole tones." In recent years the term has been applied also to the diminished fifth. Although the aug. 4 and dim. 5 span four and five staff degrees, respectively, the interval is equal to three whole tones—hence the name* tritone.

false

860. The interval D up to A♯ may be called both an aug. 5 and m6 (true/false) ____________.

M3

861. Identify the following enharmonic intervals.

dim. 4 ________

dim. 7

862.

M6 ________

WRITING ALL TYPES OF INTERVALS

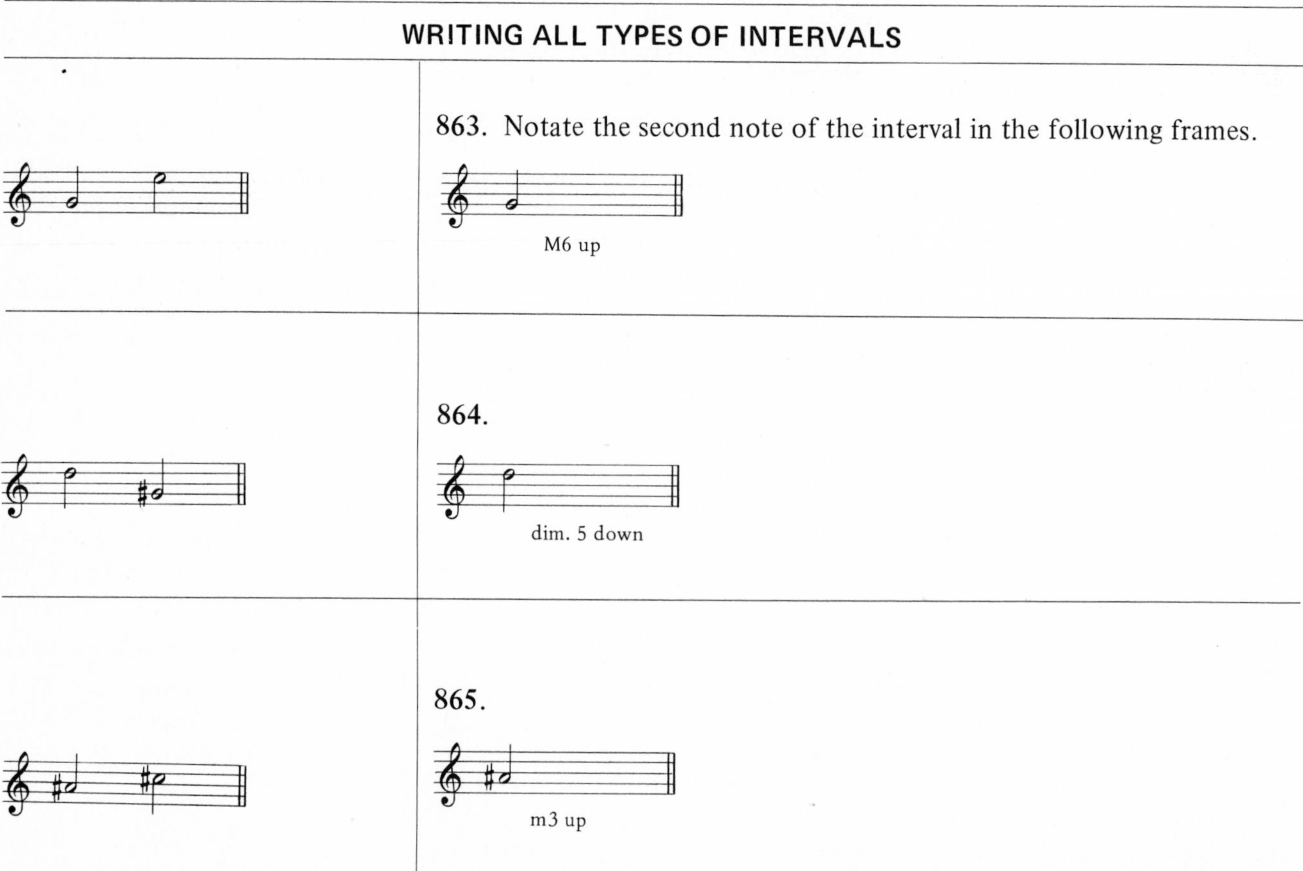

863. Notate the second note of the interval in the following frames.

M6 up

864.

dim. 5 down

865.

m3 up

866.
m7 down
867.
aug. 4 down
868.
aug. 1 up
869.
dim. 8 down
870.
aug. 2 up

INVERSION OF INTERVALS

871. The term *inversion* means the same in music as in everyday English usage: a turning upside down; reversal of position, order, or relation.

Figure (a) is turned upside down at (b).

Figure (b) is an ____________ of Figure (a).

inversion

---

872. A musical interval (a) becomes inverted (b) when rewritten with the original bottom note placed an octave higher, thus becoming the upper note, or with the original upper note placed an octave lower, thus becoming the bottom note. In either case, the resultant interval is the same:

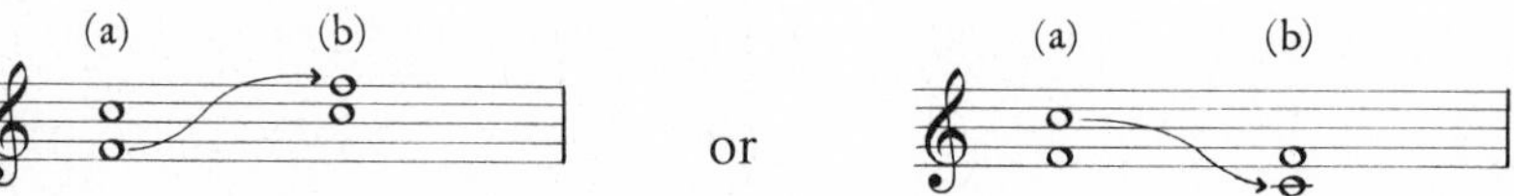

When an interval is rewritten so that the original bottom note becomes the upper or vice versa, the interval is said to be ____________.

inverted

---

873. The preceding inversions were achieved by rewriting one of the notes of the original interval either an octave higher or an octave lower. This manner of inversion is called *inversion at the octave.* Inversions at interval relationships other than the octave are also used in musical composition and are covered in more advanced studies. For our present purpose, we will consider inversion only at the octave and inversion only of simple intervals, none larger than a P8.

Invert each of the following intervals by rewriting the original bottom note an octave higher at (b):

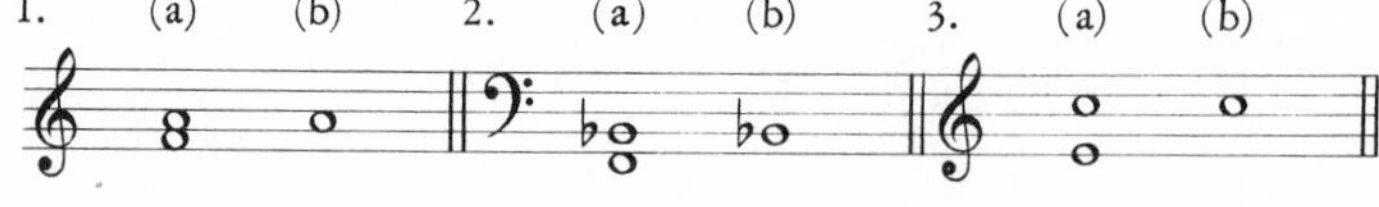

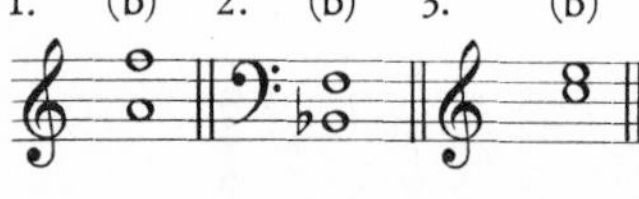

---

874. Continue to invert by rewriting the upper note an octave lower at (b).

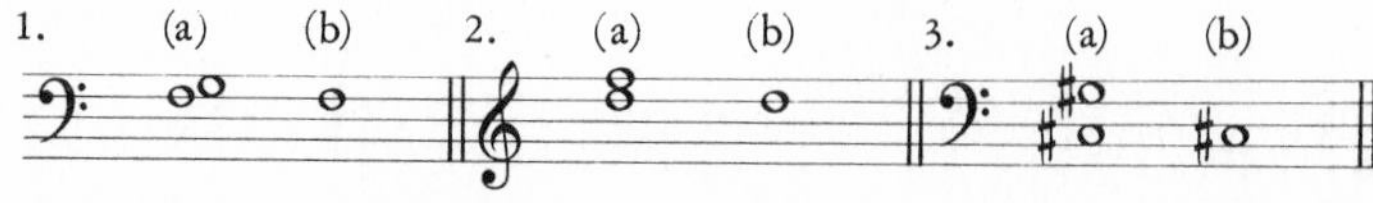

1. (b) 2. (b) 3. (b)

	875. Analyze the inversions found in Frame 873 by *quantity* names (numbers only).

	Original interval	*Inversion*
1. (b) 6	1. (a) 3	(b) 6
2. (b) 5	2. (a) 4	(b) ____
3. (b) 3	3. (a) 6	(b) ____

---

876. Analyze the inversions found in Frame 874 by quantity names.

	Original interval	*Inversion*
1. (b) 7	1. (a) 2	(b) ____
2. (b) 6	2. (a) 3	(b) ____
3. (b) 4	3. (a) 5	(b) ____

---

877. Inversion at the octave results in a mathematical ratio shown in the table below. Notice in the third column that the sum of an original interval and its resultant inversion equals an octave. Remember that in adding interval to interval, one pitch is counted twice and the resultant total is one less than the arithmetical sum (Frame 818, p. 259)

Original interval	*Inversion*	*Sum*
1	8	8 (not 9)
2	7	8
3	6	8
4	5	8
5	4	8
6	3	8
7	2	8
8	1	8

This information is useful in checking the accuracy of interval calculation.

See the inversions in Frames 873 and 874. Do all agree with the above table? ____ (yes/no).

yes

878. The *quality* of a perfect interval remains unchanged when inverted —that is, a perfect interval inverts to another perfect interval.

Fill in the blanks:

Original Interval	*Inversion*
(1) P 8	P 1
(2) P 5	____ ____
(3) P 4	____ ____
(4) P 1	____ ____

(1) P 1

(2) P 4

(3) P 5

(4) P 8

879. The quality of any interval other than perfect changes when inverted. If we consider *major* an antonym (opposite) of *minor*, and *diminished* an antonym of *augmented*, it is easy to remember the effect of interval inversion on these qualities:

Quality of Original Interval	*Quality of Inversion*
major (M)	minor (m)
minor (m)	major (M)
diminished (dim.)	augmented (aug.)
augmented (aug.)	diminished (dim.)

Fill in the blanks (use abbreviations):

Original Interval	*Inversion*
(1) M 2	m 7
(2) m 3	____ ____
(3) dim. 5	____ ____
(4) aug. 4	____ ____

(1) m 7

(2) M 6

(3) aug. 4

(4) dim. 5

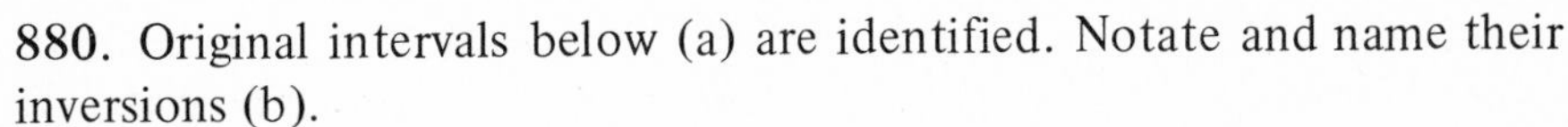

880. Original intervals below (a) are identified. Notate and name their inversions (b).

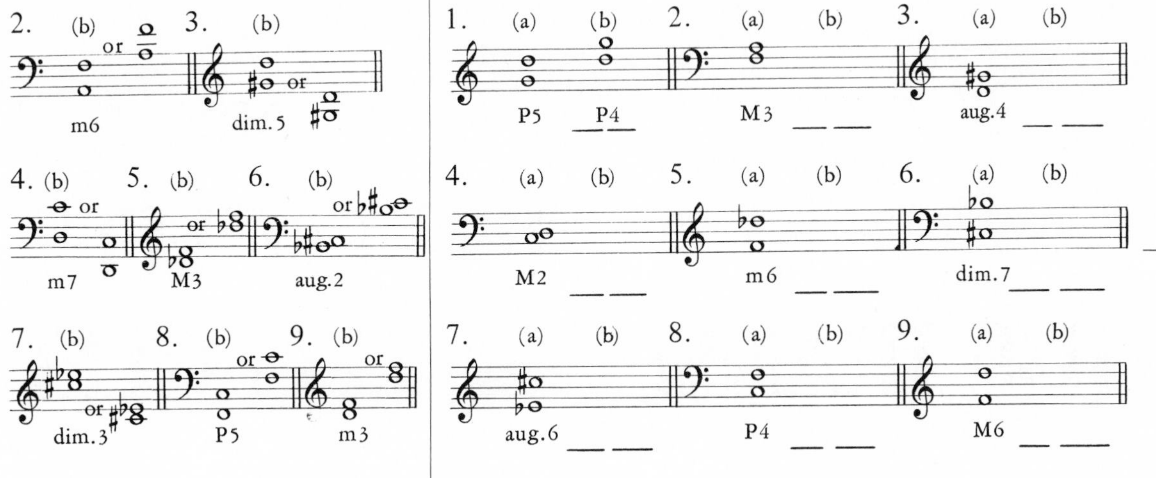

CHAPTER SUMMARY

1. A *minor interval* is one half step smaller than a major interval.

2. A *diminished interval* is one half step smaller than a minor or perfect interval.

3. An *augmented interval* is one half step larger than a major or perfect interval.

4. Any type of interval (M, m, P, dim., or aug.) is a modification by one half step of some other type of interval. By using knowledge of major and perfect intervals and modifications, we can calculate any type of interval.

5. Intervals above notes which cannot be tonics of major scales can be lowered or raised to simplify the notation or spelling. When the interval becomes apparent, return the analysis to the original notation.

6. Although intervals may be enharmonic, each must be spelled according to its own designation. C up to A♭ is a m6 and C up to G♯ is an aug. 5. Although enharmonic, one interval cannot be given the name of the other.

7. When an interval is rewritten so that the original bottom note becomes the upper or vice versa, the interval is said to be *inverted.* The constants of interval inversion are shown below:

Original interval	*Inversion*	*Original interval*	*Inversion*
P	P	1	8
M	m	2	7
m	M	3	6
dim.	aug.	4	5
aug.	dim.	5	4
		6	3
		7	2
		8	1

PRE-TEST
THE C CLEFS. THE TRANSPOSING G CLEF

1. Name this clef sign. 𝄡 ____ clef.

2. Name the clef when placed on the staff thus:

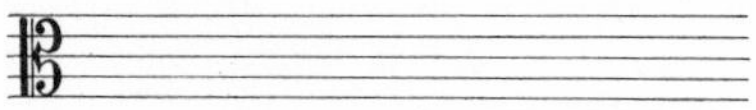

   ____________clef

3. Name the lines of the staff in question 2, beginning with the lowest line. ____ ____ ____ ____ ____

4. Name the clef when placed on the staff thus:

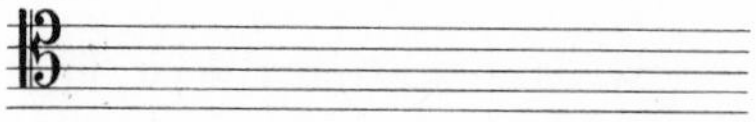

   ____________clef

5. Name the spaces of the staff in question 4, beginning with the lowest space. ____ ____ ____ ____

6. This clef, 𝄠, is used in vocal writing for the ____________ voice.

7. Place the key signature for D♭ major on this staff.

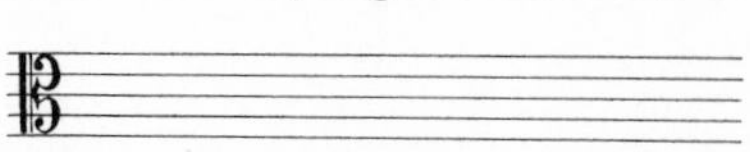

8. Place the key signature for B major on this staff.

ANSWERS

The score for each answer is given in parentheses after each answer. There is no partial credit for any answer. Place your score in the column at the right. Add this column for your total score.

	Score
1. C clef (10)	____
2. Alto clef or Viola clef (10)	____
3. F A C E G (15)	____
4. Tenor clef (10)	____
5. E G B D (15)	____
6. Tenor voice (10)	____
7. (15)	____
8. (15)	____

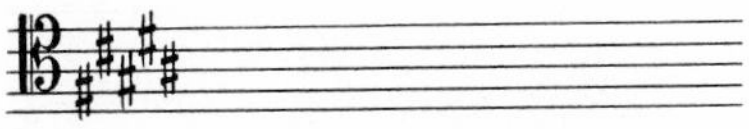

Total score: ____

Perfect score: 100

If your score is 80 or better, turn to Chapter 16, page 295. If your score is less than 80, continue with Chapter 15.

THE C CLEFS. THE TRANSPOSING G CLEF

Although the G clef and the F clef are the ones most frequently seen in music, another clef sign, the C clef, *is used in music by certain instruments, as can be seen in this example:*

Example 15.1.

Tchaikovsky, Symphony No. 4

On each of the staves for bassoon and viola you will see the clef sign 𝄡 *(also written* 𝄡 *or* 𝄡*), a C clef indicating the location of middle C on the staff. It is used in two different ways: (1) when found on the fourth line, as in the bassoon part, it is a* tenor clef, *and (2) when found on the third line, as in the viola part, it is an* alto clef *(also called* viola clef*).*

These two clefs, together with the treble and bass clefs already studied, comprise the four remaining in current usage from a system of ten different clefs in use before 1750.

Example 15.2.

Any or all of these clefs can be found in very early editions of music and in many modern publications of pre-nineteenth-century music. Only the alto and tenor clefs will be the concern of this chapter.

THE C CLEFS

881. The C clef is drawn by making two parallel vertical lines, the left line being a heavy line, ‖ to which is added a symbol resembling two Ↄ's (reversed C), one above the other.

Placed together, the complete clef is 𝄡

Draw several C clef signs.

𝄡 𝄡 etc.

882. When used on the staff, the clef is placed so that one line of the staff lies between the two Ↄ's.

𝄡

Place several C clefs on this line.

𝄡 𝄡 etc.

Answer	Frame
middle C (or c[1])	883. The line so designated by the C clef is always *middle* C (c[1]). The C clef always identifies the location of one particular C, which is ______________.
five	884. Historically, there were several uses of the C clef. In Example 15.2, page 283, how many different uses of the C clef do you find? ____.
alto clef tenor clef	885. Of these five uses, only two remain in common usage today, the *alto clef* and the *tenor clef.* Which of the two C clefs will you expect to find in music? a) ______________ clef b) ______________ clef

THE ALTO CLEF

Answer	Frame
third	886. When the C clef designates the third line of the staff as middle C, the C clef is called an *alto clef.* The alto clef identifies the__________ line as middle C.
F A C E G	887. When we know that the third line is C, we can determine the names of the other lines. F A C E G In the alto clef, the names of the lines, beginning with the first (lowest) line and spelling up, are ____ ____ ____ ____ ____

888. The names of the lines, beginning with the fifth (highest) line and spelling down, are

____ ____ ____ ____ ____

G E C A F

---

889. Identify by pitch names these notes in the alto clef.

____ ____ ____ ____ ____

F E C A G

890. With the names of the lines in the alto clef established, the names of the spaces become known.

G B D F

The names of the spaces, beginning with the first (lowest) space and spelling up are:

____ ____ ____ ____

G B D F

---

891. The names of the spaces, beginning with the fourth (highest) space and spelling down, are:

____ ____ ____ ____

F D B G

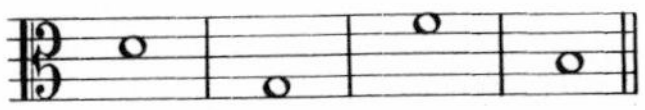

892. Identify by pitch names these notes in the alto clef.

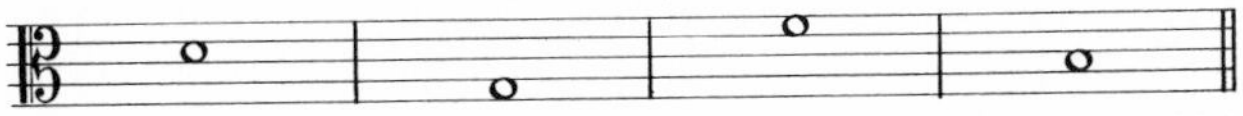

____ ____ ____ ____

D G F B

---

893. Continue as above.

____ ____ ____ ____ ____ ____

E B F F D A

894. Ledger lines and spaces may be used with the C clefs, in the same way as with the treble and bass clefs.

Fill in the remaining letter names.

G A B ___ ___ ___ ___ etc.

C D E F

895. Fill in letter names of ledger lines and spaces below the staff.

F E D ___ ___ ___ ___ etc.

Lowest note playable by the viola.

C B A G

896. The pitches middle C and above, located on the staff, are in the one-line octave, while those below middle C and on the staff are in the small octave.

Place given pitches on the staff in the correct octave registers as designated. Use whole notes.

g d^1 f g^1 b f^1

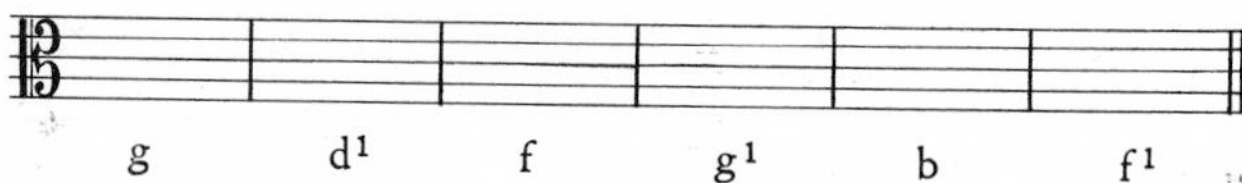

g d^1 f g^1 b f^1

897. Continue as above, adding notes in the two-line octave, and using ledger lines and spaces where necessary.

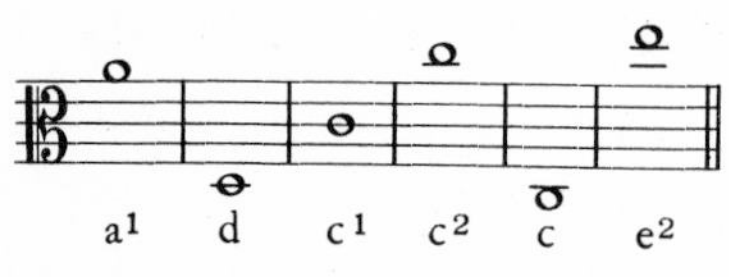

a^1 d c^1 c^2 c e^2

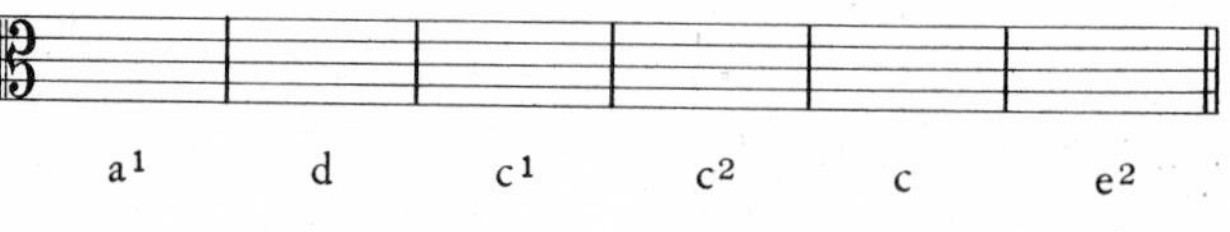

a^1 d c^1 c^2 c e^2

898. One orchestral instrument, the viola, uses the alto clef almost exclusively. This clef accommodates the range of the instrument, from c (small) to f^2 or higher with a minimum of ledger lines. To demonstrate the convenience of the alto clef to the violist, rewrite this viola part, first in the treble clef and then in the bass clef, noting in each case the need for very high or very low ledger lines. Remember that in the alto clef, the middle line is *middle c.*

Berlioz, Symphonie Fantastique

899. When you rewrite this passage in the alto clef, it will appear as the composer wrote it.

Brahms, Symphony No. 2

900. This example, rewritten in the alto clef, will appear as the composer wrote it.

Haydn, Quartet, Op. 74, No. 2

901. Key signatures in the alto clef look much the same as they do in the treble and bass clefs. The interval relationships of the accidentals are the same but are on different lines and spaces. In sharp keys, the first sharp (F♯) appears on the fourth space.

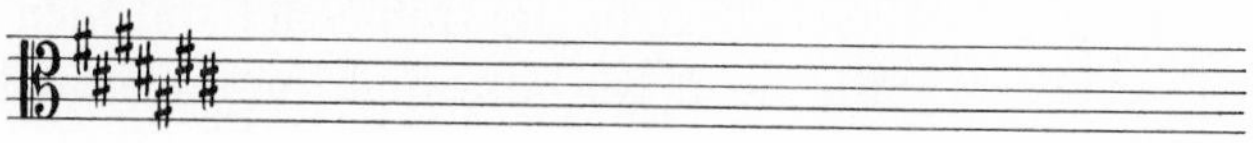

Write the signatures for these keys:

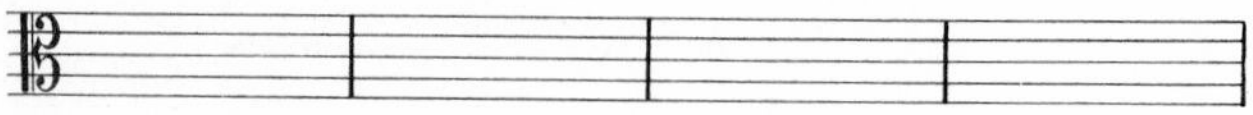

Major:	G	D	A	E
Minor:	E	B	F♯	C♯

902. Continue with these key signatures:

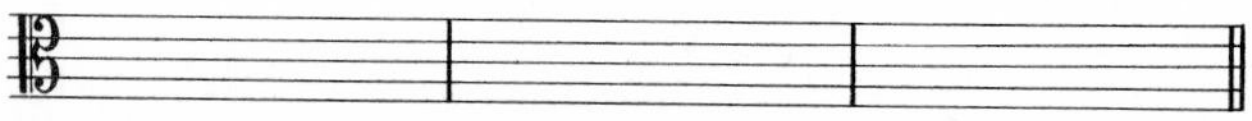

Major:	B	F♯	C♯
Minor:	G♯	D♯	A♯

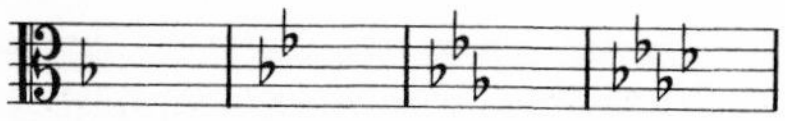

903. With flat keys, the first flat, (B♭), is placed in the second space.

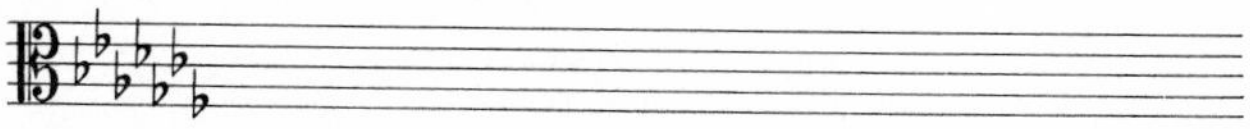

Write the key signature for these keys:

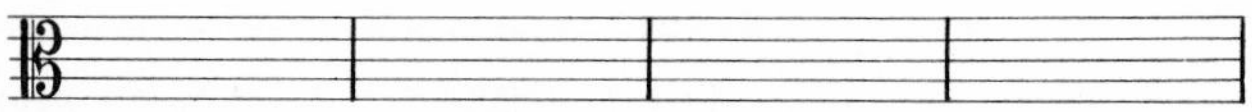

Major:	F	B♭	E♭	A♭
Minor:	D	G	C	F

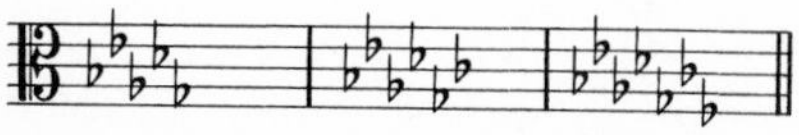

904. Continue with these key signatures:

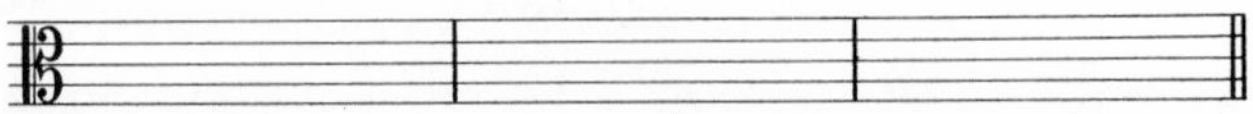

Major:	D♭	G♭	C♭
Minor:	B♭	E♭	A♭

THE TENOR CLEF

fourth	**905.** When the C clef designates the fourth line as middle C, the C clef is called a *tenor clef.* The tenor clef identifies the ______ line as middle C.
etc.	**906.** Place several C clefs on the fourth line of this staff.
tenor	**907.** On the fourth line, the C clef is known as a ______ clef.
D F A C E	**908.** When we know that the fourth line is C, we can determine the names of the other lines in the tenor clef: D F A C E In the tenor clef, the names of the lines, beginning with the first (lowest) line and spelling up, are ___ ___ ___ ___ ___
E C A F D	**909.** The names of the lines, beginning with the fifth (highest) line and spelling down, are ___ ___ ___ ___ ___
A E C D F	**910.** Identify by pitch names these notes in the tenor clef. ___ ___ ___ ___ ___

E G B D

911. With the names of the lines in the tenor clef established, the names of the spaces become known.

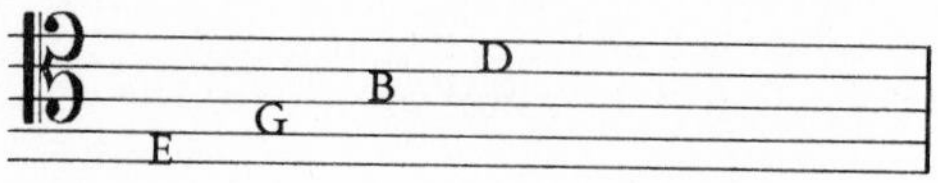

The names of the spaces, beginning with the first (lowest) space and spelling up, are:

____ ____ ____ ____

D B G E

912. The names of the spaces, beginning with the fourth (highest) space and spelling down, are:

____ ____ ____ ____

B E D G

913. Identify by pitch names these notes in the tenor clef.

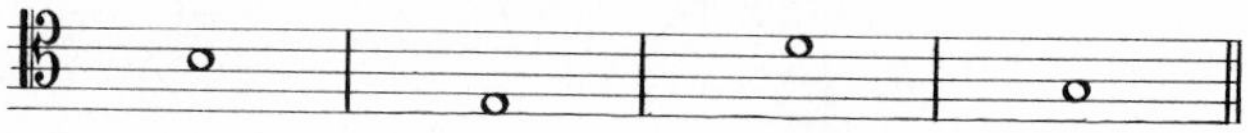

____ ____ ____ ____

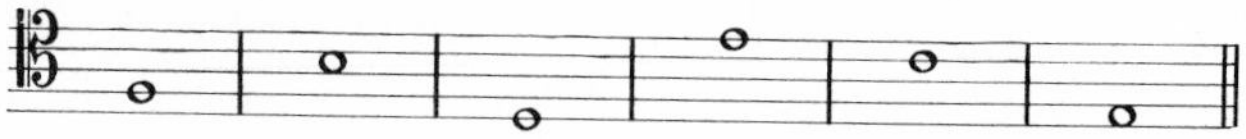

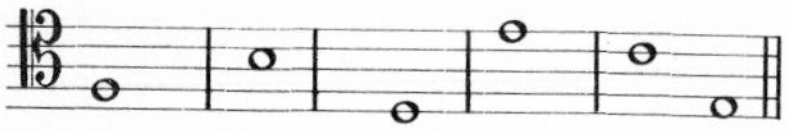

F B D E C E

914. Continue as above.

____ ____ ____ ____ ____ ____

A B C G A B C

915. Ledger lines and spaces may be used with the tenor clef. They are used sparingly below the staff, usually limited to the first one or two ledger lines and spaces, but used freely above the staff.

Fill in the remaining letter names.

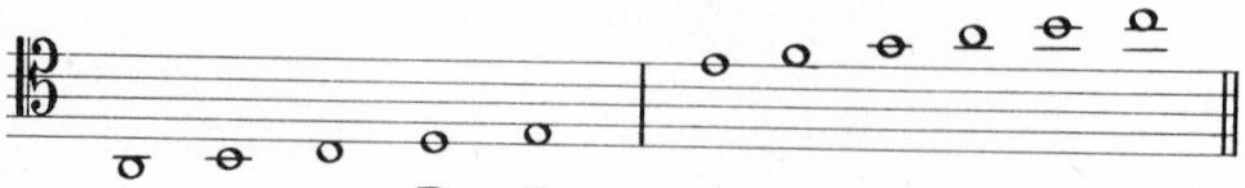

____ ____ ____ D E E F ____ ____ ____ ____

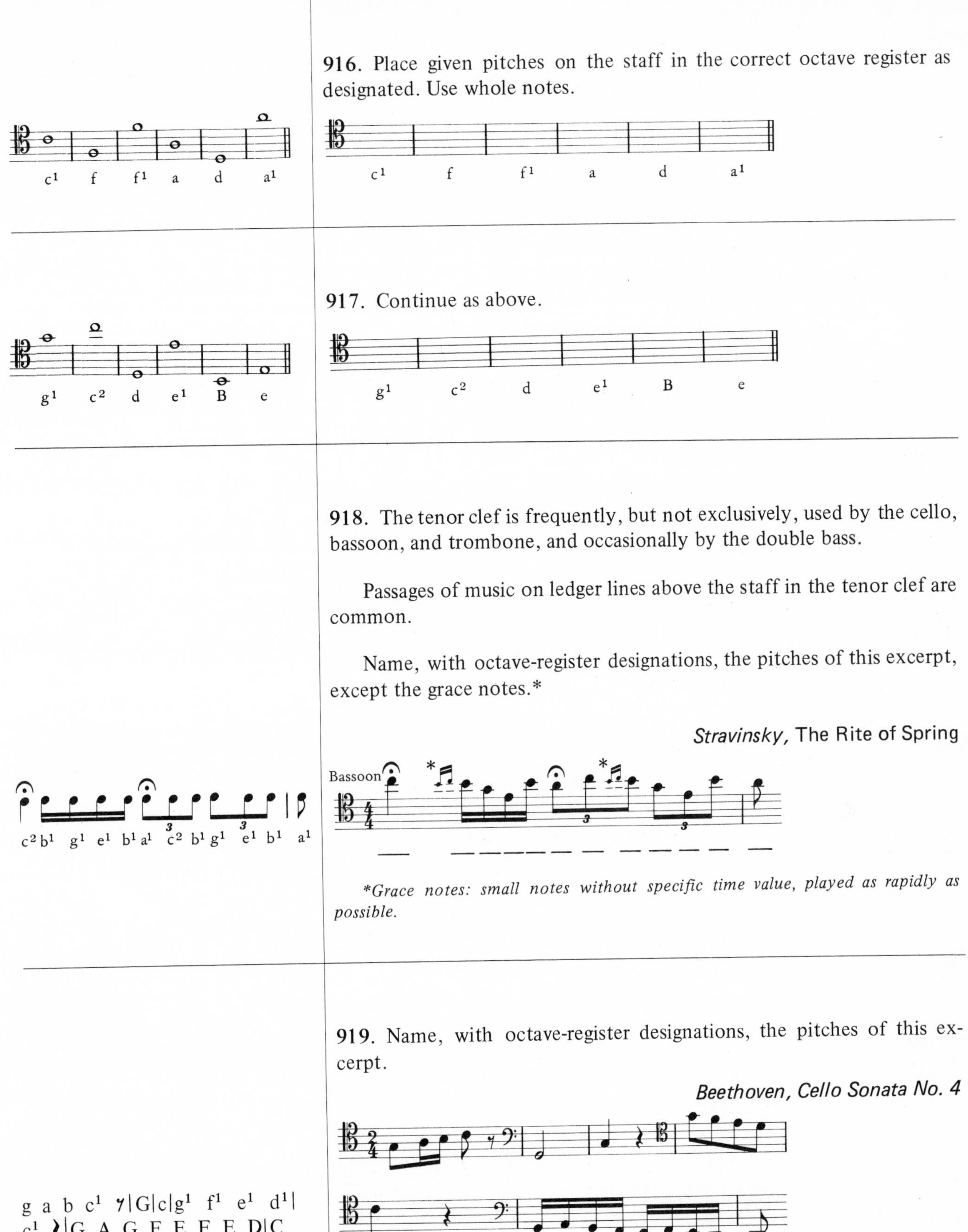

c¹ f f¹ a d a¹

916. Place given pitches on the staff in the correct octave register as designated. Use whole notes.

c¹ f f¹ a d a¹

g¹ c² d e¹ B e

917. Continue as above.

g¹ c² d e¹ B e

918. The tenor clef is frequently, but not exclusively, used by the cello, bassoon, and trombone, and occasionally by the double bass.

Passages of music on ledger lines above the staff in the tenor clef are common.

Name, with octave-register designations, the pitches of this excerpt, except the grace notes.*

Stravinsky, The Rite of Spring

Bassoon

c² b¹ g¹ e¹ b¹ a¹ c² b¹ g¹ e¹ b¹ a¹

**Grace notes: small notes without specific time value, played as rapidly as possible.*

919. Name, with octave-register designations, the pitches of this excerpt.

Beethoven, Cello Sonata No. 4

g a b c¹ 𝄾|G|c|g¹ f¹ e¹ d¹|
c¹ 𝄽|G A G F E F E D|C

920. When written with a tenor clef, this excerpt will appear as the composer wrote it.

Beethoven, Symphony No. 5

Bassoon

921. Continue as above.

Wagner, Tristan und Isolde

Cello

(See next frame for explanation of key signature.)

922. Key signatures appear differently in the tenor clef from any clef studied previously. The first sharp is placed on the second line, the second a fifth above, the third a fourth down, etc.

Write the signatures for these keys:

Major:	G	D	A	E
Minor:	E	B	F♯	C♯

923. Continue with these key signatures:

Major :	B	F♯	C♯
Minor:	G♯	D♯	A♯

924. In flat keys, the usual key signature pattern is found, with the first flat (B♭) on the third space.

Write the signature for these keys:

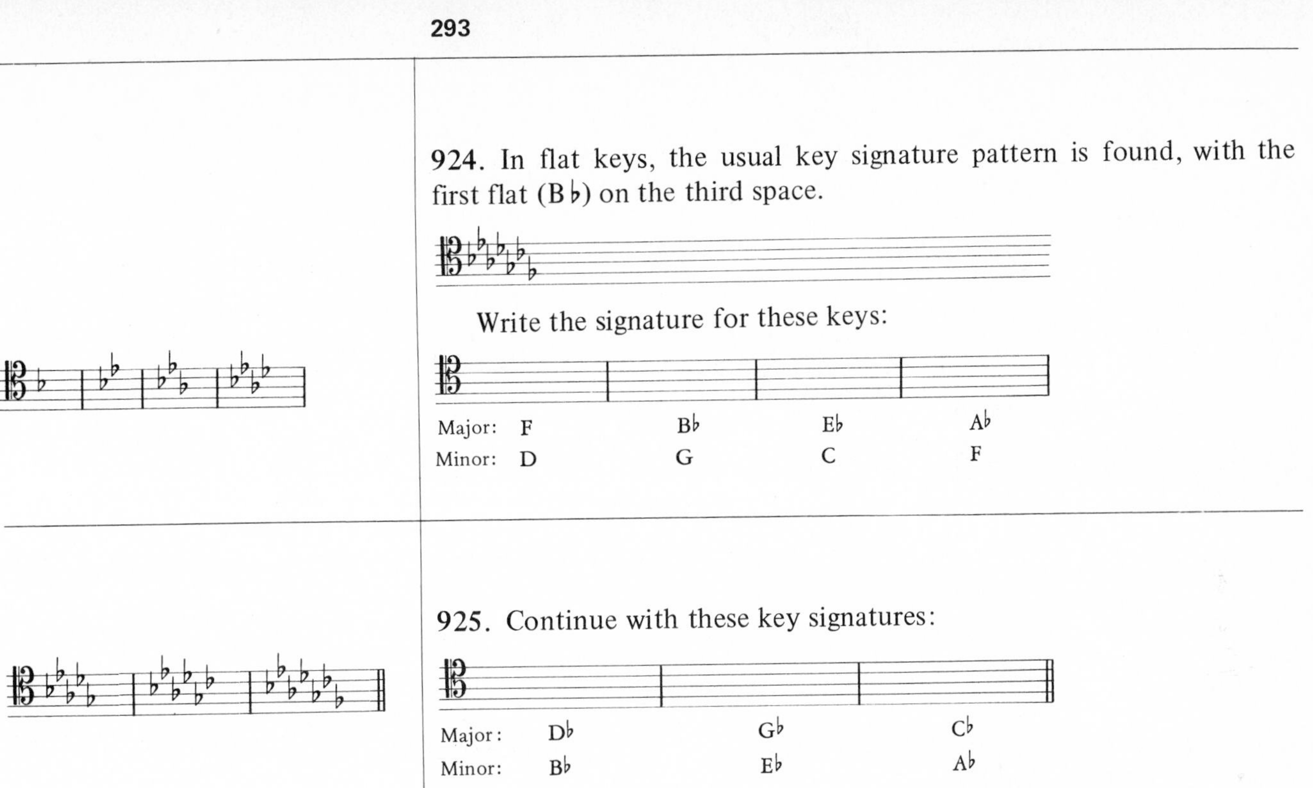

Major: F B♭ E♭ A♭
Minor: D G C F

925. Continue with these key signatures:

Major: D♭ G♭ C♭
Minor: B♭ E♭ A♭

THE TRANSPOSING G CLEF

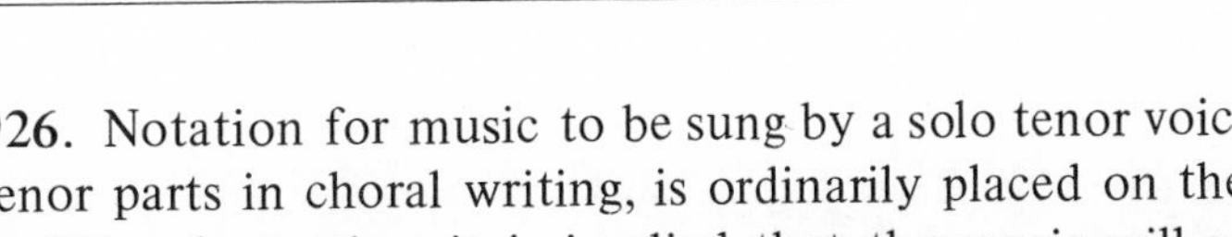

926. Notation for music to be sung by a solo tenor voice, and for most tenor parts in choral writing, is ordinarily placed on the treble clef. In traditional practice, it is implied that the music will sound an octave lower than written; hence it is a transposing clef. Besides the usual G clef, the sign 𝄠 (G clef with 8 below), indicating an octave lower than written, is widely used, while 𝄞𝄞 (double G clef) and a C clef on the third space can occasionally be found.

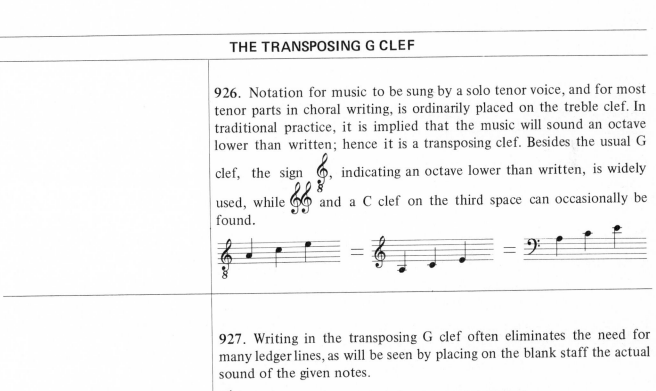

927. Writing in the transposing G clef often eliminates the need for many ledger lines, as will be seen by placing on the blank staff the actual sound of the given notes.

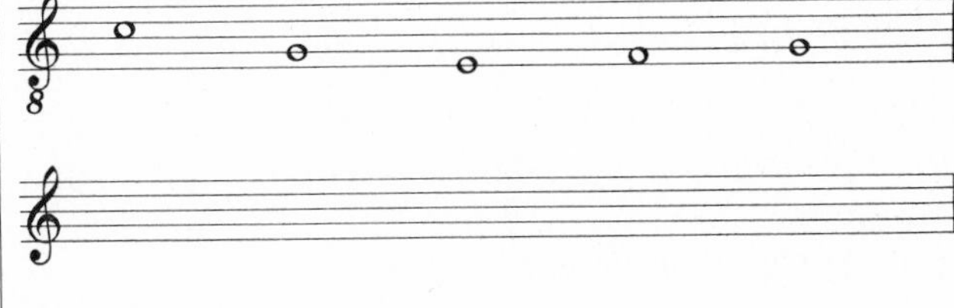

928. Continue with this example.

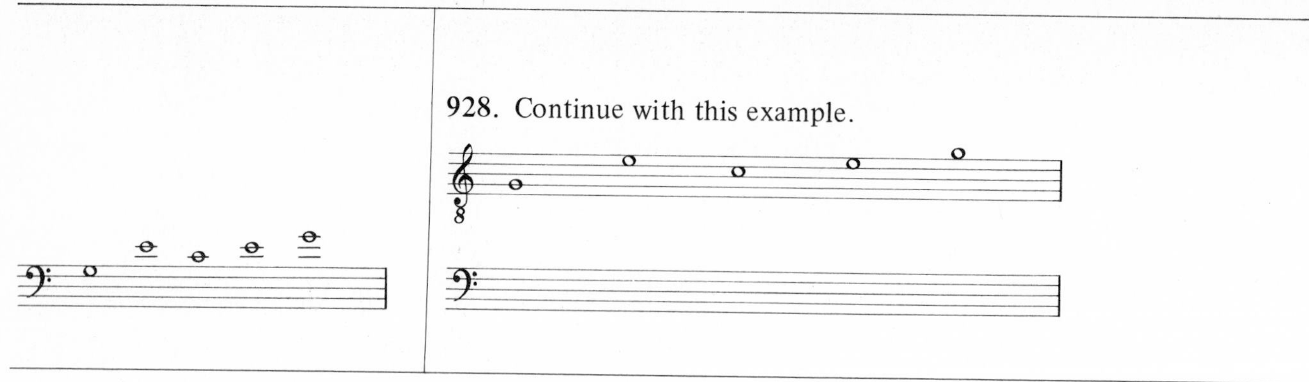

929. This excerpt, when placed on the transposing G clef, will appear as originally written by the composer. Answer appears at the end of this frame.

CHAPTER SUMMARY

1. The *C clef*, 𝄡, locates middle C on the staff.

2. When the two loops of the clef are found on either side of the third line, the clef is known as an *alto clef*.

3. When the two loops of the clef are found on either side of the fourth line, the clef is known as a *tenor clef*.

4. The C clefs are used principally by certain orchestral instruments. Use of these clefs instead of the treble and bass clefs eliminates the need for many ledger lines.

5. The *transposing G clef*, 𝄠, is used by the tenor voice and indicates that pitches sound an octave lower than written.

PRE-TEST
THE TRIAD

1. A chord consists of ____________ or more notes.

2. A triad consists of ____________ notes.

3. Chords and triads are built with consecutive intervals of the ____________.

4. Spell a major triad

   when A♭ is the root: ___ ___ ___

   when F𝄪 is the third: ___ ___ ___

   when C♯ is the fifth: ___ ___ ___

5. Spell a minor triad

   when F is the root: ___ ___ ___

   when A is the third: ___ ___ ___

   when F is the fifth: ___ ___ ___

6. Spell a diminished triad

when C♯ is the root: C♯ E G

when A♯ is the third: G A♯ C♯

when G♭ is the fifth: C E♭ G♭

7. Spell an augmented triad

when B♭ is the root: B♭ D F♯

8. The root of this triad is G.

9. In second inversion, the lowest note of the C♯ minor triad is ______.

ANSWERS

The score for each answer is given in parentheses after each answer. Place your score in the column at the right. Add this column for your score.

	Score
1. three (10)	____
2. three (10)	____
3. thirds (10)	____
4. A♭ C E♭ (5)	____
D♯ F𝄪 A♯ (5)	____
F♯ A♯ C♯ (5)	____
5. F A♭ C (5)	____
F♯ A C♯ (5)	____
B♭ D♭ F (5)	____

6. C♯ E G (5) ____

F𝄪 A♯ C♯ (5) ____

C E♭ G♭ (5) ____

7. B♭ D F♯ (5) ____

8. G (10) ____

9. G♯ (10) ____

Total score: ____

Perfect score: 100

If your score is 80 or better, you have completed the course presented in this text. You may wish to examine the music examples starting with Frame 1036, and, if you have not yet done so, study Appendix 1, Elementary Acoustics, *page 328.*

If your score is less than 80, continue with this chapter.

chapter sixteen

THE TRIAD

Harmony in music is the simultaneous sounding of two or more pitches. Music in Western culture, especially since c. 1600, is based to a great extent on the principles of harmony.

When two pitches sound together, the result is a harmonic interval. Sounding three or more pitches together results in a chord, its simplest form being a triad, which, as its name implies, consists of three different pitches. The study of the triad is the beginning of, and the basis for, the complete study of harmony.

CHORDS

930. Two different pitches sounding simultaneously produce an interval.

Sounding three or more notes of different pitch together produces a chord.

An interval consists of ________ pitches, while a chord consists of ________ or more pitches.

two, three

---

931. Chords are usually built using the interval of the third,*and, like harmonic intervals, are placed on the staff so that the notes are aligned vertically, indicating that all sound together.

1. 3rd
2. 3rd, 3rd
3. 3rd, 3rd, 3rd
4. 3rd, 3rd, 3rd, 3rd

Which of the above is not a chord? Number ____________.

This is true in most music written before the twentieth century. Later practice has added chords built in seconds, fourths, and fifths.

1 (an interval)

THE TRIAD

932. A chord consisting of three notes and built in thirds is called a *triad.*

Which chord in Frame 931 is a triad? No. ____.

2

---

933. A chord consisting of three notes and built in thirds is called a ________.

triad

---

934. Triads and other chords are usually built using intervals of a ________.

third

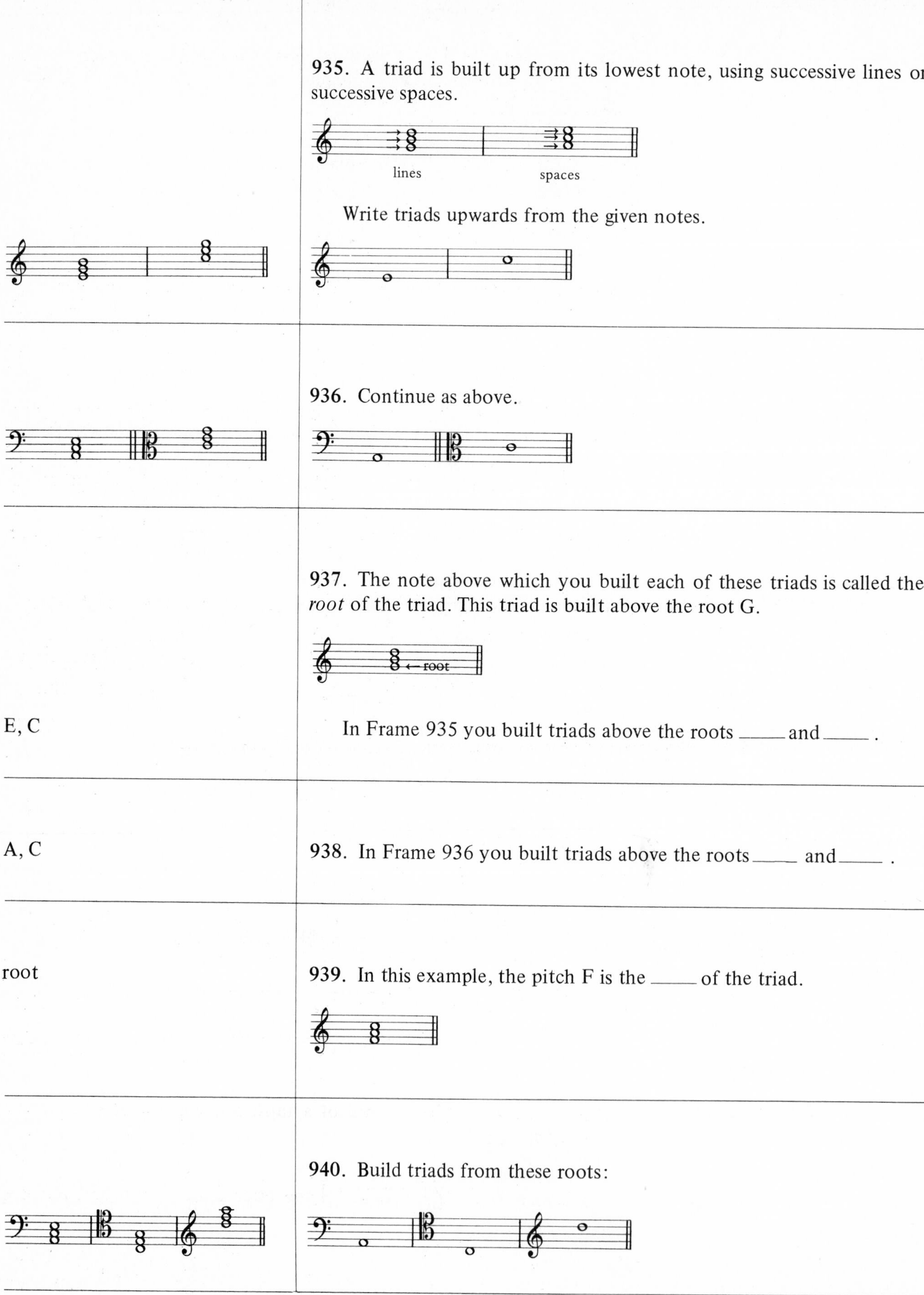

935. A triad is built up from its lowest note, using successive lines or successive spaces.

Write triads upwards from the given notes.

936. Continue as above.

937. The note above which you built each of these triads is called the *root* of the triad. This triad is built above the root G.

E, C

In Frame 935 you built triads above the roots ____ and ____.

A, C

938. In Frame 936 you built triads above the roots ____ and ____.

root

939. In this example, the pitch F is the ____ of the triad.

940. Build triads from these roots:

D

941. To spell a triad, begin with its root and continue upwards.

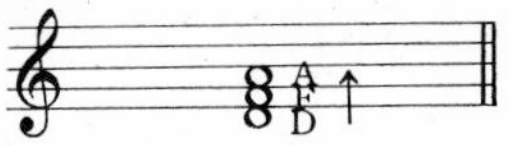

The spelling is D F A. The root is____.

A C E, C E G

D F A

942. Spell the triads you wrote in Frame 940.

____ ____ ____, ____ ____ ____,

____ ____ ____

A, C, D

943. The roots of the triads in Frame 942 are ____, ____, and ____ .

944. Spell a triad from the given root and place the triad on the staff.

Example  G ___ ___ Answer 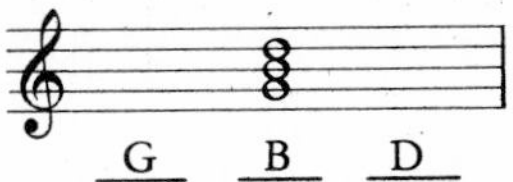 G B D

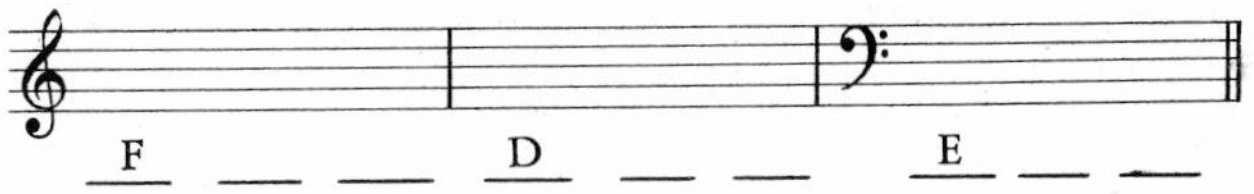

F ___ ___ D ___ ___ E ___ ___

F A C D F A or E G B

945. Continue with these.

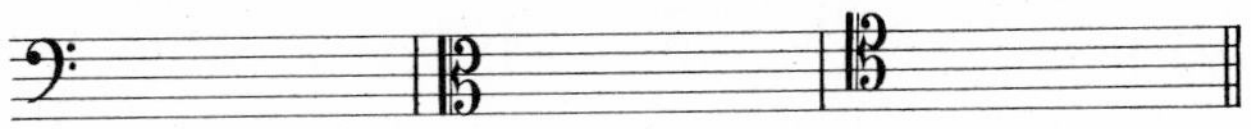

G ___ ___ B ___ ___ A ___ ___

G B D or B D F A C E

946. The note at the interval of a third above the root is called the *third* of the triad.

In this triad, 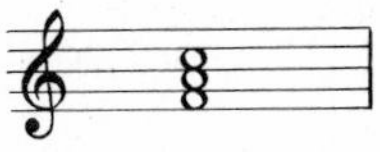 the pitch____ is the root and the pitch____ is the third.

F, A

947. In this triad, D is the ________ and F is the ________.

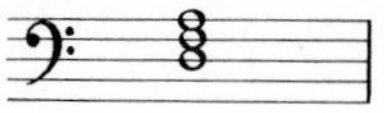

root, third

---

948. The remaining note of the triad is the *fifth* of the triad. Though it is at the interval of a third above the third of the triad, it is also at the interval of a fifth above the root of the triad.

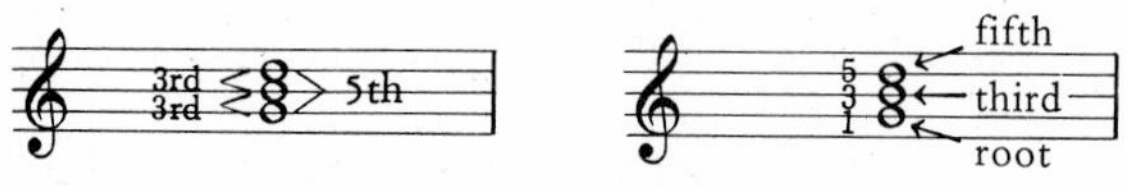

3rd 3rd 5th

5 3 1 fifth third root

The fifth of this triad is ____.

The triad is spelled ____ ____ ____.

D

G B D

---

949. Identify as root, third, or fifth the note to which each arrow points.

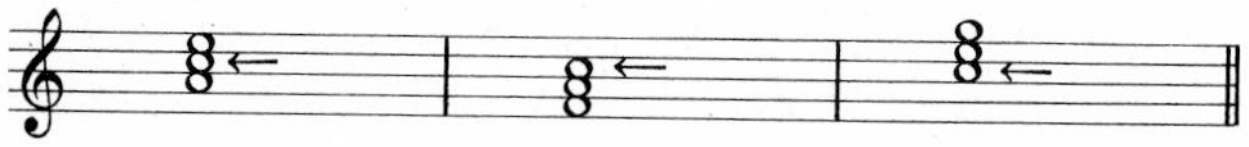

________ ________ ________

third, fifth, root

---

950. Triads consist traditionally of major and minor thirds. In the triad below, the interval from the root to the third is a ________ third, while the interval from the third to the fifth is a ________ third.

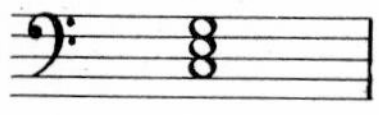

major, minor

---

951. Name the thirds in this triad.

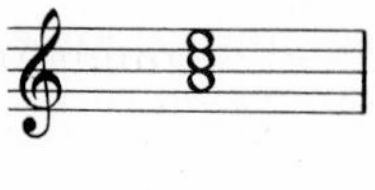

The root to the third is a ________ third.

The third to the fifth is a ________ third.

minor, major

952. Two other combinations of thirds are (1) two minor thirds and (2) two major thirds.

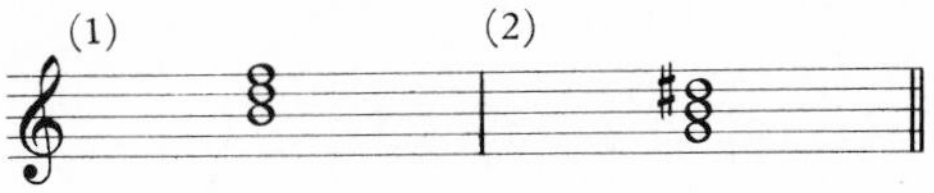

Spell the triad with two minor thirds. ____ ____ ____.

Spell the triad with two major thirds. ____ ____ ____.

B D F

G B D♯

---

953. The four combinations of thirds which will produce a triad are:

(1) major third plus minor third

(2) minor third plus ________ third

(3) minor third plus ________ third

(4) major third plus ________ third

(any order)

(1) major third plus minor third

(2) minor

(3) major

(4) major

---

954. Using the seven letters of the musical alphabet as roots, and using no accidentals, we can form seven triads.

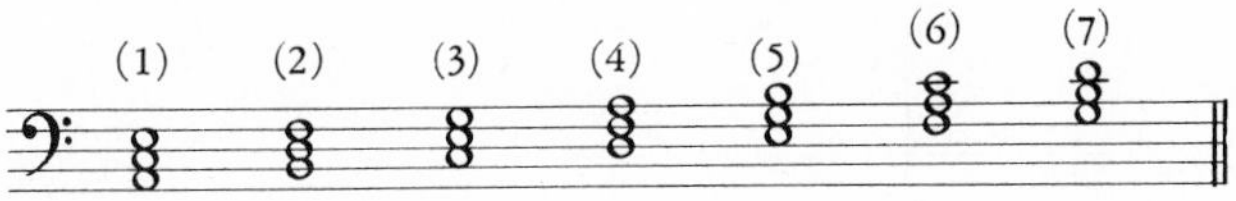

Spell each triad and name the intervals from the root up (use M for major and m for minor).

(1) A C E m3 + M3

(2) __ __ __ __ + __

(3) __ __ __ __ + __

(4) __ __ __ __ + __

(1) A C E m3 + M3

(2) B D F m3 + m3

(3) C E G M3 + m3

(4) D F A m3 + M3

---

955. Continue with the remaining triads.

(5) __ __ __ __ + __

(6) __ __ __ __ + __

(7) __ __ __ __ + __

(5) E G B m3 + M3

(6) F A C M3 + m3

(7) G B D M3 + m3

THE MAJOR TRIAD

956. A triad consisting of a major third plus a minor third (reading up from the root) is called a *major triad.*

m3
M3

In the major triad, the interval from the root to the fifth is a ________ ________ .

perfect fifth

---

957. Referring to Frame 954, circle below the roots of those triads which are major.

A B C D E F G

A B (C) D E (F) (G)

---

958. Spell major triads above these roots:

F ____ ____

C ____ ____

G ____ ____

F A C

C E G

G B D

---

959. Other spellings of major triads require accidentals. Without an accidental, the first triad below is not major. Adding a sharp to the third of the triad causes the intervals to be correct for a major triad (M3 + m3).

M3
m3

m3
M3

major triad

This major triad is spelled ____ ____ ____

A C♯ E

---

960. Make these triads major without altering the root. Place spelling below each triad. (One of these requires two accidentals).

___ ___ ___ ___ ___ ___ ___ ___ ___

E G♯ B D F♯A B D♯ F♯

961. Major triads may also be built on chromatically altered roots.

(1) (2)

m3 M3 m3 M3

Spell the triads above.

(1) ___ ___ ___ (2) ___ ___ ___

(1) F♯ A♯ C♯

(2) A♭ C E♭

---

962. Selecting degrees 1, 3, and 5 from the major scale will automatically produce a major triad.

1 3 5

M3 m3 m3 M3

Spell the major triad above.

___ ___ ___

E♭ G B♭

---

963. Spell the major triad found as 1, 3, and 5 of this scale.

1 of the scale is ___.

3 of the scale is ___.

5 of the scale is ___.

The triad is spelled ___ ___ ___.

1 is D

3 is F♯

5 is A

Triad: D F♯ A

---

964. Since there are fifteen major keys, fifteen major triad spellings may be found this way. Starting with the key of C and moving around the sharp side of the circle of fifths, spell the major triad from scale step 1 of each of these keys:

C major C E G

G major G B D

D major ___ ___ ___

A major ___ ___ ___

C: C E G

G: G B D

D: D F♯ A

A: A C♯ E

	965. Continue with these keys.
E: E G♯ B	E major ____ ____ ____
B: B D♯ F♯	B major ____ ____ ____
F♯: F♯ A♯ C♯	F♯ major ____ ____ ____
C♯: C♯ E♯ G♯	C♯ major ____ ____ ____

	966. Continue in the same way, moving from C major to the flat side of the circle of fifths.
C: C E G	C major C E G
F: F A C	F major F A C
B♭: B♭ D F	B♭ major ____ ____ ____
E♭: E♭ G B♭	E♭ major ____ ____ ____

	967. Continue with these keys.
A♭: A♭ C E♭	A♭ major ____ ____ ____
D♭: D♭ F A♭	D♭ major ____ ____ ____
G♭: G♭ B♭ D♭	G♭ major ____ ____ ____
C♭: C♭ E♭ G♭	C♭ major ____ ____ ____

968. Other pitch names with ♯ or ♭ may serve as roots of chords, and the chord may be spelled by interval, M3 + m3. Alternately, when the root carries a sharp, spell the triad as though the root were natural, and then raise all three members by one half step. Or, if the root carries a ♭, spell the triad as though the root were natural, and then lower all three members by one half step.

Example: root, D♯, D F♯A –D♯ F𝄪 A♯

E♯: ____ ____ ____

G♯: ____ ____ ____

E♯: E♯ G𝄪 B♯

G♯: G♯ B♯ D♯

---

969. Continue as above.

A♯: ____ ____ ____

B♯ : ____ ____ ____

F♭: ____ ____ ____

A♯: A♯ C𝄪 E♯

B♯: B♯ D𝄪 F𝄪

F♭: F♭ A♭ C♭

---

970. Spell each of these triads in the spaces below the staff.

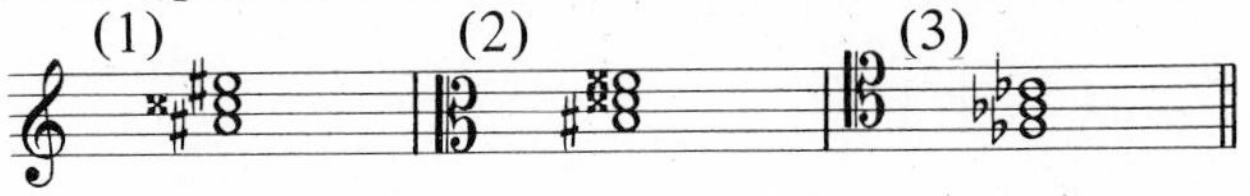

(1) (2) (3)

____ ____ ____ ____ ____ ____ ____ ____ ____

(1) A♯ C𝄪 E♯

(2) B♯ D𝄪 F𝄪

(3) F♭ A♭ C♭

---

971. Four additional major triads, each built on a doubly flatted root, can be found in music. These may be spelled by interval, or, spell the triad with a single flat on the root and then lower each member of the triad one accidental.

E♭ G B♭ E𝄫 G♭ B𝄫

Do the same with these:

B♭ ____ ____ B𝄫 ____ ____

A♭ ____ ____ A𝄫 ____ ____

D♭ ____ ____ D𝄫 ____ ____

B♭ D F, B𝄫 D♭ F♭

A♭ C E♭, A𝄫 C♭ E𝄫

D♭ F A♭, D𝄫 F♭ A𝄫

972. Spell these major triads.
A♭♭ C♭ E♭♭,
B♭♭ D♭ F♭
973. Continue with these triads.
D♭♭ F♭ A♭♭,
E♭♭ G♭ B♭♭
974. The third of a major triad is given on the staff. Notate the root and fifth. Spell the triad.
F A C D♭ F A♭ B♭ D F
975. Spell major triads when the third is given. Place the triad on the staff.
B G F×
G B D E♭ G B♭ D♯ F× A♯
976. The fifth of a major triad is given on the staff. Supply the root and third. Spell the triad.
C E G A C♯ E F♯ A♯ C♯

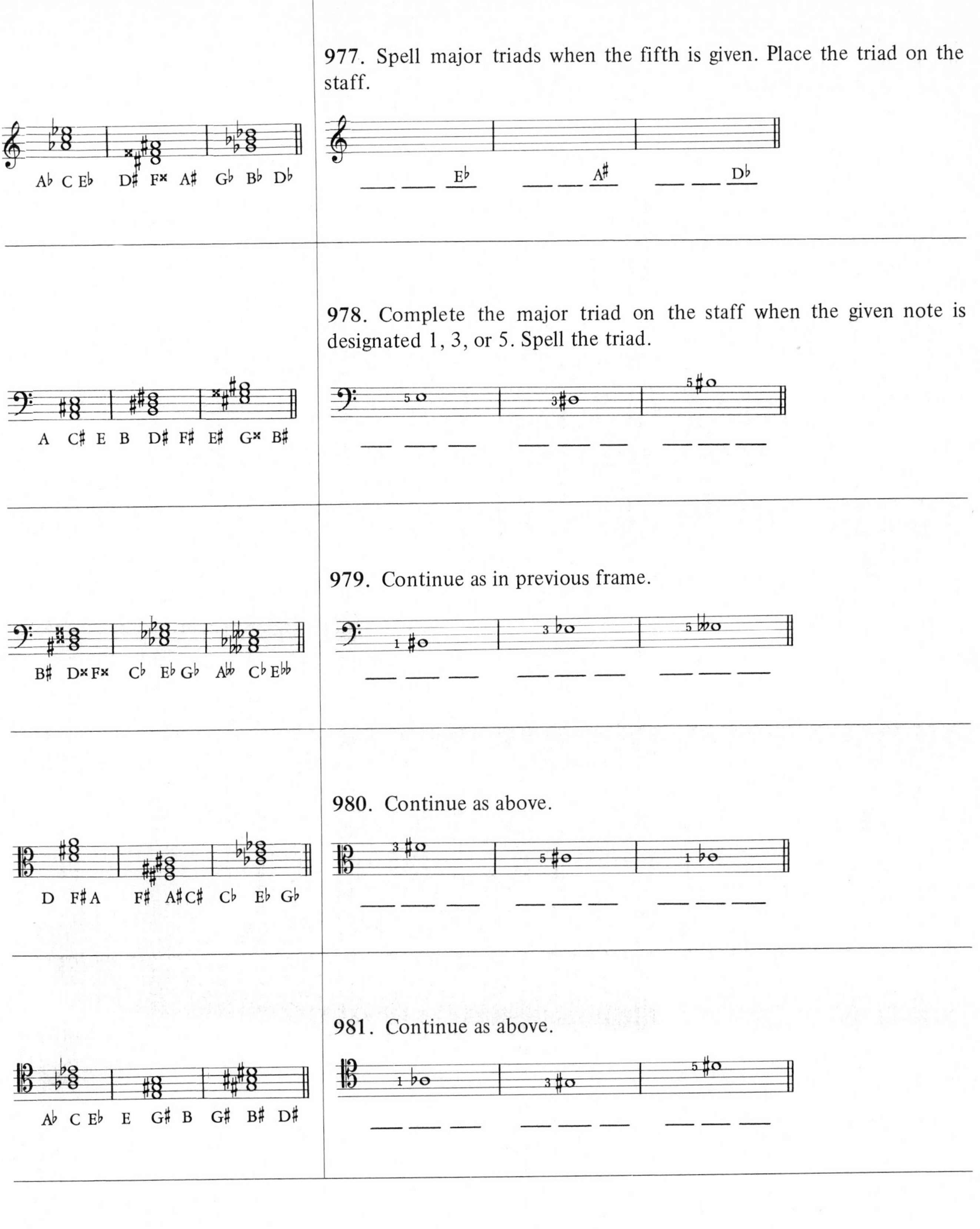
A♭ C E♭ D♯ F𝄪 A♯ G♭ B♭ D♭
977. Spell major triads when the fifth is given. Place the triad on the staff.
E♭
A♯
D♭
A C♯ E B D♯ F♯ E♯ G𝄪 B♯
978. Complete the major triad on the staff when the given note is designated 1, 3, or 5. Spell the triad.
5
3
5
B♯ D𝄪 F𝄪 C♭ E♭ G♭ A♭♭ C♭ E♭♭
979. Continue as in previous frame.
1
3
5
D F♯ A F♯ A♯ C♯ C♭ E♭ G♭
980. Continue as above.
3
5
1
A♭ C E♭ E G♯ B G♯ B♯ D♯
981. Continue as above.
1
3
5

THE MINOR TRIAD

Answer	Frame
perfect fifth	982. A triad consisting of a minor third plus a major third (reading up from the root) is called a *minor triad.* M3 m3 Like the major triad, the interval from the root to the fifth of the minor triad is a ________ ________.
Ⓐ B C Ⓓ Ⓔ F G	983. Here, repeated from Frame 954, are the triads built on the seven letters of the musical alphabet. A B C D E F G Circle those letter names which are roots of minor triads.
E G B A C E D F A	984. Spell minor triads above these roots. E ___ ___ A ___ ___ D ___ ___
C E♭ G	985. Other triads from Frame 983 may be made minor by adding accidentals which will produce a minor third and a major third successively above each root. m3 M3	M3 m3 This minor triad is spelled ___ ___ ___.
F A♭ C B D F♯ G B♭ D	986. Make these triads minor, and place minor triad spelling below the staff (do not alter the root). ___ ___ ___ ___ ___ ___ ___ ___ ___

Answer	Frame
(1) F♯ A C♯, (2) B♭ D♭ F	987. Minor triads may be built on chromatically altered roots. (1) M3 m3 (2) M3 m3 Spell these triads: (1) ___ ___ ___, (2) ___ ___ ___
F A♭ C	988. Selecting the first, third, and fifth scale steps of a minor scale will automatically produce a minor triad. 1 3 5 m3 M3 The minor triad on F is spelled ___ ___ ___.

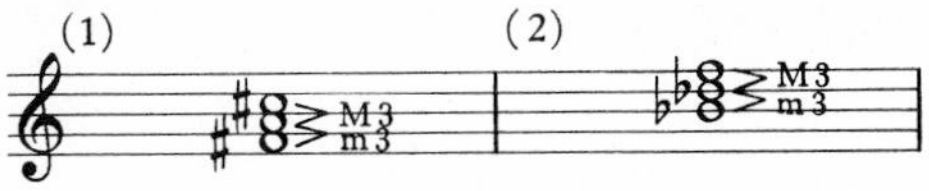

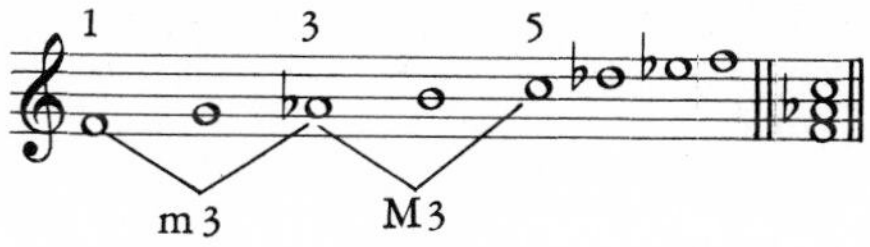

989. Starting with A minor and moving around the sharp side of the circle of fifths, spell the minor triad from 1 of the scale of each of these keys.

Answer		Frame	
A minor	A C E	A minor	A C E
E minor	E G B	E minor	E G B
B minor	B D F♯	B minor	___ ___ ___
F♯ minor	F♯ A C♯	F♯ minor	___ ___ ___

990. Continue as above.

Answer		Frame	
C♯ minor	C♯ E G♯	C♯ minor	___ ___ ___
G♯ minor	G♯ B D♯	G♯ minor	___ ___ ___
D♯ minor	D♯ F♯ A♯	D♯ minor	___ ___ ___
A♯ minor	A♯ C♯ E♯	A♯ minor	___ ___ ___

	991. Continue in the same way, moving from A minor through the flat side of the circle of fifths.
A minor A C E	A minor A C E
D minor D F A	D minor D F A
G minor G B♭ D	G minor ___ ___ ___
C minor C E♭ G	C minor ___ ___ ___

	992. Continue with these keys.
F minor F A♭ C	F minor ___ ___ ___
B♭ minor B♭ D♭ F	B♭ minor ___ ___ ___
E♭ minor E♭ G♭ B♭	E♭ minor ___ ___ ___
A♭ minor A♭ C♭ E♭	A♭ minor ___ ___ ___

993. There remain six minor triads, often found in music, whose roots are not the first steps of a scale. Spell each by interval (m3 plus M3):

C♭ E𝄫 G♭

m3 M3

or, using a minor triad built on an unaltered root, raise or lower each note of the triad a half step in the direction the root is changed:

C E♭ G — C♭ E𝄫 G♭

Continue with these:

B D F♯ B♯ D♯ F𝄪	B ___ ___ B♯ ___ ___
D F A D♭ F♭ A♭	D ___ ___ D♭ ___ ___

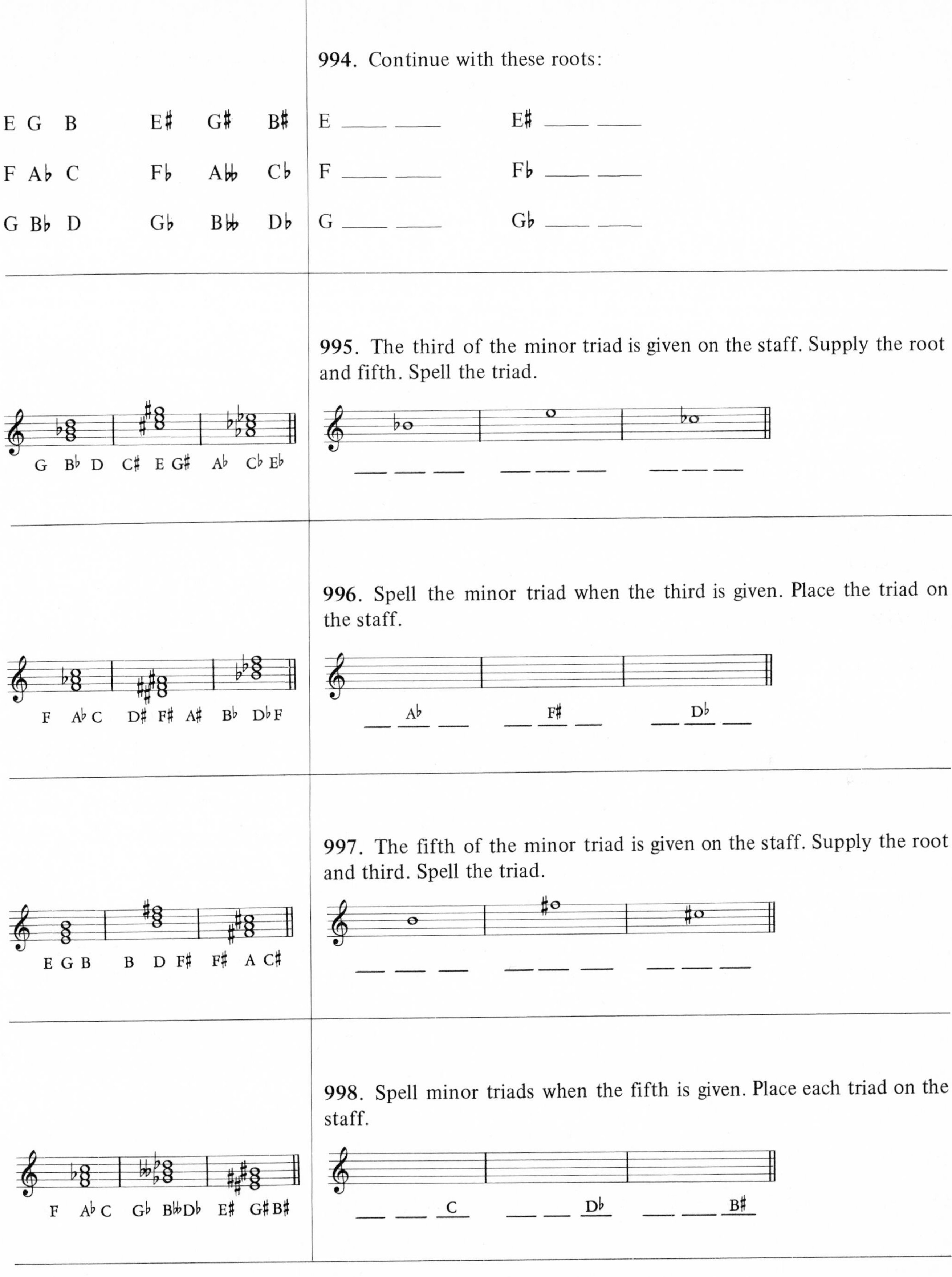

E G B E♯ G♯ B♯

F A♭ C F♭ A♭♭ C♭

G B♭ D G♭ B♭♭ D♭

994. Continue with these roots:

E ___ ___ E♯ ___ ___

F ___ ___ F♭ ___ ___

G ___ ___ G♭ ___ ___

995. The third of the minor triad is given on the staff. Supply the root and fifth. Spell the triad.

___ ___ ___ ___ ___ ___ ___ ___ ___

996. Spell the minor triad when the third is given. Place the triad on the staff.

___ A♭ ___ ___ F♯ ___ ___ D♭ ___

997. The fifth of the minor triad is given on the staff. Supply the root and third. Spell the triad.

___ ___ ___ ___ ___ ___ ___ ___ ___

998. Spell minor triads when the fifth is given. Place each triad on the staff.

___ ___ C ___ ___ D♭ ___ ___ B♯

Answer	Frame
	999. Spell major and minor triads from root, third, or fifth as indicated.

Answer	Triad	Root	Third	Fifth
B♭ D F	Major	B♭	____	____
C♯ E G♯	Minor	____	E	____
D♭ F A♭	Major	____	____	A♭
G♯ B D♯	Minor	____	____	D♯
D♯ F𝄪 A♯	Major	____	F𝄪	____

THE DIMINISHED TRIAD

Answer	Frame
diminished	1000. A triad consisting of two minor thirds is called a *diminished* triad. [staff: diminished triad with m3 / m3 labels] The interval from the root to the fifth is not a perfect fifth, as in major and minor triads, but is a ____________ fifth.
minor third minor third	1001. In a diminished triad, the interval from root to third is a ____________ ____________, and the interval from third to fifth is a ____________ ____________.
A up to E♭	1002. In Frame 1000, the interval of the diminished fifth is spelled ____ up to ____ .

D F A♭

F♯ A C

C E♭ G♭

1003. Spell these diminished triads. Be sure each interval is a minor third.

	Root	Third	Fifth
	D	___	___
	F♯	___	___
	C	___	___

D♯ F♯ A

C♯ E G

E G B♭

A♯ C♯ E

1004. Continue with these diminished triads.

	Root	Third	Fifth
	___	F♯	___
	___	E	___
	___	___	B♭
	___	___	E

C♯ E G F A♭ C♭ B♯ D♯ F♯

1005. Place diminished triads on the staff when roots are given. Spell the triad.

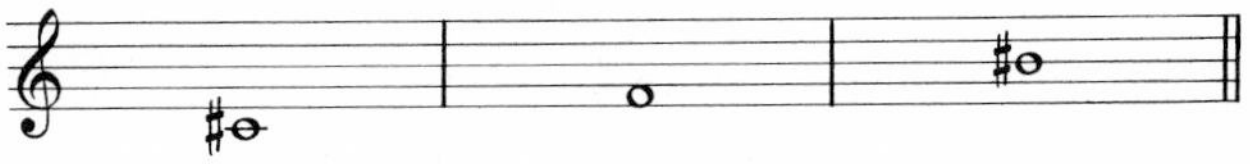

___ ___ ___ ___ ___ ___ ___ ___ ___

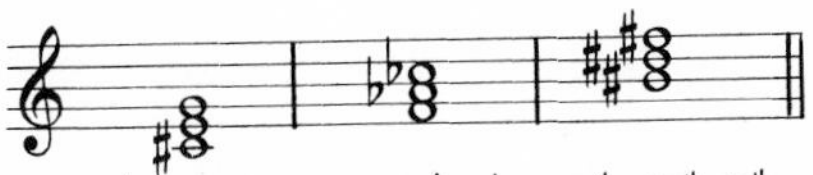

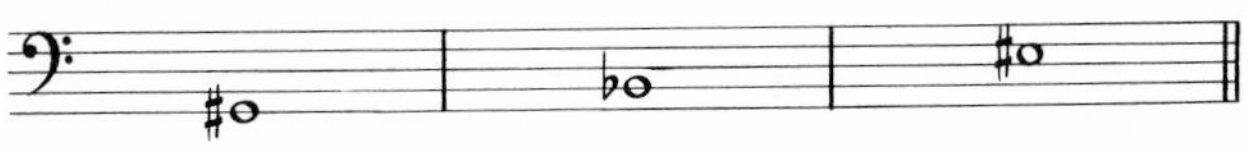

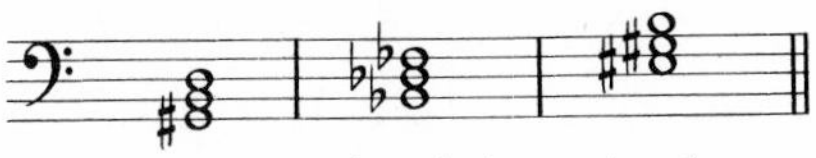

G♯ B D B♭ D♭ F♭ E♯ G♯ B

1006. Continue as above.

___ ___ ___ ___ ___ ___ ___ ___ ___

1007. Each given note is the third of a diminished triad. Place the root and fifth of each on the staff.

1008. Each given note is the fifth of a diminished triad. Place the root and third of each on the staff.

M, dim., m

1009. Identify each triad as major (M), minor (m), or diminished (dim.).

dim., dim., m

1010. Continue as above.

THE AUGMENTED TRIAD

1011. A triad composed of two major thirds is called an *augmented* triad.

augmented fifth

The interval from the root to the fifth is a half step larger than a perfect fifth, which is an __________ __________.

major third major third	1012. In an augmented triad, the interval from the root to the third is a ____________ ____________, and the interval from the third to the fifth is a ____________ ____________.
augmented	1013. The triad formed by two major thirds is an ____________ triad.
M, m, dim., aug.	1014. Identify each triad by type (use symbols M, m, dim., and aug. for augmented). ____ ____ ____ ____
m, aug., dim., M	1015. Identify each of these triads. ____ ____ ____ ____
G B D♯ E G♯ B♯ A♭ C E	1016. The root of an augmented triad is given. Place the third and fifth on the staff. Spell the triad. ___ ___ ___ ___ ___ ___ ___ ___ ___
or B♭ D F♯ D F♯ A♯ F♯ A♯ C𝄪	1017. The name of the root of the augmented triad is given. Spell the triad, and place the triad on the staff. B♭ ___ ___ D ___ ___ F♯ ___ ___

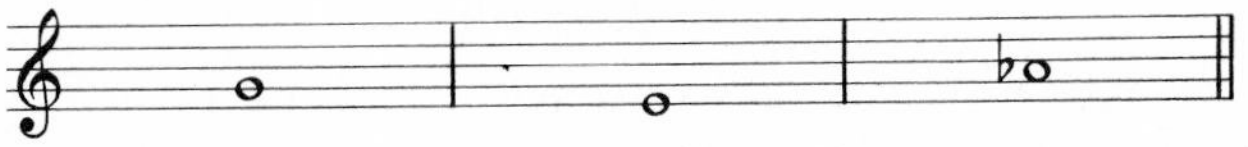

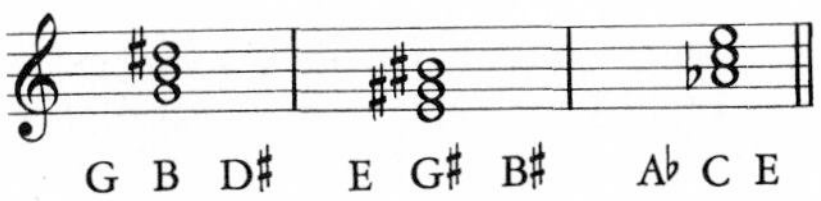

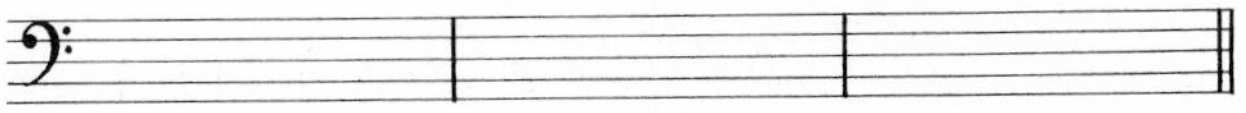

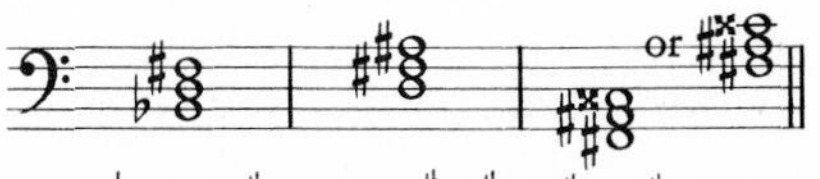

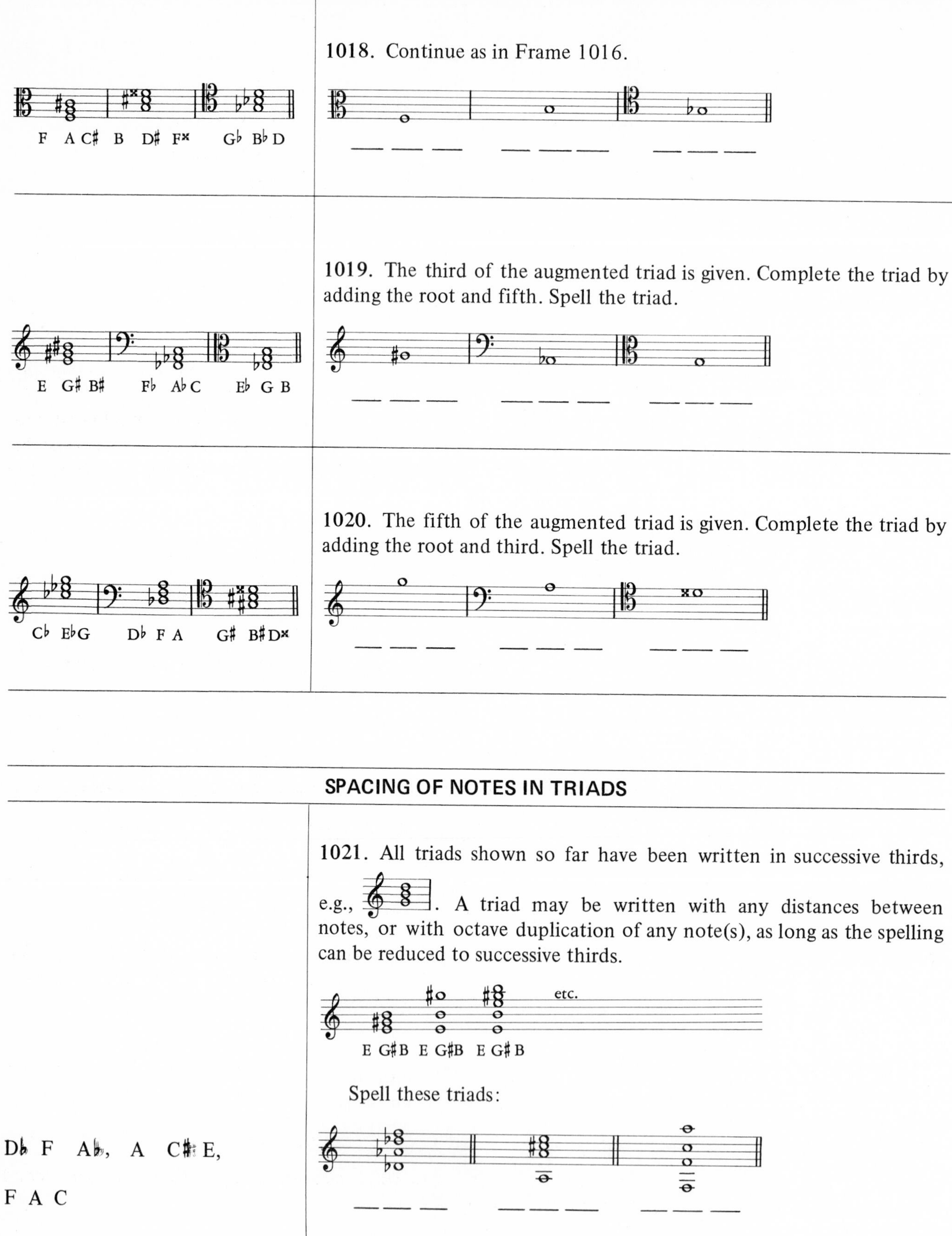

F A C♯ B D♯ F× G♭ B♭ D

1018. Continue as in Frame 1016.

___ ___ ___ ___ ___ ___ ___ ___ ___

E G♯ B♯ F♭ A♭ C E♭ G B

1019. The third of the augmented triad is given. Complete the triad by adding the root and fifth. Spell the triad.

___ ___ ___ ___ ___ ___ ___ ___ ___

C♭ E♭ G D♭ F A G♯ B♯ D×

1020. The fifth of the augmented triad is given. Complete the triad by adding the root and third. Spell the triad.

___ ___ ___ ___ ___ ___ ___ ___ ___

SPACING OF NOTES IN TRIADS

D♭ F A♭, A C♯ E,

F A C

1021. All triads shown so far have been written in successive thirds, e.g., [staff]. A triad may be written with any distances between notes, or with octave duplication of any note(s), as long as the spelling can be reduced to successive thirds.

E G♯ B E G♯ B E G♯ B etc.

Spell these triads:

___ ___ ___ ___ ___ ___ ___ ___ ___

B D F♯, G B D♯,

C♯ E G♯

1022. Continue as above.

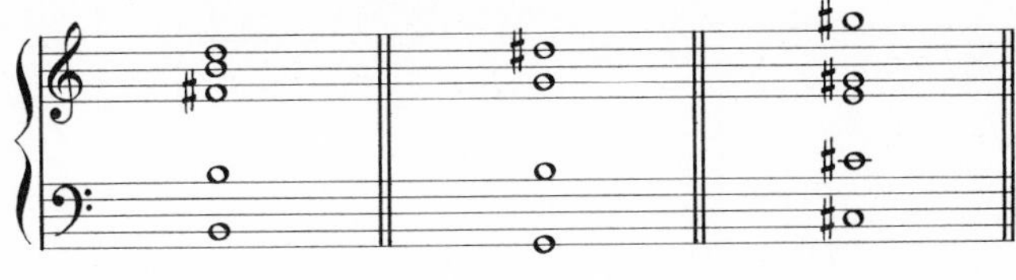

___ ___ ___ ___ ___ ___ ___ ___ ___

TRIADS IN INVERSION

2 and 3

1023. Triads may be found with the third or fifth as the lowest note. These triads are said to be in *inversion.* The spelling of each of the triads below can be arranged in the order C E G; therefore, the root of each is C, and each is a C major triad.

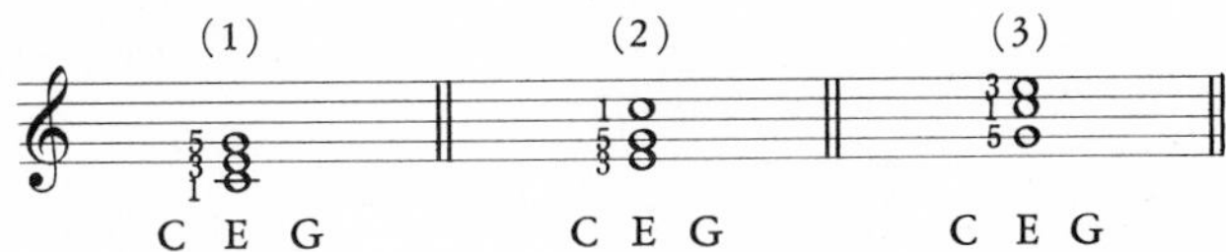

Triads in inversion are found in measures ____ and ____ above.

1

1024. A triad with its root as the lowest note is said to be in *root position.* In Frame 1023, the triad in root position is in measure ____.

2

1025. When the third of the triad is the lowest note, the triad is in *first inversion.* In Frame 1023, a triad in first inversion is seen in measure ____.

3

1026. When the fifth of the triad is the lowest note, the triad is in *second inversion.* In Frame 1023, measure ____ displays a triad in second inversion.

first inversion	1027. When the third of a triad is the lowest note, the triad is in ______ ______.
root position	1028. When the root of a triad is the lowest note, the triad is in ______ ______.
second inversion	1029. When the fifth of a triad is the lowest note, the triad is in ______ ______.
(1) second inversion (2) root position (3) first inversion	1030. Identify each triad as being in root position, first inversion, or second inversion. (1) (2) (3) (1) ______ ______ (2) ______ ______ (3) ______ ______
E♭ G B♭	1031. Each triad in Frame 1030 is spelled ____ ____ ____.

1032. Any of the four types of triads (M, m, dim., aug.) may be found in inversion. Spell each triad from its root, identify type of triad, and indicate root position or which inversion.

(1) (2) (3) (4)

(1) G B D, M, second inversion

(2) ___ ___ ___, ___, ___ ___

(3) ___ ___ ___, ___, ___ ___

(4) ___ ___ ___, ___, ___ ___

(1) G B D, M, second inversion

(2) F♯ A C, dim., first inversion

(3) A♭ C♭ E♭, m, second inversion

(4) F A C♯, aug., first inversion

1033. Continue as above with these triads in various spacings.

(1) (2) (3)

(1) ___ ___ ___, ___, ___ ___

(2) ___ ___ ___, ___, ___ ___

(3) ___ ___ ___, ___, ___ ___

(1) B D F♯, m, first inversion

(2) E G♯ B, M, root position

(3) F A♭ C♭, dim., first inversion

1034. Place first and second inversions of given triad on the staff. Use only three notes, as in Frame 1023.

root position · first inversion · second inversion

root position · first inversion · second inversion

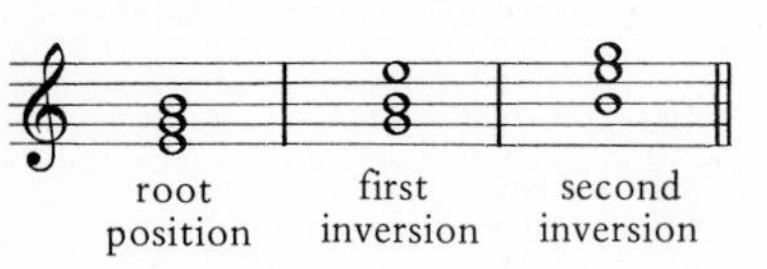

1035. Continue as in previous frame, but place the E minor triad on the staff as indicated.

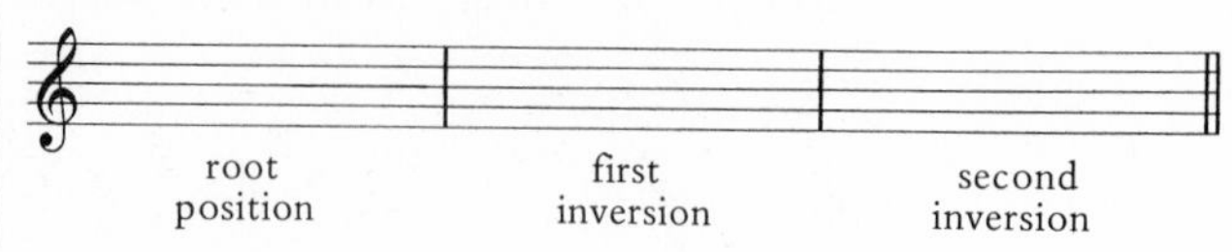

MUSIC EXAMPLES

1036. Answer questions in Frames 1037–1040 based on this example.

Ach Gott und Herr *(German hymn tune, 1625)*

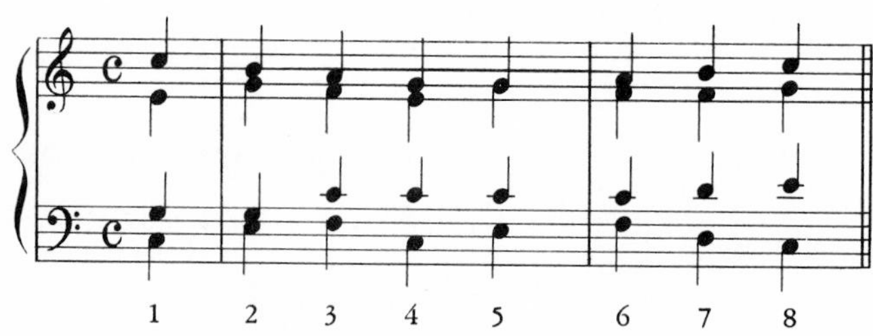

7	1037. A diminished triad is found at number ____.
2	1038. A minor triad is found at number ____.
major	1039. The remaining triads are _____ triads.
5	1040. A major triad in first inversion is found at number ____.

1041. Answer questions in Frames 1042–1044 based on this example.

Bach, O Ewigkeit, du Donnerwort

4, B♭ D F♯	1042. From Frame 1041, find an augmented triad. It is number ____, spelled ____ ____ ____.
2, E G B♭	1043. A diminished triad at number ____ is spelled ____ ____ ____.
3, 5, 6, 7	1044. Which chords in Frame 1041 are *not* triads? Numbers ______.

1045. Answer questions in Frames 1046 and 1047.

Brahms, Rhapsody, *Op. 119, No. 4*

	1046. Spell each numbered triad in Frame 1045.
1. E♭ G B♭	1. ____ ____ ____
2. B♭ D F	2. ____ ____ ____
3. A♭ C E♭	3. ____ ____ ____
4. E♭ G B♭	4. ____ ____ ____

	1047. Continue with the remaining triads.
5. E♭ G♭ B♭	5. ____ ____ ____
6. G♭ B♭ D♭	6. ____ ____ ____
7. C♭ E♭ G♭	7. ____ ____ ____
8. A♭ C♭ E♭	8. ____ ____ ____

1048. Answer questions in Frame 1049.

Schumann, Liederkreis, *Op. 39, "Waldesgespräch"*

(All notes above a bracket are to be considered a single chord.)

3 and 5 D♯ F× A♯, C♯ E♯ G♯	**1049.** The music of Frame 1048 includes two triads, at numbers ____ and ____ . They are spelled ____ ____ ____ and ____ ____ ____.

1050. Answer questions in Frames 1051–1053.

Bizet, Carmen, *Act II*

**See footnote, Frame 200.*

(1) 1, 6, or 9, F♯ A♯ C♯ (2) 3, B D♯ F♯	**1051.** In frame 1050, two different major triad spellings can be found: (1) at number ____, spelled ____ ____ ____. (2) at number ____, spelled ____ ____ ____.
6	**1052.** A triad in second inversion is located at number ____.

2 F♯ A♯ C𝄪 aug.	1053. One more triad can be found in Frame 1050. It is located at number ____. It is spelled ____ ____ ____. What type of triad is it (M, m, dim., aug.?) ________ .

1054. Answer questions in Frames 1055–1058.

Schubert, Impromptu, *Op. 142*

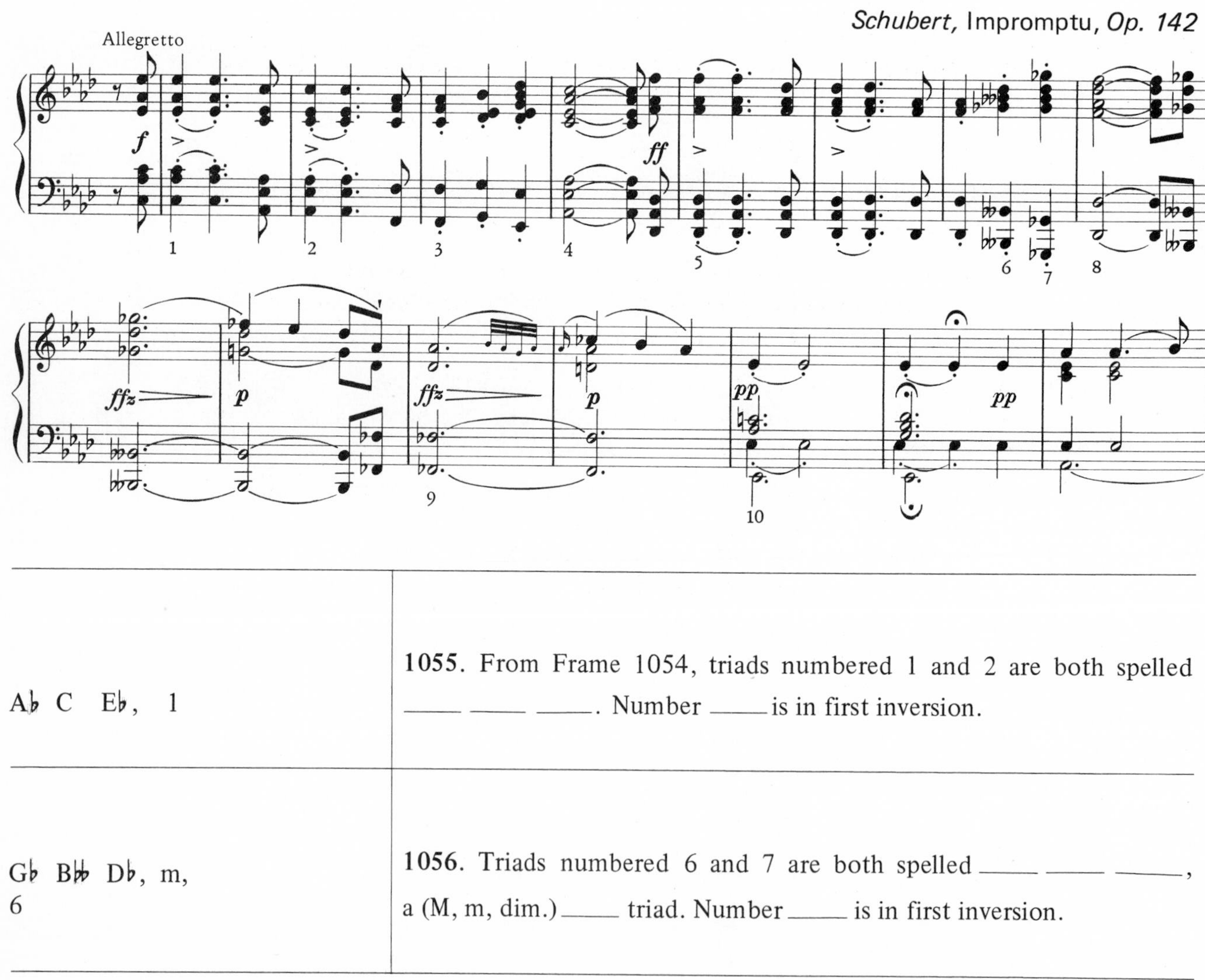

A♭ C E♭, 1	1055. From Frame 1054, triads numbered 1 and 2 are both spelled ____ ____ ____. Number ____ is in first inversion.
G♭ B𝄫 D♭, m, 6	1056. Triads numbered 6 and 7 are both spelled ____ ____ ____, a (M, m, dim.) ____ triad. Number ____ is in first inversion.

3, F A♭ C 9, D♭ F♭ A♭	1057. Locate two other minor triads: number ____, spelled ____ ____ ____, number ____ , spelled ____ ____ ____.
10, A♭ C E♭	1058. A triad in second inversion is located at number____ , and is spelled ____ ____ ____.

CHAPTER SUMMARY

1. A *chord* consists of three or more pitches, these found as consecutive intervals of the third.

2. A *triad* is a chord of three notes.

3. From its lowest note when spelled in thirds, the notes of the triad are identified as *root, third,* and *fifth.*

4. *Root position:* when the root of the triad is the lowest note.
First Inversion: when the third of the triad is the lowest note.
Second Inversion: when the fifth of the triad is the lowest note.

5. Triads are of four varieties, dependent upon the type and distribution of the thirds used. These, identified by interval construction from the root up, are:

Major triad: major third plus minor third
Minor triad: minor third plus major third
Diminished triad: minor third plus minor third
Augmented triad: major third plus major third

appendix ONE

ELEMENTARY ACOUSTICS

Sound is produced by a three-stage process. First, an object must be set in vibration. Such objects in music are a timpani head, a violin string, a clarinet reed, the human vocal chords, etc. Second, a transmission medium is necessary. Air serves this purpose by carrying vibrations from their source to the receiver. Third is the hearing process, performed by the human (or animal) auditory system, in which the ear receives the vibrations and sends their message to the brain, which instantly interprets the message as sound. The study of this three-stage process—vibrating source, transmission medium, receiver—is known as acoustics. *A knowledge of this subject will help you in future musical studies, particularly in performance, theory, composition, and orchestration.*

Answer	Frame
vibrations	**1059.** To produce vibrations, an object must be struck or in some other way set in motion. Vibrations are the back-and-forth movements of the object (vibrating body) after being set in motion. When set in motion by striking or other means, an object produces ______________.
second	**1060.** Vibrations produced by an object are usually measured in terms of number per second (*frequency* of vibration). Frequencies range from less than one (but more than zero) per second up to many thousands per second. To measure vibrations, we count the number per __________ produced by the vibrating object.
false	**1061.** Frequencies between 16 per second and 20,000 per second will affect the human auditory system,* but with considerable latitude for individual differences. A piano, for example, will produce a range of approximately 30 to 4,000 vibrations per second from its lowest note to its highest. True or false: Any number of vibrations per second will affect the human auditory system. __________. **Dogs, among other animals, are affected by a much higher range of vibration.*
No. (A vacuum is the absence of anything material, so it cannot vibrate.)	**1062.** The vibrating object will set the surrounding air in motion so that it too vibrates at the same rate as the original vibrating body. The vibrations are thereby transmitted from the object to the ear. Could the vibrations be transmitted through a vacuum? (yes or no) ______________.

1063. The vibrations of the original object and of the surrounding air when counted are expressed in terms of *cycles per second* (abbreviated *cps* or Hz[1]). The derivation of this term is not easy to describe in words, but can be seen clearly in a simple demonstration.

Take a blank sheet of paper. On it draw a straight line, the length of the long direction.

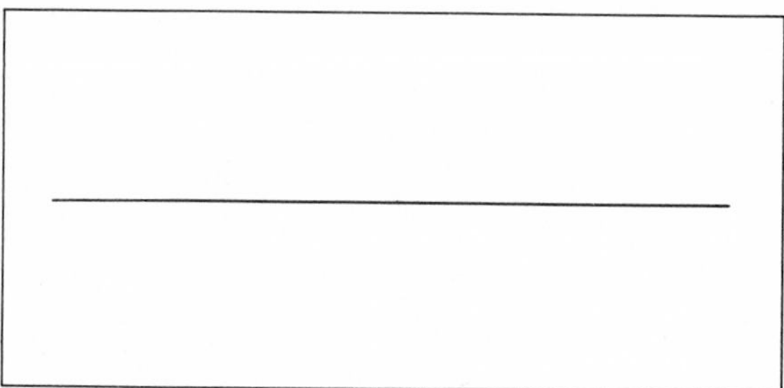

Place a pencil point on the left edge of the line. Then move the pencil vertically above the line about 1 or 2 inches, returning along the same mark and continuing below the line for the same distance. Trace back and forth several times. This represents the vibrating body, or vibrating air. You will have made only a straight mark perpendicular to the original line.

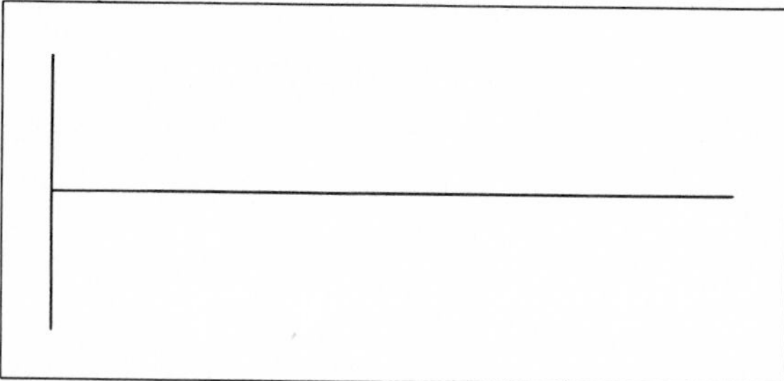

Now with your left hand (or if possible, have another person do this) grasp the left side of the sheet of paper and pull it slowly to the left while repeating the up and down action of the pencil. You should get a picture something like this:

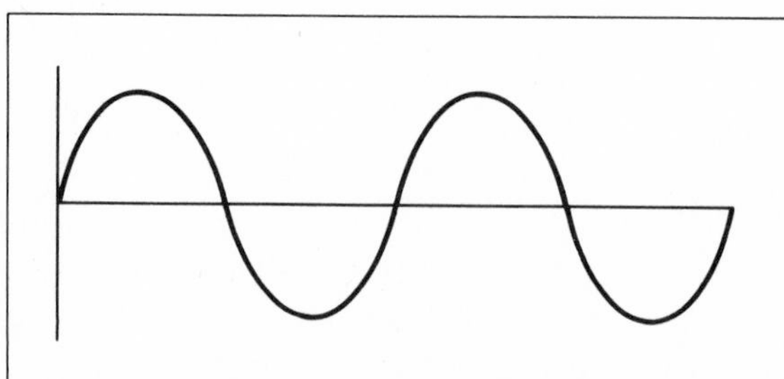

[1]*In honor of Heinrich Hertz, 1857-1894, discoverer of radio waves.*

In this picture, the original straight line represents time (how long it took to pull the paper), while each complete curve (once above the line and once below and returning to the line) is called a *cycle.* Knowing the amount of time and counting the cycles in this time period will tell you the cycles per second. In our illustration if you took one second to pull the paper you would have two cycles per second (2 cps).

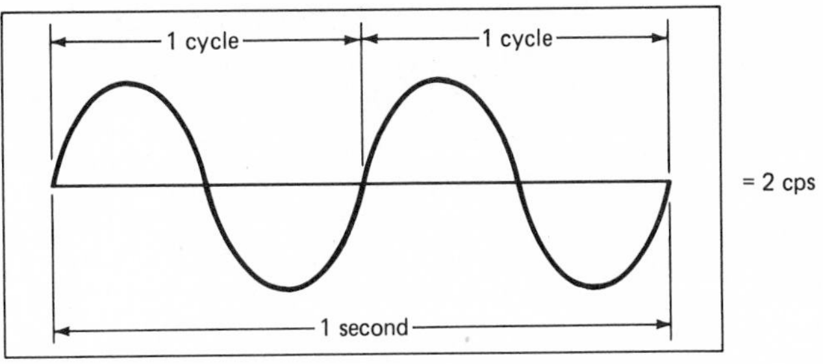

(2 cps cannot, of course, be heard. Can you visualize a picture for the highest note on the piano, 4,000 cps?)

1064. When we hear a musical sound, we think of it in terms of a "high" sound or a "low" sound, using these terms to express a property of sound, its *pitch.*

Referring to sound as high or low is a general way of referring to its

pitch ________.

1065. The pitch of a sound is specifically related to frequency of vibrations (the number of cycles per second). The higher the cps, the "higher" the pitch (remember the lower note on the piano, 16 cps, and the high note, 4,000 cps).

A "high" pitch is characterized by (fewer/more) ________ cycles per second than a "low" pitch.

more

1066. When the cps is a low number, the pitch produced will be

low ________.

higher	**1067.** A frequency of 900 cps produces a (higher/lower)________ pitch than a frequency of 300 cps.
lower	**1068.** When the frequency of two pitches is in the ratio 1:2, an octave* results. A pitch whose frequency is 800 will be an octave higher than one of 400, since the ratio of 400 to 800 is the same as 1:2. A frequency of 200 is an octave (higher/lower)________ than one of 400. **Review* octave, *Chapter 3, Frames 117–122.*
octave	**1069.** The interval represented by two frequencies with a ratio of 1:2 is called an ________.
1:2	**1070.** When two pitches are an octave apart, the ratio of their frequencies is _____.
600	**1071.** If one pitch has a frequency of 300 cps, a pitch an octave higher will be ________ cps.
1,500	**1072.** A pitch an octave lower than one of 3,000 cps will be________ cps.

1073. The interval* between any two pitches can be expressed by a mathematical ratio. For example, 2:3 refers to the interval of a fifth (easily calculated on the piano by choosing any white key, calling this 1 and counting up to 5 on white keys.**). In this instance, if the lower note were 200 cps, the higher note would be 300 cps.

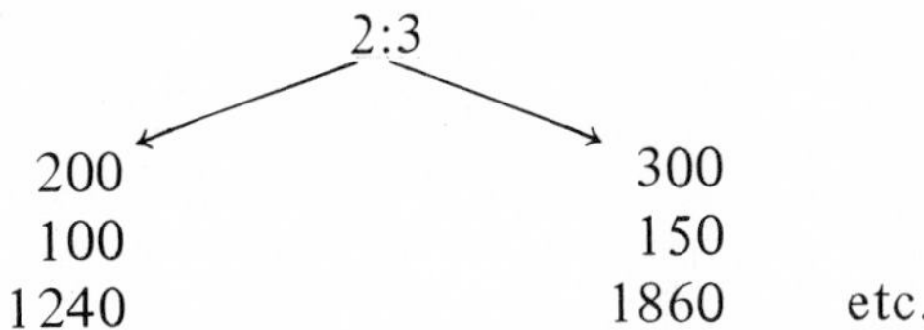

**Intervals are studied in Chapters 13 and 14 but without reference to their mathematical ratios.*

***Exception: B up to F*

If the lower note of a fifth is 600 cps, the upper note is ______

900 cps.

1074. The simplest ratios produce the intervals most used in music.

Interval name	Perfect octave	Perfect fifth	Perfect fourth	Major third	Minor third
Ratio	1:2	2:3	3:4	4:5	5:6

Partials*	1	2	3	4	5	6
Example, 1=90 cps	↑ 90	↑ 180	↑ 270	↑ 360	↑ 450	↑ 540

An interval is determined by the *ratio* of frequencies. For example, the frequency of a pitch a perfect fourth higher than a given frequency can be expressed by the ratio 3:4. In the example above, the lower pitch of a perfect fourth is given as 270. When using the ratio 3:4, the frequency of the upper pitch will be calculated to be 360.

ratio Any interval can be expressed by its particular ______.

**defined in Frame 1078*

1075. This series of ratios is coincidental with another phenomenon in sound, the *overtone series.* Simply stated, when any pitch is sounded, a series of higher frequencies is also created, sounding simultaneously. These higher frequencies, usually inaudible, are in the same ratios as the series shown in Frame 1074. Here is an overtone series based on a pitch of 90 cps. (Only the first six numbers are shown; the actual number theoretically extends to infinity.)

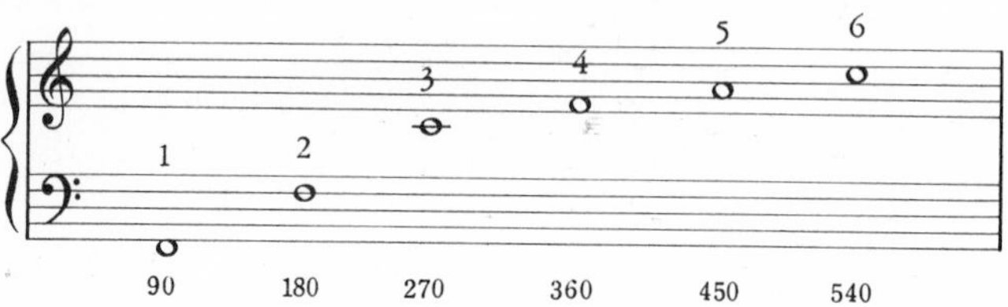

The pitches ____ and ____ are at the interval of a fifth because their ratio is ____________.

F and C; 2:3

1076. The assignment of frequency to a particular letter name is arbitrary. The frequency of tuning notes has varied at different times in history and in different countries. For example, the note a^1 has been assigned the frequency of 435 cps, 440, or 446. At an international conference in London (1939) it was agreed to assign a^1 the frequency of 440 cps. This standard "international" pitch is used today by most musicians.

International pitch is based on a^1 at _____ cps.

440

1077. The following overtone series is based on a pitch of 88 cps, slightly lower (by 2 cps) than that shown in Frame 1075. The related table lists common intervals and their ratios.

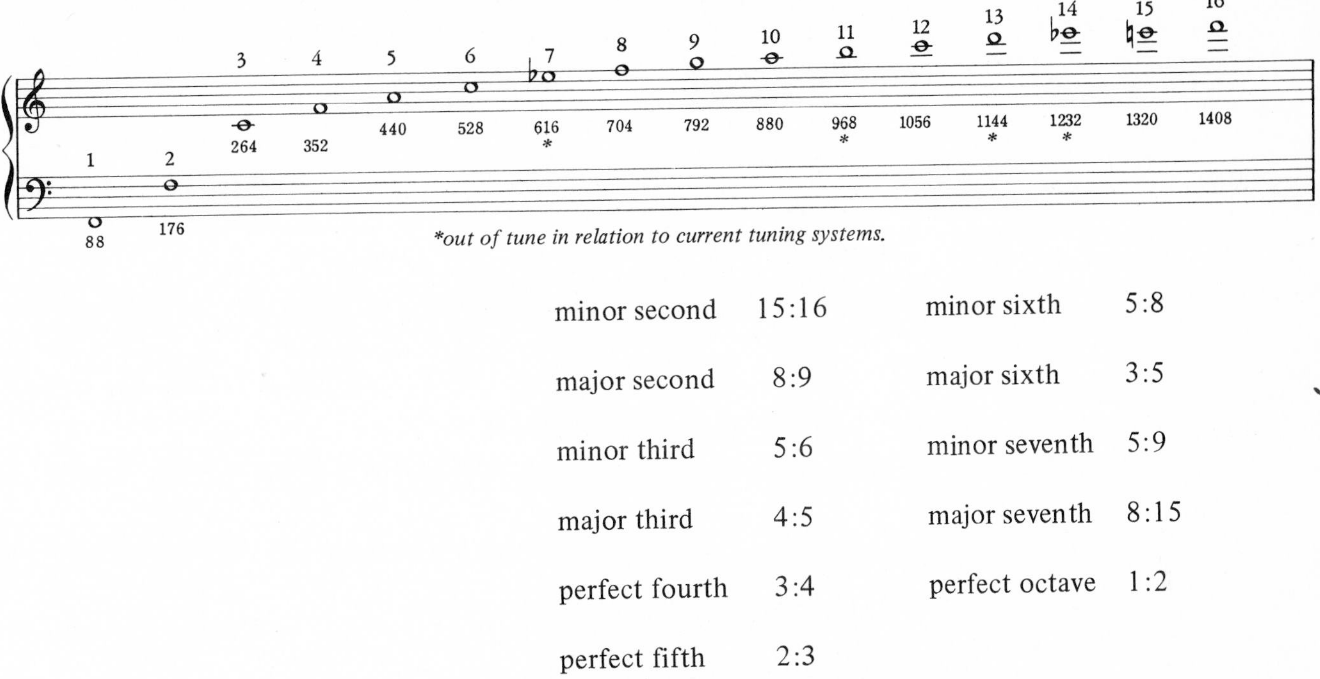

minor second	15:16	minor sixth	5:8
major second	8:9	major sixth	3:5
minor third	5:6	minor seventh	5:9
major third	4:5	major seventh	8:15
perfect fourth	3:4	perfect octave	1:2
perfect fifth	2:3		

You are not asked to memorize these ratios; rather, you are asked to remember their existence as the acoustical determinants of intervals.

1078. Number 1 of the overtone series is known as the *fundamental,* while all numbers, including 1, are known as *partials:*

1 = first partial (or fundamental)
2 = second partial, etc.

All numbers including the fundamental are known as ________.

partials

1079. The fundamental and the ________ partial are identical.

first

1080. The first partial is also called the ________.

fundamental

octave	1081. The first and second partials are in the ratio 1:2 and therefore represent the interval of the ________.
fourth	1082. In another terminology, the word *overtone* from the overtone series is used to describe each partial numbered 2 and higher. 1 = fundamental = first partial 2 = first overtone = second partial 3 = second overtone = third partial etc. The third overtone is the same as the ________ partial.
first	1083. The second partial is the same as the ________ overtone.
lower	1084. The lower the number of the partial, the (lower/higher) ________ will be the frequency implied.
(2) 1:2 (3) 3:6	1085. The overtone series shown in Frame 1077 within the first six partials shows three intervals of the octave, at the ratios of: (1) 1:2 (2) 2:4, which is a ratio equivalent to ____ (3) ____, which also is equivalent to the ratio 1:2 (Any two numbers, one twice the other, will be in the ratio 1:2)

1086. The importance of partials to musical sound is dependent upon knowledge of one more property of sound, *intensity*. This term refers to loudness or softness of a pitch. Intensity is directly related to the *amplitude* or the size of the vibration. The greater the amplitude, the louder, or more intense, will be the sound.

A difference in the amplitude of vibration will result in a difference in ____________ in a sound.

intensity

1087. In this example, both a) and b) show 2 cps. At a), the distance traveled above and below the line (the amplitude) is much less than at b). Therefore a) represents a softer sound than b). (Understand, of course, that 2 cps is inaudible at any amplitude, but is convenient for demonstration.)

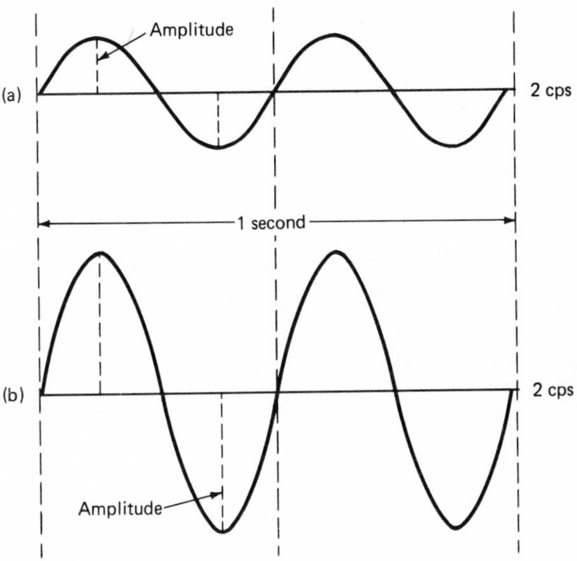

In this example above, the intensity is greater at (a or b)____ than at____ .

b, a

1088. Sounds which are soft have a relatively (wide or narrow)_______ amplitude.

narrow

amplitude	1089. Intensity of sound is dependent upon the ______ of vibration.
higher, softer	1090. (a) (b) 1 second — Compared to b), the sound at a) is ______ in pitch and ______ in intensity.
higher, louder	1091. (a) (b) 1 second — Compared to b), the sound at a) is ______ in pitch and ______ in intensity.

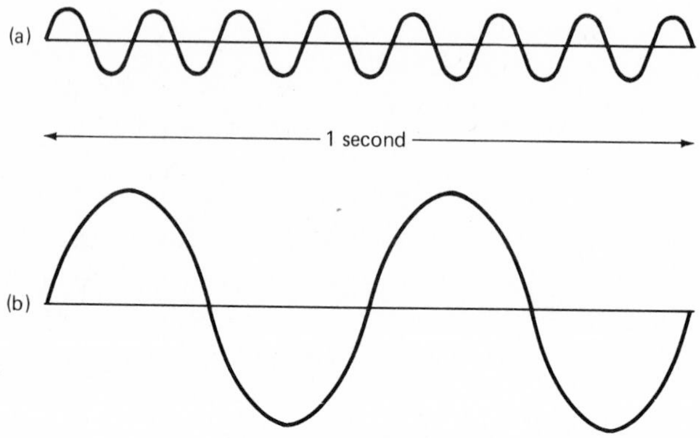

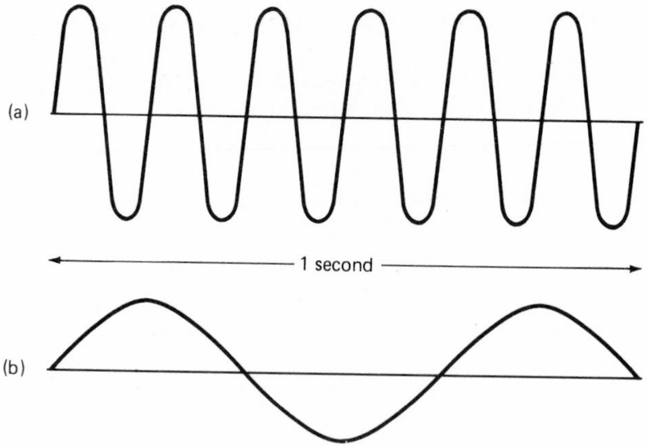

weaker	**1092.** Return to the overtone series (from Frame 1077). When a pitch is sounded, all overtones (or partials) are not of the same intensity. Generally, the higher the number, the weaker the intensity. Upper partials tend to be ________ in intensity.
timbre	**1093.** Two instruments each playing the same pitch (same cps) will produce a different quality of sound. The quality of a sound is known as its *timbre.* (The sound of a violin and a trumpet each playing the same pitch differs in timbre.) A French horn and a cello each has its own distinctive quality of sound known as ________.
timbre	**1094.** The difference in timbre between two different sound sources producing the same pitch is caused by a difference in the intensity of the partials. A given partial for one instrument may be more or less intense than the same partial on another instrument. In some cases, some partials may be missing entirely. The important point is that the relative intensity of the partials of a given pitch determines its timbre. When two pitches differ in the intensity of their partials, the pitches will be heard as having a difference in ________.
intensity	**1095.** Timbre is determined by the relative ________ of the partials of a given tone.
timbre	**1096.** If the fundamental of two pitches is the same, but the partials differ in intensity, the result is a difference in ________.

1097. If the distance above the horizontal line represents intensity of partials, which two are identical in timbre?

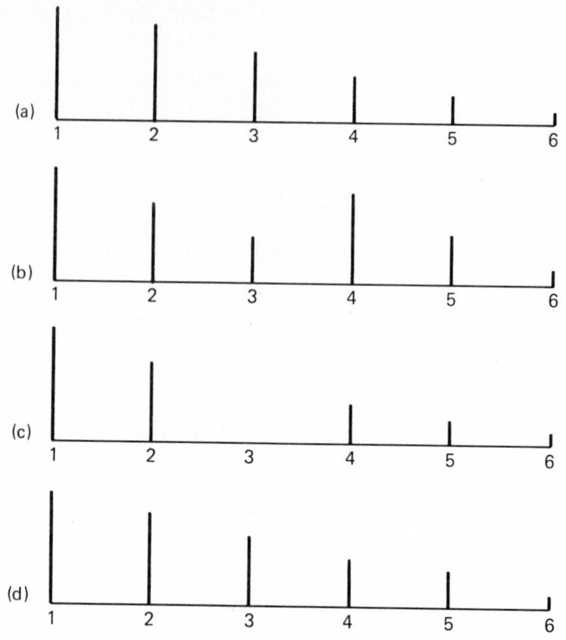

(a) 1 2 3 4 5 6

(b) 1 2 3 4 5 6

(c) 1 2 3 4 5 6

(d) 1 2 3 4 5 6

a and d

_____ and _____

1098. We have discussed three properties of sound, pitch, intensity, and timbre, from an acoustical viewpoint. The fourth quality is *duration*—the length of a sound or a silence. The succession of durations of sound produces rhythm, one of the important compositional elements in music.

durations

Rhythm is the study of the succession of __________.

---

four

1099. We have studied how many properties of sound? ________

(any order)
pitch
timbre
intensity
duration

1100. Name the properties of sound:

____

____

____

____

HISTORICAL DERIVATION OF MAJOR AND MINOR SCALES

EARLY SCALES

The structures of both our present-day major and natural minor scales are identical to two scales in earlier music history. Eight-note scale systems in Western music evolved as early as the eighth century A.D., and by 1600 music was commonly written in a system of six different scales, called *modes.* These six modes can be found quickly on the piano keyboard by playing up an octave from each note given below, Ex. A2.1, using only white keys. You will observe that each mode consists of five whole steps and two half steps, and that the half steps are always E–F and B–C, but each mode differs from the others because of the varying locations of the half steps. These differences, together with the name of each mode, are shown in Example A2.1.

IONIAN AND AEOLIAN: MAJOR AND MINOR

Through evolutionary processes, the number of scale systems was reduced to two by the mid-seventeenth century. The Ionian mode became the pattern for the major scale. The Aeolian mode was also retained, and became the pattern for the basic minor scale: the pure, or natural, form of the minor scale.

THE ROLE OF *"MUSICA FICTA"* IN SCALE DEVELOPMENT

Of the seven possible modal scales, only two, the Ionian and the Lydian, contain a leading tone. This lack of a leading tone in ascending

Ex. A2.1. *Modes.*

First note	White-key scale	Mode
A	A B C D E F G A (½ between 2 3 B–C; ½ between 5 6 E–F)	Aeolian
(B)[1]		(Locrian)
C	C D E F G A B C (½ between 3 4 E–F; ½ between 7 8 B–C)	Ionian
D	D E F G A B C D (½ between 2 3 E–F; ½ between 6 7 B–C)	Dorian
E	E F G A B C D E (½ between 1 2 E–F; ½ between 5 6 B–C)	Phrygian
F	F G A B C D E F (½ between 4 5 B–C; ½ between 7 8 E–F)	Lydian
G	G A B C D E F G (½ between 3 4 B–C; ½ between 6 7 E–F)	Mixolydian

forms of the other modes was recognized very early in the history of the use of modes. Performers often preferred the sound of leading tone to tonic rather than a whole step, and, in performance of music written with an ascending whole step between 7 and 8, would sometimes raise the seventh scale step to create a leading tone. This practice, part of a system known as *musica ficta* (false music), was condoned by performers and composers alike.[2]

By adding a leading tone, the Mixolydian mode displays the same scale structure as major:

G A B C D E F♯ G;

the Aeolian the same as minor, harmonic form:

A B C D E F G♯ A;

and the Dorian the same as minor, melodic form:

D E F G A B C♯ D.

[1] Theoretically, a mode called Locrian can be constructed on B, but it was not used in musical practice.

[2] This principle was not applied to the Phrygian mode. For more detailed information, consult articles under the heading *musica ficta* in music dictionaries, or in music history books, chapters on Medieval and Renaissance music.

Ex. A2.2 shows a melodic line in the Aeolian mode, with the seventh scale degree G raised to G♯. The sharp *above* the note indicates that it was *not* written by the composer but rather reflects the probable performance based on known principles of *musica ficta.*

Ex. A2.2. *Use of Musica Ficta.*

Palestrina (1525–1594), Missa de Feria

In another practice common to *musica ficta,* B was lowered to B♭ in certain circumstances. When applied to the Lydian mode, the resulting scale structure is the same as major:

F G A B♭ C D E F.

When applying both varieties of *musica ficta* (B♭ and ♯7[3]) to the Dorian, the resulting scale structure is the same as minor, harmonic form:

D E F G A B♭ C♯ D.

Thus the three forms of the minor scale are simply a result of performance practices applied to modal structures. Even today, the minor key signature is that for Aeolian mode, while changes in the sixth and seventh scale degrees are placed in the music itself.

CHARACTERISTICS OF THE HARMONIC MINOR SCALE

In the harmonic form of the minor scale, the raised seventh (leading tone) has a strong tendency to ascend, and the sixth scale step has a strong tendency to descend. When, in a piece of music in minor, the seventh scale step ascends and the sixth descends, these characteristics identify the form of the scale used for the composition as harmonic minor.

Ex. A2.3. ***Characteristics of the Harmonic Minor Scale.***

Mozart, Sonata for Violin and Piano, K. 304

[3]The symbol ♯7 indicates *raised seventh.*

CHARACTERISTICS OF THE MELODIC FORM OF THE MINOR SCALE

When the sixth scale degree of the harmonic minor scale ascends, the next scale tone, the leading tone, is more than a whole step up. This interval of three half steps (a step and a half[4]) has been found objectionable in melodic writing by most composers and performers. To eliminate this offending interval, the sixth scale degree is raised, eliminating the awkward step and a half between 6 and 7 of the harmonic form of the scale. The interval between 6 and 7 becomes a whole step and, at the same time, the desired leading tone is present. This accounts for the ascending form of the melodic minor scale with its raised sixth and seventh degrees.

Ex. A2.4. ***Difference Between Harmonic and Melodic Forms of the Minor Scale.***

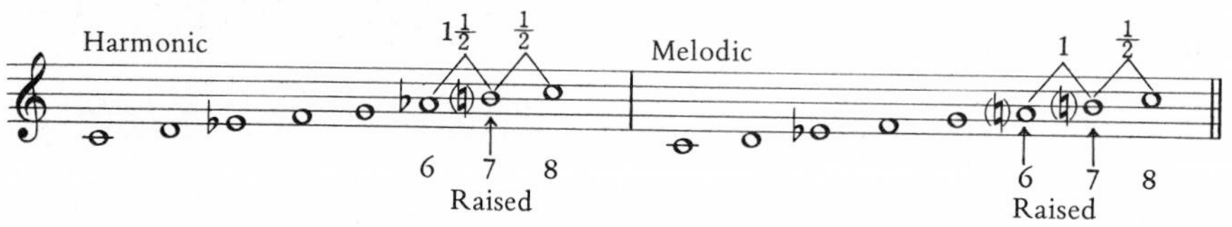

The sensation of leading tone is peculiar to ascending melody; on the other hand, when a melody descends from the tonic note, there is no need for the leading tone. Accordingly, the descending form of the melodic minor scale is found with both the sixth and seventh scale steps lowered, and is identical to the natural form of the scale. When, in a piece of music, both raised and lowered sixth and seventh scale steps occur, these characteristics identify the form of the scale used for the composition as melodic minor.

Ex. A2.5. ***Characteristics of the Melodic Minor Scale.***

Bach, Suite for Lute in F Minor

SUMMARY

(1) The natural minor scale is a hold-over from an earlier scale system and is identical to the Aeolian mode (just as the major scale is identical to the Ionian mode); (2) the harmonic form evolved from the musical practice of raising the seventh scale degree to allow for a leading tone; and (3) the ascending melodic form resulted from raising the sixth (along with the seventh) in order to eliminate the awkward interval of a step and a half in the harmonic form; descending, the sixth and seventh tones were lowered to conform with natural minor.

[4] Called *augmented second;* included in the study of intervals, Chapter 14.

FOREIGN WORDS AND MUSICAL TERMS

Most music commonly performed at the present time contains directions for performance, particularly in reference to tempo and dynamics. These directions are often found in the Italian language, a custom dating back to the seventeenth century. It was at that time that such markings were first added to the music score, and because of the prevalence of Italian music, these markings became standard in all languages.

In the late nineteenth century, composers began using directions from their native languages, such as French, German, and English, though the older Italian terms continue to be commonly used.

This list presents a selection of terms most frequently encountered in music. Unless indicated otherwise, the language is Italian. Fr = French, G = German, L = Latin.

A

a, à (Fr)—by

accelerando—getting faster

adagietto—slightly faster than adagio

adagio—slow, leisurely

ad libitum (L)—at will (abbr. *ad lib.*)

agitato—agitated

al—to

all', alla—to the, at the, in the, in the style of

all' ottava—at the octave; play an octave higher (when above the notes); play an octave lower (when below the notes)

all' unisono—play in unison

allargando—growing broader, slowing down with fuller tone (abbr. *allarg.*)

allegretto—moderately fast; slower than allegro

allegro—lively, fast

andante—moderately slow

andantino—slower than andante

animato—animated
animé (Fr)—animated
a piacere—freely
appassionato—with passion
assai—very
assez (Fr)—enough, rather
a tempo—return to original tempo after a change
attacca—begin next section at once
aussi (Fr)—as

B

ben—well
bien (Fr)—well, very
brio—vivacity, spirit, fire

C

cantabile—in a singing style
coda—end of piece
col, coll', colla, colle—with
comodo, commodo—comfortable tempo
con—with
crescendo—increasing in volume (abbr. *cresc.*)

D

da capo—from the beginning (abbr. *D.C.*)
dal segno—from the sign (abbr. *D.S.*)
declamato—in declamatory style
decrescendo—decreasing in volume (abbr. *decresc.*)
diminuendo—decreasing in volume (abbr. *dim.*)
dolce—soft
doppio—double
douce, doux (Fr.)—soft, sweet

E

einfach (G)—simple, plain
ernst (G)—earnest, serious
espressivo—expressive
et (Fr.)—and
etwas (G)—somewhat

F

feierlich (G)—solemn
fine—end
forte—loud (abbr. *f*)
forte-piano—loud, then immediately soft (abbr. *fp*)
fortissimo—very loud (abbr. *ff*)
forzando—with force (abbr. *fz*)
frisch (G)—brisk, lively
fröhlich (G)—glad, joyous
fuoco—fire

G

gai (Fr)—gay, brisk
gesangvoll (G)—in a singing style
giocoso—playful
giusto—correct
gracieusement (Fr)—graciously
gracieux (Fr)—gracious
grandioso—grand, pompous
grave—slow, ponderous
grazia—grace, elegance
grazioso—graceful
gut (G)—good, well

H

heimlich (G)—mysterious
herzlich (G)—heartily, affectionate

I

immer (G)—always
innig (G)—heartfelt, fervent
innigkeit (G)—deep emotion
istesso—same
istesso tempo—same tempo; after a change of time signature, the value of either the measure or the beat note remains the same

J

joyeuse, joyeux (Fr)—joyous

K

klagend (G)—mourning
kurz (G)—short, crisp

L

langoureuse, langoureux (Fr)—languorous
langsam (G)—slow
langsamer (G)—slower
largamente—broadly
larghetto—not as slow as largo

largo—slow and broad, stately
lebhaft (G)—lively, animated
legato—smoothly connected
leger (Fr)—light
leggiero—light (abbr. *legg.*)
leicht (G)—light
leise (G)—soft
lent (Fr)—slow
lenteur (Fr)—slowness
lento—slow
liberamente—freely
lieblich (G)—with charm
l'istesso tempo—same as istesso tempo
lustig (G)—merry, gay

M

ma—but
mächtig (G)—powerful
maestoso—with majesty or dignity
malinconico—in a melancholy style
marcato—marked, emphatic
marcia—march
marziale—martial
mässig (G)—moderate
même (Fr)—same
meno—less
mesto—sad
mezzo—half (mezzo forte, *mf;* mezzo piano, *mp*)
misterioso—mysteriously
mit (G)—with
moderato—moderately
modéré (Fr)—moderately
molto—much, very
morendo—dying away
mosso—"moved"; (*meno mosso*—less rapid; *più mosso*—more rapid)
moto—motion
munter (G)—lively, animated

N

nicht (G)—not
non—not
non tanto—not so much
non troppo—not too much
nobilmente—with nobility

O

ossia—or
ottava—octave

P

parlando—singing in a speaking style
pas (Fr)—not
pas trop lent (Fr)—not too slow
pesante—heavy
peu (Fr)—little
peu à peu (Fr)—little by little
piano—soft (abbr. *p*)
pianissimo—very soft (abbr. *pp*)
più—more
plus (Fr)—more
poco—little
presto—fast, rapid
prima, primo—first

Q

quasi—as if, nearly (*andante quasi allegretto*)

R

rallentando—slowing down (abbr. *rall.*)
rasch (G)—quick
rinforzando—reinforcing; sudden increase in loudness for single tone, chord, or passage (abbr. *rfz*)
ritardando—slowing down (abbr. *rit.*)
rubato—performed freely
ruhig (G)—quiet

S

sanft (G)—soft
scherzando—playfully
sans (Fr)—without
schnell (G)—fast
secco—dry
segue—follows; next section follows immediately, or, continue in a similar manner
sehr (G)—very
semplice—simple
semplicemente—simply
sempre—always
senza—without
senza misure—without measure
sforzando—forcing; perform a single note or chord with sudden emphasis (abbr. *sfz*)
simile—similarly; continue in the same manner (abbr. *sim.*)

sostenuto—sustained
sotto—under
sotto voce—in an undertone, subdued volume
spirito—spirit
staccato—detached, separate
stark (G)—strong
stringendo—pressing onward
subito—suddenly

T

tant (Fr)—as much
tanto—so much
tempo giusto—correct tempo
tendrement (Fr)—tenderly
teneramente—tenderly
tenuto—held
tranquillo—tranquil
traurig (G)—sad
très (Fr)—very
triste (It, Fr)—sad
trop (Fr)—too much
troppo—too much

U

un, uno—one, an, a
una corde—one string; on the piano, *use soft pedal* (abbr. *u.c.*)
unisono—unison
un peu (Fr)—a little

V

vif (Fr)—lively
vite (Fr)—quick
vivace—very fast
vivo—lively

Z

zart (G)—tender, delicate
ziemlich (G)—somewhat, rather

REPEAT SIGNS

(1) Double Bar and Dots. A repeat sign consists of a double bar preceded by two dots around the third line, and indicates a repetition of the music preceding the sign. Upon reaching the repeat sign the second time, continue on to the next measure.

Ex. 4A.1. ***Repeat Sign at the End of a Measure.***

When the section to be repeated ends before the end of the measure, the repeat sign (double bar with dots) will be found between the two single bar-lines of the measure.

Ex. 4A.2. ***Repeat Sign (Double Bar and Dots) Within a Measure.***

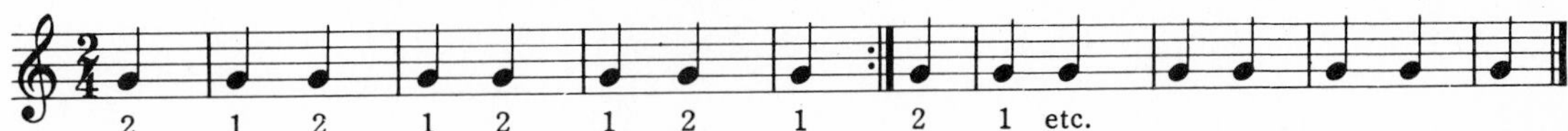

If the section to be repeated begins after the beginning of the composition, the section is enclosed by double bars, the first with dots to the right of the double bar and the second with the dots to the left of the double bar.

Ex. 4A.3. *Indication of Repetition of a Section Within a Composition.*

(2) First and Second Endings

Ex. 4A.4. *First and Second Endings.*

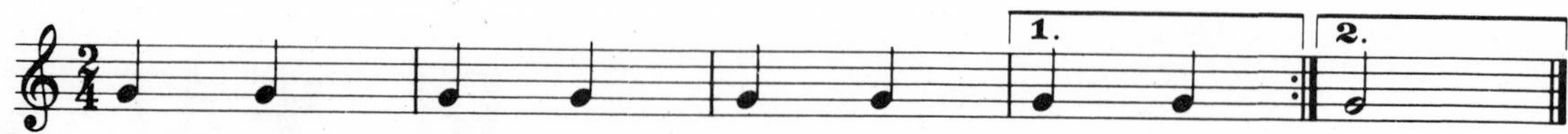

The first ending (1.) indicates a return to the beginning, or to a previous repeat sign (𝄆). During the repetition, the music of the first ending is skipped and the piece continues with the second ending (2.).

(3) D.C., D.S., and *Fine*

(a) Da capo (It. *da capo,* literally, "from the head"), abbreviated D.C., indicates a repeat from the beginning of the composition. See Example 4A.5.

(b) Dal segno (It. *dal segno,* "from the sign"), abbreviated D.S., indicates a repeat from the sign 𝄋. See Example 4A.6.

(c) Fine (It. *fine,* "end," pronounced *fee'-nay*) indicates the place where the composition ends after using D.C. or D.S. These combinations are often used: *D.C. al fine* (from the beginning, then to the end) and *D.S. al fine* (from the sign, then to the end). A double bar is used with the *fine.* See Examples 4A.5 and 4A.6.

Ex. 4A.5. *The Da Capo.*

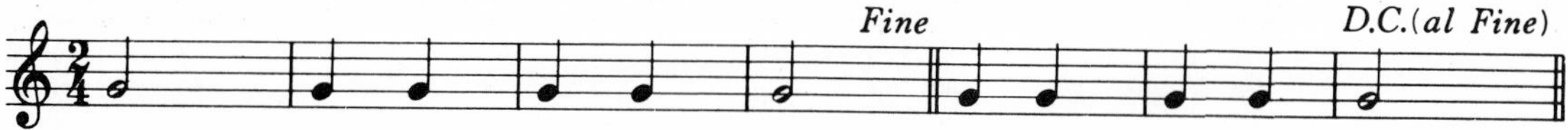

Ex. 4A.6. *The Dal Segno.*

Several of the devices for musical repeats are shown in the three folk-songs following:

Ex. 4A.7. ***Examples of Repeat Signs.***

INDEX

Numbers refer to frame numbers unless preceded by P for page number.